Cocaine, Literature, and Culture, 1876–1930

Critical Interventions in the Medical and Health Humanities

Series editors
Stuart Murray, Corinne Saunders, Sowon Park and Angela Woods

Critical Interventions in the Medical and Health Humanities promotes a broad range of scholarly work across the Medical and Health Humanities, including both larger-scale intellectual projects and argument-led provocations, to present new field-defining, interdisciplinary research into health and human experience.

Titles in the series
Abortion Ecologies in Southern African Fiction, Caitlin E. Stobie
COVID-19 and Shame, Fred Cooper, Luna Dolezal and Arthur Rose
Medical Humanities and Disability Studies, Stuart Murray
Relating Suicide, Anne Whitehead

Forthcoming titles
Autism and the Empathy Epidemic, Janet Harbold
Reproductive Health, Literature, and Print Culture, 1650–1800, Ashleigh Blackwood

Cocaine, Literature, and Culture, 1876–1930

Douglas R. J. Small

BLOOMSBURY ACADEMIC
LONDON • NEW YORK • OXFORD • NEW DELHI • SYDNEY

BLOOMSBURY ACADEMIC

Bloomsbury Publishing Plc, 50 Bedford Square, London, WC1B 3DP, UK
Bloomsbury Publishing Inc, 1385 Broadway, New York, NY 10018, USA
Bloomsbury Publishing Ireland, 29 Earlsfort Terrace, Dublin 2, D02 AY28, Ireland

BLOOMSBURY, BLOOMSBURY ACADEMIC and the Diana logo are trademarks of
Bloomsbury Publishing Plc

First published in Great Britain 2024
This paperback edition published in 2025

Copyright © Douglas R. J. Small, 2024

Douglas R. J. Small has asserted his right under the Copyright, Designs and Patents Act,
1988, to be identified as Author of this work.

Series design by Rebecca Heselton
Cover image © *Cocaine!...One Step*, published by A. Forlivesi, c.1927
© Aymon de Lestrange / Bridgeman Images

This work is published open access subject to a Creative Commons Attribution
4.0 licence (CC BY 4.0, https://creativecommons.org/licenses/by/4.0/). You may re-use,
distribute, reproduce, and adapt this work in any medium, including for commercial
purposes, provided you give attribution to the copyright holder and the publisher,
provide a link to the Creative Commons licence, and indicate if changes have been made.

Open access was funded by The Wellcome Trust.

All rights reserved. No part of this publication may be: i) reproduced or transmitted in any form,
electronic or mechanical, including photocopying, recording or by means of any information
storage or retrieval system without prior permission in writing from the publishers; or ii) used or
reproduced in any way for the training, development or operation of artificial intelligence
(AI) technologies, including generative AI technologies. The rights holders expressly reserve
this publication from the text and data mining exception as per Article 4(3) of the Digital Single
Market Directive (EU) 2019/790.

A catalogue record for this book is available from the British Library.

Library of Congress Cataloging-in-Publication Data
Names: Small, Douglas R. J., author.
Title: Cocaine, literature, and culture, 1876–1930 / Douglas R.J. Small.
Description: London ; New York : Bloomsbury Publishing, 2024. |
Series: Critical interventions in the medical and health humanities ; vol 5 |
Includes bibliographical references and index.
Identifiers: LCCN 2023030476 (print) | LCCN 2023030477 (ebook) |
ISBN 9781350400092 (hardback) | ISBN 9781350400139 (paperback) |
ISBN 9781350400108 (pdf) | ISBN 9781350400115 (ebook)
Subjects: LCSH: Drugs in literature. | Cocaine abuse in literature.
Classification: LCC PN56.N18 S63 2024 (print) | LCC PN56.N18 (ebook) |
DDC 809/.933561–dc23/eng/20230830
LC record available at https://lccn.loc.gov/2023030476
LC ebook record available at https://lccn.loc.gov/2023030477

ISBN: HB: 978-1-3504-0009-2
PB: 978-1-3504-0013-9
ePDF: 978-1-3504-0010-8
eBook: 978-1-3504-0011-5

Series: Critical Interventions in the Medical and Health Humanities

Typeset by Newgen KnowledgeWorks Pvt. Ltd., Chennai, India

For product safety related questions contact productsafety@bloomsbury.com.

To find out more about our authors and books visit www.bloomsbury.com
and sign up for our newsletters.

Contents

List of Figures	vi
Acknowledgements	vii
Introduction	1
1 Coca leaves, Edward Weston, and the Victorian origins of sports doping	21
2 Conquerors of pain: Cocaine anaesthesia and the ideal medical man	47
3 Brutal fashions: Cosmetic surgery and tattooing at the fin de siècle	79
4 Cocaine bugs and the horrors of addiction	107
5 Sherlock Holmes and cocaine in canon and comedy: Profession, pleasure, and the Zany	141
6 White powder, White fears: Race, sex, and masculinity in the jazz age	175
Conclusion	211
Bibliography	223
Index	243

Figures

0.1	Alphonse Mucha, Advert for 'Vin Des Incas' (1890–9)	4
0.2	Albert Robida, Frontispiece for *History of Coca: 'The Divine Plant' of the Incas* (1901)	5
2.1	Dr Halifax coolly examines Molly Stafford in 'The Red Bracelet' (1895)	74
5.1	Holmes (played by William Gillette) injects himself with cocaine, 1900	157
5.2	Sheerluck Jones (played by Clarence Blakiston) parodies Holmes's cocaine habit, 1902	161
5.3	Dr Watson faithfully dogs Sherlock Holmes with syringe at the ready. Peter Arno, 1923	162
5.4	Coke Ennyday (Douglas Fairbanks) in his office, *The Mystery of the Leaping Fish*, 1916	164
5.5	Coke Ennyday's collection of syringes, 1916	165

Acknowledgements

This book is the result of help from more friends, institutions and colleagues than I can ever hope to adequately thank here.

The Wellcome Trust generously supported the research and writing of this work under grant no: 200353/Z/15/Z, and I would particularly like to thank Gavin Miller, David Shuttleton and Megan Coyer for their enormously patient and incisive advice throughout the application process. I am also indebted to numerous friends and colleagues at the Edge Hill University, the University of Glasgow and beyond for their help and guidance: Abigail Boucher, Alyson Brown, Rebecka Klette, Robert Maslen, Andrew McInnes, Bob Nicholson, Hannah Tweed and Molly Ziegler.

Earlier versions of parts of this book have previously appeared in *English Literature in Transition* ('Sherlock Holmes and Cocaine: A 7% Solution for Modern Professionalism,' *English Literature in Transition*, 58.3, 2015) and the *Journal of Victorian Culture* ('Masters of Healing: Cocaine and the Ideal of the Victorian Medical Man,' *Journal of Victorian Culture*, 21.1, 2016); all this material has since been significantly revised and expanded. I would like to thank the editors of these journals – Robert Langenfeld and Trev Broughton – as well as their readers and reviewers for their invaluable assistance. I would also like to thank Ben Doyle, Laura Cope and the rest of the editorial team and anonymous reviewers at Bloomsbury, whose efforts have gone into making this a better book.

Finally, my deepest thanks go to my family. My parents Drummond and Elizabeth deserve all the love and gratitude that I can give, as does my indefatigably fantastic sister, Lynsay. I would like to thank my parents-in-law Helen and David for their support and for consistently keeping me well-caffeinated. Finally, and most of all, I would like to thank my wife, Laura Eastlake: this book's most insightful reader, my best friend and by a wide margin the best human being I have ever met.

Introduction

Cocaine is the perfect drug. If God were to give us a drug, it would be the perfect drug. Since cocaine is perfect, it is God's gift to man.

These words were recorded in 1983 by the American psychopharmacologist Ronald K. Siegel in the course of an interview with a young man named Eddie Love. Love had recently been arrested after embarking (as Siegel described it) on a three-week-long combination crime spree and 'religious crusade', robbing banks to fund his 'cocaine sacrament'. Cocaine, Love said, made him feel 'as happy as a king, the way I'm supposed to be'; shifting excitedly against his prison restraints, he continued: 'When I take cocaine into my body, I am partaking of God himself. … I've had every drug conceivable. Cocaine is *God*.'[1]

These remarks capture, in particularly dramatic style, an essential image of cocaine and of its effects that continues to predominate in modern popular culture. As a central nervous system stimulant, cocaine (taken recreationally) produces intense feelings of energy and euphoria, and it magnifies joy, confidence, sexuality, and disinhibition. Eddie Love's fist injection of cocaine had been enough to convince him that God had somehow become materialized in those glittering, feather-light crystals, and that He had passed through the needle into Eddie's own flesh. In 1974, almost a decade before Siegel and Love's interview, the *New York Times* magazine ran an expansive multi-page article on the drug under the headline, 'Cocaine: The Champagne of Drugs'.[2] To this day, many of the most widespread conceptions of cocaine still derive from its representation in the 1970s and 1980s – an era when the drug's effects seemed

---

[1] See Ronald K. Siegel, 'Cocaine and the Privileged Class', *Advances in Alcohol & Substance Abuse*, 4.2 (1984), 37; and Ronald K. Siegel, *Intoxication: The Universal Drive for Mind-Altering Substances* (Rochester, NY: Park Street Press, 2005), 250.
[2] Ann Crittenden and Michael Ruby, 'Cocaine: The Champagne of Drugs', *New York Times*, 1 September 1974, 14.

to precisely match the tenor of the times. In late-twentieth-century America and Britain, cocaine came to figure in the popular imagination as the ideal 'party drug', a compound that perfectly synergized with 'both the eroticised 1970s and the risk-taking, entrepreneurial fever of the early 1980s'.[3] Visions of this period continue to predominate in popular perceptions of cocaine: aggregated images of wealth and 'privilege';[4] arch pretentiousness and criminal excess; the lithely coked-up 'glitter people'[5] of the Disco Age; the operatic violence and self-annihilation of Brian De Palma's *Scarface* (1983); and legions of money-hungry, 'hard-charging ... Yuppies'.[6] Since the late twentieth century, cocaine has often been taken to 'represent the aristocracy of drug-users',[7] while also acquiring a reputation as the quintessential indulgence of the parvenu. Cocaine stands at once as 'The Rich Man's Drug' and 'The Pimp's Drug',[8] both the glamourous, snow-white distillation of 'initiative, energy, frenetic achievement and ebullient optimism'[9] and the poseur diversion of 'smug advertising executives'.[10]

The enduring power of these more modern images, however, has the effect of obscuring the cultural–historical complexity of cocaine in the first period of its popularity: the last decades of the nineteenth century and the first decades of the twentieth. Prior to this time, European experiences with cocaine came principally from the Spanish conquests of South America in the sixteenth century. Cocaine occurs naturally in the leaves of the coca plant (*Erythroxylum coca*)[11] which was cultivated extensively by the Incan Empire of the western Andes and was 'central' to both the civil and religious infrastructure of the Incan state.[12] The conquistador Pedro Cieza de León observed in 1552:

> Throughout Peru the Indians carry this coca in their mouths; from morning until they lie down to sleep they never take it out. When I asked some of these

---

[3] David Farber, *Crack: Rock Cocaine, Street Capitalism, and the Decade of Greed* (Cambridge: Cambridge University Press, 2019), 33.
[4] Siegel, 'Cocaine and the Privileged Class', 38.
[5] Crittenden and Ruby, 'Cocaine: The Champagne of Drugs', 14; and 'Against Benign Neglect', *New York Times*, 22 September 1974, 252.
[6] Farber, *Crack*, 33.
[7] George R. Gay, Darryl S. Inaba, Richard Tobin Rappolt, George F. Gushue, and John James Perkner, '"An' Ho, Ho, Baby, Take a Whiff on Me": La Dama Blanca Cocaine in Current Perspective', *Anaesthesia & Analgesia*, 55.4 (July 1976), 584.
[8] Ibid.
[9] George R. Gay and Darryl S. Inaba, 'Acute and Chronic Toxicology of Cocaine Abuse', in *Cocaine: Chemical, Biological, Clinical, Social, and Treatment Aspects*, ed. S. J. Mule (Cleveland: CRC Press, 1976), 251.
[10] Dominic Streatfeild, *Cocaine* (London: Virgin Books, 2007), ix.
[11] NB: The majority of Victorian sources spell the name '*Erythroxylon coca*'.
[12] Lidio M. Valdez, Juan Taboada, and J. Ernesto Valdez, 'Ancient Use of Coca Leaves in the Peruvian Central Highlands', *Journal of Anthropological Research*, 71.2 (January 2015), 232.

Indians why they carried these leaves in their mouths, which they do not eat, but merely hold between their teeth, they replied that it prevents them from feeling hungry, and gives them great vigour and strength.[13]

Coca's capacity to increase stamina, suppress appetite, and intensify resilience contributed to its primacy in Incan cultural life. It was kept and distributed to labourers from government-run storage facilities throughout the Incan domains; the leaves were placed in the mouths of the dead before burial and given to 'capacocha sacrificial victims'; cultivation of the plant drove Incan 'colonis[ation of] the tropical rainforest east and north of Cuzco'; and the religious offerings of the leaves were made at shrines and important landmarks across the Empire.[14] Incan religious veneration of the plant was picked up on and imitated in later descriptions. One of the earliest representations of coca in English comes from Abraham Cowley's 1662 poetry collection *Six Books of Plants*. Book Five of Cowley's work imagines a competition between the classical gods of the old world and those of the new continents of America to see which pantheon has produced the greatest of botanical wonders. It is coca that leads the American vanguard. The Incan goddess Pachamama declares:

> Our *Varicocha* first this Coca sent,[15]
> Endow'd with Leaves of wondrous Nourishment,
> Whose Juice suce'd [sucked] in, and to the Stomach tak'n
> Long Hunger and long Labour can sustain;
> From which our faint and weary Bodies find
> More Succour, more they cheer the drooping Mind,
> Than can your *Bacchus* and your *Ceres* join'd;
> Three Leaves supply for fix days march afford,
> The *Quitoita*[16] with this Provision stor'd
> Can pass the vast and cloudy Andes o'er.[17]

This creative association between the 'wonderous nourishment' of coca and the exotic divinities of the Incan Empire continued into the fin de siècle. In the 1890s, Alphonse Mucha produced his floridly art nouveau advert for 'Vin des Incas' – a French brand of coca wine. Mucha's painting shows an Incan goddess imperiously refusing to share a bottle of the product with her worshippers

---

[13] Quoted in ibid., 231.
[14] Ibid., 232.
[15] Varicocha is the name of the Incan creator god.
[16] An inhabitant of Quito, the capital of modern-day Ecuador.
[17] Abraham Cowley, *The Second and Third Parts of the Works of Mr Abraham Cowley* (London: Charles Harper, 1700), 121.

Figure 0.1 Alphonse Mucha, Advert for 'Vin Des Incas' (1890–9).

('Divinité Incas refusant la coca à son peuple' as the advert's subscript puts it), preferring instead to keep the drink's wondrous effects for herself. Albert Robida's frontispiece for William Golden Mortimer's *History of Coca: 'The Divine Plant' of the Incas* (1901) shows a similar, though more magnanimous, divinity, 'Mama Coca' (a deified form of the coca plant), ceremonially offering the revitalizing leaves to the peoples of the old world (see Figures 0.1 and 0.2).

Throughout the nineteenth century (intensifying from the 1850s onwards), there were periodic revivals of medical and popular interest in the coca leaf and its 'extraordinary qualities'.[18] Horticulturalists noted that the chewing of the leaves allowed users to undertake 'great muscular exertion' and that '[their use] impart[s] a sense of cheerfulness and happiness'.[19] In 1867, *The Ladies' Treasury* wrote excitedly about the possibility of creating a world of 'Life and Labour Without Fatigue' if only the leaf – with its 'almost divine properties' – could be successfully imported from South America and kept free from adulteration along the way.[20] Richard Verity penned a letter to *The Lancet* in 1872 to recommend the plant:

> I have personally used [coca] for the last twenty five or thirty years, and found it exceedingly useful, specially [*sic*] in hot weather, as a stimulant and reviver. It

---

[18] 'The Coca Leaf', *Dublin Evening Mail*, 5644 (21 February 1855), 1.
[19] 'Horticulture', *Hampshire Advertiser*, 1995 (23 November 1861), 2.
[20] E. J. W. F., 'Life & Labour without Fatigue, without Food', *The Ladies' Treasury: An Illustrated Magazine of Entertaining Literature* (1 August 1867), 355–6.

MAMMA COCA PRESENTING THE "DIVINE PLANT" TO THE OLD WORLD.
[From an Aquarelle by Robida.]

Figure 0.2 Albert Robida, Frontispiece for *History of Coca: 'The Divine Plant' of the Incas* (1901).

is very good also when added in small quantity to ordinary tea. A digestive and truly 'pick-me-up' liqueur is made of it, and would be a boon to many if they knew the advantages which can be derived from its use.[21]

Leaves could, Verity said, be obtained – with some expense – from the British and Foreign Pharmacy in Warwick Street, London.[22] Two of the British public's most impactful encounters with coca (examined in detail in the first chapter of this book) took place in the spring of 1876. In the span of a couple of months, the renowned American athlete Edward Payson Weston revealed that he chewed coca leaves during his races to strengthen his powers of endurance, and the pioneering toxicologist and medical jurist Sir Robert Christison published 'Observations on the Effects of Cuca, or Coca, the Leaves of Erythroxylon Coca' in the *British Medical Journal*.

Throughout this time, though, the concentrated cocaine alkaloid remained relatively unknown to those outside of the specialized realms of botanical chemistry. Between 1858 and 1860, the German chemist Albert Niemann successfully isolated pure cocaine from the leaves of the coca plant, but it was only in 1884 that the substance was to emerge into the fullness of its celebrity. On the 15th of September of that year, the congress of the Heidelberg Ophthalmological Society received word that Karl Koller, a twenty-seven-year-old ophthalmological intern on the staff of the Vienna General Hospital (the 'Allgemeine Krankenhaus'), had discovered that a mild solution of cocaine introduced into the eye would deaden the nerves' sensitivity to pain. Thus, cocaine became known to the world as the first effective local anaesthetic.

Koller had been inspired to begin experimenting with cocaine by some work of Sigmund Freud's, who was at the time still a young man himself and a friend of Koller's at the Vienna General. (In publishing his discovery, Koller had felt it appropriate to express, in a general way, his gratitude to Freud by observing that cocaine had 'been brought to the front' of therapeutic research by his friend's investigations.[23]) Freud's initial researches into cocaine – which he published

---

[21] Richard Verity, 'Erythroxylon Coca', *Lancet*, 100.2549 (6 July 1872), 31. For details of other medical explorations of coca leaves, see: 'Coca', *Lancet*, 81.2060 (21 February 1863), 222; 'Medical News', *Lancet*, 88.2242 (18 August 1866), 195; 'Medical News', *Lancet*, 88.2257 (1 December 1866), 625; 'Coca', *Lancet*, 99.2544 (1 June 1872), 746.

[22] Richard Verity, 'Erythroxylon Coca', *Lancet*, 100.2555 (17 August 1872), 248.

[23] Carl Koller, 'On the Use of Cocaine for Producing Anaesthesia of the Eye', *Lancet*, 124.3197 (6 December 1884), 990. Some later publications followed Koller's lead in acknowledging that the ophthalmologist's 'attention was called to the probable power of cocaine' by Freud's study, but in the long term the credit for the discovery of cocaine anaesthesia remained almost entirely with Koller alone. See James E. Pilcher, 'Cocaine as an Anaesthetic; Its Status at the Close of the First Year of Its Use', *Annals of Surgery*, 1.3 (January 1886), 52.

in July 1884 in the medical journal *Centralblatt für die Gesamte Therapie* under the title 'Ueber Coca' – were heavily influenced by earlier accounts of the effects of coca leaves, both descriptions of Incan coca use and the experiences of medical authors such as Robert Christison. 'Ueber Coca', as such, focusses almost entirely on the systemic effects of cocaine as a stimulant and strength-giver. Freud confidently states that the 'main use' of the drug will 'undoubtedly remain that which the Indians have made of it for centuries … to increase the physical capacity of the body'.[24] Indeed, Freud's description of cocaine seems to be largely predicated on the assumption that the alkaloid is basically a purified or concentrated form of the coca leaf itself. Cocaine is, according to Freud, 'the true agent of the coca effect',[25] and he often represents the drug as producing a truer, more refined, intensification of coca's action on the body. Freud likewise uses the names 'coca' and 'cocaine' interchangeably throughout the article, suggesting that the two compounds were functionally coterminous in his estimation.[26] 'Ueber Coca' depicts cocaine primarily as a technological evolution of coca, the extracted essence of the leaf, which produces the same systemic effects but with greater efficiency.

Despite his later international renown, Freud's focus on the psychotropic and physically stimulating effects of cocaine had relatively little impact on late Victorian perceptions of the drug compared with Koller's discovery.[27] The precise sequence of events involving the two medical men is hard to identify, partly because Koller and Freud appear to have given slightly different accounts at different points in their lives. According to Koller, in the summer of 1884, Freud had invited him to participate in 'a series of experiments [on] the physiological systemic effects of cocain [*sic*]' and the two had begun 'taking the drug by mouth'

---

[24] Sigmund Freud, *The Cocaine Papers*, ed. K. Donoghue and James Hillman (Vienna: Dunquin Press, 1963), 14.

[25] Ibid., 7.

[26] It is worth noting that this discursive conflation of coca and cocaine persists throughout the period of this study. While the cocaine alkaloid makes up only a small percentage of the coca plant, Victorian and early-twentieth-century observers tended to recognize only a hazy and loosely defined separation between the two. Advocates for the use of the leaf, like William Golden Mortimer, complained that 'cocaine … is commonly regarded as the sole active principle of Coca'. (William Golden Mortimer, *Peru: History of Coca, 'The Divine Plant' of the Incas* (New York: J.H. Vail, 1901), 402–3.) Other commentators, like Aleister Crowley, viewed coca as merely the 'crude form' of cocaine. (Aleister Crowley, 'Cocaine', *The International*, 11.10 (October 1917), 292.) This work, as such, focusses primarily on the discursive interconnection between the two substances, detailing how the cultural associations of both compounds influenced the reception of the other.

[27] For a more detailed examination of Freud's works on cocaine, his personal history with the drug, and the ways in which subsequent discourses of psychoanalysis were 'mediated' through Freud's encounters with cocaine see Dušan I. Bjelić, *Intoxication, Modernity, and Colonialism: Freud's Industrial Unconscious, Benjamin's Hashish Mimesis* (New York: Palgrave, 2016), 1–21, 31–56, and 67–75.

and recording their physical responses.[28] During the course of these experiments, Koller noted the numbing effect that cocaine had on the tongue, and it occurred to him that the drug might have a similar action if applied directly to the eye. Freud left on a month-long visit to see his fiance in late August and while he was away Koller independently continued with his experiments, successfully anaesthetizing first the eye of a frog, then a guinea pig, and finally his own eye.[29] (Later, in *The Interpretation of Dreams*, Freud was to somewhat ruefully claim that he 'had hinted at this use [ie. local anaesthesia] of the alkaloid in my publication, but I was not sufficiently thorough to pursue the matter further'.[30]) Releasing the potential surgical applications of the discovery, Koller hastily wrote up a report of his findings and passed the communiqué to his associate Dr Joseph Brettauer to present on his behalf at the Heidelberg conference.

The medical community's response was immediate and elated. Koller, reflecting on his discovery after a lapse of over forty years and a move across the Atlantic to New York, recalled how: 'Knowledge of the new remedy spread quickly, and in looking over the medical and the lay press of the time, daily and periodical, one will encounter a perfect flood of communications on cocain and local anesthesia'.[31] *The Lancet*'s yearly summary of medical news (the 'Annus Medicus') for 1884 confessed to feeling somewhat overwhelmed by the sheer number of 'flattering testimonies advanced in favour of the drug', concluding that: 'Cocaine has occupied so much of our recent space that there is no need to dilate further on its properties in this place'.[32] In the first half of 1885, the *British Medical Journal* and *The Lancet* carried a combined total of over 130 articles on cocaine and its various applications. 'The medical press,' one correspondent dryly observed, 'is full of cocaine just now.'[33] The volume of

---

[28] Carl Koller, 'Personal Reminiscences of the First Use of Cocain as a Local Anesthetic in Eye Surgery', *Anesthesia and Analgesia*, 7.1 (February 1928), 10.
[29] See Ronald S. Fishman, 'Karl Koller: The Introduction of Local Anesthesia', in *Foundations of Ophthalmology: Great Insights that Established the Discipline*, ed. Michael F. Marmor and Daniel M. Albert (New York: Springer, 2017), 120–1; and Koller, 'Personal Reminiscences of the First Use of Cocain', 10.
[30] Sigmund Freud, *The Interpretation of Dreams*, ed. A. A. Brill (New York: Macmillan, 1913), 143. Several authors also note that before departing on his holiday, Freud proposed to Leopold Königstein – another colleague in the Vienna General's ophthalmology department – that he should 'research the use of cocaine in painful diseases of the eye such as iritis and trachoma'. Königstein apparently observed that the drug mitigated the discomfort of these conditions, but 'failed to investigate the cause or draw further conclusions'. See A. López-Valverde, J. de Vicente, L. Martínez-Domínguez, and R. Gómez de Diego, 'Local Anaesthesia through the Action of Cocaine, the Oral Mucosa and the Vienna Group', *British Dental Journal*, 217.1 (11 July 2014), 42; and Bjelić, *Intoxication, Modernity, and Colonialism*, 151.
[31] Koller, 'Personal Reminiscences of the First Use of Cocain', 11.
[32] 'The Annus Medicus 1884', *Lancet*, 124.3200 (27 December 1884), 1152.
[33] 'Cocaine', *Lancet*, 125.3201 (3 January 1885), 43.

this commentary was equalled by its enthusiasm. Henry Power, the president of the British Medical Association's ophthalmology and otology section, asserted that: 'In the discovery of cucaine [sic], a new era seems to have dawned.'[34] To contemporaries, cocaine appeared to have 'flashed like a meteor' across the horizon of modern medicine; the drug's effects seemed to promise that fin de siècle therapeutics had at last attained a hitherto unimagined 'Ultima Thule of anaesthetics', and grasped one of the best and most 'splendid triumphs of science'.[35]

As for Koller, it was to be some time before he was able to enjoy the practical rewards of this international elation. On 6 January 1885 (while medical papers were still full of news of his success), he had the misfortune to run across a surgical intern at the Vienna General Hospital named Friedrich Zinner. An argument over the treatment of a patient's bandaged finger escalated until Zinner called Koller an 'impudent Jew' and Koller struck him in the face. Both men were medical lieutenants in the army reserve, so Zinner challenged Koller to a duel, which Koller won handily. In the aftermath, though, the Vienna public prosecutor brought charges against both men, with the result that Koller was unable to continue his work at the hospital. Consequently, Koller moved abroad and for the next few years he worked at the Utrecht Eye Hospital under the famed Dutch neurologist and ophthalmologist Franciscus Cornelius Donders before emigrating to New York in 1888. In the United States he was better able to capitalize on his renown, opening a 'thriving' ophthalmological practice and becoming both 'the first head of ophthalmology at the Montefiore Hospital' and (in 1922) the first recipient of the Lucien Howe Medal for achievements in ophthalmology.[36]

Cocaine itself experienced similarly mixed fortunes over the following years. The initial sense of ecstatic possibility associated with the substance was to become increasingly tempered by an awareness of its potential dangers. Early commentators had suggested that the worst reactions that might be expected

---

[34] Henry Power, 'An Address Delivered at the Opening of the Section of Ophthalmology and Otology', *British Medical Journal*, 2.1283 (1 August 1885), 207.
[35] 'Cocaine', *Chambers's Journal*, 3.114 (6 March 1886), 145; 'Coca and Cocaine', *Lancet*, 124.3198 (13 December 1884), 1063.
[36] See Fishman, 'Karl Koller: The Introduction of Local Anesthesia', 124–7. Further biographical details for Koller's later life (as well as a transcript of the Vienna public prosecutor's indictment of Zinner and Koller in the original German) can be found in M. Goerig, 'Aus dem Nachlass von Carl Koller: Aufzeichnungen zu seinen Experimenten mit Kokain', *Der Anaesthetist*, 64.6 (June 2015), 470–4. For more information on wider cultures of Jewishness and anti-Semitism in the Viennese medical establishment of this period, see: Tatjana Buklijas, 'Surgery and National Identity in late nineteenth-century Vienna', *Studies in History and Philosophy of Biological and Biomedical Sciences*, 38.4 (December 2007), 756–61.

from the substance were probably no worse than 'those attending a boy's first experience of tobacco'.³⁷ But as the 1880s wore on, the risks – both of cocaine poisoning and of addiction – began to figure more prominently in popular and medical discourse. The opening of J. B. Mattison's 1887 article 'Cocaine Dosage and Cocaine Addiction' summarizes the drug's ambivalent position in the years following its introduction into common usage:

> No advent in the therapeutic arena during the last decade has been attended with such varied and extensive claims for favour as cocaine. Its marvellous effect in ophthalmic surgery roused a spirit of experimental research in other directions which has added largely to its well-proved power for good; but, as has been well observed, a potency for good implies a potency for harm, and the risk impends of its ardent advocates being carried by over-enthusiasm beyond the limit of a safe regard for the welfare of their patients or themselves, that may imperil an otherwise well-founded success. Surely it is high time to draw the line, to revoice a warning as to the use and abuse of this valued but at the same time toxic drug.³⁸

Other contemporary medical accounts reiterate this image of cocaine as simultaneously 'marvellous' and perilous. Cocaine, in the words of one medical author, had the dubious distinction of 'showing how readily the latest additions to the means of relieving human suffering are seized upon as means of self-indulgence, however dangerous'.³⁹ According to J. B. Mattison, the 'free and frequent use' of cocaine carried with it a danger of addiction 'more marked and less hopeful than that from alcohol or opium'.⁴⁰ The month before Mattison's article appeared in *The Lancet*, news had reached the UK of a remark made by the German neurologist Friedrich Albrecht Erlenmeyer: that cocaine had overshot the established dangers of opium and alcohol to become 'the third scourge of humanity'.⁴¹ By the early twentieth century, accounts of the terrible, scourging effects of cocainism were to become a common feature of the British press. 'The effects of cocaine,' as one paper described them, 'while delightfully exhilarating, are so evanescent that the individual soon passes all bounds in its use. Mental and physical ruin, if not actual death, are certain results if the habit is continued. ... This habit is fearfully on the increase, and if doctors do

---

³⁷ R. Shalders Miller, 'Remarks on the Employment of Cucaine', *BMJ*, 1.1314 (6 March 1886), 439.
³⁸ J. B. Mattison, 'Cocaine Dosage and Cocaine Addiction', *Lancet*, 129.3325 (21 May 1887), 1024.
³⁹ 'New Forms of Narcotism', *BMJ*, 1.1482 (25 May 1889), 1186. Large parts of this article were also reproduced in the popular press. See 'A New Form of Intoxication', *Trewman's Exeter Flying Post*, 6870 (25 May 1889), 8 and 'A New Form of Intoxication', *Blackburn Standard and Weekly Express*, 22 June 1889, 2.
⁴⁰ Mattison, 'Cocaine Dosage and Cocaine Addiction', 1026.
⁴¹ 'Scraps', *Manchester Times*, 1554 (23 April 1887), 8.

not do something shortly it will become a plague.'[42] Fears about this 'plague' of cocaine addiction were to continue to build in the national imagination until the outbreak of the First World War, and the passage of section 40b of the Defence of the Realm Act (DORA) in 1916, which criminalized the sale and possession of cocaine by anyone other than specific 'authorised persons'. These restrictions were later reworked into the Dangerous Drugs Act of 1920, which solidified the legal prohibitions surrounding cocaine into peace-time law.

This is the arc followed by most critical and historical accounts of cocaine in the late nineteenth and early twentieth centuries: the brief but passionate affair of the 1880s, quickly succeeded by decades of lingering recrimination and regret. The purpose of this book is, in part, to elaborate this narrative, to examine the simultaneous co-existence and interaction of multiple different cocaine discourses across this period. To take one relatively straightforward example, descriptions of cocaine in these years do not rapidly and smoothly progress from characterizing it as a marvel of science to a dangerous drug of addiction. In 1885, the ophthalmologist Henry Power had seen in cocaine the inauguration of a 'new era' for the profession.[43] Based on subsequent remarks in the *British Journal of Ophthalmology*, that 'new era' might be said to have endured until at least 1928. According to the journal: 'In spite of the repeated trials of other drugs cocaine easily holds the field as the best local anaesthetic for eye work; and although it is nearly 44 years since it was first used, and in spite of the advocacy of butyn, borocaine, etc., nothing more satisfactory has yet been found to take its place in ophthalmic surgery.'[44] In 1929, W. E. Dixon, reader in pharmacology at the University of Cambridge, reached a similar conclusion in the pages of the *British Medical Journal*. 'No drug,' Dixon wrote, 'produces local anaesthesia so well as cocaine.'[45] This continuing medical admiration for the virtues of cocaine was likewise accompanied by a surprisingly persistent strain of resentment at its criminalization. Throughout the 1910s and 1920s, many writers for the *Chemist and Druggist* were of the opinion that both DORA 40b and the Dangerous Drugs Act were the 'absurd' work of 'some highly placed amateur'.[46] Other commentators for the journal maintained that the 'proper and medicinal use' of drugs like morphine and cocaine had 'become mixed in official minds with abuse by a few degenerates,

---

[42] 'Taking Cocaine', *Burnley Express*, 4059 (31 July 1909), 2.
[43] Power, 'An Address Delivered at the Opening of the Section of Ophthalmology and Otology', 207.
[44] 'Carl Koller and Cocaine', *British Journal of Ophthalmology*, 12.5 (May 1928), 263.
[45] W. E. Dixon, 'Physiology the Basis of Treatment', *BMJ*, 2.3577 (27 July 1929), 142.
[46] 'The Cocaine Muddle', *Chemist and Druggist*, 89.1938 (17 March 1917), 51.

and the result is a growing suppression of these drugs and dependence on inferior remedies'.[47] Though 'exceedingly valuable' as a remedy, cocaine had, its defenders claimed, fallen prey to 'wildly extravagant and sensational' accounts of its evils and to 'an alarmist and panicky demand for extreme legislative restrictions'.[48]

The English biochemist Henry Hallett Dale (who was later to be awarded the Nobel Prize for Medicine in 1936) articulated some of the diffuseness and complexity of cocaine discourse when, in 1924, he observed that:

> We must admit, I think, that the case of cocaine is in some respects unique. There are other drugs of addiction; but cocaine appears to be the only one in which the therapeutic value depends upon an action of a different type from that which leads to the vicious habit. In therapeutics only its local actions have any serious value, whereas the action desired by the addict is one produced, after absorption, upon his central nervous system.[49]

For contemporary observers, cocaine seemed to be possessed of a 'unique' duality of actions. Applied locally, it was a 'powerful' instrument of medical therapy and pain relief, one which 'after almost half a century of use has not been supplanted'. In contrast to this, however, were the drug's potentially 'deplorable' systemic effects.[50] As one police surgeon put it: 'It is a stimulant and exhilarating, but it is a dangerous thing. ... If taken habitually [it] produces mental and moral degeneration, and becomes dangerous and demoralising to the community.'[51] Even in the context of its recreational uses (or abuses) cocaine seemed to be uniquely capable of multiplying its own actions and aspects. In his 1924 survey of narcotics and stimulants, *Phantastica*, Louis Lewin described how: 'no other substance has as many different modes of application as cocaine, from injection under the skin to drinking cocaine wine or cocaine champagne, to smoking cocaine cigars, from being brushed into the nose or taken as a snuff, to being rubbed into the gums or the anus. Each of these forms has its lovers.'[52] Thus,

---

[47] 'International Legislation', *Chemist and Druggist*, 109.20 (17 November 1928), 604–5.
[48] 'Dangerous Drugs Act Regulations', *Chemist and Druggist*, 94.2143 (19 February 1921), 52.
[49] H. H. Dale, 'The Possible Substitutes for Cocaine', *BMJ*, 1.3299 (22 March 1924), 511.
[50] Dale, 'The Possible Substitutes for Cocaine', 511; and Koller, 'Personal Reminiscences of the First Use of Cocain', 11.
[51] 'Evils of Cocaine', *Illustrated Police News*, 2990 (2 June 1921), 6.
[52] 'Kein anderes zeigt in der Verwendungsart so viele Varianten wie Kokain, von der Einspritzung unter die Haut an, bis zum Trinken von Kokainwein oder Kokain-champagner, bis zum Rauchen von kokainisierten Zigarren, zum Einpinseln in die Nase oder dem Gebrauche als Schnupf-pulver, zum Einreiben in das Zahnfleisch oder an den After. Für jede dieser Formen gibt es Liebhaber'. Louis Lewin, *Phantastica: Die Betäubenden und Erregenden Genussmittel* (Berlin: Georg Stilke,

beginning in the fin de siècle and continuing into the early twentieth century, cocaine carries with it a powerful sense of multiplicity. From the 'miraculous invigoration'[53] of coca leaves, to its introduction as a local anaesthetic – one of the foremost 'miracles of the nineteenth century'[54] – to its stigmatization and criminalization, cocaine existed in the popular imagination as a combination of distinct (sometimes confusingly contradictory-seeming) effects, different modes of application, and the diverse uses to which the drug might be put.

It is these cultural receptions and imaginative connotations of cocaine that are the focus of this book. Most existing studies of cocaine tend to concentrate on the social and legal processes that led to the drug's international prohibition.[55] Other critics treat with cocaine more incidentally, examining it as a part of broader analyses of historical discourses on addiction and substance abuse.[56] This work, by contrast, uses an approach and methodology drawn from the medical humanities. Rather than being straightforwardly a work of social history or taking cocaine addiction as its primary focus, this book, instead, concentrates on cocaine as it appears in metaphor and fictional narratives in the late nineteenth and early twentieth centuries. To quote Susan Sontag's introduction to *Illness as Metaphor*, this book is less concerned with the practical applications of cocaine and the direct experiences of its users, than it is with 'the punitive or sentimental fantasies that are concocted about' these experiences and applications. Sontag famously considers 'the uses of illness as a figure or metaphor', detailing the processes by which 'figurative meaning ... [is] projected onto a disease and the disease (so enriched with meanings) is projected onto the world'.[57] This book – unlike other more explicitly historical accounts of the

---

1924), 72–3. See also: Louis Lewin, *Phantastica: A Classic Survey on the Use and Abuse of Mind-Altering Plants* (Rochester: Park Street Press, 1998), 68.

[53] 'Round Lancaster Castle', *Lancaster Gazette*, 6052 (15 February 1890), 8.

[54] Benjamin Ward Richardson, 'The Mastery of Pain: A Triumph of the Nineteenth Century', *Longman's Magazine*, 19.113 (1 March 1892), 510.

[55] See, for example, Joseph F. Spillane, *Cocaine: From Medical Marvel to Modern Menace in the United States* (Baltimore, MD: Johns Hopkins University Press, 2000); James H. Mills, 'Drugs, Consumption, and Supply in Asia: The Case of Cocaine in Colonial India, c. 1900–c. 1930', *Journal of Asian Studies*, 66.2 (May 2007), 345–62; James H. Mills, 'Cocaine and the British Empire: The Drug and the Diplomats at the Hague Opium Conference, 1911–12', *Journal of Imperial and Commonwealth History*, 42.3 (2014), 400–19. This book treats less with the specific effects of the First World War than previous works largely because Virginia Berridge and Marek Kohn both offer extensive and detailed accounts of the impact of the war on receptions of cocaine and the development of drug prohibition legislation. See Virginia Berridge, 'War Conditions and Narcotics Control: The Passing of Defence of the Realm Act Regulation 40B', *Journal of Social Policy*, 7.3 (July 1978), 285–304; and Marek Kohn, *Dope Girls: The Birth of the British Drug Underground* (London: Granta Books, 2001).

[56] See Susan Zieger, *Inventing the Addict: Drugs, Race, and Sexuality in Nineteenth-Century British and American Literature* (Amherst: University of Massachusetts Press, 2008), 177–8 and 233–40.

[57] Susan Sontag, *Illness as Metaphor and AIDS and Its Metaphors* (London: Penguin Books, 2002), 3 and 60.

drug – adapts Sontag's approach to disease to examine the historical reception of cocaine as a transformative medical technology and the imaginative responses that this generated among contemporary observers.

Across the fin de siècle and the first part of the twentieth century, cocaine both receives and bequeaths metaphorical significance. Contemporary understandings of cocaine – as a surgical anaesthetic, home remedy, stimulant, euphoriant, drug of enhancement, and so on – cannot be disentangled from the narratives, symbols, metaphors, and moral fables that accumulate around it. Similarly (and recalling Sontag's discussion of tuberculosis, cancer, and AIDS), this book examines how cocaine is itself used as a metaphor: how it becomes a figure by which emotion and meaning can be projected onto other discourses, situations, and personalities (both real and fictional) not immediately connected with the substance. Thus, this book aims to detail how a particular drug can become 'aestheticize[d]', how its various uses and patterns of consumption can be translated into different 'manner[s] of appearing' and new 'tropes for new attitudes towards the self'.[58]

This cross-connection of selfhood and substance use is directly addressed in the first chapter, which begins this book's account of cocaine in 1876, with the first major upsurge of British popular interest in the drug. In March of that year, papers began to report that the internationally famous 'pedestrian' (a form of competitive long-distance walking), Edward Payson Weston, had chewed coca leaves during some of his races to improve his performance. This incident is sometimes identified in modern histories as the first sports doping scandal,[59] but an examination of Victorian sources demonstrates that most saw nothing immoral in Weston's use of coca to assist him in competition. This chapter sets out to explain this reaction – to answer the question of why Weston's contemporaries didn't see drug use in sport as either dishonest or cheating. Many journalists, in fact, commended Weston for his ingenuity while other sportsmen hurried to try the leaves for themselves. I argue that performance-enhancing drugs in general (and coca in particular, due to its strengthening and energizing effects on the body) could be easily accommodated into underlying Victorian conceptions of the sporting individual and their performance. In the 1870s, performance-enhancing drugs could be combined with an athlete's

---

[58] Sontag, *Illness as Metaphor and AIDS and Its Metaphors*, 20, 28–9.
[59] Steven B. Karch, *A Brief History of Cocaine* (London: Taylor and Francis, 2006), 27; Paul Dimeo, *A History of Drug Use in Sport: 1876–1976: Beyond Good and Evil* (London: Routledge, 2007), 3 and 19–21; and Vanessa Heggie, 'Bodies, Sport, and Science in the Nineteenth Century', *Past and Present*, 231 (May 2016), 193.

physical training, expertise, and emotional fortitude to produce an ideal model of the sporting self.

Chapters 2 and 3 move from sporting ideals to medical ones. After cocaine's local anaesthetic function was discovered in 1884, the drug quickly acquired a reputation as one of the greatest, most humanely beneficial discoveries of fin de siècle science. With the capacity to remove pain without rendering the patient unconscious, cocaine appeared to sidestep the anxieties associated with older general anaesthetics like ether and chloroform. Chapter 2 analyses how the public and practitioners alike became emotionally and ideologically invested in cocaine in this period. I argue that, as the twentieth century drew nigh, it seemed that modern science had at last succeeded in producing a modern panacea.[60] Consequently, the virtues of cocaine – its ease of use, its effectiveness in abolishing pain, and the swiftness with which it took effect – offered a particularly striking template for the virtues of the ideal fin de siècle medical practitioner. In medical papers, popular journalism, and in works of fiction like L. T. Meade's 'The Red Bracelet' (1895), cocaine – presented as the perfect drug – was depicted as manifesting the character of the perfect medical man.

Chapter 3 continues to explore the ramifications of cocaine anaesthesia in the last years of the nineteenth century and the early 1900s. In this chapter I suggest that – by making anaesthesia easier – cocaine removed a major obstacle to purely cosmetic medical procedures. Cocaine enabled a range of minor operations that allowed patients to modify the aesthetic qualities of their own bodies, to change the outlines of their features, smooth and retouch their countenances, and remove any blemishes or imperfections that they desired. The most obviously spectacular aesthetic application of cocaine was to the art of tattooing, as fin de siècle tattooists took up the new drug to promise their 'patients' the most extensive and elaborate designs without the least discomfort.[61]

---

[60] Modernity is a notoriously ambiguous and contested phenomenon to define, not least because – as Peter Wagner points out – one of its apparently central contradictions is the fact that different societies at different points in history have regarded themselves as 'modern societies', while the modernity of the past is 'radically different from the modernity of our present'. (Peter Wagner, *Modernity: Understanding the Present* (London: Polity, 2012), x.) Throughout this work, I have used terms such as 'modernity' and 'modern society' not primarily to designate a particular technological, political, or economic epoch but rather to signify, in the words of Jean Baudrillard, 'a characteristic mode of civilisation'. According to Baudrillard, modernity represents 'a social practice and way of life articulated on change and innovation – but also on anxiety, instability, [and] continual mobilization'. Modernity, in this formulation, expresses the ideation of the new, both as progress and as crisis. (See Jean Baudrillard, 'Modernity', *Canadian Journal of Political and Social Theory*, 11.3 (December 1987), 63–5.) This understanding of modernity as a civilizational 'mode' helps to explain why cocaine could – as we shall see – be discursively associated with modernity in both the 1880s–1890s and the 1920s, despite the differences in each period's specific manifestations and conceptions of 'the modern'.

[61] 'A Visit to a Professional Tattooer', *Chums: An Illustrated Paper for Boys*, 2.81 (28 March 1894), 485.

This chapter details several points of tension within Victorian and Edwardian cosmetic medicine. In being applied to cosmetic (or decorative) ends, cocaine could be regarded as having crossed over into an ambiguous territory between medicine and fashion. Indeed, I argue, many observers within this period came to regard tattooing itself as an especially disconcerting and chaotic form of medical procedure. Similarly, fictional representations of cocaine and cosmetic operations from this period often combine the hope of a more easily modified and beautifully decorated body with a strain of gothic horror: the prospect of a body free to be 'changed at will'[62] also implied a body deprived of the necessary limits imposed by pain and subjected to endless, directionless transformation.

Chapter 4 concentrates on discourses of cocaine addiction at the turn of the century and details how these came to be associated with a narrative of medical over-confidence – the sense that, despite having so enthusiastically advocated for it, '[the medical profession] in general [did] not understand the possibilities of this drug for evil.'[63] While there is an obvious overlap between representations of cocainism and more general discourses of substance abuse in this period, this chapter argues that specific images and tropes came to define cocaine habituation in the popular consciousness. Cocaine addiction was often characterized by a rhetoric of newness, of unprecedentedly horrifying danger. The drug's effects as an aphrodisiac and the hallucinatory affliction known as 'cocaine bugs' – a delusional conviction on the part of the victim that their skin was full of crawling insects – were often identified as evidence of the drug's unique and radical hazards. The main literary case study of this chapter analyses how this interweaving of skin, sexuality, and hallucination is reworked into a source of supernatural horror in Arthur Machen's 'The White Powder' (1895).

Recent sociological studies of substance use (particularly in the field of chemsex studies) have moved away from exclusively 'foregrounding [narratives of] stigma, trauma, and abuse' and towards interrogating the ways in which drugs constitute 'site[s] of joy and pleasure' for their users.[64] The concluding chapters of this book take a similar approach to analysing the cultural history of cocaine in the late Victorian and early Modernist periods. Chapters 5 and 6

---

[62] 'Changed at Will', *Hampshire Telegraph*, 5875 (31 March 1894), 11.
[63] W. Scheppegrell, 'Editorial', *Laryngoscope*, 5.6 (December 1898), 374.
[64] Kristian Møller and Jamie Hakim, 'Critical Chemsex Studies: Interrogating Cultures of Sexualised Drug Use beyond the Risk Paradigm', *Sexualities*, https://doi.org/10.1177/13634607211026223. See also, Kiran Pienaar, Dean Anthony Murphy, Kane Race, and Toby Lea, 'Drugs as Technologies of the Self: Enhancement and Transformation in LGBTQ Cultures', *International Journal of Drug Policy*, 78 (April 2020), 1–2; and Kane Race, 'Thinking with Pleasure: Experimenting with Drugs and Drug Research', *International Journal of Drug Policy*, 49 (July 2017), 144–9.

interrogate some of the ways in which contemporary subjects interacted with the pleasures of cocaine outside of the more familiar paradigm of addiction.

Chapter 5 examines the depiction of cocaine in Arthur Conan Doyle's Sherlock Holmes stories as well as the broader receptions of Holmes's cocaine habit among the reading public. Some of the richest responses to the great detective's cocainism appear in the many Sherlock Holmes parodies and comic pastiches that followed the wake of Doyle's initial success. As such, this chapter argues that where Doyle's original stories portray Holmes's cocaine habit as being inherently connected to his unwavering, machine-like professional focus, later comic writers convert the detective's drug use into the vicarious thrill of self-indulgent dissipation. Doyle's Holmes demands nothing more from life than that it should 'give [him] work' and only turns to his famous 7 per cent solution 'as a protest against the monotony of existence when cases were scanty and the papers uninteresting'.[65] The many Holmes caricatures that take shape in the newspapers, novels, and silent cinema of the late nineteenth and early twentieth centuries are, by contrast, relentlessly committed to the pursuit of pure enjoyment. This strain of headlong, delirious hedonism can, I suggest, be most effectively read through Sianne Ngai's analysis of the comic aesthetic of 'zaniness'. Ngai's framing of the zany – a comic style that is at its heart 'about work' and about the 'ambiguous erosion of the distinction between playing and working'[66] – allows us to understand both Doyle's original stories and their parodies as equally preoccupied with the same underling issues of modernity, professionalism, and the pleasures of drug-taking.

Chapter 6 elaborates on depictions of cocaine euphoria, considering its connections with racial unease in the wake of the international criminalization of cocaine in the early twentieth century.[67] In Britain, cocaine had since the fin de

---

[65] Arthur Conan Doyle, *The Sign of Four*, ed. Peter Ackroyd and Ed Glinert (London: Penguin, 2001), 6; Arthur Conan Doyle, *The Memoirs of Sherlock Holmes*, ed. Christopher Roden (Oxford: Oxford University Press, 2009), 53.
[66] Sianne Ngai, *Our Aesthetic Categories: Zany, Cute, Interesting* (Cambridge, MA: Harvard University Press, 2012), 188.
[67] Throughout this work, and most notably in Chapter 6, I have made the decision to capitalize the word 'White' when it appears as a racial identifier. The rationale behind this decision is not to obscure the fundamentally racist and hierarchical associations inherent in the concept of 'Whiteness', nor is it to suggest an equivalence between the identities of White subjects and the 'specific cultural and liberatory identity captured by the word "Black"'. Rather, the intention is to emphasize how, throughout the early twentieth century, the use of cocaine by White individuals is often deliberately linked to the active construction and performance of a White racial identity. The White authors examined in Chapter 6 purposefully articulate Whiteness through the performative enjoyment of cocaine pleasure. Thus, I argue, the taking of cocaine by White subjects becomes a considered 'choice … about how to understand and actualise (perform) their racial identit[y]'. The capitalization of White is, as such, intended to highlight these acts of choice and performance in the context of White

siècle been viewed as a characteristically American drug, its chaotic energy, joy, and over-stimulation seeming to capture the hectic experience of a civilization 'in the van of human progress'.[68] By the 1920s, though, cocaine had come to be seen as a drug specifically connected with Black American populations. Even when used by White people in the bars and nightclubs of London, cocaine was still thought to be inherently tied to Black culture. This racial, and fundamentally racist, logic resulted in a peculiar and apparently contradictory complex of ideas centred on the drug in the early Modernist period. This chapter argues that cocaine, in common with other Black-aligned cultural products of the 1920s like jazz and modern dance, came to be seen as simultaneously a 'product of machine-age modernity' and 'as something [supposedly] elemental or natural or primitive'.[69] In the White imagination of the period, cocaine appeared to merge the cutting edge of technological modernity with the primal excitement of sexual pleasure. This combination of associations meant that cocaine represented a distinct threat to White masculinity in this period, as White men found their position of racial and cultural primacy undermined by the newly sophisticated yet elemental pleasures of cocaine. For some, the natural response was to aggressively stigmatize the use of the drug, but for others – most notably Aleister Crowley in his 1923 novel *The Diary of a Drug Fiend* – a different solution presented itself: to regain their former position of security and ascendancy, the White man would have to acquire a masterful familiarity with the dynamically modern and primitively carnal pleasures of cocaine. Thus, this chapter examines how cultural and legal constructions of drug pleasure can be made to serve the ends of racist hegemony.

Throughout its history, cocaine has become a receptacle for many fantasies, both grandiose and fearful. It creates confidence and ecstasy so 'perfect' as to seem like 'God's gift to man'.[70] In the aftermath of the First World War, Aleister Crowley was to nostalgically reflect that: 'Cocaine, removes all hesitation. ... When one is on [cocaine], one is really, to a certain extent, superior to one's fellows. ... The British Empire is due to this spirit.'[71] When the drug's anaesthetic function was discovered in the 1880s, one paper responded with the claim that: '[Christ] is

drug use and to foreground the conscious integration of drug pleasure into a schema of White racial domination. (See Tommy J. Curry, 'Shut Your Mouth When You're Talking to Me: Silencing the Idealist School of Critical Race Theory through a Culturalogic Turn in Jurisprudence', *Georgetown Law Journal of Modern Critical Race Studies*, 3.1 (2012), 1; and Veronica T. Watson, *The Souls of White Folk: African American Writers Theorize Whiteness* (Jackson: University of Mississippi Press: 2013), ix.)

[68] 'Chit-Chat', *Sheffield Evening Telegraph*, 803 (7 January 1890), 2.
[69] James Donald, *Some of These Days: Black Stars, Jazz Aesthetics, and Modernist Culture* (Oxford: Oxford University Press, 2015), 65.
[70] Siegel, 'Cocaine and the Privileged Class', 37.
[71] Aleister Crowley, *The Diary of a Drug Fiend* (London: W. Collins, 1923), 44–5.

the Patron of infirmaries, hospitals, and homes, and cocaine is one of the blessed instruments of his pain-removing and peace-instilling mission.'[72] For different users, cocaine could crystallize diverse images of godlike bliss, the self-assurance of Empire, and the promise of a divine medical science that might finally and absolutely conquer pain. These were accompanied (and are still accompanied) by other, more alarming imaginaries: the gothicized horrors of addiction and more pejorative fantasies of legal coercion and punishment. In 1922, questions were raised in newspapers and in parliament about the possibility of giving 'twelve strokes of the cat [o' nine tails]' to any convicted cocaine dealer.[73] In August 2021, the UK Home Secretary Priti Patel announced her determination that the police should '"make an example" out of middle-class cocaine users'.[74] This book aims to illuminate the ways in which multiple tropes, aesthetics, and ideals can be imposed onto a single drug, and how these narratives intersect with its real-life uses, the perceived risks of its use, and the forces of law brought to bear upon it.

---

[72] 'Cocaine', *The Scotsman*, 29 August 1887, 7.
[73] '"Cat" for Cocaine Sellers', *Pall Mall Gazette*, 17754 (27 April 1922), 4. See also *Hansard Parliamentary Debates*, HC Deb, 4 May 1922, vol. 153, c.1549.
[74] 'Priti Patel wants to "make an example" out of middle-class cocaine users', *Independent*, 16 August 2021, https://www.independent.co.uk/news/uk/politics/priti-patel-middle-class-cocaine-b1903337.html

1

Coca leaves, Edward Weston, and the Victorian origins of sports doping

Before Karl Koller's discovery of cocaine's anaesthetic properties, British public conceptions of the coca leaf were largely shaped by a series of events in the spring of 1876. In January of that year, the American athlete Edward Payson Weston (1839–1929) and his wife Maria set out on the two-week Atlantic crossing to England. Back in the United States, Weston was already famed as a long distance competitive walker – or 'pedestrian' – and his aim in undertaking the Atlantic voyage was to spread his renown to the mother country. Over the coming months, Weston was to compete against British pedestrians in a series of highly popular and widely reported endurance races. At his first event in the British Isles – a 24-hour-long contest from February 8 to 9 against the English champion walker William Perkins[1] – a crowd of five thousand spectators assembled at the London Agricultural Hall to watch the start of the race.[2] By the end, Weston alone had lasted the full twenty-four hours, accomplishing a distance of 109½ miles, while Perkins – in 'lamentable condition', and with 'the blood ooz[ing] through his shoes'[3] – had been forced to resign at 11.50 pm the previous night, having managed only 65½ miles.[4] Weston's victory over his English rival won him a mixture of journalistic admiration and humorously resigned patriotic chagrin. The *Daily News* called Weston's walk a 'marvellous performance' accomplished with 'astonishing dash and vigour'.[5] *The Sporting Gazette* devoted two columns to its account of the contest, writing that the international visitor was 'gifted with the most indomitable perseverance and extraordinary ability to go on without

---

[1] F. W. Pavy, 'The Effect of Prolonged Muscular Exercise on the System', *Lancet*, 107.2739 (27 February 1876), 319.
[2] Nick Harris, Helen Harris, and Paul Marshall, *A Man in a Hurry: The Extraordinary Life and Times of Edward Payson Weston, the World's Greatest Walker* (London: deCoubertin Books, 2012), 118.
[3] 'International Walking Match', *Birmingham Daily Post*, 25.5486 (10 February 1876), 8.
[4] Pavy, 'Effect of Prolonged Muscular Exercise', 319.
[5] 'The International Walking Race', *Daily News*, 9298 (10 February 1876), 3.

stopping for an indefinite distance'. Though the American's style of walking was 'something most peculiar', disconcertingly poised between 'a postman's walk [and] the twitching of a galvanized corpse', his determination coupled with 'the way he kept pegging along, lap after lap and mile after mile, was the theme of universal admiration'.[6] *The Sporting Times* paid Weston the double compliment of having enacted 'certainly one of the greatest pedestrian feats on record' and of proving that 'our American cousins are "spry" in other matters besides the manufacture of cocktails'.[7]

More than one paper remarked upon Weston's avowed teetotalism. The staff of the comic magazine *Fun* pretended to believe that the 'overthrow of English pedestrian prominence' would have been even more emphatically accomplished if not for the fine British traditions of immoderate smoking and drinking. The 'agony endured by Mr Weston at the sight of the crowds round the refreshment bars ... [and] by the smell from innumerable pipes and cigars' had, the writer claimed, so badly upset 'the gentleman from America' that it had saved British athleticism from an even worse defeat. Whatever Weston's private thoughts might have been about his audience's love of 'intoxicating drinks' and 'the noxious weed',[8] however, he was soon to become involved in a more expansive public discussion of substance use and sporting performance. On 18 March 18 1876 (in response to a rash of articles that appeared in *The Lancet*, the *British Medical Journal*, and the popular press), Weston wrote to *The Lancet* to declare that: 'During my first trial in London on the 9th of February ... I chewed coca leaves freely.'[9]

By the 1870s, there had been relatively little sustained scientific examination of either coca leaves or of the cocaine derivative. The most consistent sources of information were travellers' tales and accounts of life in South America, which frequently related both the plant's powers as a restorative and a sustainer of physical strength, as well as the prevalence of the coca habit among the Native American populace. In the 1820s, the famous English general William Miller (known in Latin America as Guillermo Miller) was noted to have 'often chewed [coca]' during his service under Simon Bolivar in the Peruvian War of Independence. (Though accounts were unclear as to whether this was because of the plant's own properties or because 'cigars were a luxury not within the reach

---

[6] 'Athletic Notes', *Sporting Gazette*, 14.718 (12 February 1876), 158.
[7] 'Notes and Notions', *Sporting Times*, 605 (16 February 1876), 91.
[8] *Fun*, 23 (16 February 1876), 78.
[9] Edward Payson Weston, 'Mr Weston on the Use of Coca Leaves', *Lancet*, 107.2742 (18 March 1876), 447.

of the patriot army'.[10]) Later descriptions emphasized that: '[coca] has no equal in its power of stimulation ... The Indians of Bolivia and Peru travel four days at a time without taking food, their only provision consisting of a little bag of coca.'[11] The leaf could, it was said, endow its user with 'an increased disposition to muscular action [and], with great power of endurance', so that 'locomotion can be performed with more than ordinary facility and continued without fatigue for a long period during the mastication of coca'.[12] Near-identical descriptions appeared in medical papers. In 1872, *The Lancet* wrote: 'Extraordinary stories are told of the wonderful properties of coca in enabling those who chew it to overcome the feeling of hunger, and to undergo great muscular exertion and fatigue. ... The Incas and Indians, who constantly masticate coca, are said to go through excessive labour with ease, and to require very little food.'[13] Inspired by such accounts, Weston had apparently chewed coca leaves during his duel with Perkins to increase his powers of endurance and stave off fatigue, and his sporting celebrity excited British popular interest in the plant like never before. In addition to reportage in magazines, newspapers, and medical journals, the American pedestrian claimed to 'daily receive scores of letters asking me if I believe in the efficacy of coca leaves'.[14] The pioneering Edinburgh toxicologist Sir Robert Christison – who was known to be an authority on the action of the coca leaf – was likewise pressed by 'numberless references to me by friends and strangers in all parts of the kingdom for information as to its effects'.[15] Weston's experiences with coca, however, were destined not only to spread public awareness of the drug but also to shape much of the discourse that came to surround it.

In 'Drugs as Instruments' Christian Müller and Gunter Schumann argue that non-addictive drug use represents 'a functional adaptation to modern environments', particularly modern working environments.[16] In their analysis, Müller and Schumann view drugs as being 'instrumentalised' – tools that allow users to, for instance, purposefully 'change mental states', 'improve cognitive performance', and 'counteract fatigue'.[17] This instrumentalized approach

[10] John Miller, *Memoirs of General Miller in the Service of the Republic of Peru*, Vol. 2 (London: Longman, Rees, Orme, Brown, and Green, 1829), 229 and 174.
[11] 'New Vegetable Stimulant', *Hampshire Advertiser*, 1995 (23 November 1861), 2.
[12] 'Scientific Miscellany', *Manchester Times Supplement*, 24 November 1866, 375.
[13] 'Coca', *Lancet*, 99.2544 (1 June 1872), 746.
[14] Weston, 'Mr Weston on the Use of Coca Leaves', 447.
[15] Robert Christison, 'Observations on the Effects of Cuca, or Coca, the Leaves of the Erythroxylon Coca', *BMJ*, 1.800 (29 April 1876), 527.
[16] Christian P. Müller and Gunter Schumann, 'Drugs as Instruments: A New Framework for Non-Addictive Psychoactive Drug Use', *Behavioural and Brain Sciences*, 34.6 (December 2011), 293.
[17] Ibid., 298, 299, 311.

posits that: 'in industrialised societies, an individual's workload [requires them to perform] many different behaviours with contrasting types of effort' and to rapidly transition between a wide variety of 'strong[ly] differentiated microenvironments' both at home and at work.[18] Under these conditions, drug consumption allows users to artificially augment 'behavioural flexibility' and produce a limited form of 'self-induced, time-restricted personality change'.[19] Müller and Schumann's theorization of 'instrumental'[20] drug use and modernity (though written from the point of view of neurology and behavioural evolution) has much in common with Brenda Mann Hammack's discussion of the 'chemically inspired intellectual'[21] in late-Victorian culture. Hammack delineates a pervasive association between fin de siècle depictions of drug use and notions of intense, or excessive, intellectual activity and labour. Substances with stimulant or hallucinatory effects on the brain were often thought to be resorted to by exhausted 'brain workers' (such as authors, doctors, lawyers, and other intellectual professionals) to supply mental energy or creative inspiration.[22] Like Müller and Schumann, Hammack describes an 'instrumentalised' use of psychoactive drugs to optimize cognitive performance and improve the professional individual's ability to do their work.

Müller, Schumann, and Hammack, however, focus their analysis specifically on psychoactive drugs and their potential use as mental enhancements. In this chapter, by contrast, I want to argue that coca was initially characterized by physical effects and discourses. Impelled by Weston's highly publicized use of the leaf, coca was portrayed as acting predominantly on the body, rather than on the mind: while representations of other compounds foreground the cognitive or emotional responses they excited in their users, coca was thought to augment the body's capacity for muscular exertion, to temper the body's need for food and rest, and to fortify its power of endurance. By intensifying the body's capabilities, coca was associated with images of improved, or superior, physicality – particularly the heightened physical exertions of sport and sportsmen. As such, this chapter analyses early receptions of coca in the light of contemporary constructions of sporting performance, alongside nascent questions as to the morality of chemically enhancing that performance.

---

[18] Ibid., 297.
[19] Ibid., 297, 299.
[20] Ibid., 295.
[21] Brenda Mann Hammack, 'Phantastica: The Chemically Inspired Intellectual in Occult Fiction', *Mosaic: A Journal for the Interdisciplinary Study of Literature*, 37.1 (2004), 83–100; accessed 1 April 2019, http://literature.proquest.com/.
[22] Ibid.

Most critical commentary on Weston's coca chewing in his race against Perkins has tended to position him as part of (or, indeed, as the originator of) the tradition of sports doping and illegal use of performance-enhancing substances. Vanessa Heggie refers to the revelation of Weston's coca chewing as 'the first recorded incident of a complaint about doping in modern sports'.[23] Steven B. Karch goes even further, calling Weston, 'the first known athlete to cheat using drugs'.[24] There has, however, been relatively little examination of the reactions which Weston's coca use provoked among his contemporaries.[25] Rather than the 'furore'[26] which Karch suggests was sparked by the discovery, the predominant reaction – in both the medical and sporting communities – was one of interest coupled with cautious excitement. The *York Herald* and the *Huddersfield Daily Chronicle* agreed that 'the extraordinary sustaining power' of the coca leaf was 'very interesting' and likely to have many 'popular applications'.[27] The *Northern Echo* joked that the South American plant might prove itself an inestimable ally of the temperance movement: 'If only half of the marvellous properties of this leaf are correct, alcohol has got a most formidable rival, whose services should at once be enlisted by the teetotallers.'[28] And the *Glasgow Herald* wound up a report on Weston's latest athletic triumph with the remark that: 'if it be indeed true that Weston during his long walks habitually chews a piece of coca leaf, the plant is clearly one to which scientific men cannot too soon turn their attention.'[29]

Signally absent from these reports is any suggestion that Weston might have enjoyed an unfair advantage over his opponents by chewing coca. Commentators were ready to 'attribute some of [the American Pedestrian's] marvellous capacity for endurance'[30] to his use of the leaf, but there was little-to-no sense that Weston had violated the ethics of either his sport or of fair competition by 'doping' to support his own abilities. John Gleaves and Matthew Llewellyn attribute the

---

[23] Vanessa Heggie, 'Bodies, Sport, and Science in the Nineteenth Century', *Past and Present*, 231 (May 2016), 193.
[24] Steven B. Karch, *A Brief History of Cocaine* (London: Taylor and Francis, 2006), 27.
[25] Paul Dimeo's *A History of Drug Use in Sport: 1876–1976* takes its initial starting point in 1876 from Edward Weston and Sir Robert Christison's experiences with coca, but concentrates primarily on later trends in sports ideology responsible for 'turn[ing] the socially approved quest for stimulants into a tense standoff between "official" sanctions and "unofficial" doping.' (See Paul Dimeo, *A History of Drug Use in Sport: 1876–1976: Beyond Good and Evil* (London: Routledge, 2007), 3 and 19–21.) Similarly, while Vanessa Heggie touches on Weston's coca chewing, the primary focus of her article is on Weston's contribution to Victorian medical debates about sport, exertion, and nutrition, rather than on his coca consumption. (See Heggie, 169–72 and 193–4.)
[26] Karch, *A Brief History of Cocaine*, 29.
[27] 'The Art of Walking', *York Herald*, 5957 (13 March 1876), 8; 'The Great Walking Match', *Huddersfield Daily Chronicle*, 2683 (13 March 1876), 3.
[28] 'The American Scandals', *Northern Echo*, 1929 (14 March 1876), 3.
[29] 'The 500 Miles Walk', *Glasgow Herald*, 12098 (11 March 1876), 5.
[30] 'The American Scandals', *Northern Echo*, 3.

rise of anti-doping sentiment in the early twentieth century to the widespread adoption of a Victorian 'amateur ethos'[31] of sporting competition. Victorian sport was (according to Gleaves and Llewellyn) divided between amateur and professional sportsmen – professionals being predominantly (though not exclusively) working-class individuals who were paid for appearances or who competed for cash prizes, while the amateur self-consciously 'played the game for the game's sake, disavowed gambling and professionalism, and competed in a composed and dignified manner'.[32] Drug use was widely accepted among professional sportsmen and was 'portrayed as a tool to assist professional athletes in doing their job'. Victorian commentators 'did not see doping as unfair or cheating, but simply contrary to the gentlemanly amateur code that governed middle- and upper-class sport'.[33] Analysis of Weston's coca chewing partially corroborates this professional framing of sport and performance enhancement. Contemporary reports can be seen to be comparatively accommodating to Weston's use of 'artificial stimulants' like coca, in part because the drug could be regarded as a demonstration of the sportsman's own practical expertise in how to get the best results out of his own body.

This chapter, however, also aims to broaden our understanding of Victorian conceptions of the morality of drug use for sporting performance enhancement. I argue that contemporary reactions to Weston's coca use are dependent upon the construction of his sporting performance more generally. Weston's athletic performance was, at the time of his coca chewing, presented as a synthesis of a diverse range of different factors. His physical capabilities, his expertise, specialized knowledge, emotional temperament, and force of will were all alloyed together to produce Weston's individual, multifaceted identity, and it was this aggregated sporting selfhood which was portrayed as responsible for his victories. Put simply, Weston's exceptional achievements as an athlete were thought to materialize his exceptional inner nature as a sportsman. An important corollary to this can be seen in the fact that coca was often depicted as coordinating or realigning the body's own natural functions in a way that replicated the ideally coordinated selfhood of the sportsman; in its chemical action, coca was presented as balancing the operations of the system in the same way that the athlete had to balance strength, knowledge, and emotional

---

[31] John Gleaves and Matthew Llewellyn, 'Sport, Drugs and Amateurism: Tracing the Real Cultural Origins of Anti-Doping Rules in International Sport', *Journal of the History of Sport*, 31.8 (May 2014), 845.
[32] Ibid., 840.
[33] Ibid., 843.

fortitude to ensure victory. In this context, amateur sportsmen could and did make use of coca to produce the (to paraphrase Gleaves and Llewellyn) 'composure and dignity'[34] essential to the amateur ethos. This chapter, then, examines depictions of Weston's coca chewing alongside other contemporary medical and sporting discussions of the drug to illuminate coca's role in constructions of athletic performance and the origins of sporting drug use. Professional and amateur use of coca in this period serves to (in Müller and Schumann's terminology) 'instrumentalise' the body and the body's alignment with the self.

The expert sportsman

Edward Weston's career was, as *The Lancet* was to reflect some years later, one which was often played out 'on the borderland between Physiology and Sport'.[35] Weston's coca habit had come to light because – first in his race against Perkins and then in subsequent events – he had allowed a number of medical authorities to record his physical responses (and to collect samples of his urine) with a view towards clarifying the relationship between nutrition, exercise, and fatigue.[36] In attendance at the races were the physiologist Frederick William Pavy (1829–1911); Frederick Akbar Mahomed (1849–1884), pathologist for St. Mary's Hospital, Paddington; and John Ashburton Thompson (1846–1915) – who was later to become a world authority on leprosy and bubonic plague. Pavy's observations were published in *The Lancet*, while Thompson and Mahomed published their own medical commentaries in the *British Medical Journal*.[37] On the 11th of March, in the course of an article reporting on Weston's fourth competitive walk in Britain (an attempt by Weston and two other men to walk five hundred miles in six days), Thompson noted:

---

[34] Ibid., 840.
[35] 'The Annus Medicus 1884', *Lancet*, 124.3200 (27 December 1884), 1161.
[36] Various papers – both British and American – questioned the sincerity of Weston's devotion to the cause of science, seeing in his participation another instance of his 'Yankee', 'high falutin' style' of self- publicity (see 'The Anglo-American Walking Match', *The Penny Illustrated Paper and Illustrated Times*, 755 (12 February 1876), 106). *Forest and Stream* claimed to 'recognise [Weston's] old dodge of inviting members of the medical profession to be present' from his former 'grandiloquent' performances in America ('Weston in England', *Forest and Stream*, 6.4 (2 March 1876), 56), while *The Sporting Gazette* reported the 'suggestive' rumour that Weston's British lodgings were on the premises of Barnum's American Circus ('Athletic Notes', *Sporting Gazette*, 158).
[37] For a more detailed account of these physiological investigations and of their context in the history of nineteenth-century theories of metabolism, energy, and exertion, see Heggie, 'Bodies, Sport, and Science in the Nineteenth Century'.

> At intervals as he persistently pursues his route, Weston may be seen to go through the action of chewing; and a brown stain upon his lips ... On these occasions, he is masticating a substance which, although credited with some of the properties of tobacco, is the most serviceable of its class for use under exertion. That substance is the dried leaf of the Erythroxylon Coca.[38]

Thompson went on to contend that, since coca was widely reported to 'diminish the waste of the tissues', 'affect the pulse and respiration', and reduce body temperature and urinary excretion, these effects 'must be taken into consideration before drawing any conclusions from the elaborate and careful analysis ... now in course of publication by Dr Pavy'.[39]

Thompson's main concern in publishing his observations had been to account for coca's effects on the ongoing physiological trials, but his exposure of Weston's coca habit was rapidly picked up and republished in the popular papers. Consequently, the following week, on the 18 March, Pavy and Weston both published vehement rebuttals of Thompson's claims in *The Lancet*,[40] and the *BMJ* printed a letter William Pavy had written to its editorial staff disputing Thompson's critique of his physiological investigations.[41] Pavy (with evident irritation), 'regretted that, before advancing such a proposition, Mr Thompson did not obtain more precise information'.[42] In all three articles, Weston and Pavy's position was that Thompson had jumped to the wrong conclusion. Weston's position was that he had only used coca during his first British walk against Perkins, and never afterwards. Pavy further asserted that the urine samples taken from Weston during this first race had been discarded, 'through a mishap', before inspection and analysis took place. This meant that Pavy's physiological conclusions were based only on samples taken during later races when Weston had been (ostensibly) coca-free. The overall accuracy of Pavy's results was seemingly thus preserved.[43]

Thompson then prepared a further statement for the *BMJ*, where he diplomatically attempted to both defend his own observations and conciliate Weston and Pavy.[44] Wrote Thompson:

---

[38] J. Ashburton Thompson, 'Weston's Fourth Walk', *BMJ*, 1.793 (11 March 1876), 335.
[39] Ibid.
[40] See F. W. Pavy, 'The Effect of Prolonged Muscular Exercise on the System', *Lancet*, 107.2742 (18 March 1876), 429–30; and Weston, 'Mr Weston on the Use of Coca Leaves', 447.
[41] J. Ashburton Thompson, 'The Coca Leaf', *BMJ*, 1.794 (18 March 1876), 362.
[42] Pavy, 'The Effect of Prolonged Muscular Exercise', 18 March 1876, 429.
[43] Ibid.
[44] NB: Thompson, Weston, and Pavy had been in communication privately during the week after the 11th, so Thompson's own response, Pavy's letter to the *BMJ*, and Weston and Pavy's statements in *The Lancet* all appeared on the same day: 18 March 1876.

> I stated last week, in positive terms, that Mr Weston was in the habit of chewing the leaf of the erythroxylon coca during his exertions. I based that statement upon observations which I made, not during the first walk alone, but during every one of the four walks. I am now informed by Mr Weston that my inference from those observations is correct with regard to the first walk, but that it is not correct as far as the second, third, and fourth walks are concerned. … My statement of last week must now, therefore, submit to qualification. I modify it with pleasure; but I regret the occasion.[45]

Thompson likewise regretted that the investigators had not been appraised of Weston's coca use from the beginning. 'For some reason or other,' wrote Thompson, 'he thought it inadvisable to advertise his use of the plant; and this (under the circumstances) most probable source of error was not guarded against by those who are gravely responsible to the profession for their accuracy.'[46] The statement's final sentiment, though, was that thanks to the happy accident of the discarded urine sample, no lasting harm had been done, and Thompson's statement effectively ended any overt questions about the accuracy of Pavy's results.

It is worth observing that the controversy around Weston's coca chewing was focussed almost entirely on what it might signify for the accuracy of Pavy's physiological trial. The dispute was one which centred on professional and experimental standards, rather than on the standards of fair play in the races themselves; Thompson's critique of Weston – that for some indeterminate reason of his own he had elected not 'to advertise his use of the plant' – was rooted in the implications that Weston's actions might have had for Thompson and Pavy's own 'grave responsibility' to their profession. The acrimony that played out in the pages of *The Lancet* and the *BMJ* arose in response to the threat of medical professional embarrassment and the questioning of Pavy's experimental integrity. What was not in question (perhaps curiously from a modern perspective) was Weston's integrity as a sportsman. Observers were, in fact, keen to point out that Weston's athletic triumphs were in no sense diminished by his use of coca. One reader of *The Lancet*, S. M. Bradley, wrote to the journal to express his concern that public interest in the plant might end up overshadowing public appreciation of Weston's achievement. 'In the name of common sense,' wrote Bradley 'it is but just to say that it is simply absurd to distract attention from the pedestrian feat which has astonished the country to a little detail of this kind.'[47]

---

[45] Thompson, 'The Coca Leaf', 361.
[46] Ibid.
[47] S. M. Bradley, 'Coca-Leaf on the Brain', *Lancet*, 107.2744 (1 April 1876), 519.

For Bradley, it seemed that readers' ephemeral, hyperbolic interest in coca risked doing an injustice to the more substantial, authentic marvellousness of Weston's athleticism. It was a violation of 'common sense', and self-evidently 'absurd', to imply that Weston's performance might be compromised in some way by his use of coca.

Bradley's letter might have seemed like a partisan defence of the American pedestrian were it not that J. Ashburton Thompson, in disclosing Weston's coca chewing, had similarly been at pains to portray the drug as merely one factor among many that had contributed to Weston's success. Thompson clearly felt it appropriate to censure Weston for keeping his habit a secret from his medical observers, but approved of Weston's actions as a sporting competitor. He affirmed: 'There is no obvious reason why Mr Weston should not take advantage of every aid which his superior knowledge places at his disposal. Already he is clothed, fed, and tended in such a scientific manner as leaves but little room for improvement.'[48] Thompson refers to coca as offering an 'advantage' to Weston but not an unfair one. Rather, coca is legitimated on the grounds that it represents a practical application of specialized 'superior knowledge'. Thompson positions coca alongside the 'scientific' optimization of Weston's diet, clothing, and training as factors which 'aid' Weston's abilities and which illustrate the extent to which he has cultivated his professional expertise. Weston's character as a superior sportsman is, in part, attributable to his superior understanding of how to get the best results out of his own body. In this context, Weston's use of coca to fortify his stamina and endurance serves as an example of a highly developed technical expertise – a practical scientific proficiency that marked Weston as belonging to the premier echelon of sportsmen.

For Thompson, Weston's exceptionalism as a sportsman was due to his being a more expertly informed sportsman: he was the possessor of greater knowledge, combined with a better capacity to put that knowledge to use. This idea recurs throughout various journalistic discussions of Weston's coca chewing. In reporting the American pedestrian's habits as a successful sportsman, most papers divided the bulk of their coverage between Weston's use of coca and his techniques for 'the care of the feet in walking', since both factors represented information which 'might be expected [to be] … useful to pedestrians generally'.[49] Like J. Ashburton Thompson, the mainstream press

---

[48] Thompson, 'The Coca Leaf', 361.
[49] 'The 500 Miles Walk', *Glasgow Herald*, 12098 (11 March 1876), 5. Over the following days, near-identical remarks appeared in the *York Herald* ('The Art of Walking', *York Herald*, 5957 (13 March 1876), 8), *Huddersfield Daily Chronicle* ('The Great Walking Match', *Huddersfield Daily Chronicle*,

equated Weston's coca chewing to other techniques and 'superior knowledge' that the pedestrian used to improve his performance, such as the special care and attention he gave to his feet and footwear. Weston, it was reported, 'observes a definite series of precautions from want of which his competitors have suffered severely'. Among other procedures, his boots were specially shaped to reduce foot strain; when he did begin to feel footsore he 'poured large quantities of whiskey into his boots by means of a funnel'; and during brief intervals he bathed his feed in warm salt water for exactly five minutes, piercing blisters with a fine needle, but leaving the skin in place.[50] These reports emphasized the competitive advantage these elaborate 'precautions' offered Weston over his fellows, their failure being partly attributed to the 'want' of such actions. *The Sporting Times*'s account of Weston's race against Perkins attributed Weston's victory not only to his exceptional physical 'condition' but also to the fact that 'the American wisely elected to perform in thicker shoes on clay and gravel, whilst [Perkins] walked injudiciously in thin shoes on [bare] boards'.[51] In these reports Weston's superiority as a sportsman proceeds from his ability to implement superior, specialized knowledge and techniques. In so doing, Weston was able to arrange both the conditions of his environment and the condition of his own body in his favour – competing, according to *The Sporting Times*'s description, almost literally on his own ground. Weston's understanding of his body, how to optimize its performance, minimize its disadvantages, and maintain its smooth functioning under extreme stress, was regarded as one of his most distinctive and admirable characteristics. In this light, his use of drugs to reinforce his system and the elaborate preparations used to fortify his feet are essentially the same: expert 'precautions' derived from highly cultivated professional knowledge.

Sport and selfhood

Allied with this admiration for Weston's cultivated expertise, though, there was also the more expansive idea that Weston's athletic feats were the result of his uniquely cultivated selfhood as a sportsman. Reports of Weston's victories presented the view that his performance was the result of a complex,

---

2683 (13 March 1876), 3), and *Lancaster Gazette* ('Weston's Attempt to Walk 500 Miles in Six Days', *Lancaster Gazette*, 4636 (15 March 1876), 4).
[50] 'The 500 Miles Walk', *Glasgow Herald*, 5.
[51] 'Notes and Notions', *Sporting Times*, 91.

ideally aligned collection of attributes – his pedestrian exploits were the 'unprecedented'[52] results of Weston's own individual nature. Weston's use of coca was accepted as a legitimate instance of professionally specialized and applied information, but it was also legitimized on the grounds that it was thought to be an individual factor amid the multitude that contributed to the sportsman's victory. Weston displayed such exceptional prowess because he had balanced within himself an exceptional assortment of virtues and characteristics: Victorian observers prioritized Weston's individual identity as the primary determiner of his athletic performance, and the effects of coca were viewed as but a single constituent of an idealized whole.

A rhetoric of personal uniqueness permeates many of the reactions to Weston's coca chewing. In *The Lancet*'s editorial on 'Weston's Last Feat' from 18 March 1876, the journal observed: 'It would be wrong not to point out how unique are Mr Weston's powers.'[53] In like manner, the *Northern Echo* counselled its readers that, as potent as the effects of coca were, they should bear in mind that: 'Of course, the mere chewing of the leaf will not make a counter-jumper a Weston.'[54] For the paper, it was important to establish that Weston's feat was specific to himself, that coca alone would not allow the mere jobbing shop-clerk or 'counter-jumper' to rival his attainments. No drug could, unaided, make a lesser man into 'a Weston'. It is revealing to observe that Weston's avowed teetotalism (and its effects on his athletic performance) was presented to readers in language that was strikingly similar to that used in discussions of his coca chewing. In the early 1880s Weston returned to Britain to undertake a series of walks in support of the temperance movement. After one particularly 'prodigious' exhibition of his abilities (walking fifty miles a day for one hundred days), *The Lancet* wrote:

> Men who cultivate physical health and strength may well consider the significance of Mr Weston not only going through such a walk, but going through it so well, and with such an equilibrium of function at the end. ... A splendid physical achievement has been wrought without alcohol ... Not that teetotalism will enable any man to do what Weston has done, which is essentially a personal feat.[55]

The same sentiment underpins both *The Lancet* and the *Northern Echo*'s remarks: the two performances are presented as peerless 'personal feat[s]',

---

[52] 'Weston's Last Feat', *Lancet*, 107.2742 (18 March 1876), 440; and 'Weston's Last Feat', *Daily News*, 9329 (17 March 1876), 6.
[53] 'Weston's Last Feat', *Lancet*, 439.
[54] 'The American Scandals', *Northern Echo*, 1929 (14 March 1876), 3.
[55] 'Mr. Weston's Feat', *Lancet*, 123.3160 (22 March 1884), 540.

attainments wrought from the 'equilibrium' and 'strength' of Weston himself and inherently expressive of his individuality. *The Lancet* wrote that the physical difficulty of the temperance walk combined with 'the element of mental worry and anxiety' created 'conditions that would have disabled almost any man but Weston'.[56] The same logic is used to reinforce the singular distinctiveness of Weston's performance both in the presence of coca and in the absence of alcohol: the use or disuse of any particular substance is imagined to be incidental to the truly 'unique' and 'essentially personal' nature of Weston's victories. Weston's use of coca was immaterial when weighed against the substance of Weston's own selfhood.

This model of Weston's sporting performance (and its relationship with drug use) is repeated in J. Ashburton Thompson's articles for the *British Medical Journal*. Thompson consistently attributes Weston's successes not merely to the American's bodily strength and fortitude but to a combination of rigorous training with more abstract virtues of emotion, temperament, and mentality. Thompson emphasizes Weston's character as the main determining factor for the outcome of his races. In this framework, extraneous influences – like Weston's use of coca – could be regarded as comparatively unimportant. Writes Thompson:

> There is nothing nefarious, so far as I know, about the use of coca under the present circumstances; nor, I presume, would any person attribute all Mr Weston's powers to the use of some drug suddenly introduced into his system from without. Could they persuade themselves to do so, his mental powers – his foresight, his energy, and his perseverance – to which he owes so much, would still remain to be accounted for. These are natural qualities of Mr Weston's mind, which he not only knows himself to possess, but which he has cultivated to best advantage.[57]

Although Weston's achievement is a physical one, Thompson stresses that it is contingent upon more nebulous 'mental powers' and 'qualities of mind' – it is 'foresight', 'energy', and 'perseverance' that consistently propel Weston to victory. Indeed, Weston's mental determination might (in Thompson's view) provide him with an almost literal propulsive force. Elsewhere, Thompson described how the athlete could, in the extremes of tiredness, '*think* of each step, and steadfastly *oblige* himself to keep moving … progressing at the expense of his brain-power entirely'.[58] The force of Weston's 'brain-power' was sufficient to compel his body

---

[56] Ibid.
[57] Thompson, 'The Coca Leaf', 361.
[58] J. Ashburton Thompson, 'Physiological Memoranda on E. P. Weston's Third Walk', *BMJ*, 1.792 (4 March 1876), 298.

into action, the energy of his mind surmounting the depletion of the rest of his system. Thompson's description is ambiguous as to whether this process represents an actual transfusion of cerebral energy from Weston's brain into his body, or whether it is the more abstract force of Weston's character that allows him to overcome physical exhaustion. His depiction of coca is far less equivocal, however: the compound is 'introduced from without' and separated from the 'natural qualities of Mr Weston's mind' that define his performance. Thompson also stresses that these qualities are simultaneously 'natural', or innate, to Weston's mind, and 'cultivated' through rigorous self-examination and training. In this way, Thompson emphasizes that Weston's sporting ascendancy is heavily mediated through a range of closely interconnected emotional, physical, and mental factors: Weston is the beneficiary both of qualities that are inborn, or inherent, to himself and possessed of the capacity to painstakingly work to augment those same qualities. 'The introduction of some drug into his system from without' might have added to Weston's powers, but it was only a single constituent in the athlete's uniquely blended alloy of training, technique, and determined self-tempering. These virtues – uniquely coalesced in Weston himself – were the real source of his victory.

Later medical commentaries on Weston picked up and expanded the notion that the operation of the athlete's body was connected to (and, indeed, might be indistinguishable from) the nature of his character. In his analysis of exercise and athleticism, 'On Systematic Exercises; Their Value in the Prevention of Disease' (1878), Edward T. Tibbits invited his readers to:

> Note the admirable swim of Webb[59] and the prolonged walk of Weston, both feats of prodigious and unexampled endurance. In each case there was undoubtedly an intense feeling of fatigue, amounting to severe pain, and yet they were enabled by a powerful exercise of the will, greatly aided by, if not actually arising out of muscular development, to bring their labours to a wonderfully successful termination.[60]

Tibbits depicts Weston's 'unexampled' success as the outcome of physical strength allied to 'a powerful exercise of the will'. The language of these lines, however, also indicates the overlapping nature of body and mind. Weston's mental fortitude is not only 'aided' by 'muscular development', it appears to 'actually

---

[59] Matthew Webb, the first swimmer to make an unsupported solo crossing of the English Channel in 1875.
[60] Edward T. Tibbits, 'On Systematic Exercises; Their Value in the Prevention of Disease', *Lancet*, 112.2874 (28 September 1878), 436.

arise out of [it]'. Tibbits represents willpower as functioning in tandem with physical discipline, the will to action strengthening as the muscles themselves are strengthened through action. Tibbits portrays the mind (particularly the mind of the sportsman) in physical terms, the 'exercise of the will' conforming to the same processes of exertion, training, and fitness as the body. The article explicates this mental and physical connection in another passage:

> It is generally supposed that the brain is the organ of the mind. But the mental operations carried on within the skull could not take place independently of the senses. Hence, mind appears to include not only the centres, but the peripheral portions of the nervous system. We might even say that it exists in the muscles, and to a certain extent in every organ of the body; that, in fact, it includes the body – that the latter is part of the mind.[61]

Tibbits represents the brain and body existing on a form of continuum – the brain, 'the organ of the mind', is diffused throughout the tissues, organs, and (most importantly for the nature of athletic performance) the muscles, to the extent that the body may be regarded as 'part of the mind'. Force of will and muscular force are seen as extensions of each other. The supposed diffusion of mental processes into the fabric of the body[62] meant that the mental and physical dimensions of sport were closely (even materially) interconnected; 'professional athletes' aligned 'good physique' with 'great volitional control' – a coterminous 'exercise' of mind and body in which each strengthened the other.[63]

Reception of Weston's coca chewing, therefore, took place in an environment where the athlete's physical abilities were only ambiguously separated from the attributes of his mind and character. If the operations of mind (and brain) could be regarded as being distributed throughout the muscles and organs of the physical body, then the heightened physicality of sporting exertion seemed to depend as much on psychological coherence as it did on physical fitness. Without this deeper, 'mental and moral' self-training the athlete was (to borrow an image from Tibbits) like 'a vessel classed A1, thoroughly well furnished with efficient machinery, able seamen, and judicious officers, but without helm, compass, or chart'.[64] Like a vessel embarked upon a voyage to a distant continent, the successful athlete needed to synthesize a wide variety of qualities into a

---

[61] Tibbits, 'On Systematic Exercises', 435.
[62] For more information on late-nineteenth-century brain science and theories as to the embodied nature of consciousness, see Anne Stiles, *Popular Fiction and Brain Science in the Late Nineteenth Century* (Cambridge: Cambridge University Press, 2014), 50–61.
[63] Tibbits, 'On Systematic Exercises', 436.
[64] Ibid.

cohesive, operational whole in order to achieve his end. He had to dutifully train his body; had to furnish himself with specialized knowledge, equipment, and preparations; had to 'cultivate' the 'natural qualities of [his] mind';[65] and needed to temper his emotion and volition to best direct his energies. Reports of Weston's abilities as a sportsman presented the view that his performance was the result of a highly varied constellation of attributes harmoniously aligned in Weston himself – his pedestrian feats were the 'unprecedented'[66] results of Weston's own individual nature. The American visitor's unique selfhood seemed to be embodied in the uniquely triumphal outcome of his races.

In 'The Amateur Body and the Middle-Class Man', Richard Holt describes the way in which the idea of physical equilibrium was held up as a core tenet of amateur sportsmanship. Equilibrium was, Holt writes, 'central to the [amateur] ideal of body', constituting a 'balance both between the different elements of the human anatomy and the inner and outer self'.[67] Far from being an exclusively amateur ideal, though, we can see from the case of Weston that the composed and equipoised 'self' was also regarded as integral to excellence in professional sporting performance. An ideally structured equipollence between body, character, and mind was regarded as the definitive marker of Weston's many successes. Aligned with this, however, were the specific effects of coca itself. Various contemporary observers described coca's main operation to be one of ordering or composing the body's diverse functions. In this way, coca seemed uniquely suitable as a sporting enhancement, because it produced the sportsman's longed-for 'equilibrium' in its very chemical action. Coca appeared to not only improve physical performance, it also served to forward the pursuit of a broader sporting ideal.

Coca and coherence: Amateur excellence and professional expertise

While the successful sportsman was presented as possessing an inherently ordered selfhood, accounts of coca's effects similarly represented the drug as an agent of order, a compound that could realign the body's various functions into a concordant whole. Coca, it seemed, might produce the 'inner and

---

[65] Thompson, 'The Coca Leaf', 361.
[66] 'Weston's Last Feat', *Lancet*, 440; and 'Weston's Last Feat', *Daily News*, 6.
[67] Richard Holt, 'The Amateur Body and the Middle-Class Man: Work, Health, and Style in Victorian Britain', *Sport in History*, 26.3 (2006), 361.

outer'⁶⁸ coherency that was vital to sporting performance. Alongside Edward Weston, the figure most commonly associated with coca in the British popular consciousness of the 1870s was Sir Robert Christison (1797–1882) of the Royal College of Physicians of Edinburgh. Famed as a groundbreaking toxicologist and medical jurist (he had enjoyed a particularly memorable 'surge of fame as a star witness in the Earl of Mar life insurance case' in 1832⁶⁹), Christison had served early in his career as Physician in Ordinary to Queen Victoria, and was awarded a baronetcy in 1871. In 1870 Christison began a series of experiments with coca leaves with a view towards verifying their legendarily 'restorative and preventative virtues'.⁷⁰ Between 1870 and 1875, Christison and a coterie of student volunteers chewed the leaves in a series of protracted walks of between fifteen and sixteen miles a day for several days.⁷¹ The experiments culminated in September 1875 when the Baronet – now seventy-eight years old – made two ascents of Ben Vorlich in the South Highlands while under the influence of the drug. Christison's conclusion was that his observations 'set at rest all doubts [about] the more important effects of cuca [sic]';⁷² 'The chewing of cuca removes extreme fatigue, and prevents it.'⁷³

Christison made an initial announcement of his results in an address to the Botanical Society of Edinburgh in November 1875, and his celebrity as a medical grandee ensured that, when Edward Weston's coca chewing came to light, many papers turned to Christison's experiences to verify the leaves' incredible effects. Alongside its narrative of Weston's coca chewing, the *Lancaster Gazette* described

---

⁶⁸ Ibid.
⁶⁹ Barry Milligan, 'Morphine-Addicted Doctors: The English Opium-Eater, and Embattled Medical Authority', *Victorian Literature and Culture*, 33.2 (2005), 545. See also: Virginia Berridge, 'Opium Eating and Life Insurance', *Addiction*, 72.4 (April 1977), 371.
⁷⁰ Robert Christison, 'Observations on the Effects of Cuca, or Coca, the Leaves of the Erythroxylon Coca', *BMJ*, 1.800 (29 April 1876), 527.
⁷¹ Christison, 'Observations on the Effects of Cuca, or Coca', 529–30. See also: 'Opening Address by the President (Sir Robert Christison, Bart.)', *Transactions of the Botanical Society*, 12 (November 1873–July 1876), 408–9.
⁷² Throughout his 'Observations' Christison consistently refers to 'coca' as 'cuca', explaining that:

> I have ventured to restore to the commercial article its original name, cuca. This was its Indian name, which the Spaniards corrupted into coca. But there is no reason why other nations should adopt a Spanish corruption; and there is a very good argument against transferring it to our own tongue, inasmuch as we have already two totally different vegetable products, cocoa and cacao, which, as indiscriminately pronounced in ordinary speech, coco and coca, are undistinguishable from the corrupt name of this new invention. I hope, therefore, that others will second me in attaching a characteristic name to an article which seems very likely to come ere long into general use among our countrymen at home. (Christison, 'Observations on the Effects of Cuca, or Coca', 527)

For the sake of accuracy, I have retained Christison's spelling in quotations.
⁷³ Christison, 'Observations on the Effects of Cuca, or Coca', 527 and 530.

the medical nobleman's 'remarkable' conquest of Ben Vorlich, executed with 'firmness and juvenile elasticity' despite Sir Robert's being 'well advanced in years'.[74] The *Glasgow Herald* confirmed that the 'hale septuagenarian' had 'also stated that, with the assistance of the coca leaf, he could walk considerable distances without fatigue, which would otherwise be beyond his powers of endurance'.[75]

The following month, the *British Medical Journal* printed an expanded report of Christison's experiments under the title 'Observations on the Effects of Cuca, or Coca, the Leaves of Erythroxylon Coca'. Throughout the article, Christison characterizes coca as a plant which 'has a really wonderful power in supporting the strength under prolonged fatigue without food'.[76] Signally, though, Christison avoids any suggestion that coca's effects might represent a mere suppression or distortion of the body's natural actions. Christison's first round of experiments with coca had involved two medical students – identified in their reports to their teacher by the initials 'A.B.' and 'R.B.L.' – who walked from Edinburgh to Musselburgh and back (approximately fifteen miles) in an afternoon, taking no more food than 'an ordinary breakfast' in the morning and 'a London Bun (about 2.30 pm)'.[77] On their return in the evening, rather than eating any dinner, they took an infusion of coca leaves, 'drinking it slowly and quietly as one usually does tea'.[78] Christison described the effects of the infusion in his article:

> They were very hungry, but refrained from food, and took each an infusion of two drachms of cuca ... Presently, hunger left them entirely, all sense of fatigue soon vanished, and they proceeded to promenade Prince's Street for an hour; which they did with ease and pleasure. On returning home their hunger revived with great intensity; and they made an excellent dinner; they felt alert all the subsequent evening, slept soundly all night, and the next morning awoke quite refreshed and active.[79]

Christison reported comparable results from later experiments with another, larger group of students: 'All found their hunger cease for a time; but shortly

---

[74] 'Weston's Attempt to Walk 500 Miles in Six Days', *Lancaster Gazette*, 4.
[75] 'The 500 Miles Walk', *Glasgow Herald*, 5.
[76] 'Christison, 'Observations on the Effects of Cuca, or Coca', 528.
[77] 'Erythroxylon: Trial of its Action by A.B. and R.B.L.', Notebook, Edinburgh University Library Special Collections, GB 237 COLL-237, 1.
[78] Ibid.
[79] 'Christison', Observations on the Effects of Cuca, or Coca', 529.

afterwards neither appetite nor digestion was at all impaired.'[80] And the professor's own experiences on Ben Vorlich tallied with those of his pupils:

> I had taken neither food nor drink of any kind after breakfasting at half past eight in the morning; but I continued to chew my cuca till I finished the sixty grains when halfway down the mountain. … At the bottom, I was neither weary, nor hungry, nor thirsty, and felt as if I could easily walk home four miles; but that was unnecessary. On arriving home at five o'clock, I still felt no fatigue, hunger, or thirst. At six, however, I made a very good dinner. During the subsequent evening, I was disposed to be busy, and not drowsy; and sound sleep during the night left me in the morning refreshed and ready for another day's exercise.[81]

Christison interprets the effects of coca in such a way as to suggest that the drug does not act to crudely subordinate hunger and the need for rest – instead, the drug apparently channels these natural appetites into more properly ordered and healthful patterns. Both Christison and his students report experiencing 'neither hunger, nor fatigue' under the effects of coca, and the article emphasizes that, rather than feeling drained or enervated when the demands of hunger and exertion reassert themselves, their appetites return in refreshingly productive and vigorous forms. The subjects make enthusiastically 'excellent' dinners; they are 'alert' and 'disposed to be busy' throughout the evenings; and sleep, when it comes, is peaceful, 'sound', and leaves them 'refreshed and ready for another day'. Coca (in Christison's 'Observations') acts to coordinate energy, activity, and appetite without 'impair[ing]' any of them. While other stimulants and soporifics might defraud the body into unnatural patterns of hyper-alertness or over-sleep, Christison depicts coca as essentially balancing and regulating the body's systems to healthful and normalizing effect. The body under coca is a precisely aligned body: neither over-exerted or underworked, neither starved nor overfed, energized but not agitated. Coca's chief action is to restore the body to a naturally optimal alignment.

Other amateur sportsmen (and medical experimenters) energetically embraced coca as a means of regulating and improving their own performances. The *Glasgow Medical Journal* observed that, since 'Sir Robert Christison found by experience that eating the coca leaves prevented fatigue … it has been greatly used by athletes, bicyclists, and others'.[82] Adverts for coca leaves, 'The Peruvian

---

[80] Ibid.
[81] Ibid., 530.
[82] J. Crawford Renton, 'Cocaine in Ophthalmic Surgery', *Glasgow Medical Journal*, 23.1 (January 1885), 28.

Restorative', addressed 'To Tourists, Pedestrian, &c.' began to appear in sporting papers almost as soon as Weston's experiences became public knowledge.[83] Sir George Chetwynd, fourth Baronet Chetwynd and famous racehorse owner, recalled that he 'procured a bottle of coca tincture … and gave a horse possessed of a very uncertain temper a dose of it, two teaspoonfuls in a wine-glass of water. … At the same time my brother and I each took a dose of it before we set out on our walk up to the downs. It certainly produced an exhilarating effect on us, and the horse ran straight as a die.'[84]

In September 1876 (six months after the revelation of Weston's coca use) a Devonshire doctor and sportsman signing himself 'A.L.' wrote to *The Lancet* to describe 'A New Use for Coca'. Though a keen hunter, A.L.'s enjoyment of his hobby was not untroubled:

> I confess to belonging to that class of sportsmen, a class more numerous than is commonly known, because the admission is not always made, whose nervous system is badly adapted for steady shooting. I have, in fact, often felt that if it were possible to exist without a heart I would be a better marksman. It is this organ which, when the dogs point steadily, and the utmost composure is necessary for steady aim, by its unruly throbs, disturbs my whole frame, and secures immunity for the fleet and whirring covey.[85]

A.L. however (like the illustrious George Chetwynd) found an answer to his difficulties by 'filling [his] flask with coca tincture'. The experiment proved successful:

> As soon as the dogs pointed, I expected the usual inward commotion with its usual results; but, to my surprise, nothing of the kind happened, and down went the birds left and right. 'Eureka', I said to myself; the coca has made me a steady shot. So, in fact, it subsequently proved, to the wonder and pleasure of my host, who is more gratified at seeing his friends enjoy good sport than in having the sport himself. … Coca in sufficient doses would seem to be a powerful nervine tonic; and as its effects appear to be entirely harmless, if my observations are confirmed by others, its use will be hailed as a boon by many a brother sportsman.[86]

---

[83] 'To Tourists, Pedestrians, &c.' *Athletic News*, 2.65 (26 August 1876), 8.
[84] George Chetwynd, *Racing Reminiscences and Experiences of the Turf*, Vol. 1 (London: Longmans, Green, 1891), 164–5.
[85] A.L., 'A New Use for Coca', *Lancet*, 108.2769 (23 September 1876), 449.
[86] Ibid.

'A New Use for Coca' expresses a problem which, on the surface, appears to be a simple one: the writer is a poor shot because he is of a nervous and excitable temperament. In describing the issue, though, A.L. also stresses the ambiguous and multifarious causes of his difficulty. The article's opening sentences, for example, begin by conflating the actions of the nervous system and the heart: A.L. opens with the confession that his 'nervous system is badly adapted for steady shooting' but immediately moves on to attribute his disturbance to the undisciplined and 'unruly throbs' of his heart. In this context, his wistful remark that he would be a better shot if he could 'exist without a heart' – seemingly longing to be more 'heartless' – smacks as much of a desire for unconcerned emotional equipoise, as it does for physical stability. A.L.'s 'unruly' heart signifies his being both mechanically and emotionally shaken. Thus, the problem of being a poor shot partakes equally of physical, psychological, and nervous causes. In effect, A.L. presents us with a systemic problem, the 'disturb[ance of his] whole frame', that coca solves by conferring 'utmost composure' upon his system. Much as Christison represented coca as rebalancing the body's operations to improve its health and performance, A.L. describes coca as 'steady[ing]' his body's various systems into an expansive equilibrium and composedness.

This somatic reordering in turn carries over into social restoration. A.L.'s host is delighted to see his guest enjoy the 'good sport' he has provided, and which we are told matters more to him than his own direct enjoyment. When A.L. claims, then, that he belongs to 'a class more numerous than is commonly known' because few are willing to make 'admission' to their constitutionally poor marksmanship, this acknowledgement also comes with an undertone of shame – he is unable to properly oblige his friend by enjoying the amusement he offers. In this sense, coca functions to not only enhance the user's sporting performance, it also enhances the amateur sportsman's social performance – it makes possible the polite exchange of 'composed [and] dignified'[87] pleasantries between host and guest. The 'good sport' which is enabled by coca represents a conjunction of individual performance and collective enjoyment – the poise and stability that coca brings to A.L.'s aim is reflected in the social stability that it bestows upon the amateur sportsman's friendship group. This sense of ordered community is further extended in the letter's final line. The assertion that coca 'will be hailed as a boon by many a brother sportsman' serves not only to affirm coca's practical usefulness but also functions as an invocation

---

[87] Gleaves and Llewellyn, 'Sport, Drugs and Amateurism', 840.

of sporting fraternity and camaraderie. Throughout 'A New Use for Coca' the tincture is portrayed as an agent of order and coordination: it organizes thought, emotion, and physical action; it facilitates mutual enjoyment between friends; and, in this concluding line, it apparently confirms A.L.'s sense of himself as a sportsman among brother sportsmen. Rather than running 'contrary to the gentlemanly amateur code that governed middle- and upper-class sport',[88] coca could become a means by which to fulfil that code in its highest form. In 'composing' the amateur sportsman's body, coca also confirmed the ordering principle of the amateur sporting ethos.

Other sources went so far as to apply coca's promise of bodily cohesion to Edward Weston himself. *The Star* newspaper expressed the view that Weston's coca chewing actually served to legitimate the American pedestrian's sporting performance – using coca to redouble his fortitude and stamina seemed to preserve Weston (and other sportsmen) from the dangerous moral and physical consequences of athletic exertion. The paper readily conceded that Weston's exploits were 'enough to stamp him as a man of consummate pluck and most abnormal powers of physical endurance', but begged leave to ask, 'for what good purpose have all these feats been attempted or performed?' It continued:

> The practical good attained will, we fear, be but little, and the evil which may follow may be very great, if the example of Weston's leads, as it very likely will, to a whole host of imitators in the professional and amateur world of athleticism. We do not want to know the extreme limits of human endurance in walking and running, or in any other recognised exercise, any more than we want to know how long a man can stand on one leg … or, like an Indian Fakeer, endure suspension on a hook inserted through the muscles of his back.

Coca, however, seemed to ameliorate the potential dangers of pushing human physiology to its limits. As *The Star* mused:

> But perhaps we are expending some warmth of expression and feeling on a matter which after all is not a subject for it; for if it turns out that the virtues of the leaf of the *Erythroxylon Coca*, said to have been nearly continuously chewed by Weston, are almost miraculous in sustaining the human body under exertion, the feat performed ceases to be very wonderful, or a subject for objection on the score of its exceeding the legitimate stresses which may be put upon our powers of endurance … There are [numerous] instances on record of [coca's]

---

[88] Ibid., 843.

great sustaining powers. It would seem, then, that to put athletes on an equality, its use must either be tabooed or adopted by all.[89]

The Star evinces a conflicted view of Weston's races – painting them simultaneously as 'wonderful' sporting achievements and physically excessive grotesqueries. This contrast can be seen in the fact that Weston's 'consummate pluck' is (apparently subconsciously) juxtaposed with his 'abnormal' physical endurance – one is faultless, the other freakish. The comparisons to a man perpetually standing on one leg or hanging from a hook through the flesh of his back push the perception of Weston's endurance towards a kind of wilful self-mutilation and monstrosity, the human body distended beyond the limits of normal operation. Against this backdrop, coca serves an emphatically regularizing role, since it preserves athleticism from moral 'objection[s]' by restoring bodily normality. In 'A New Use for Coca' A.L. claimed that his 'unruly' system was brought into proper alignment by the use of coca. *The Star* similarly portrays Weston as having an 'unruly' body – one that 'exceed[s] the legitimate stresses' that might safely be put upon the well-balanced individual – which is, however, tempered and restrained by the drug he consumes. Under the influence (and aegis) of coca, Weston's feats are no longer excessive but are reincorporated into the realm of 'legitimate stresses' that can be healthily placed on the human body. Behind the paper's final suggestion that 'to put athletes on an equality', coca must be 'tabooed or adopted by all', there is the sense that either would be an acceptable alternative. *The Star*'s primary concern here is not fair play (or the notion of clean competition) but the hope that putting all athletes 'on an equality' will lead to the return of a healthy, morally acceptable normality. 'Equality' here signifies a physical equanimity that frees the sporting community from the disturbing excrescence of extreme athletic spectacles like those practised by the American pedestrian. In *The Star*'s view, Weston's body is guilty of a type of unbalanced or intemperate physicality, which is restrained and composed by the effects of coca. The 'wonder' and 'extrem[ity]' of Weston's performance are moderated by the influence of the leaf and refined into a dignified equilibrium.

As such, coca seemed not only an excellent tool to fortify the professional athlete, it also worked to enhance the wider ideals of sportsmanship in general. Coca composed the systems of the sportsman's body and the constituents of his self; coca conferred an optimized and elevated physicality. In strengthening its users' capacity for sporting performance, the drug simultaneously appeared to

---

[89] 'The Walking Match', *The Star*, 106 (16 March 1876), 1.

rectify, or purify, the nature of that performance. Coca served both amateur and professional sporting ideals.

Conclusion: Before 'doping'

Ironically, in the midst of all the journalistic and medical attention focussed on Edward Weston's coca chewing, the one significant voice to speak out against the advisability of coca use in professional sport was Weston's own. The week after J. Ashburton Thompson published his observations of Weston's coca consumption, the pedestrian responded by penning a letter to *The Lancet*. Weston's statement was that:

> During my first trial in London on the 9th of February, while walking from the sixty-fifth to the seventy-fifth mile, I chewed coca leaves freely, acting under the advice of my medical adviser in America. I found that they did not have the effect expected; that is, they would not keep awake or in the least stimulate my efforts, but, to the contrary, they acted as an opiate, and forced me to sleep; … hence I abandoned them, *and have not even tasted them since my first trial in London, which closed on the evening of February 9th*. I deem it my duty to thus make public this explanation … in justice to the efforts of Dr. Pavy, whose investigations would have been somewhat disturbed had I allowed myself the use of any false stimulant.
>
> In conclusion, permit me to add that, after an experience of upwards of eight years in public life, during which time I have walked *over 14,000 miles*, experience has taught me that Nature should not be outraged by the use of artificial stimulants in any protracted trial.[90]

In his letter, Weston's disavowal of coca leaves rests primarily on the assertion of his own professional expertise and personal experience: having walked 'over 14,000 miles' he is expertly qualified to judge the practical benefits of any medical advice he receives; and in any case, the leaves were useless to him, inclining him to sleep, rather than activity. Intriguingly, though, the conclusion of Weston's letter subtly moves towards rejecting coca (and, indeed, any other drug) on the grounds of health and the essential integrity of the sporting body. Evident moral overtones begin to creep into Weston's language – coca is labelled a 'false stimulant' and an 'outrage' against 'Nature'.

---

[90] Weston, 'Mr Weston on the Use of Coca Leaves', 447.

It is difficult to exactly parse Weston's account, here, because it is difficult to know how far his description of his experiences with coca are accurate and honest. Weston's claim that he had used coca only once – and that during a period for which Pavy's urine samples had 'through a mishap' been discarded[91] – had the happy effect of preserving the appearance of integrity in Pavy's physiological trials. At least one observer of Weston's later races claimed to have seen the American chewing coca on those occasions as well.[92] Regardless of the truth of Weston's statement, though, it is worth noting that his rhetorical framing of coca in his conclusion was eventually to become the accepted, orthodox view of performance-enhancing drugs in professional sport. Weston's letter presents coca as 'falsifying' the sportsman's performance. Coca (and, by extension, any performance-improving drug) is represented as alien to that performance – the 'artificial' drug versus the sportsman's integral and 'natural' body. In this logical construction, the body's normal (or unalloyed) operations might be construed as being (in Weston's terminology) 'outraged' or defrauded by the use of drugs. Paul Dimeo, in his study of the evolution of the ideology of 'clean competition' (ie drug-free competition) in professional sports, describes how, beginning in the early decades of the twentieth century, sporting drug use was increasingly characterized as 'unhealthy and dishonest', resulting inexorably in 'unethical victories won by fraud'.[93] This language of fraudulence, deception, and bodily pollution[94] is prefigured in Weston's assertion of the 'false' nature of coca, and his warning that 'Nature should not be outraged by the use of artificial stimulants'.

For Weston's Victorian contemporaries, though, his body seemed to testify more eloquently than his words: despite his protestations about the wrongness of taking coca (disingenuous or not) his prodigious successes and the role that the South American leaf appeared to have played in them were compelling validations of the drug. Even fifty years later, old sportsmen could still recall 'when the American, Edward Payson Weston, created a sensation by long distance walking in this country he used to chew coca leaves' and point to it as

---

[91] See Pavy, 'The Effect of Prolonged Muscular Exercise', 18 March 1876, 429.
[92] See 'Latest News', *Freeman's Journal*, 9 April 1877, 6; and 'Latest News', *Freeman's Journal*, 10 April 1877, 5.
[93] Paul Dimeo, 'The Myth of Clean Sport and Its Unintended Consequences', *Performance Enhancement and Health*, 4 (2016), 106.
[94] For more discussion of the image of the sporting body corrupted by drugs, see Kathryn E. Henne, *Testing for Athlete Citizenship: Regulating Doping and Sex in Sport* (New Brunswick, NJ: Rutgers University Press, 2015). Particularly worthy of note is her argument that drug testing and punishment in professional sport serves the ideological function of 'condemning polluted bodies and distinguishing them from so-called pure ones' (53).

an exemplar of the time 'before dopes were forbidden'.[95] For Victorian observers coca was legitimated by the very professional expertise that Weston himself leaned upon to disavow it. More broadly, coca was thought to correspond to a particular ideal of both amateur and professional athleticism. The chewing of the leaf not only enhanced the body, it facilitated a flawless equilibrium of body and selfhood. In later decades, 'doping' was to come to be popularly defined as being 'in contradistinction to the essence of sport' and to be thought to 'contravene something essential and vital about sport itself'.[96] In 1876, however, rather than contravening the fundamental ethos of sport, the coca leaf promised to propel the sportsman towards the finest type of competition and the best version of his self.

---

[95] 'John O' Gaunt', *The Sportsman*, 16971 (16 January 1924), 5.
[96] Dimeo, 'Myth of Clean Sport', 106 and 107.

2

Conquerors of pain: Cocaine anaesthesia and the ideal medical man

On 2 January 1886, the *British Medical Journal*'s first edition of the new year carried a brief but distressing report on the effects of cocaine. The journal's correspondent described: 'A poor fellow (a physician)' who had become consumed with 'his earnest desire to investigate [cocaine's] wonderful properties, [and] become a *habitué*, and drugged himself and his family down to the lowest depths of degradation'. The one moral of this sad incident, opined the author, was to alert the medical community that '[cocaine] this sweet rose of our therapeutic bouquet, has its bitter thorn'.[1] The *British Medical Journal*'s article gives us a taste of the vexed relationship between cocaine, addiction, and medical professionals that was to be increasingly widely reported over the coming decades.[2] Cocaine's introduction as the first functional local anaesthetic in 1884 had dramatically increased awareness of the drug among the public and medical communities alike. Relatively soon thereafter, however, reports began to proliferate of its potential for toxicity and addiction. Indeed, medical practitioners were thought to be particularly vulnerable to cocaine habituation. Connolly Norman, the renowned Irish psychologist and superintendent of the Richmond District Lunatic Asylum, wrote in 'A Note on Cocainism' in 1892 that 'up to the present time the largest number of [cocaine's] victims appear, unfortunately, to have been medical men'.[3] Norman and other contemporary addiction specialists often ascribed the 'heavy tribute' that the medical fraternity

---

[1] 'Special Correspondence', *British Medical Journal*, 1.1305 (2 January 1886), 40.
[2] For a more in-depth examination of the discourses surrounding substance addiction and medical men in the late Victorian period, see Brenda Mann Hammack, 'Phantastica: The Chemically Inspired Intellectual in Occult Fiction', *Mosaic: A Journal for the Interdisciplinary Study of Literature*, 37.1 (2004), 83–100; Barry Milligan, 'Morphine-Addicted Doctors: The English Opium-Eater, and Embattled Medical Authority', *Victorian Literature and Culture*, 33.2 (2005), 541–53; and Susan Zieger, *Inventing the Addict: Drugs, Race, and Sexuality in Nineteenth-Century British and American Literature* (Amherst: University of Massachusetts Press, 2008), 127–55.
[3] Connolly Norman, 'A Note on Cocainism', *Journal of Mental Science*, 38.161 (April 1892), 195.

paid to addiction to 'their ready access' to dangerous drugs, and to the fact that their profession demanded a greater burden of work and responsibility than other similarly educated gentlemen.[4] Cocaine addiction, the 'bitter thorn' disguised in the 'therapeutic bouquet', was a lurking threat to practitioners' personal and professional standing: a temptation which might entice its unwary victim away from the rigours of work and down into 'drugged degradation'.

It is, however, important to understand the varied reception of cocaine in the late Victorian and Edwardian periods. Describing early cocaine use in the United States of America, Joseph F. Spillane comments that 'evidence of early medical praise for the benefits of cocaine and the subsequent concerns over its dangers can be misread as a simple progression from the former to the latter'.[5] In this period – both in Britain and overseas – cocaine was simultaneously understood to be a potentially dangerous, addictive substance and an extraordinary medical discovery. When its anaesthetic effects were uncovered, it was widely applauded as having 'immediately wrought a complete revolution'[6] in medicine and announced as 'a discovery to captivate the imagination of mankind'.[7] The chemical was hailed as a glorious and transformative achievement of modern medical science, and the knowledge that it could be misused did comparatively little to dispel the glamour surrounding it. When word of two further medical victims of cocaine ('Dr. W–' and 'Dr. B–') reached the *Midland Medical Miscellany* in March 1886, the paper noted that the drug was clearly 'as powerful for evil as for good', but nevertheless remained 'a therapeutic agent of indisputable power'.[8]

Cocaine had a similarly double significance for the image of the fin de siècle medical man. While it conveyed the threat of addiction, cocaine was also frequently represented as one of (if not *the*) iconic feats of nineteenth-century medical–scientific endeavour. This technological radiance transferred itself in turn to representations of the medical gentlemen who employed it. In both medical and popular depictions, the physician who could dispense cocaine to banish discomfort or relieve the agony of surgery seemed the heroic incarnation of a set of scientific and personal virtues, an ideal image of professional authority, individual self-discipline, and medical expertise. In contemporary sources,

---

[4] J. J. Graham Brown, 'Notes on the Treatment of the Diseases of the Nervous System', *Scottish Medical and Surgical Journal*, 4 (January–June 1899), 499.

[5] Joseph F. Spillane, *Cocaine: From Medical Marvel to Modern Menace in the United States* (Baltimore, MD: Johns Hopkins University Press, 2000), 25.

[6] Simeon Snell, 'Presidential Address on Some Points of Progress in Ophthalmic Surgery', *BMJ*, 2.1489 (13 July 1889), 58.

[7] Alfred J. H. Crespi, 'Some Recent Scientific Advances', *The Gentleman's Magazine*, 1906 (October 1889), 391.

[8] *The Midland Medical Miscellany and Provincial Medical Journal*, 5.51 (1 March 1886), 125.

cocaine is afforded a totemic role in defining the fin de siècle's sense of its own unparalleled modernity, and the innovative brilliance of the age is imaginatively manifested in the form of the practitioner who could bring the drug to bear in aid of his patients.

This chapter examines an alternative strand present in the discourse surrounding cocaine use and the medical professional: as well as degradation and failure, cocaine could illustrate the astonishing moral and scientific successes of the medical man. For almost twenty years after the revelation of its anaesthetic function, cocaine was enthusiastically received by both the therapeutic and lay communities. The result of this was that the alkaloid acquired a deeply personal significance for the public image as well as the self-image of medical personnel; among physicians and patients alike, the notion developed that the consummate power of the modern medical man was best represented by cocaine, the 'consummation'[9] of modern medicinal chemistry. This idea also informs portrayals of the drug in fiction, and I conclude with an analysis of L. T. Meade's 1895 short story, 'The Red Bracelet', as an example of the way in which cocaine functions as an almost mystical materialization of the physician's unassailable moral primacy and Aesculapian exceptionalism.

Pain threshold: Cocaine and the discovery of local anaesthesia

The discovery of cocaine's anaesthetic influence was to radically alter perceptions of the compound on the part of both the medical profession and the public at large. Karl Koller had first announced his results at the Heidelberg Ophthalmological Congress in September 1884. Being too poor to afford the trip from Vienna to Heidelberg himself, he had asked his senior colleague Dr Joseph Brettauer (head of ophthalmology at Trieste hospital) to read his paper for him and repeat his experiments before the assembled delegates.[10] Koller's work demonstrated several obvious advantages of cocaine anaesthesia for optical surgery: awake, but immune to pain, a patient could cooperate with the operating surgeon and keep them apprised of their progress; the drug likewise eliminated the risk that the patient's unconscious movement would damage the eye being operated on, or that the post-operative vomiting produced by general anaesthesia would destroy the surgeon's work. While cocaine was to have its most immediate and

---

[9] 'The Operation for Cataract', *Newcastle Weekly Courant*, 11447 (9 June 1894), 5.
[10] Koller, 'On the Use of Cocaine for Producing Anaesthesia of the Eye', 990.

enduring impact in the field of ophthalmology, it was received with such intense enthusiasm that it was rapidly applied to numerous other medical disciplines. *The Lancet*'s 'Annus Medicus' for 1884 was moved to conclude that, across the year's work in all branches of medical science, the introduction of cocaine looked emphatically to be 'the one grand triumph of the year'.[11]

Cocaine possessed such strong attractions for the medical community as a whole because the compound appeared to realize a long-standing – almost immemorial – aspiration of medical practice: it could not only remove pain, but do so without apparent effort, needing only a few drops of liquid solution to take effect. In July 1884, only three months before Koller's cocaine research was made public, *The Midland Medical Miscellany and Provincial Medical Journal* had invited its readers to consider the wider implications of pain for the medical profession. 'What,' the *Miscellany* asked, 'does the world when ill cry out for? Relief from pain.' The 'true relief of disease and pain' was, in the journal's view, 'the great aim of medicine'. Accordingly, the paper maintained that:

> Scientific medicine, if it means anything at all, must aim at the relief of pain. … With the attitude of the public expecting relief, our duty is clear – to afford it. Still more, our duty lies in ascertaining how far we can do so with certainty, and in finding out the best remedies.[12]

For the *Midland Medical Miscellany*, the easy and scientifically exact amelioration of pain was the healer's overriding mandate, the one accomplishment that might allow medical science to 'mean anything at all'. Alongside this humanitarian 'duty', the journal was also sensitive to the financial considerations at stake in the doctor's ability to alleviate pain. Those 'philosophical physicians' who contented themselves with simply instructing their clients to 'grin and bear it' were likely, the *Miscellany* thought, to 'find their studies empty'.[13] Pain relief, then, was not only essential for how practitioners perceived themselves – how well they might feel themselves to be fulfilling their 'great aim' – but also for how well they thought (or feared) they might appear in the eyes of the public. The discovery of cocaine was a boon on both counts. Stephanie J. Snow makes the observation that the introduction of ether and chloroform into surgical practice in the mid-Victorian period meant that 'patients had become accustomed to a medical culture in which … pain relief was understood to be a primary function

---

[11] 'The Annus Medicus 1884', *Lancet*, 124.3200 (27 December 1884), 1152.
[12] *The Midland Medical Miscellany and Provincial Medical Journal*, 3.31 (1 July 1884), 208.
[13] Ibid.

of medical care'.[14] Cocaine's contribution to analgesic science appeared all the greater because it offered the possibility of removing pain without any of the inconveniences attendant upon these previous anaesthetics.

A recurrent feature of late Victorian discourse on cocaine is the implied contrast between the safety and efficiency of the new drug, and the danger and stupefaction that were widely believed to be inherent to the use of chloroform, ether, and nitrous oxide. Chloroform had been widely used as an anaesthetic for almost forty years by the time cocaine entered the public consciousness. But its first introduction into the operating room in 1847 was followed, 'within months', by its first fatality.[15] Anaesthetic death remained a consistent (though comparatively rare) danger of surgical activity until the end of the century. In 1894, Dr J McNamara wrote (somewhat melodramatically) to the *British Medical Journal* to proclaim that 'the records of death by chloroform are monstrous in their frequency' and that it was time to 'put an end to the human sacrifice that is weekly offered on [its] alter'.[16] By the time cocaine began to be popular, conventional anaesthesia was still in the eyes of both doctors and patients 'a dangerous and unreliable practice'.[17]

There were also less obviously fatal anxieties associated with chloroform. Contemporary works on anaesthesia warned physicians that:

> One of the most annoying results from [chloroform] anaesthesia is the production of erotic hallucinations, which occur during recovery from the narcosis; and, as is the rule in subjective impressions, they are very vivid. This danger, if there were none other, would be sufficient to necessitate the presence of a second medical man during the administration of an anaesthetic.[18]

General guides for those newly embarked upon a medical career – such as Jukes De Styrap's *The Young Practitioner* (1890) – issued similar cautionary advice: 'In all cases in which it is necessary to produce anaesthesia,' wrote De Styrap, 'take care to have another practitioner present, more especially if the patient be a female, with the view, moreover, to disprove, if necessary, possible hallucinations in regard to improper language or action, and so to avoid scandal.'[19] These risks

---

[14] Stephanie J. Snow, *Operations without Pain: The Practice and Science of Anaesthesia in Victorian Britain* (Basingstoke: Palgrave Macmillan, 2005), 99.
[15] Ian A. Burney, *Bodies of Evidence: Medicine and the Politics of the English Inquest, 1830–1926* (Baltimore, MD: Johns Hopkins University Press, 2000), 138–9.
[16] J. Mcnamara, 'Deaths from Chloroform', *BMJ*, 2.1762 (6 October 1894), 795.
[17] Burney, *Bodies of Evidence*, 141. For further discussion of debates earlier in the century surrounding anaesthetic fatalities and the balancing of pain relief with the risk to patients' lives see: Snow, *Operations without Pain*, 94–110.
[18] George Foy, *Anaesthetics Ancient and Modern* (London: Baillière, Tindall, and Cox, 1889), 114.
[19] Jukes De Styrap, *The Young Practitioner* (London: H.K. Lewis, 1890), 127.

of 'scandal' and 'annoyance' were accompanied by further concerns. Some commentators expressed the worry that, by annulling not only the patient's pain but also their consciousness, chloroform might consequently annul the surgeon's ability to see their patient as a fellow human being. Ian A. Burney describes the fear that:

> The anaesthetised patient could neither through a conscious act of will nor through the corporeal language of pain resist the surgeon's actions; the surgeon, on the other hand, might view the patient as a mere object, the surgical scene evacuated of the beneficial limitations imposed by human empathy.[20]

When compared with the threat of chemically enforced passivity and dehumanization, cocaine seemed a pleasing alternative. Under the influence of cocaine, the patient remained awake, remained aware, and – in a sense – remained human, throughout the operation being performed on them. When the *Wesleyan-Methodist Magazine* first learned of cocaine, it enthused that such an anaesthetic – one that would dispense with 'the risk and disturbance' necessitated by ether, chloroform, and nitrous oxide – was all the more welcome for having 'been long sought'.[21] In this light, the climactic characterization of cocaine becomes easier to understand: not only did the revelation of its effects come with dramatic suddenness, they appeared to be the substantiation of a discovery long hoped-for. For many observers, cocaine fulfilled an epochal, almost miraculous, expectation and the medical world responded accordingly.

Transformative technology

In the year after the Heidelberg Ophthalmological Congress, there was a rush to identify and publish new uses for the drug. In the first six months of 1885, there were sixty-seven pieces on cocaine in the pages of the *British Medical Journal*, proselytizing its value in 'operations on the vagina and urethra, in dentistry, ophthalmic surgery, in vaccination, in operations on the nose and larynx, vomiting, mammary abscess, in cancer, scalds, circumcision, neuralgia,

---

[20] Burney, *Bodies of Evidence*, 145. Rob Boddice makes a similar point about the introduction of anaesthesia into vivisectionist experiments, and the possibility that it might lead to a 'numbing of the physiologists' own [emotional] sense'. See Rob Boddice, 'Species of Compassion: Aesthetics, Anaesthetics, and Pain in the Physiological Laboratory', *19: Interdisciplinary Studies in the Long Nineteenth Century*, 15 (2015), https://doi.org/10.16995/ntn.628.

[21] See W. H. Dallinger, 'Notes on Current Science', *Wesleyan-Methodist*, 9 (January 1885), 67; and 'Notes on Current Science', *Wesleyan-Methodist*, 9 (February 1885), 148.

hay fever, senile gangrene, nymphomania [and] sea sickness'.²² To mark the end of the first year of its use, the surgical periodical *Annals of Surgery* published a comprehensive survey of the drug and its applications. To the list of uses enumerated in the *British Medical Journal* it added (among others) cocaine's efficacy as a mild antiseptic, its value to women whose nipples were sore or chapped from nursing, and its properties as a tonic for digestive troubles and against wasting syndrome. The article reiterated a suggestion made the previous year by (the still-young) Sigmund Freud that the drug would make a valuable therapy for morphine and alcohol addiction, described its utility in relieving the pain of caustic injections for syphilis, its efficacy as a therapy for chronic asthma and coryza, and (significantly for the drug's later career) its use as a stimulant and an aphrodisiac.²³ Improving on the 2 per cent solution used in early experiments, it could now be administered via hypodermic injection, cocainized Vaseline, cocaine-impregnated gelatine disks, or a specially designed hydraulic spray.²⁴ The article confidently concluded: 'As the sum of the whole, it may be said that, so broad is its application, and so frequently is it indicated by reason of its power to substitute ether and chloroform … [that cocaine] occupies the position of an ideal anaesthetic more nearly than any other drug now know.'²⁵

Medical investigators scrambled to obtain samples of the fêted new substance, and prices spiked dramatically until supply could catch up with demand. In late 1884, cocaine climbed above £32 an ounce, falling to 23s. 6d. by 1892 and 'not very much more than one-half that amount' by 1896.²⁶ The white powder was, for a time, even 'dearer than gold'.²⁷ Meanwhile, stories circulated 'of an Edinburgh professor who, anxious to become possessed of a small quantity of the drug for experimental purposes, told a chemist to send him home three or four ounces. The cocaine arrived, and with it a bill for between £60 and £70, much to the professor's amazement.'²⁸ Such was the extent of the medical community's enthusiasm for cocaine that *Fun*, the weekly comic magazine, quipped: 'The

---

[22] Virginia Berridge, *Opium and the People: Opiate Use and Policy in Nineteenth and Early Twentieth Century Britain* (London: Free Association Books, 1999), 221.

[23] See James E. Pilcher, 'Cocaine as an Anaesthetic; Its Status at the Close of the First Year of Its Use', *Annals of Surgery*, 1.3 (January 1886), 58–61. For Freud's suggestion that cocaine might allow the recovering addict to 'withstand, at the cost of only insignificant symptoms, the withdrawal of morphine', see Sigmund Freud, *The Cocaine Papers* (Vienna: Dunquin Press, 1963), 21.

[24] Ibid., 54.

[25] Ibid., 66.

[26] See 'Commercial and Financial Notes', *Manchester Guardian*, 15474, (16 March 1896), 8.

[27] 'Address by Professor Botkin on the Circumstances attending the Suicide of the late Professor Kolomnin', *Lancet*, 128.3303 (18 December 1886), 1196.

[28] 'Au Courant', *Eddowes's Shrewsbury Journal*, 4852 (9 June 1886), 4.

Solution of cocaine is becoming extremely popular with physicians and surgeons. A doctor has just used it successfully in a case of rolpoperineorrhaphy. We are profoundly ignorant of the above complaint, but we are informed that it must not be confounded with rolypolyjampuddingporkchopgastritis.'[29] In its own retrospective of cocaine's first year on the world's stage, the *Dublin Journal of Medical Science* wrote:

> Cocaine [has] flashed out from previous obscurity upon the medical world, and at once secured a place in therapeutics which can scarcely be paralleled in the history of any other drug. Already it counts a literature of its own so extensive and so many-sided that it is difficult to deal with it summarily.[30]

Thanks to its unique properties, cocaine not only appeared to be the 'ideal anaesthetic' but held out the promise that modern science had, in the last years of the nineteenth century, brought forth a modern panacea.

Cocaine also possessed added attractions for researchers in more specialized medical–scientific fields. Cocaine's power to selectively annul sensation made it a useful tool for those experimentalists working to comprehend the mechanisms of the human brain and nervous system. Within a few months of the discovery of cocaine anaesthesia, the journal *Mind: A Quarterly Review of Psychology and Philosophy* carried a report by Henry Donaldson on the action of different nerve structures and the possible means by which they might carry different sensory information. Donaldson described 'the action of cocaine as bearing directly on this question'[31] since many patients whose eyes were anaesthetized with the drug nevertheless reported being able to 'recognise the presence of the knife on the eye by a sensation of cold'.[32] Repeating these experiments on himself, Donaldson found that: 'By means of a 5 per cent. solution of cocaine the eye was rendered completely insensitive to pain or contact, but still readily felt heat and cold.'[33] The possibility that cocaine might selectively repress the sense of pain, but not temperature, opened up new avenues of inquiry into the action of the nervous system and its interconnectivity with the brain. In 1894, *Mind* published the results of a similar set of experiments wherein cocaine anaesthesia reportedly effected the taste buds' (and associated nerves') ability to properly perceive

---

[29] 'Knicknacks', *Fun*, 43.1088 (17 March 1886), 121.
[30] Walter G. Smith, 'Report on Materia Medica and Therapeutics', *Dublin Journal of Medical Science*, 80.6 (December 1885), 506.
[31] Henry Herbert Donaldson, 'On the Temperature Sense', *Mind: A Quarterly Review of Psychology and Philosophy*, 10.39 (July 1885), 415.
[32] Ibid., 413.
[33] Ibid.

bitter and sweet sensations.³⁴ The study of local anaesthesia had – as Augustus D. Waller put it in *Brain: A Journal of Neurology* in 1896 – opened up 'a maze of possibilities'³⁵ for neurological investigation, giving medical scientists a valuable new tool to explore the brain and the senses.

The possibilities cocaine afforded the science of neurology were still being actively examined after the turn of the twentieth century. In 1900, surgeons working at Chicago's Cook County Hospital perfected a technique to inject cocaine into the spinal canal, thus allowing severe operations to be carried out without the use of chloroform, since the injection directly anaesthetized the central nerves in the spine. While the technique (in the words of the *Scottish Medical and Surgical Journal*) attracted 'considerable attention' from the surgical community in general, it also implied the further development of more complex cerebrospinal techniques. The neural specialist J. J. Graham Brown suggested that the spinal aesthetic process might yield a possible treatment for life-threatening epileptic seizures. Based on previous researches, Brown posited that 'medicines introduced into the spinal dura are diffused by the cerebro-spinal fluid and ... are in this way conveyed to the brain'. The anaesthetization of spinal tissue might, by this mechanism, allow practitioners to anaesthetize those sections of the brain responsible for epileptic convulsions. If instant heroic measures were called for to save the patient, more radical options were possible: 'In a case of dangerous infantile convulsions it might perhaps be permissible to inject cocaine in a weak solution through the fontanelle. In a case of the status epilepticus which appeared about to end fatally, might it not be justifiable to make a small trephine opening over the cortex and inject the cocaine solution directly.'³⁶ The fact that cocaine could paralyse individual nerves (or sections of nerves) led, in Brown's reasoning, to the possibility that it might similarly neutralize the operations of the brain itself. The selective deactivation of the individual sensation of pain suggested the idea that individual reflexes and brain functions might, eventually, be rendered susceptible to medical control.

For fin de siècle medicine, cocaine appeared to not only have a multitude of therapeutic applications – so many, in fact, that the *Dublin Journal of Medical Science* found it difficult to summarize them all³⁷ – but to be a vital tool for the

---

[34] 'Philosophical Periodicals, etc.' *Mind: A Quarterly Review of Psychology and Philosophy*, 3.11 (July 1894), 433.
[35] Augustus D. Waller, 'On the Influence of Reagents on the Electrical Excitability of Isolated Nerve', *Brain: A Journal of Neurology*, 19.2 (1896), 297
[36] J. J. Graham Brown, 'Notes on the Treatment of Diseases of the Nervous System', *Scottish Medical and Surgical Journal*, 8 (January–June 1901), 493.
[37] Smith, 'Report on Materia Medica and Therapeutics', 506.

advancement of the most complex and pioneering discipline of medical science. Local anaesthesia provided a means by which to explore the phenomena of pain and sensation, as well as the interpretation of that sensation by the brain, the organ of the mind itself. 'The whole subject of the action of drugs in subduing pain' might have been, even to its specialist examiners, 'very obscure', but the most modern of anaesthetics provided a means by which to 'wade through many perplexities and complications' and obtain the underlying 'elementary simplicity'[38] of understanding.

The medical triumphalism surrounding cocaine quickly communicated itself to mainstream journalism. The correspondent for *Chambers's Journal* excitedly confided to his readers that '[cocaine] is of such importance to the general public that I make no apology for stating my experience with this new drug in the public press'. The article added that, since the introduction of general anaesthesia a third of a century ago, no other discovery could claim to 'equal [cocaine] in importance' or accrue such 'great benefits' to 'suffering humanity'.[39] The *Glasgow Herald* was equally confident of cocaine's essential significance for the lay public. The paper's first coverage of cocaine appeared on Boxing Day 1884, and began: 'The progress of medical science and research is a matter in which the public are bound to take a deep and lasting interest, for the plain reason that such progress affects in the most immediate manner the wellbeing of mankind'. The scientific primacy of cocaine could hardly fail to be 'readily appreciable by the public at large' and they had duly 'turned with interest to note the characters of the drug which has certainly leapt into frame at one bound'. Both *Chambers's Journal* and the *Glasgow Herald* thought it only natural and proper for cocaine to assume a place of honour in society's estimation of modern medicine and its accomplishments. The *Herald*'s article concluded with the apotheosizing sentiment that: 'It may truly be said of such a discovery, that it illustrates anew the axiom that the victories of peace are infinitely greater than those of war.'[40] Other publications followed suit – in papers, journals, and magazines, cocaine inspired an almost sacerdotal enthusiasm. Headlines proclaimed 'The Latest Cocaine Miracle' and nominated it 'the wonderful medicament'.[41] The *Scotsman* newspaper declared that: '[Christ] The Divine Healer is the Patron of infirmaries,

---

[38] J. J. Graham Brown, 'Notes on the Treatment of Diseases of the Nervous System', *Scottish Medical and Surgical Journal*, 12 (January–June 1903), 104; and Donaldson, 'On the Temperature Sense', 433.
[39] 'A New Anaesthetic', *Chambers's Journal*, 2.61 (28 February 1885), 144.
[40] 'Cocaine', *Glasgow Herald*, 310 (26 December 1884), 6.
[41] 'Latest Cocaine Miracle', *Hampshire Telegraph and Sussex Chronicle*, 5454 (26 December 1885), 12; and 'Occasional Notes', *Leeds Mercury*, 14703 (23 May 1885), 1.

hospitals, and homes, and cocaine is one of the blessed instruments of his pain-removing and peace-instilling mission.'[42]

This rapturous approval was sustained not only by cocaine's benefits as a surgical technology but also by the fact that cocaine – as the *Glasgow Herald* had predicted – penetrated into the everyday lives of the wider public in a variety of surprisingly 'intimate'[43] ways. Outside of the operating room, one of the most consistent uses of cocaine was as a remedy for cold and flu symptoms. David B. Lees of St Mary's Hospital remarked in 1886 that cocaine 'affords exactly what we require' from a cure for catarrh, since it 'both causes local anaesthesia and diminishes local congestion'. Acting as both a painkiller and vasoconstrictor, cocaine, applied 'by means of a camel's hair brush gives instant relief, and on one occasion, at all events, this measure sufficed completely to arrest a cold without the aid of any other remedy whatever'.[44] In 1890, the author Robert Louis Stevenson wrote to his friend Dr Thomas Bodley Scott to confide that he had made 'a medical discovery':

> I find I can (almost immediately) fight off a cold with liquid extract of coca; two or (if obstinate) three teaspoonfuls in the day ... sees the cold generally to the door. I find it at once produces a glow, stops rigour, and though it makes one very uncomfortable, prevents the advance of the disease. Hearing of this influenza, it occurred to me that this might prove remedial; and perhaps a stronger exhibition – injections of cocaine, for instance – still better.
>
> If on my return I find myself let in for this epidemic, which seems highly calculated to nip me in the bud, I shall feel very much inclined to make the experiment.[45]

By the 1890s, Burroughs, Wellcome and Co. supplied a portable cocaine nasal spray for colds and flu that was 'so small as to be easily carried in the waistcoat pocket'.[46] The drug also did faithful service to travellers as a cure for sea sickness. Voyagers susceptible to *mal-de-mer* found that cocaine (taken either as a lozenge or in a solution mixed with sugar or alcohol) could 'render a miserable journey comfortable and even enjoyable'.[47] Men, women, and children could claim to

---

[42] 'Cocaine', *The Scotsman*, 29 August 1887, 7.
[43] 'Cocaine', *Glasgow Herald*, 310 (26 December 1884), 6.
[44] David B. Lees, 'The Neurotic Treatment of Catarrh', *Lancet*, 127.3261 (27 February 1886), 394.
[45] Robert Louis Stevenson, *The Letters of Robert Louis Stevenson to His Family and Friends*, ed. Sidney Colvin (London: Methuen, 1901), 176.
[46] 'New Preparations and Scientific Inventions', *Dublin Journal of Medical Science*, 98.3 (September 1894), 272.
[47] Watson Smith, 'The Cocaine Cure for Sea-Sickness', *Manchester Guardian*, 12531 (12 October 1886), 7.

benefit from the 'truly magical' restorative effects of the drug which allowed them to eat, drink, play, and socialize aboard ship.[48] As such, for many people cocaine represented not only the elevated realms of specialized surgery but a tonic to overcome the day-to-day aggravations of illness and discomfort in the modern world.

Triumph of the century

As the nineteenth century drew to a close, the pervasive lionization of cocaine (and its various medical applications) was accompanied by a broader sense that the drug could serve as a powerful symbol for an oncoming era of modernity and innovation. Scientific and medical commentators frequently represented cocaine as the culmination of nineteenth-century medical technology and suggested that the drug's most significant innovation – the effortless conquest of pain – could embody a century's worth of benevolent scientific discovery. In 1900, the *Daily News* began its report on the discovery of cocainized spinal anaesthesia with a rhetorical flourish: 'When the question is asked, "What is the greatest discovery of the nineteenth century?" the reply not infrequently made is, "The suppression of pain in surgical operations."'[49] J. L. McCartney, writing in *The New Century Review* in October 1900, described the radical changes that had intervened between 'the scientific horizon of the man who stood at the opening of the 19th century' and that of the man who stands at the opening of the 20th century'.[50] In the realm of medicine and surgery, McCartney inquired of his readers: 'Can we imagine that the stumps of sailors were plunged into hot pitch at Trafalgar to stop haemorrhage? Now the most intricate, critical and serve surgical operation can be performed while the patient is utterly oblivious to pain. ... The use of cocaine in rendering local immunity to pain is of inestimable value.'[51]

In the same vein, the doctor and journalist Alfred J. H. Crespi expressed his awe at the 'meteor-like rapidity' with which cocaine had sped from the fringes of discovery to become 'the prized possession of millions' and an 'invaluable' weapon in 'the armoury of the modern scientific surgeon'. For Crespi, the conversion of Brazilian or Peruvian coca leaves into cocaine and the ever-decreasing cost of

---

[48] 'Cocaine in Sea-Sickness', *Lancet*, 126.3236 (5 September 1885), 451; and 'Cocaine in Seasickness', *Manchester Times Supplement*, 19 September 1885, 8.
[49] 'Painless Surgery', *Daily News*, 17016 (6 October 1900), 5.
[50] J. L. McCartney, 'Flash Lights on the Progress of the Century or The Scientific Horizon of 1800 to 1900', *New Century Review*, 46 (October 1900), 249.
[51] McCartney, 'Flash Lights on the Progress of the Century', 258.

the process mirrored the power of modern engineering to transmit electricity over 'vast distances' at a 'rapidly decreasing cost'.[52] In Crespi's view the same modernizing rhetoric of distance, economics, and utility could be applied to describe both electricity and cocaine. Crespi imbues cocaine with a galvanic dynamism, so that it captures the insubstantial energies of the age in a material, medicinal form.

The sense that cocaine might capture the excelsior ascent of Victorian technological progress was most explicitly spelled out in a poem which appeared in *The London Reader* in 1902. Titled 'Progress of the Nineteenth Century', the work presented itself as a kind of centennial panegyric – a glorious commemoration of the numerous advances attained over the preceding hundred years. It began:

> This century received from its predecessors the horse; we bequeath the bicycle, the locomotive, and the automobile.
> We received the goosequill; we bequeath the fountain pen and the typewriter.
> We received the scythe; we bequeath the mowing machine.
> We received the sickle; we bequeath the harvester.
> We received the hand printing press; we bequeath the rotary.
> We received twenty-three chemical elements; we bequeath eighty.
> We received the tallow drip; we bequeath the arc electric light.
> We received the sailing ship; we bequeath the steamship.

After sixteen similar contrasts the final two lines conclude:

> We received unalleviable pain; we bequeath asepsis, chloroform, ether, and cocaine.
> We received the average duration of life of thirty years; we bequeath forty years.[53]

Throughout, 'Progress of the Nineteenth Century' maintains a consistent format: the impoverished technological legacy of the eighteenth century contrasted with the wonders attained during the nineteenth, and now ready to be bestowed upon the twentieth. The piece builds through the arts, through agriculture, through physics, chemistry, and industry, until it reaches its conclusion in the medical sciences. Here, cocaine becomes the crescendo of nineteenth-century innovation: as the unflagging march of progress ascends from the reign of King George III to the death of Queen Victoria, it attains its summit in a new lifespan of forty years instead of the thirty which began the

---

[52] Crespi, 'Some Recent Scientific Advances', 398–9.
[53] 'Progress of the Nineteenth Century', *The London Reader*, 78.2021 (25 January 1902), 377.

century.⁵⁴ The verses transform a panoply of scientific discoveries into a single endeavour, with a single, profoundly humanitarian achievement at its end. Figured like this, cocaine stands for the culmination of one hundred years of industrial and scientific revolution.

The perfect drug and the ideal practitioner

If cocaine could be viewed as the zenith of Victorian social and scientific improvement, it was not difficult to assign this same consummate quality to the medical gentleman who put the drug into service. Equipped with an ideal implement of healing, the practitioner could seem to embody a professional and personal ideal.

This idealism can be clearly seen in the accounts of visitors to specialized ophthalmic hospitals, both at home and abroad. In 1893 the traveller and journalist J. Errol described the work of Professor Hermann Pagenstecher at the Augenklinik (eye hospital) at Wiesbaden. Faced with the pathetic spectacle of a small child almost completely blinded by cataract, Errol was amazed that, after a quick application of cocaine to deaden the eye, the professor then set to work 'with such skill and celerity' and with such 'delicate and masterly manipulation' that the surgery was concluded in 'a few minutes'. His work accomplished, Errol recounts that the surgeon passed instantly onwards to other patients who 'sat awaiting the visit of one who, if any human being could, would avert the calamity menacing them'.⁵⁵ The same images of assured speed, masterful dexterity, and

---

⁵⁴ It is worth noting that the closing lines of 'Progress of the Nineteenth Century' reflect a general mood of optimism about substantially increasing lifespans throughout the 1800s and early 1900s. Pat Jalland writes that,

> Life expectancy at birth in England and Wales began to rise from about 40 years in 1850 to about 52 for males and 55 for females by 1911–12. The death-rate began to decline slowly from 22 per 1,000 in the 1870s to 13 per 1,000 by 1910'. Similarly, the percentage of the British population over 65 rose from 4.7% in 1861 to 5% by 1901.

See Pat Jalland, *Death in the Victorian Family* (Oxford: Oxford University Press, 1996), 143. Commentators consistently remarked on these changes throughout the last decades of the nineteenth century. As comparatively early as 1881, *The Spectator* wrote: 'We all know that whatever be the truth throughout the world, the "expectation of life", that is, the chance of longevity, has, in the well-drained and carefully-fed cities of the West, increased to a perceptible degree.' 'The Improvement of Human Health', *The Spectator*, 2796, (23 July 1881), 11. J. L. McCartney also prefaced his celebration of the progress made in medical science throughout the nineteenth century with the observation that: 'The average term of human life has been lengthened to forty instead of thirty years in civilised countries' (McCartney, 'Flash Lights on the Progress of the Century', 257).

⁵⁵ J. Errol, 'A Visit to Professor Dr Hermann Pagenstecher's Augenklinik', *London Society*, 63.375 (March 1893), 292–3.

near-instantaneous anaesthesia also feature in Marian von Glehn's description of her visit to the Royal London Ophthalmic Hospital in *The Leisure Hour* in February 1890. Von Glehn's writes that, while speaking to one of the nurses:

> A messenger interrupted asking the nurse to get her patients ready, as Mr – (the operating surgeon) would be upstairs in about ten minutes. One could not escape an involuntary shudder. And yet, such are the wonderful properties of the newly discovered cocaine, that the operating theatre is robbed of half of its terrors ...
>
> [In the lobby-room outside the operating theatre] I watched the nurses with their quiet manner inspiring their patients with courage and confidence as they dropped the magic drug into the eye which was to deaden and allay the pain ... Thoughts must turn to prayer before such spectacles of human suffering and endurance.
>
> Nor was the endurance displayed by the patients alone striking. To anyone unfamiliar with hospital life, it might well seem noteworthy that operations requiring the greatest nerve and technical dexterity should be performed by the same surgeons who for hours already had been giving the most concentrated attention to the out-patients' cases below.[56]

Von Ghlen equates the therapeutic effectiveness of cocaine with the capabilities of both the nurses and the surgeons. The 'magic' of the drug mingles with the inspiring – almost seraphic – competence and compassion of the women who apply it, so that both appear to develop organically out of each other. The rapidity and ease with which the drug takes effect, having to be but lightly 'dropped' into the eye, mirrors the evanescent presence of the nurses who flit with gentle efficiency through the lobby outside the operating room, easily dispensing both cocaine and a reaffirmed confidence in the power of medical science. Significantly, the religious timbre of the writing also strongly suggests the image of the nurses as a body of female angels (or a community of *religieuses*) dedicated to the service of God-like male practitioners. These men are, in turn, inexhaustible, commanding, and encircled with a refined atmosphere of isolation and anonymity. They, like Errol's Professor Pagenstecher, are seemingly isolated from the rest of mankind, enfolded in their supernaturally magisterial duty to 'avert' a catastrophic sickness that lies beyond the skill of 'any [other] human being'. That they accomplish this august responsibility with brisk professionalism and 'celerity' of technique only intensifies the observers'

---

[56] Marian Von Glehn, 'A Day in a Hospital', *The Leisure Hour*, February 1890, 279.

sense of wonder. To onlookers the (male and female) staff of both hospitals reflect an underlying superhuman excellence which is ultimately enabled by 'the wonderful properties' of cocaine.

The ophthalmologists of the Royal London Hospital and Wiesbaden Augenklinik are remote divinities, but a more affable medical ideal can be found in the person of the heroic Dr Campbell from Harry Stillwell Edwards's 1896 novel, *Sons and Fathers*. At one point, Campbell and his assistant Edward are called upon to perform a delicate operation to save the sight of a wife and mother of two, by removing her glaucoma. The chapter in which the surgery takes place is given the distinctly messianic title of 'The Hand of Science'.[57] It is Campbell's own hand that wields the cocaine and the surgical scalpel, but both he and the drug he administers take on an aspect of supernatural intervention; together, the doctor and the drug are portrayed as the avatars of an almost deified scientific majesty. When Stillwell Edwards describes Campbell entering his patient's home, he writes: 'The famous practitioner, a tall shapely figure, entered, and as he removed his glasses he brought sunshine into the room, with his cheery voice and confident manner.'[58] Physically graceful, charismatic, and reassuring, Campbell metaphorically returns 'sunshine' to the family home, just as he will soon use cocaine and surgical skill to return light to the lady of the house in a more literal sense.

The doctor takes only the briefest interval to make his diagnosis, and so 'deliberate' is he, 'in every word and action', that 'the occasion was already robbed of half its terrors, so potent are confidence, decision, and action'.[59] Campbell and Edward immediately go to their business:

> There was no chloroform, no lecture. With the simplicity of a child at play, the great man went to work. Turning up the eyelid, he dropped upon the cornea a little cocaine, and selecting a minute scalpel from his case, with two swift, even motions cut downward from the centre of the eye and them from the same stating point at right angles. The incisions extended no deeper than the transparent epidermis of the organ. Skilfully turning up the angle of this, he exposed a thin, white growth – a minute cloud it seemed to Edward.
>
> 'Another drop of cocaine please', the pleasant voice of the oculist recalled him, and upon the exposed point he let fall from the dropper the liquid. Lifting the little cloud with keen pincers, the operator removed it, restored the thin

---

[57] Harry Stillwell Edwards, 'Sons and Fathers', *Nottinghamshire Guardian*, 2682 (10 October 1896), 6.
[58] Ibid.
[59] Ibid.

epidermis to its place, touched it again with cocaine and replaced the bandage. The strain of long hours was ended; he had not been in the house 30 minutes.[60]

The entire passage not only emphasizes Campbell's personal skill but also creates an equivalence between his surgical incisiveness and the efficacy of the cocaine. Campbell's cuts are swift and precise, and the narration imitates this by progressing in rapid, succinct clauses and statements. The surgery is punctuated by efficient drops of cocaine that form the counterpoint to Campbell's quickness by instantly annulling the pain of the operation.

The initial mention of chloroform is also significantly phrased. Not only does it imply the comparative safety of the operation (since it removes the risks associated with the older drug), it also affirms that Campbell's presence in the house is a consoling, compassionate one. As we have seen, chloroform was connotative not only of the risks of surgery but also of a dehumanizing distance between practitioner and patient.[61] The absence of chloroform is tied to the absence of any unpleasant attribute in Campbell's character; just as he does not employ the soporific chloroform, Campbell does not coldly stand upon dignity or delay to 'lecture'. He operates on his patient, Mrs Montjoy, with quickness and confidence, and this assured speed of action is also the wider hallmark of his personality. In the same manner, the 'great man' is seen to act 'with the simplicity of a child at play', an image which testifies to Campbell's technical *sprezzatura*, while also imbuing him with a humane, even domestic aspect. Cocaine and Campbell's surgical adroitness transform a difficult operation into easy playfulness. After his work is concluded, he happily dandles the Montjoys' youngest son on his knee, further establishing a familial intimacy between patient and practitioner.[62] In Stillwell Edwards's novel, cocaine permits a type of treatment which is both emotionally comforting, yet technologically astounding. Thirty minutes of cocaine and professional expertise are all it takes for Campbell to restore sight to his patient and joy to her family. The manners of the ideal practitioner evolve from the mechanism of cocaine.

Harry Stillwell Edwards and Marian von Glehn in effect combine cocaine and medical personnel into a fantasy of scientific sanctity. While theirs was a view from outside the magic circle of surgery, medical men themselves also used cocaine as a way to articulate their own identities as practitioners – the drug became a symbol through which to express the professional conditions of their

[60] Ibid.
[61] See Burney, *Bodies of Evidence*, 145.
[62] Stillwell Edwards, 'Sons and Fathers', 6.

lives and their emotional responses to those conditions. Perhaps surprisingly, it was not only the elite of ophthalmic specialists who developed a personal investment in the employment of cocaine, the humble general practitioner did as well. In discussing the drug, many of these men focused their observations on the contrast between cocaine and older varieties of anaesthesia, and on how the newer compound might promote a better relationship between them and their patients. In 1900, J. Eustace Webb, a general practitioner in Aberdeenshire, submitted a paper to the *Scottish Medical and Surgical Journal* called 'The Use of Hydrochlorate of Cocaine in Private Surgical Practice'.[63] For the previous six years, Webb had used cocaine anaesthesia almost exclusively for the minor surgeries commonly required of a general practitioner, because, 'In general private practice the dread of the patient to take a general anaesthetic, and often the difficulty of getting an administrator [anaesthetist] are felt as distinct disadvantages to operative work being done.'[64] From Webb's point of view, cocaine not only negated the practical obstacles associated with other drugs, it was more reassuring for patients as well.

Another general practitioner, William Semple Young, reached the same conclusions. Working in a small country practice in Garlieston in the west of Scotland, he found that: 'There are many people who dread chloroform so much, that they decline to take it, unless practically coerced into doing so.'[65] Semple Young was so impressed with the drug that when, in 1898, the time came for him to produce his MD thesis for the University of Glasgow, his subject was 'Cocaine as a Local Anaesthetic'. Like J. Eustace Webb, he applauded the benefits that cocaine could offer the general practitioner: 'Cocaine has this advantage over chloroform, that no assistant is required. It is also safer, as the patient is conscious all the time, and can give timely warning in case of any untoward symptoms coming on. Its price is also (which to many patients is a serious item) very much less than that of chloroform.'[66] The fact that cocaine was cheaper to use, less dangerous, and more easily administered than other anaesthetics made it obviously appealing to the general practitioner. Without chloroform, the general practitioner was no longer a potential figure of 'dread' to his clients.

These practical considerations were also accompanied by a more personal investment in the drug on the part of some medical professionals. Semple

---

[63] J. Eustace Webb, 'The Use of Hydro-Chlorate of Cocaine in Private Surgical Practice', *Scottish Medical and Surgical Journal*, 7 (July–December 1900), 46.
[64] Ibid.
[65] William Semple Young, *Cocaine as a Local Anaesthetic: With Special Reference to its Use in Tooth Extraction* (Glasgow: 1898), 51.
[66] Ibid., 36–7.

Young's MD thesis contains a short but significant passage where he explains why he selected cocaine as his subject. The work begins with his reminiscences of a boyhood terribly afflicted by toothache and goes on to explain: 'When as a student I heard such glowing reports of the use and action of cocaine in tooth extraction, I determined, that if ever I had the opportunity, I would study the action of the drug in this particular direction.'[67] Semple Young's initial consideration of cocaine as a dental anaesthetic expands into an assessment of how 'invaluable'[68] the alkaloid is to all branches of modern medicine. Semple Young establishes at the outset that his interest in cocaine derives from the pains of his childhood – pains which medicine was then powerless to alleviate. When he hears about cocaine as a student, it is an inspiring moment for him since it illustrates how far fin de siècle medicine has come and what it is now capable of. Behind his analysis of its physical capabilities, Semple Young imbues the drug with an emotional resonance, since it signifies not only the progress of medical science but also his own progress as a doctor. There is a professional and personal intimacy inherent in the thesis's description of the drug: cocaine not only provides a consoling connection between his childhood distress and his adult vocation, but – by making it the subject of his dissertation – cocaine is now about to make him an MD, furthering his standing once again. The introduction to Semple Young's thesis implies a sort of professional bildungsroman, in which cocaine plays a defining part; as a practitioner, his assessment of cocaine is blended with his ideas about his life and work.

A similar presentation of the compound can be seen in 'Recent Advances in Surgery and Medicine', an article which appeared in the *Edinburgh Review* in October 1888. The piece unites a discussion of how cocaine has 'revolutionised'[69] medicine with detailed depictions of the personality, social status, and professional situation of the medical man. The piece documents the many inconveniences that the practitioner could face in his vocation, but it also paints a picture of how cocaine – as an iconic medical technology – could combine with the practitioner's heroic nature to help him transcend these obstacles. The opening pages state that:

> [The life of the medical man] is peculiarly a life of untiring warfare; he is always in the thick of the battle with disease, and, moreover, he has to exert himself strenuously to hold his own among his brethren and to earn a livelihood. The

---

[67] Ibid., 3–4.
[68] Ibid., 39.
[69] 'Recent Advances in Surgery and Medicine', *Edinburgh Review*, 168.344 (October 1888), 506.

doctor is almost the only educated man claiming to be treated and regarded as a gentleman, and often having the tastes and instincts of that class, who commonly works for and looks for payment to classes far beneath his own in the social scale. ... A medical career consequently lacks, and must always lack, those social amenities and advantages which attract able and accomplished men in such numbers to other liberal callings.[70]

This summary of the problems inherent in the late Victorian medical profession is fairly straightforward: the medical man must constantly 'battle' to preserve his patient from disease; then battle almost as hard to get that patient to pay him; and, finally, struggle to retain his own sense of himself as a respectable middle-class gentleman. 'Untiring warfare', 'exertion', 'strenuousness', and 'conflict' are the defining activities of a life where *déclassé* is almost as fierce an enemy as disease. The prevalence of these obstacles can be seen from Roy Porter's remark that, by the 1880s, 'few [doctors] secured a competent living before they were approaching forty'.[71]

Amidst these larger anxieties there were also more specific irritations that doctors might encounter. 'Recent Advances' addresses the concern that, while other branches of medical practice could delight in a torrent of new devices and discoveries, the general practitioner might feel himself depressed by the comparative plainness of his day-to-day employment:

It has been said that the advance in [traditional] medicine has not equalled that in surgery, and can hardly be placed in comparison with it. ... Medicine, moreover, has had its field greatly curtailed of late. Many obscure and obstinate diseases, which were included in its province, and for which until recently comparatively little could be done, have been transferred to the realm of the surgeon; and, while obstinately intractable as long as medicines were alone administered, are found to admit of ready and successful treatment at the hands of the surgeon. Physicians can no longer claim to be the gentlemen and scholars of the profession, and to regard surgeons as their humble dependents.[72]

This passage expresses an alarming possibility: in being left behind technologically, the physician might also be left behind socially. It suggests that the once-dependable hierarchies of the medical profession could be disrupted by the altered circumstances of a new age.

---

[70] Ibid., 491–2.
[71] Roy Porter, *Disease, Medicine and Society in England, 1550–1860* (Basingstoke: Macmillan, 1993), 51.
[72] 'Recent Advances in Surgery and Medicine', 510–11.

But 'Recent Advances in Surgery and Medicine' was quick to reassure its readers that physicians were not mere relics of the past – they too could participate in the era of technological medicine. After the passage above, there follows the remark: 'Still, there have been triumphs, of which we may mention a few: the treatment of rheumatic fever with salicylate of antipyrin, the induction of sleep with chloral, paraldehyde, urethane, and hypnone, and the introduction of cocaine, the last invaluable as an internal remedy.'[73] These new drugs – particularly the 'invaluable' cocaine – are held out as evidence that the work of the physician has not stood still while other fields have leapt ahead. These chemicals are tied to the professional and social status of physicians: the drugs fortify their position against the vicissitudes of the modern world and infuse the general practitioner's work with a precious quantum of technological lustre. Just as surgical specialists had had their abilities 'immensely enlarged'[74] by cocaine, general practitioners could also claim the drug as a source of pride in themselves and their work.

On a wider scale, the economic and social disadvantages that practitioners suffered through could be said to pale before the medical man's own personal virtues. The business of medicine was 'a most useful occupation, one affording unbounded scope to the most enlightened and far-reaching mind [… and offering] the most complete and constant union of those three qualities which have the greatest charm for pure and active minds – novelty, utility and charity'.[75] Financial concerns are also presented as being immaterial, since the work of medicine is 'carried out without that slavery to it which greed begets and fosters'.[76] A sense of noble, charitable endeavour is imagined to ameliorate the practitioner's labour. This superiority also communicates itself to the mind and body: 'He has scope for muscular exercise; he has always to be acquiring new information, which keeps the mental organism employed; and as he soon discovers that to make his presence endurable to the sick he must be serene and cheerful, he acquires a temper of serenity and cheerfulness.'[77] Furthermore, the medical professional enjoyed a more robust physicality than the average man. In medicine, 'Recent Advances' maintained 'the average of health, though not the duration of life, is far above the common average in other professions'.[78] The medical gentleman's moral and intellectual capacities were also more finely developed: 'It is surely fair

[73] Ibid., 511.
[74] Ibid., 507.
[75] Ibid., 492.
[76] Ibid., 494.
[77] Ibid.
[78] Ibid., 493.

to hold that as in every search for knowledge we may strengthen our intellectual power, so in every practical employment of it we may, if we will, improve our moral nature.'[79] More than any alternative career, in medicine a man might rely upon his work to enhance his nature. While his employment might put him beyond many of the comfortable sureties of middle-class life, the practitioner could reassure himself that he, in his person, represented the heroic ideal of middle-class professional masculinity: knowledgeable, physically fit, and morally assured.

'Recent Advances in Surgery and Medicine' enfolds its discussion of cocaine's technological cachet into a larger depiction of the superior nature of the medical individual. Cocaine revolutionizes surgery and compensates physicians for their 'curtailed field',[80] but this is only a small part of a narrative in which technical innovation and individual exceptionalism combine to dispel the annoyances of medical work. Together, cocaine and the selfhood of the practitioner form two sides of the same coin, one which repays the medical man for the obstacles of his chosen career. From surgical specialists to family doctors, the drug is unified with the personality of the practitioner who uses it; cocaine is presented as the most 'invaluable'[81] of modern therapeutic innovations, and the medical professional possesses the most incomparable of modern selves.

L. T. Meade's 'The Red Bracelet'

The idea that the medical man constituted the apex of middle-class personal and professional existence is taken to an even greater extreme in L. T. Meade's short story, 'The Red Bracelet' (published in *The Strand Magazine* in January 1895). Here, we are presented with a doctor whose morality and scientific assuredness are so potent that he can combine cocaine and surgical intervention to bestow these qualities upon another character. In Meade's story, cocaine occupies a pivotal position, as it manifests the practitioner's idealized personal virtues and allows them to affect his patient both physically and emotionally.

'The Red Bracelet' is one of a series of medical mystery tales – with the overarching title *Stories from the Diary of a Doctor* – that Elizabeth Thomasina (or 'L. T.') Meade produced for the *Strand* between 1893 and 1895. These narratives

---

[79] Ibid.
[80] Ibid., 511.
[81] See 'Recent Advances in Surgery and Medicine', 511; Crespi, 'Some Recent Scientific Advances', 399; and Semple Young, *Cocaine as a Local Anaesthetic*, 39.

revolve around patients suffering from particularly mysterious or outré ailments and the attempts of the gifted physician, Dr Clifford Halifax, to diagnose their condition. In a metatextual move, the *Stories from the Diary of a Doctor* were advertised as being a collaboration between Meade and 'Clifford Halifax, M.D' himself – an act which was clearly supposed to buttress their appearance of medical authenticity. Despite the unreality of Clifford Halifax, Meade really did obtain medical details for the stories from the Metropolitan Police Surgeon Edgar Beaumont.[82] Indeed, throughout her career, Meade was keenly attuned to the narrative allure of new technologies and medical procedures. Janis Dawson remarks that Meade's work was characterized by a high degree of 'literary marketplace savvy'.[83] Not only was she 'particularly adept at following literary trends', but early in her career she 'learned to exploit sensational incidents and topical issues to construct best-selling [stories]'.[84]

This sense of exciting scientific contemporariness is particularly evident in the various works that Meade produced for *The Strand Magazine*. In her novel *The Brotherhood of the Seven Kings*, for example, one of the victims of the villainous Madame Koluchy is found to have mysterious star-shaped wounds on his face and neck, which are later revealed to have been caused by exposure to 'constant powerful discharges of cathode and X-rays'.[85] Likewise, not only were Meade's *Stories from the Diary of a Doctor* 'inspired by the phenomenal success of Arthur Conan Doyle's Sherlock Holmes series'[86] but each story was prefaced by the statement: 'These Stories are written in collaboration with a medical man of large experience. Many are founded on fact, and all are within the region of practical medical science. Those stories which may convey an idea of the impossible are only a forecast of an early realisation.'[87] Meade's medical mystery stories are, therefore, specifically written to attract readers through a combination of literary and scientific fashionableness. The portrayal of cocaine in 'The Red Bracelet' not only illustrates its technologically topicality but also manifests the rational and moral capability of Dr Clifford Halifax.[88]

---

[82] Janis Dawson, 'Rivaling Conan Doyle: L. T. Meade's Medical Mysteries, New Woman Criminals, and Literary Celebrity at the Victorian Fin de Siècle', *English Literature in Transition*, 58.1 (2015), 57.
[83] Ibid., 69.
[84] Ibid., 55.
[85] See L. T. Meade, 'The Brotherhood of the Seven Kings', *The Stand Magazine*, 15 (January–June 1898), 664.
[86] Dawson, 'Rivaling Conan Doyle', 56.
[87] L.T. Meade, 'The Red Bracelet', *The Strand*, 9 (January–June 1895), 545.
[88] The appearance of cocaine in the story may also be similarly intended to hark back to the drug's appearance in the early Sherlock Holmes stories. For more detailed discussion of Sherlock Holmes's relationship with cocaine see Chapter 5.

The case at the centre of the story is partly medical, partly supernatural, and partly a domestic drama. Dr Halifax is consulted by a man named Stafford who is deeply concerned about his daughter, Molly. She suffers from congenital blindness and although Mr and Mrs Stafford have taken her to the finest oculists in Europe, nothing can be done to cure her. Molly has also recently fallen under the control of an unscrupulous man by the name of Basil Winchester. After a chance encounter, Winchester has been able to hypnotize Molly, so that she longs only to be with him and is incapable of thinking of anything else. Stafford asks Halifax to counter Winchester's control of his daughter, since her hypnotic obsession is seriously threatening her health. When Halifax arrives at the Staffords' home in Yorkshire, it is revealed that Basil Winchester is able to project his influence into Molly's mind through a red coral bracelet that he has given her. Though unfamiliar with hypnotic techniques, Halifax is able to use his personal aura of authority to get Molly to eat and rest a little. She remains sick, however, and Halifax theorizes that it is Molly's blindness that makes her unusually vulnerable to Winchester's power.

The break in the case comes when Halifax realizes that, though her vision is so severely impaired that she is effectively blind, Molly has a subliminal perception of the presence of light and darkness. He deduces that her eyes are really perfectly intact, but obscured behind a dense, fleshy layer of tissue. With the aid of cocaine, Halifax performs a rapid operation to remove the obstruction. Her sight restored, Molly is freed from her false lover's influence and when Winchester next meets her, Molly rejects him. He is soon thereafter arrested for forgery. At the story's end, Molly sends the red bracelet to Halifax as a gesture of thanks.

At the heart of the story is an explicitly moral message, but this moralizing is conveyed almost entirely through a series of densely interlinked metaphors and symbolic associations. Although Molly has been hypnotized by Winchester, the hypnosis does not result merely in his having a zombie-like control over her. Rather, it causes her to become emotionally fixated on him. The story uses purposefully ambiguous language to describe Winchester's mesmeric power. He is persistently referred to as possessing an 'influence' over Molly or as having created a 'strange craze' or 'infatuation' in her.[89] Even more tellingly, her father laments that: 'Badly as [Winchester] has treated her, her overpowering passion for him is beyond all reason.'[90] By describing the hypnosis in explicitly

---

[89] Meade, 'The Red Bracelet', 546, 558, 556.
[90] Ibid., 549.

emotional terms, Meade obscures the distinction between mesmerism and a more conventional romantic obsession. Coupled with these descriptions, there are frequent references to Molly's refusal to submit to her parents' well-meaning instructions that she should break off her attachment to Winchester. At their first meeting, Mr Stafford tells Halifax that '[Molly] is deaf to our entreaties. She thinks of nothing morning, noon, or night, but this man.'[91] Halifax later incredulously urges Molly to 'think of your parents', but she flatly responds, 'My father and mother were opposed to our marriage, but I cared nothing for their opposition.'[92] Here, Molly's hypnosis is clearly identified as a metaphorical rendering of an unsuitable attachment. Underlying the medical mystery of 'The Red Bracelet' is a moral and domestic issue: a highly emotional young woman is deceived into forming a connection with an unworthy man, she abandons filial obedience for desire, and his eventual mistreatment causes her to distress and sicken herself. The hypnosis is a pseudo-scientific disguise for a consuming passion that destroys Molly Stafford's power of rational thought and causes her to defy social and domestic propriety.

This interpretation is reinforced by the fact that – even before she meets Winchester – Molly is characterized as emotionally disordered and vulnerable. In her 'overpowering passion' for him, she is alternately described as 'laughing wildly', 'giving way to hysteria', and piteously clinging to her mother like a child.[93] Molly's blindness is explicitly identified as the origin of her emotional state. She mournfully recalls that, 'I never thought that love – love of this sort – could come into the life of a blind girl.'[94] After examining her, Halifax gives a comprehensive analysis of her condition:

> Few doctors believe in the well-known phrase 'a broken heart', but if anyone was likely to die of this malady, the girl over whom I was now watching would be the one. Her blindness and her particularly nervous and highly strung temperament would all conduce to this effect. … Her illness is due to a strange and overstrained condition of the imagination. All her thoughts are turned inwards. Her blindness adds much to this condition. If only I could give her back her sight![95]

This diagnosis conjoins Molly's blindness, her unhealthy emotional introversion, and her susceptibility to Winchester's malign influence. Her defective sight is the underlying factor, and in restoring it, Halifax also restores her emotional

---

[91] Ibid., 547.
[92] Ibid., 553.
[93] Ibid., 551.
[94] Ibid., 553.
[95] Ibid., 555.

coherence and frees her from Winchester's mesmeric affliction. Molly's lack of sight is, therefore, also a lack of insight; unable to see, she is also symbolically unable to perceive Basil for the scoundrel he really is. In this vein, there are numerous faintly punning references in the text to the fact that, in lacking the sense of sight, Molly also lacks common sense. Halifax calmly informs his patient that: 'You have parted for the time being with common sense … I mean to bring that precious possession back to you.'[96] In the final pages of the story, Molly's restored eyes are twice referred to as 'her new possession.'[97] In allowing the girl to possess the power of sight, Meade establishes that Halifax has gifted his patient with a new self-possession; in remedying a physical ailment, he has undone a social and emotional malignity.

In this context, the use of cocaine to remedy Molly's deformed eyes is also a means by which to restore moral and domestic correctness. The symbolism in the story is constructed around cocaine's physiological properties, since without the drug it would be impossible to accomplish the surgery that realigns Molly's visual and social acuity. In 'The Red Bracelet' cocaine is an agent of both technological and a moral advancement, a refinement in medical technology that effects a more refined personal conduct. Meade highlights the moral superiority of cocaine by contrasting it with the older anaesthetic chloroform. When Halifax suggests the surgery to Molly's parents, her mother anxiously enquires:

> 'Will the operation be painful? Will it be necessary for you to use chloroform?'
>
> 'No [Halifax responds]; I shall put cocaine into the eye – don't be alarmed, Miss Stafford will feel no pain'.

Mrs Stafford's question explicitly differentiates Halifax's employment of cocaine from the 'dangerous and unreliable'[98] threat of chloroform anaesthesia. It allows L. T. Meade to confirm the more developed condition of modern medicine which has done away with the crude instruments and practices of the past. Given the metaphorical significance of Molly's blindness, though, the contrast between cocaine and chloroform also reiterates the story's larger contrast between moral and immoral behaviour, between the light of social awareness and the darkness of irresponsible desire. Chloroform, which rendered the subject unconscious and which could provoke delusional erotic fantasies,[99] is easily relatable to the blackness surrounding Molly, both because of her defective eyes and because of

---

[96] Ibid., 552.
[97] Ibid., 560.
[98] Burney, *Bodies of Evidence*, 141.
[99] See Foy, *Anaesthetics Ancient and Modern*, 114.

the hypnotic occlusion of her perceptions by Winchester. Cocaine, on the other hand, conveys physical and social cognizance.

To further develop this contrast, it is worth noting that fin de siècle discussions of anaesthetic hypnosis frequently juxtaposed the hypnotic condition with the action of cocaine. The topic was one to which both neurologists and the Society for Psychical Research recurred throughout the 1890s. In 1891, F. W. H. Myers broached the subject in the *Proceedings of the Society for Psychical Research*, suggesting that it might be possible to artificially create, through hypnosis, 'the analgesia or insensitiveness to pain which runs wild in hysteria'. Myers stressed that hypnosis produced an effect wholly distinct from the 'anaesthetisation of some particular segment of the body or some particular group of nerve endings – such as [with] cocaine'.[100] Dr J. Milne Bramwell reiterated the distinction between 'hypnotic suggestion' and cocaine anaesthesia some years later in *Brain: A Journal of Neurology*.[101] C. M. Barrows, who elaborated upon F. W. H. Myers's work (and also published in the *Proceedings of the Society for Psychical Research*), not only stressed the divergent actions of hypnosis and cocaine but also stated that hypnotic influence was closely aligned with 'telepathic suggestion or so-called thought transference'.[102] The differing depictions of cocaine and hypnosis in 'The Red Bracelet' reflect these wider juxtapositions. Advocates of hypnosis in the *Proceedings of the Society for Psychical Research* were keen to portray the analgesia it produced as one which could be achieved with precise control, and without resorting to drugs. But even these positive descriptions positioned hypnosis unnervingly close to 'hysteria' and 'telepathic suggestion' – elements which form the core of its portrayal in Meade's story, since Molly's own hysterical predisposition renders her vulnerable to the contaminating influence of Basil's telepathic control. By contrast, cocaine represents the exactitude of chemical and neurological precision. In juxtaposing cocaine and hypnosis, Meade affirms cocaine's status as a tool of moral clarity and self-consciousness. In 'The Red Bracelet', cocaine confirms that innovations in medical technology can also engender improvements in moral nature.

Simultaneously, Meade also makes it clear that cocaine is a type of material synecdoche for the idealized virtues of Halifax's own personality. In fact, before he uses cocaine to open Molly's eyes, the main way in which he treats her is through

---

[100] F. W. H. Myers, 'The Subliminal Consciousness: Chapter 2 – The Mechanism of Suggestion', *Proceedings of the Society for Psychical Research*, 7 (1891–2), 330–1.
[101] J. Milne Bramwell, 'On the Evolution of Hypnotic Theory', *Brain: A Journal of Neurology*, 19.4 (1896), 530.
[102] C. M. Barrows, 'Suggestion without Hypnotism', *Proceedings of the Society for Psychical Research*, 12 (1896–7), 30–1.

" WHO ARE YOU ?"

Figure 2.1 Dr Halifax coolly examines Molly Stafford in 'The Red Bracelet' (1895).

imposing his own unflinching rationality and moral authority onto her. The story's illustrations show Halifax examining Molly with unruffled composure while his unfortunate patient stares wildly, and uncomprehendingly, into nothingness (see Figure 2.1). 'The Red Bracelet' establishes a clear opposition between Basil Winchester, the evil hypnotist, and Clifford Halifax, the good doctor. (Indeed, the differentiation of the two characters recalls wider discursive differentiations between the hysterically inflected techniques of hypnosis and the scientifically exact 'anaesthetisation of nerve-endings' effected by cocaine.[103]) While Basil influences Molly towards selfishness and passion, Halifax influences her towards self-control and domestic deference; where Winchester uses deception and mesmerism, Halifax uses his own personal rectitude and willpower. When Molly tells him that she is too distraught to eat, Halifax calmly counters: 'No, that is folly. You are giving way to a feeling of hysteria. This is causing your father and mother great unhappiness. Your throat is not closed, you only imagine it.' Molly obediently goes to eat, and Halifax remarks, 'She didn't even attempt to struggle against my stronger will.'[104] Later, in conversation, he tells her:

> 'I am going to exercise my will over yours'.
>
> 'You have done so already', she answered. 'I eat when you tell me; I sleep when you wish me to; I don't feel wicked when I am with you. I even begin, just a little, a very little, to take an interest in my father and mother again. Basil used to make all the rest of the world a blank.'[105]

Halifax's will has the power to restore Molly's sense of right and wrong and her awareness of her social obligations. As a doctor, Halifax perfectly encapsulates the middle-class, professional, and masculine virtues of self-restraint, rationality, and ethical firmness. He is so potent an ideal that, when Molly succumbs to girlish emotion and hysteria, he can transfuse his moral conviction into her and restore her to physical and psychological coherence. For L. T. Meade the medical professional represents the supreme apotheosis of middle-class values, and in curing bodily ills, the medical man also cures the infirmities of the soul.

Cocaine, then, is really Halifax's moralizing will condensed into material form. Through the innovative new drug, Halifax is able to excise the sclerotic membrane that veils Molly's eyes and purge the moral infection of hypnosis. Interestingly, Winchester has a comparable metonymic relationship with the titular red bracelet that he gives to Molly. The hypnotist is absent for the majority of the story, and he transmits his desires to the girl through the bracelet. Molly describes it as 'a part of the man I love',[106] and it is 'a link between her and him'.[107] If the red bracelet manifests Basil's wicked influence over Molly, then cocaine

---

[103] See Bramwell, 'On the Evolution of Hypnotic Theory', 530.
[104] Meade, 'The Red Bracelet', 551.
[105] Ibid., 556.
[106] Ibid., 553.
[107] Ibid., 549.

has a similarly talismanic connection to Dr Halifax. When the physician drops the cocaine into her eye, the drug forms a chemical connection between Molly's weakened nature and his superior one. In 'The Red Bracelet', medicine is seen to be a social and moral process, as much as it is a physical one. As a doctor, Halifax becomes the superhuman realization of middle-class professional and personal virtues, and cocaine becomes the incarnation of his miraculous, curative will.

Conclusion: 'A Wonder of the Age'

In March 1886, *Chambers's Journal* published an article in praise of cocaine, 'the new discovery which [had] agreeably startled the world of medicine towards the end of the year 1884'.[108] It proudly announced the new drug to be the heir of chloroform and ether, and an anaesthetic that had now freed physicians, surgeons, and patients from the 'discomforts' and 'inconveniences' of those older compounds.[109] The article's final lines announced:

> In the present prosaic condition of the world, when the surfeit of new discoveries seems to have bred in this connection the familiarity which produces the conventional contempt, it is refreshing to draw attention to a discovery which has surpassed the ordinary standard of greatness sufficiently to enable it to figure as a wonder of the age. Cocaine flashed like a meteor before the eyes of the medical world, but, unlike a meteor, its impressions have proved to be enduring; while it is destined in the future to occupy a high position in the estimation of those whom duty requires to combat the ravages of disease.[110]

Cocaine's destiny was to be more conflicted than *Chambers's Journal* foresaw, however. The following year, *The Illustrated Police News* had wryly responded to the first reports of cocaine poisoning by remarking: 'cocaine is getting into discredit'.[111] This discreditation was to persist as medical and popular writers became increasingly aware of the drug's 'dangerous and alluring'[112] charms and of the 'hopeless, endless chain'[113] of addiction that it might forge around the unwary.

---

[108] 'Cocaine', *Chambers's Journal*, 3.114 (6 March 1886), 145.
[109] Ibid.
[110] Ibid., 147.
[111] 'Everybody's Column', *The Illustrated Police News*, 1242 (3 December 1887), 2.
[112] Norman, 'A Note on Cocainism', 196.
[113] 'Old and New', *The Scots Observer*, 3.64 (8 February 1890), 334.

For many, though, cocaine was still haloed 'like a meteor', with the celestial luminescence of discovery, and this same light also encircled the practitioner who made use of the drug in his daily work. Employed for healing, rather than for recreation, cocaine could signify the monumental achievements of fin de siècle medicine, and the transcendent stature of the medical man. For writers like Alfred J. H. Crespi, the neat syringe or pipette that held the chemical seemed to contain all the aggregated triumphs of a century of technological innovation. Among medical men and patients alike, the drug articulated a glamourous image of the practitioner's superior selfhood. And for authors like L. T. Meade, the solution of cocaine became a moral solution, a dissolved form of the medical professional's exalted ideal. In fin de siècle fiction, medical literature, magazines, and journals, cocaine formed part of a beatific constellation of virtues contained within the medical gentleman.

3

Brutal fashions: Cosmetic surgery and tattooing at the fin de siècle

Victorian observers were (as we saw in the previous chapter) often keenly sensitive to the fact that theirs was the first age in which the requirements of surgery had been liberated from the inevitability of agony. October 1896 marked the fiftieth anniversary of the first successful use of general anaesthesia in surgery, and one of the men tasked to commemorate the occasion was Dudley Buxton, anaesthetist to University College Hospital. Though wary of the 'facile jingle[s]' that 'the daily press' was wont to compose in praise of new medical discoveries, Buxton conceded that:

> The fifty years that have elapsed since that eventful day … have revolutionised surgery, have altered completely men's minds as regards surgical operations.
>
> In pre-anaesthetic days recourse to the knife was an alternative to death or to a living misery even more terrible to contemplate. Now … ills cosmetic, or ills too hideous for endurance may be mended without fear, hurry, or strain to patient or surgeon.[1]

Buxton's mention of the still young discipline of cosmetic surgery, though brief, gives us a useful starting point for a discussion of cocaine anaesthesia and aesthetic procedures in this period. Buxton's retrospect begins by observing that anaesthetics have produced not only a practical revolution in surgical techniques but a conceptual one as well – the preceding fifty years having altered both the physical conditions of surgery and the condition it assumes in 'men's minds'. Earlier in the century, in the absence of effective pain relief, surgery could be embarked upon only when the patient was faced with the threat of immediate mortality or some protracted suffering more dire than the operation itself. The

---

[1] Dudley W. Buxton, 'Fifty Years of Anaesthetics', *British Medical Journal*, 2.1868 (17 October 1896), 1144.

effect of anaesthetic innovation, as Buxton described it, was not only to make surgery more likely to succeed but also to make patients and practitioners more likely to turn to surgical remedies for less severe ailments. By the 1890s, the bar for surgical initiative had been substantially lowered – lowered so far, in fact, that it now accommodated ills which were purely 'cosmetic' in nature. According to the *BMJ*'s retrospective, the effect of fifty years of anaesthetics had been to turn surgery from an act of desperation into a matter of first resort for ever more superficial bodily ills. The introduction of local anaesthesia by cocaine dramatically intensified this turn.

By the 1890s, cocaine was well established in its character as an essential instrument of contemporary therapeutic surgery. Simultaneously, though, cocaine also enabled a host of minor operations that allowed patients to more easily alter the aesthetic qualities of their own bodies. Sander L. Gilman points to the advent of cocaine anaesthesia – first for ophthalmology in the 1880s and then later for spinal and epidural application – as the essential prerequisite necessary for the development of aesthetic surgery as a speciality.[2] Cosmetic surgery was most commonly enacted under cocaine for the practical reason that it allowed such comparatively non-essential operations to be performed without the risk of death associated with general anaesthesia. As early as 1887, the New York doctor John Orlando Roe, 'the father of aesthetic rhinoplasty',[3] advertised an operation by which patients whose noses had the unfashionably 'aspiring tendency to turn upwards at the end' could – with the aid of cocaine anaesthesia – have them surgically resculpted into the 'desired aquiline shape'.[4] Almost thirty years later, in the early 1920s, practitioners could still maintain that the performance of these kinds of superficial surgeries was 'intimately wrapped up with the subject of local anaesthesia', and that 'as a local anaesthetic, cocaine is probably unsurpassed'.[5]

Cocaine appears in late-nineteenth-century accounts as a foundational technology for cosmetic medicine. Freed from the certainty of pain on the one hand and from the fear of anaesthetic death on the other, fin de siècle ingenuity responded by popularizing a multitude of cosmetic procedures. Enterprising

---

[2] Sander L. Gilman, *Making the Body Beautiful: A Cultural History of Aesthetic Surgery* (Princeton, NJ: Princeton University Press, 2000), 16–17.
[3] Blair O. Rogers, 'John Orlando Roe – Not Jacques Joseph – The father of Aesthetic Rhinoplasty', *Aesthetic Plastic Surgery*, 10.1 (December 1986), 63.
[4] 'Educating a nose', *Bow Bells*, 46.1200 (27 July 1887), 139. For more sustained commentary on Roe's techniques and on the racial implications of late-nineteenth-century rhinoplasty, see Gilman, 85–118 and 134–6.
[5] 'Possible Substitutes for Cocaine', *Lancet*, 203.5247 (22 March 1924), 597; E. Watson-Williams, 'Cocaine and Its Substitutes', *BMJ*, 2.3283 (1 December 1923), 1018.

practitioners offered techniques by which patients might rework the contours of their nose; change the colour of the eyes; excise moles, blemishes, and birthmarks; cull unsightly hairs; and recolour their complexions. The fashion for tattooing that sprang up in the 1890s and the early twentieth century was one of the period's most frequently remarked-upon intersections of personal aesthetics and medical science. Tattoo artists like the nationally renowned Sutherland MacDonald of Jermyn Street were quick to incorporate the new anaesthetic into their craft, with fascinated journalists assuring their readers that: 'by the use of cocaine, which is injected under the skin, the operation causes not the slightest pain'.[6] The proliferation of these procedures, however, also initiated a complex of wider questions about their moral and physical hazards. If medical procedures were undertaken for entirely aesthetic – rather than curative – reasons, did this in some way invalidate the underlying therapeutic mission of medicine? Could, indeed, the surgically aestheticized body itself come to be seen to be somehow invalid or artificial? And if these questions were answered in the affirmative, who was ultimately responsible for these lapses – the physicians who stooped to 'satisfy the vanity of their patients'[7] or the patients themselves who demanded that medical techniques and technologies be (mis)applied to purely cosmetic ends?

This chapter examines the varying receptions of cocaine anaesthesia and cosmetic procedures in the late-Victorian and Edwardian era. In doing so, I want to argue that – with the coming of cocaine – fin de siècle onlookers were confronted with a peculiar historical moment in which the elimination of pain seemed to herald the removal of once-rigid limitations on bodily form. The imaginative potential of this idea was strongly mixed. For some, cocaine anaesthesia appeared to proffer a future of unlimited bodily motility – the possibility that one's features might be infinitely remade to the economic, social, cosmetic, and romantic advantage of their possessor. Conversely, these possibilities could be read as possessing a more alarming emotional and ethical valence: unfettered by cocaine anaesthesia, the body became vulnerable to the prospect of grotesque, gothic disintegration, a hideous 'self-mutilation and self-destruction'[8] enacted in the 'cause of vanity'.[9] This chapter considers both of these figurations of cocaine and cosmetic procedures in the medical and popular imagination of the late 1800s and early 1900s. It concludes with an analysis of

---

[6] 'An English Tattooer', *The Pall Mall Gazette*, 7525 (1 May 1889), 7.
[7] George M. Gould and Walter L. Pyle, *Anomalies and Curiosities of Medicine* (Philadelphia: W. B. Saunders, 1900), 746.
[8] Ibid., 743.
[9] 'Rosy Cheeks', *Irish Independent*, 3679 (18 November 1904), 2.

the role of cocaine and medical–cosmetic techniques in W. C. Morrow's darkly comic 1897 short story 'Two Singular Men' – a narrative that illustrates both the emancipatory and destructive potential of cocaine anaesthesia in this period: the simultaneous prospect that cosmetic medicine might liberate the body to be individually customized and endlessly remade to order, and that this malleability might collapse into purposeless mutation and mere freakishness.

About face: Cocaine and cosmetic surgery

Max Beerbohm's famously ironic essay 'A Defence of Cosmetics' (one of the leading lights of the first issue of *The Yellow Book* in April 1894) begins with the puckishly prophetic announcement that: 'The Victorian era comes to its end and … the portents warn the seer of life that we are ripe for a new epoch of artifice.'[10] How many of Beerbohm's contemporaries would have taken this prognostication seriously is difficult (if not impossible) to gauge fully. For many fin de siècle citizens, however, it appeared plausible that the transitional years between the nineteenth and twentieth centuries would be marked by the ever more inventive artifices of the cosmetic 'beauty doctor'[11] and the 'beauty specialist'.[12] 'The world,' wrote the *Daily Mirror* in 1904, 'understands the process whereby on men and women ornamental surgery removes wrinkles, straightens crooked noses, and sets close to the head ears that stick out.'[13] Many aesthetic surgical techniques originated in the older and more general discipline of plastic surgery, which focussed primarily on the functional restoration of badly damaged or distorted anatomy. The introduction of cocaine anaesthesia, however, made it more likely that these techniques would be applied to purely 'ornamental' ends. Some of the earliest popular efforts in fin de siècle cosmetic surgery can be seen in the field of rhinoplastic operations. In 1887 the *British Medical Journal* observed that: 'For a short time, while the *beauté du diable* lasts, the tip-tilted nose may be forgiven in a woman, but for the greater part of existence it is a continual source of social agony to its unfortunate possessor. Such sufferers will rejoice to hear that their sad case is not beyond the reach of plastic surgery.' Having once 'deadened the sensitivity of the interior of the nose with cucaine [*sic*]', the surgeon could cut away 'superfluous tissue' and cartilage

---

[10] Max Beerbohm, 'A Defence of Cosmetics', *The Yellow Book*, 1 (April 1894), 65.
[11] 'Making Women Beautiful', *Birmingham Daily Post*, 9396 (7 August 1888), 5.
[12] 'Rosy Cheeks', *Elgin Courant and Morayshire Advertiser*, 5328 (9 August 1904), 6.
[13] 'The Dogs' Beauty Doctor', *Daily Mirror*, 57 (8 January 1904), 11.

to remake the organ anew.¹⁴ Similar operations were refined and iterated upon over the following decades. 'A broken nose,' wrote the *Review of Reviews* in 1902, 'is unsightly and may injure the prospects of a person in life.' Such unfortunate sufferers could, though, have their damaged tissues 'benumbed with cocaine' and reshaped by an injected mixture of paraffin wax and Vaseline. Reluctant patients who feared that the operation might leave its own telltale marks upon their faces could have the paraffin mixture 'tinted with carmine to relive the white of scars'. The entire process, the *Review of Reviews* assured its readers, was: 'quite simple, practically painless and harmless … [and] applicable to other deformations of the body'.¹⁵

With the aid of cocaine anaesthesia, numerous other bodily 'deformations' and 'the social agon[ies]' they produced could be revised into newly attractive forms. The journalist, electrolysist, and 'lady-specialist [in] Health and Beauty' Ada S. Ballin more than once told the story of a patient of hers whose nose was badly swollen and 'disfigured by the appearance of red veins'. For eight years, the young man had 'suffered greatly' from his reddened nose 'which was hindering him in his profession (the law) as giving rise to the idea that he drank … [when] it had been started by scarlet fever when he was quite a boy'. For such cases, Ballin stated: 'Electrolysis is the only cure. Cocaine may be used to render it painless, and there is no mark or scar left when I do it.'¹⁶ Under local anaesthesia, the imperfections, stains, and rebellious irregularities of the complexion could be easily corralled back into tranquillity at the patient's instruction. The advice columns of *The Girl's Own Paper* counselled women concerned about blemishing moles or port-wine birthmarks that they might have them expunged by surgical electrolysis or electro-puncture. Such operations, the paper wrote, 'can be very readily done under cocaine … can often be finished in half an hour, and the patient will be as well as ever with everything healed in a week or ten days'.¹⁷ Deborah Primrose, the health and beauty correspondent for *Hearth and Home*, regularly advised her lady readers that the best way to deal with excessive or unsightly hair growth was to: 'get a small quantity of cocaine and a pair of ivory tweezers from your chemists. Rub the cocaine in first to numb the skin, and then pluck out the hairs with the tool.' Cocaine was particularly helpful because, in

---

¹⁴ 'Tip-Tilted Noses', *BMJ*, 1.1381 (18 June 1887), 1345.
¹⁵ 'Restoring Broken Noses', *The Review of Reviews*, 25.146 (February 1902), 146.
¹⁶ See Ada S. Ballin, 'Health and Beauty', *Womanhood*, 9.52 (March 1903), 299; and Baroness De Bertouch, 'Mrs Ada S. Ballin and her Work', *Hearth and Home*, 13.338 (4 November 1897), 1035.
¹⁷ 'Answers to Correspondents', *The Girl's Own Paper*, 1079 (1 September 1900), 767.

Primrose's view, 'with a little cocaine, you will have no pain whatever, and can go to the very root of the matter'.[18]

If errant hair could be easily taken out, then it was almost as simple to 'transplant' hair to a more pleasing location. The year 1899 offered a new possibility to those whose eyelashes and eyebrows were not quite all that could be desired: 'If your eyes are unattractive you may make them irresistible by transplanting the hair. Transplanted eyelashes and eyebrows are the latest things in the way of personal adornment.' First taking a long hair from the patient's head and threading it through a fine needle, the operator would rub the border of the eyelid with a solution of cocaine and 'by a few skilful touches run his needle through the extreme edges of the eyelid between the epidermis and the lower border of the cartilage of the tragus'. The substitute eyelashes would then be trimmed to shape, curled, and bandaged to encourage them to take root and grow in their new location. Thanks to this 'sewing of hair' the most pedestrian set of eyes could be enchanted into 'irresistible' lustrousness: 'By means of the new process, it is said, eyes which are at ordinary times only passable become languishing in their expression, while eyes which were previously considered fine have their beauty much enhanced.'[19] Other, more apparent, imperfections of the eye could also be addressed. One nurse who signed herself 'Very Worried' wrote to *Womanhood* magazine to ask if anything could be done to remedy a squint. 'The operation might be done under cocaine,' came the reply, '[and] I am quite certain that you ought to have it done, because for a nurse to squint in ever so slight a degree, would prevent her from getting such a good engagement as otherwise. ... You will not look at all unsightly after this is done, as it consists only in cutting a tiny muscle, which is hidden behind the eyelids.'[20] As with the young man with the unfortunately red-veined nose, cocaine here holds out the promise that unattractive – and, therefore, potentially professionally disadvantageous – parts of the body might be surgically purified and smoothed over. Under cocaine anaesthesia, even the most seemingly obscure of bodily embarrassments could be undone. Professional singers, for instance, who worried that a particularly low-hanging uvula might make for an unappealing sight during their performances were advised (apparently as a matter of course)

---

[18] For examples of Primrose's frequent recommendations of cocaine in her 'Health and Beauty' column, see Deborah Primrose, 'Health and Beauty', *Hearth and Home*, 308 (8 August 1897), 924; 'Health and Beauty', *Hearth and Home*, 332 (23 September 1897), 784; 'Health and Beauty', *Hearth and Home*, 411 (30 March 1899), 846; and 'Health and Beauty', *Hearth and Home*, 336 (21 October 1897), 970.

[19] 'Irresistible Eyes', *Dundee Courier*, 14361 (6 July 1899), 4.

[20] Ada S. Ballin, 'Health and Beauty', *Womanhood*, 7.40 (March 1902), 323.

to 'go to a specialist' to have it 'snipped or shortened by means of a galvano cautery. ... The operation is a very slight one, and with pervious application of cocaine, perfectly painless.'[21] In these articles, cocaine combines with cosmetic (or plastic) medical techniques to produce a rhetoric of comprehensive effortlessness. Surgery smooths the subject's way through life, enhancing beauty and removing professional obstacles, but the surgeries themselves are also characterized by their simplicity and painlessness: the patient feels no discomfort at the operation, they recover quickly, and such scars as are left behind can be straightforwardly painted out or concealed. The overarching telos of these fin de siècle operations is the production of a kind of frictionless beauty: an easy process that is itself productive of further easiness.

The effect of cocaine anaesthesia was to suggest an image of cosmetic-surgical serenity. Beyond this, though, the possibility of easy beauty also contained the potential for the easy individualization of that beauty – the notion that the body might be efficiently, fashionably tailored to order. The promise of yet more sophisticated forms of physical customization is apparent in an article entitled 'Changed at Will' that appeared in March 1894, only the month before Max Beerbohm's 'Defence of Cosmetics' was first printed. Confidently jovial in its assessment of modern cosmetic surgery, the article commenced with the flamboyant remark that: 'If Cleopatra were alive to-day, the length of her nose would have little to do in determining her career.' Such, the piece went on, was 'the present advanced state of surgery' that the features of the face were now (or very soon would be) capable of being utterly 'changed at will' – determined only by the whims of their possessor. The cutting and sewing of the surgeon meant that large mouths could now be 'transformed into dainty shapes'. Likewise: 'If a Roman nose gives one the air of being too dominant, the hump is removed by making an incision ... If a pug nose does not harmonise with the other features of the face or with a pensive disposition, it is easily changed by removing a wedge-shaped piece between the nostrils.' Each of these procedures, the journal concluded, could – thanks to cocaine – be 'done without pain', the operation being rendered 'a mere detail'. 'Changed at Will' closes with the promise of even greater changes to come, writing that: 'The surgeon who is the authority for these statements says that the time will come when skin-grafting will be so easily managed that another countenance may be ordered, like a new bonnet.'[22]

---

[21] 'Questions and Answers', *The Musical Herald*, 515 (1 February 1891), 58.
[22] 'Changed at Will', *Hampshire Telegraph*, 5875 (31 March 1894), 11.

The sentiments expressed in 'Changed at Will' articulate several closely interconnected surgical ideals. At their core is the notion that the modern body – or, more specifically, the modern face – is highly amenable to surgical transformation; it can be easily remoulded not only to conform to the dictates of aesthetic unity but also to conform to the personal preferences of its owner. The physical structures of the face are now as flexible as individual expressions, so that, whether an individual is pensive or passive, their exterior appearance can now be made to more agreeably conform to their interior disposition. Related to this is a distinct emphasis on the patient's personal agency and self-determination. The article's opening sentiment is a revision of the seventeenth-century French mathematician Blaise Pascal's famous, punning remark on the role of accident in history – that if Cleopatra's nose had been shorter, the entire face of the world would have been different.[23] The inversion of Pascal's sentiment hints at the idea that modern surgery has inverted the established relationship between the body and the fortunes of that body's owner. The happenstance of Cleopatra's beauty had once ruled not only her fate but also the fate of the world. Fin de siècle surgery, however, might now allow the individual to take control over the condition of their body and, by implication, take control over the circumstances of their destiny. The ancient Cleopatra had been Cleopatra only by chance, but modern surgery held out the possibility that anyone might rule their own fortunes and make themselves into a new Cleopatra by an act of will – provided that they had the assistance of an appropriately dextrous surgeon. Presented in this way, cosmetic surgery seemingly promised a more sustained and expansive liberation than just the liberation from ugliness; freedom from the constraints of the body is implied to produce the more far-reaching freedom of complete self-determination.

For 'Changed at Will' then, the main appeal of cosmetic surgery is not so much that it might make people more beautiful, as that it might allow them to more ideally assert their personal autonomy.[24] This privileging of the patient's selfhood (or 'will') had, in turn, important implications for the relationship between patient and practitioner. 'Changed at Will' closes with a fantastical image of the future state of aesthetic surgery – a world in which 'another countenance may be ordered, like a new bonnet'. It is significant that the closest analogue that the writer can find for this imagined future surgeon is

---

[23] See Blaise Pascal, *Pensées* (London: Penguin, 1995), 120.
[24] See Gilman, *Making the Body Beautiful*, 17–20 for a more extensive discussion of autonomy as a core value of aesthetic surgery.

the tailor. Indeed, the language and imagery of tailoring recurs throughout the piece – it depicts the surgeon 'cutting', 'sewing', and remodelling the body as its fabric is chosen to order, 'trimmed to fit, sewed, and properly bound'.[25] The notion that the body might be, as it were, hand-tailored to the patient's peculiar specifications gives rise to the idea that the surgeon might assume the role of the artisan. Rather than a medical authority supervising the patient's care, the cosmetic surgeon is imagined to relate to the patient as a craftsman – one who is paid to execute a technical commission, and who is subservient to his customer's requirements and desires. 'Changed at Will', by implication, forecasts that the new conditions of plastic surgery will displace existing hierarchies of medical expertise and control. The medical man might, in this new configuration, be reimagined as a bespoke artificer, and the doctor–patient relationship be reframed as a more explicitly capitalist exchange. Cocaine was the key ingredient in this new formulation: cocaine anaesthesia (applied to cosmetic operational ends) had made the body into a flexible, modifiable object. But in transforming the body into a subject for couture, cocaine had also potentially made it into an object of consumerism and a subject of fashion.

The tattoo

The 'fashionable craze'[26] for tattooing that sprang up in fin de siècle Britain is most often attributed to the examples of Edward VII and the future George V, both of whom had (in their youths) been tattooed on overseas trips to Jerusalem and Japan respectively.[27] 'It is,' wrote one paper, 'one of the smartest fashions now-a-days to be tattooed.'[28] Others observed that: 'The latest craze is tattooing. Fashionable women are getting their shoulders and arms covered with all sorts of gaudy devices.'[29] In 1892 *The Globe* magazine ran a lengthy

---

[25] 'Changed at Will', *Hampshire Telegraph*, 11.
[26] 'Tattooers and Tattooed', *Pall Mall Gazette*, 8441 (9 April 1892), 1.
[27] Jordanna Bailkin, 'Making Faces: Tattooed Women and Colonial Regimes', *History Workshop Journal*, 59 (2005), 43–4. Victorian and Edwardian contemporaries also suggested the opening up of Japan (with its long tradition of tattoo art) to increased international contact and – later – British support for their Asian ally in the 1904 Russo-Japanese war as potential contributions to the fad. Whatever its exact origins, it was clear by the 1890s that the art of the tattoo was an integral part of Britain's fashionable scene. See 'The Growth of Tattooing', *Pall Mall Gazette*, 7543 (22 May 1889), 2; and 'Skin Pictures', *Irish Independent*, 3819 (16 May 1904), 2.
[28] 'The Fashion to Be Tattooed', *Hull Daily Mail*, 2239 (11 November 1892), 3.
[29] 'Now and Then', *Evening Herald* (Dublin), 9.264 (12 January 1901), 5.

feature on the new tribe of 'Fashionable Savages' that seemed to be roaming the streets of Britain's largest cities. For the 'young swells' of the metropolis, the paper claimed, the invitation to 'Come and have a tattoo with me!' had now risen to equal ascendancy with 'that other equally fashionable suggestion of American moderns, "Come and have a drink?" '[30]

The self-consciously voguish modernity of the invitation to 'Come and have a tattoo!' might seem to sit uneasily alongside *The Globe*'s suggestion that there was something inherently 'savage' about the practice. Indeed, many of the fin de siècle journalists who remarked on the fashion for tattoos felt similarly compelled to wrestle with the art's apparently antediluvian character. For the travel writer Clement William Scott there was, despite the 'wide and potent' nature of the craze, nevertheless 'something suggestive of the galley slave, the branded convict, and the ancient Britain and cave-dweller in the tattooed man'.[31] One correspondent for the *Pall Mall Gazette* lamented: 'It has come to this: tattooing, the most primitive form of personal adornment as practised by the natives in the backwoods of America, is quickly becoming one of the fine arts and fashionable crazes of civilised life.'[32] Much critical analysis of fin de siècle tattooing and its savage connotations has concentrated on the work of the Italian criminologist and degeneration theorist Cesare Lombroso. For Lombroso and his disciples, 'the attraction to tattoos was evidence of savage and criminal tendencies'[33] – in large part because the tattoo served as evidence of the recipient's willingness to endure pain in order to gratify their hunger for mere decoration. 'Obtuse' submission to pain was, in Lombroso's view, a definitive marker of personal degeneration – a sign that the recipient lacked 'delicacy and refinement' and that their tastes ran 'contrary to progress'. Lombroso was particularly disturbed by the fashionability of tattoos among upper-class British women, since – in his conception – the preference for elaborate and painful ornamentation bespoke 'something atavistic and savage in their hearts'.[34] Consequently, savages, 'criminals, and aristocratic women were linked by their propensity to mark themselves in irrational and painful ways'.[35] In this analysis, the painfulness of tattooing intrinsically connected the art with moral regression

---

[30] 'Fashionable Savages', *The Globe*, 30385 (21 October 1892), 3.
[31] Clement Scott, 'Tattooing in Japan', *The Illustrated London News*, 103.2837 (2 September 1893), 287.
[32] 'Tattooers and Tattooed', *Pall Mall Gazette*, 1.
[33] Pamela Gilbert, *Victorian Skin: Surface, Self, History* (Ithaca, NY: Cornell University Press, 2019), 324.
[34] See 'Tattooing the Body', *Supplement to the Cork Daily Herald*, 40.1195 (16 May 1896), 2.
[35] Bailkin, 'Making Faces: Tattooed Women and Colonial Regimes', 49.

and impassive dullness – the characteristic signifiers of savagery, stupidity, and criminality.[36]

The introduction of cocaine anaesthesia into the practice of fin de siècle tattooing, however, serves to somewhat complicate this reading. Numerous sources from the 1880s through to the early twentieth century emphasize the importance of the drug to both amateur and professional tattooists in making the new fashion painless. One paper covering the trend wrote: 'Some years ago it was a very painful operation, but the discovery of cocaine has made it a painless one.'[37] One writer for *Chums: An Illustrated Paper for Boys* described how, after tracing the design onto the client's skin, 'Cocaine is next hypodermically injected all round the surface of the drawing so as to numb the nerves in that locality and so prevent the subject from feeling pain.'[38] Of the period's celebrity tattoo artists, Sutherland MacDonald was one of the most consistent in advertising his use of the drug. Clients who asked MacDonald whether the decoration was likely to be a painful experience were assured: 'Not at all, because I inject cocaine under the skin at the part upon which I am going to operate, and use more cocaine directly the effects of the first injection have passed away.'[39] Other papers reported that the internationally feted Hori Chyo of Yokohama (who had allegedly been paid 'the princely salary of £2,400' to travel to New York and tattoo an American millionaire) kept a 'silver hypodermic' of the anaesthetic ready to hand for 'when the [skin's] surface is required to be deadened'.[40] Alongside these professionals, Victorian papers wrote fascinatedly about the newly fashionable 'Tattooed Countesses'[41] and their turn from first being tattooed to becoming tattoo artists themselves:

> Other hitherto favourite pastimes for ladies are giving place, we are assured, to the barbaric art of hypodermic decoration. A trustworthy correspondent tells us that in the shop of a London instrument-maker she was recently shown a small Russia leather case, bearing a silver plate, engraved with the name of a well-known lady of title. The case contained a complete set of tattooing instruments, comprising needles mounted in ivory handles, non-poisonous inks of various colures, and a tiny bottle of cocaine to render the operation painless. …

[36] See Gilbert, *Victorian Skin: Surface, Self, History*, 189–90; and Bailkin, 'Making Faces: Tattooed Women and Colonial Regimes', 48–50 for more extensive discussion of Lombroso's thinking on pain, gender, and primitivity.
[37] 'Now and Then', *Evening Herald*, 5.
[38] 'A Visit to a Professional Tattooer', *Chums: An Illustrated Paper for Boys*, 2.81 (28 March 1894), 485.
[39] 'The Fashion to be Tattooed', *Hull Daily Mail*, 3. See also: 'Sporting Pictures on the Human Skin', *Country Life Illustrated*, 7.160 (27 January 1900), 109.
[40] 'On Tattooing', *Newcastle Courant*, 11677 (5 November 1898), 6.
[41] 'Tattooed Countesses', *Hearth and Home*, 77 (3 November 1892), 821.

It was, our correspondent was informed, one of nearly a hundred cases of similar patterns, which have been manufactured to order within the last twelve months.[42]

In rendering the operations of the tattooist 'painless' cocaine had the effect of resolving several of the practical and philosophical objections to the new pastime. Not only would the client not have to bear the pain of the procedure unaided, they were also implicitly freed from having to consider what their willingness to endure such pain might imply about their character. This is not to dismiss the savage or 'barbaric' connotations of tattooing in this period, but I want to suggest that the perceived primitivism of the tattoo was (at least in the context of cocaine anaesthesia) more directly rooted in aesthetic considerations than in the tattooed subject's atavistic willingness to endure pain. The modification and adornment of the body by tattooing was seen as a custom originating in 'a very early stage of the evolution of mankind',[43] but this did not necessarily make it an unambiguously immoral one. Various critics have demonstrated that the 'restoration' of 'primitive'[44] styles and practices might (paradoxically) be received by fin de siècle audiences as markers of youthful vitality and even of progressive energy.[45] The very barbarity of the tattoo, with its 'strange devices [and] divers colours' gave it 'a certain fantastic charm' for some observers.[46] At the same time, the tattoo was often depicted in contemporary sources as a highly specialized application of medical–cosmetic technologies. Tattooing was – I argue – simultaneously perceived to be a return to barbaric and discordant forms of 'bodily ornamentation'[47] and a particularly striking variety of aesthetic medicine, where the body might be individually recrafted and decorated by means of modern science. Even more vividly than the cosmetic procedures

[42] 'Editorial Notes', *Pick-Me-Up*, 46 (17 August 1889), 314.
[43] 'A Revival in Tattooing', *Yorkshire Evening Post*, 4379 (14 September 1904), 2.
[44] See Bradley Deane, *Masculinity and the New Imperialism* (Cambridge: Cambridge University Press, 2014), 164.
[45] Bradley Deane, for example, argues that the image of the 'barbarian' could be interpreted as a model for the optimum form of British imperialist endeavour, so that a modern man's taste for barbarous fashions could be approvingly read as a 'primal expression of enduringly manly qualities'. By the end of the century, in Deane's words: 'atavism could be imagined as a sign of strength rather than weakness, exoticism as one of virility rather than effeminacy, and the relapse into barbarism as an empowering fantasy rather than a paralyzing anxiety' (see Deane, *Masculinity and the New Imperialism*, 8, 147–50, and 164–70). Similarly, in the developing field of late-nineteenth-century eugenic medicine, recurrence to the 'savage' practice of human sacrifice could be seen as a necessary precondition for the production of a more perfect form of future human heredity. (See Douglas R. J. Small, 'Primitive Doctor and Eugenic Priest: Grant Allen, M.P. Shiel, and the Future of the Victorian Medical Man', *Journal of Literature and Science*, 11.2 (2018), 40–61.)
[46] 'A Visit to a Professional Tattooer', *Chums*, 485.
[47] 'The Dress Question in Times Past', *The Ladies' Treasury: An Illustrated Magazine of Entertaining Literature*, 1 March 1895, 181.

detailed in the preceding section, the tattoo could be understood as an especially arresting interstice between modern medicine and contemporary fashion.

It was not uncommon for the tattoo artist's techniques of inking and colouring to be applied directly to the ends of cosmetic medicine. Following the introduction of cocaine to eye surgery, ophthalmologists discovered that the eye could itself be tattooed and recoloured. 'The operation of tattooing is first performed by treating the eye with cocaine until it becomes absolutely senseless to pain. ... The tattooing is then performed by means of a little electric machine, which operates a specially made needle.'[48] Upon its discovery in 1897, writers stressed the reparative value of the operation, but by 1905 it was being reported that the procedure was now available for purely cosmetic reasons: 'After having induced insensibility by the use of cocaine, [the surgeons] make a number of tiny incisions in the cornea. Into these tiny holes they drop a minute portion of a special colouring pigment – blue, grey, black, or brown, as may be desired.'[49] A more accessible operation involved the tattooing of a 'delicate rose colour' onto the cheeks of women who wanted a permanent version of the fashionably rouged complexion of the day. Men – while they might eschew the 'soft' pinkness favoured by women – could be tempted by the reproduction of a 'brown' and rugged suntan. 'A large number of men,' wrote the *Irish Independent*, 'have undergone the procedure.' Neither sex was, however, 'called upon to suffer any sensation of pain, as cocaine is mixed with the paint. Many clients indifferently read a book during the process.'[50]

These operations to recolour the eyes and the skin fit comfortably alongside other 'ornamental surgeries'[51] that aimed to bring the patient's body into aesthetic harmony. Intriguingly, though, even explicitly decorative, or pictorial, styles of tattooing tend to be described in this period using terminology and allusions drawn from the world of medical science. Tattooing was, in effect, figured as a type of cosmetic medicine. The use of anaesthesia was the most obvious parallel between the procedures of the tattooist and those of the practitioner. In 1892, *The Globe*'s correspondent fascinatedly watched Sutherland MacDonald at work: 'Dipped in ink, the needle was drawn like a pencil along the lines traced on the arm ... In each separate line cocaine was injected by the same methods

---

[48] 'Tattooing the Human Eye', *Hampshire Telegraph and Sussex Chronicle*, 6045 (24 July 1897), 12. See also: 'Tattooing the Human Eye', *Northern Daily Mail*, 5931 (24 July 1897), 6; and 'Fact and Fancy', *Weekly Telegraph*, 1843 (7 August 1897), 15; and 'Corneal Tattoos', *BMJ*, 2.1923 (6 November 1897), 74.
[49] 'Re-Colouring the Eyes', *Huddersfield Daily Examiner*, 11511 (8 February 1905), 2.
[50] 'Rosy Cheeks', *Irish Independent*, 3679 (18 November 1904), 2.
[51] 'The Dogs' Beauty Doctor', *Daily Mirror*, 57 (8 January 1904), 11.

by which morphine is injected by physicians.'[52] More generally, both professions seemed to call for the same manual dexterity, the same conscientiousness in avoiding pain and infection, and for similarly skilled applications of chemicals and instruments. To many onlookers, the execution of a tattoo seemed more like a surgical operation than an artistic commission, a meticulous remodelling – not of canvas or of clay but of a patient's body. 'The tattooer,' one paper noted, 'never operates upon the same patient for more than two hours at a sitting lest it should cause an unhealing sore or in any way injure the blood.'[53] Tattooing, like surgery, was accomplished with its own selection of strange, sharpened instruments and accompanied by similar rituals of sterilization and anaesthesia. When the tattoo craze reached the north of England in 1905, the *Yorkshire Evening Post* observed:

> The expert tattoo artist is extremely careful in the use of his instruments and material. The impressions are made with a variety of instruments. Some consist of two very fine needles; others, for shading purposes, of as many as a score of needles. There are fitted at the end of a wooden holder. The steel 'prickers' are kept clean by boiling, and also by placing in an antiseptic solution, carbolic being preferred. The part of the skin operated upon is also carefully washed in carbolic or some other antiseptic after the operation.[54]

The superficial affinity between the decorative injection of ink and the therapeutic injection of drugs suggested further comparisons between the two disciplines. The tattooist was sometimes jokingly figured as a strange, far-flung relative of 'the vaccinator'[55] and the tattoo itself acquired a curiously medical inflection in descriptions of it as a 'hypodermic stain' or a 'hypodermic decoration'.[56]

For fin de siècle observers, tattooing seemed to exert a deeply oxymoronic fascination, simultaneously redolent of barbarous mutilation and of the technical finesse of contemporary medicine. The process seemed one of 'extreme contrasts' – primitive and unruly in its associations but intensely modern in its implementation. An 1898 article 'On Tattooing' concluded:

> The extreme contrast to the [barbarian races], whose crude dexterity with a fish bone or shell or other rude implement we have adverted to, is furnished by the English operators in luxuriously furnished rooms, in 'swagger' parts of the Metropolis, pricking their designs with an electric needle, on a circumscribed

---

[52] 'Fashionable Savages', *The Globe*, 3.
[53] 'A Visit to a Professional Tattooer', *Chums: An Illustrated Paper for Boys*, 2.81 (28 March 1894), 485.
[54] 'A Revival in Tattooing', *Yorkshire Evening Post*, 4379 (14 September 1904), 2.
[55] 'A Japanese Tattooer', *Liverpool Mercury*, 13720 (26 December 1891), 6.
[56] 'Science Notes', *Pall Mall Gazette*, 9634 (10 February 1896), 1; and 'Editorial Notes', *Pick-Me-Up*, 46 (17 August 1889), 314.

area of the anæsthetised skin of a wealthy client, who will pay highly for an exclusive design.⁵⁷

In 1908, a decade later, journalists were still engrossed by the same contrasts: 'It is rather curious that the arts of adornment practiced by the most uncultivated savages and one of the most modern outcomes of our civilisation should become intimately connected, and yet in the electric tattoo machine we have an example of the way in which extremes meet.'⁵⁸ This sense of chaotic juxtaposition is at its most obvious in descriptions of fashionable tattooists' own premises and work rooms. Clement Scott described the 'sanctum' of one noted practitioner:

> It is a veritable cabinet of curiosities, partly library of reference, partly surgeon's consulting room. There is the easy chair for the patient, in which he reposes during the weary hours necessary to transform the skin in which he was born into the decorated mass of eccentricities devised by man. Close by the chair are ranged lamps and burners of every imaginable strength, such as we see at the aurist's and the fashionable throat doctor's. On a table close by the chair, handy for the artist-tattooer, are the thousands upon thousands of needles requisite to prick and punch your epidermis into pattern according to taste. The operation is tedious, comparatively painless, but extremely simple.⁵⁹

The Globe's account of London's 'Fashionable Savages' contained a similarly elaborate sketch of the basement room in Jermyn Street occupied by Sutherland MacDonald:

> It was a room that in odours and furniture suggested odd occupations. There was the aroma of brandy subdued by the faint smell of a hospital ward. It was a distinct smell, as yet unnamed in any dictionary; something between a chemist's shop and Spiers and Pond's establishments. There were armchairs, dwarfed by little legs, but in a breadth, depth, and amplitude of body almost equal to a sofa. Then there were the ordinary chairs that one finds in a hall way. From the ceiling hung an incandescent light, and strewn about on the large square table were Japanese horrors traced on parchment, vials of cocaine, coloured inks, an electrical machine that looked like a bomb connected with a fuse under the table, an empty champagne bottle, and a box of the best Nubian cigarettes.⁶⁰

Here, the tattooist's operating room is characterized most distinctly by its 'eccentricities' and disorder – surgical lamps crowded up against 'Japanese

---

⁵⁷ 'On Tattooing', *Newcastle Courant*, 11677 (5 November 1898), 6.
⁵⁸ 'Electric Pin-Pricks', *Weekly Telegraph*, 2427 (17 October 1908), 17.
⁵⁹ Scott, 'Tattooing in Japan', *The Illustrated London News*, 287.
⁶⁰ 'Fashionable Savages', *The Globe*, 3.

horrors', cushioned (albeit curiously deformed) armchairs side by side with keen and pricking needles, the mingled waft of the hospital ward and the popular restaurant, champagne and cocaine. Tattooing is presented in these sources as an activity of lurid, though fascinating, confusion and discord: medical devices haphazardly muddled with the appurtenances of fashionable amusement. Tattooing is portrayed in these works as a kind of wild, hedonistic medicine. For the fin de siècle, the tattoo represented a practice in which medical techniques and technologies might be crudely grafted onto the quest for pleasure – the harsh 'lamps and burners' of the 'surgeon's consulting room' shining down on brightly patterned and riotous bodies.

For late Victorians and Edwardians, then, tattooing seemed to take on the guise of a compelling but bacchanalian new variety of medicine, one which was 'savage', spectacular, anarchic, and subordinated to the wispish dictates of fashion. The tattoo was – in many ways – a particularly hyperbolic exaggeration of the discourses attached to contemporary cosmetic medicine. We have previously seen how the work of the 'beauty doctor'[61] could be easily compared with the art of the tailor: the body being individually decorated, trimmed, and outfitted to the customer's specifications. For the tattooer, this parallel seemed even more readily applicable. The needle was both the tool of the tailor and of the surgeon, and the tattooist had recourse in his profession to 'thousands upon thousands of needles'.[62] By a transposition of ideas, many sources from this period tend to refer to the tattoo either as a kind of clothing or as a weird (faintly magical) substitution of the skin for some other ostentatious fabric. Clement Scott's impression was that the function of the tattoo was 'to transform the skin' into a 'decorated mass of eccentricities'.[63] Journalistic descriptions of tattooed men and women often affect an exaggerated confusion on being confronted with beings who are simultaneously clothed and unclothed, who appear human and artificial. According to one report, tattooed skin 'appears as if covered with some "loud" patterned fabric. A tattooed man never looks unclothed. He seems constantly clad in the same Harlequin costume, and must surely feel that he goes to bed without undressing.'[64] During an 1892 interview with the professional tattoo artist 'Professor' John Williams and his wife, the *Pall Mall Gazette*'s correspondent described the couple's appearance:

---

[61] 'Making Women Beautiful', *Birmingham Daily Post*, 5.
[62] Scott, 'Tattooing in Japan', *The Illustrated London News*, 287.
[63] Ibid.
[64] *The Standard*, 19266 (13 April 1886), 5.

[The young lady's] shoulders and arms down to her wrists were covered with black lace. Was it lace, though, this fanciful design that looked so pretty upon the round arm and against the necklace of pearls? In was not: it was the ornament which, once put on, can never be doffed again.

And now the professor appeared, bare down to his bright coloured belt, but clothed in the Indian ink and vermillion that coiled and wound and twisted and spread in a thousand forms over his chest, and back, and arms, and shoulders.[65]

One visitor to Sutherland MacDonald's studio was confronted with a young, half-naked army officer waiting for the image of a large griffin on his torso to finish drying, and pretended to a momentary confusion as to where the substance of the monster left off and the substance of the 'young captain of foot' resumed: 'The coloured scales of this creature glistened with damp colours, and completely usurped the identity of the human skin.'[66] Griffin and man are here unified together into a single new and glittering 'creature'. Exaggerated for dramatic effect as these moments of confusion might be, they signal the tattoo's potential to ambiguate natural and artificial elements of the body. Elaborately working on 'anæsthetised skin',[67] the tattooist's needle suggested the same possibilities as 'Changed at Will' – that the time might come when 'another countenance may be ordered, like a new bonnet'.[68] Fashionable yet barbaric, 'strange and fantastic-looking',[69] painless because 'injected with cocaine',[70] the tattoo seemed to dramatically encapsulate the immanent potential for the body to be decorated, patterned, and modified to preference. Behind this possibility, however, there remained the risk that this new body might be one that was 'usurped' by unnatural and artificial elements, menacing its health, and even the clarity of its humanity.

The moral problems of aesthetic surgery

Fin de siècle medical authorities were sensitive to the moral and ideological issues provoked by new (largely cocaine-enabled) innovations in cosmetic surgery. In 1888, Sir William MacCormac began an address to the Midland Medical Society

---

[65] 'Tattooers and Tattooed', *Pall Mall Gazette*, 1.
[66] 'Fashionable Savages', *The Globe*, 3.
[67] 'On Tattooing', *Newcastle Courant*, 6.
[68] 'Changed at Will', *Hampshire Telegraph*, 11.
[69] 'Tattooers and Tattooed', *Pall Mall Gazette*, 1.
[70] 'Fashionable Savages', *The Globe*, 3.

by 'defining plastic surgery as that branch of the art which has as its object the relief of deformity or the restoration of a lost function, ... as well as to replace parts destroyed by accident or disease'. After this assured opening, though, MacCormac apparently felt himself less secure of his ground, doubling back to justify his choice of topic: 'He quoted Dieffenbach's[71] statement that plastic surgery is one of the highest achievements of the art, as an apology, if one were needed, for his choice of subject, and mentioned the names of the many famous surgeons who had devoted their best attention to the matter.'[72] MacCormac's wariness in commencing his address – his need to be seen to both clearly delineate his subject and to 'apologise' for it – indicates some of the insecurity that plastic surgery engendered in the late-nineteenth- and early-twentieth-century medical profession. In lecturing on 'Plastic Operations and Their Place in Surgery,' MacCormac's foremost imperative was to reassure his audience that the 'place' of plastic operations was an irrefutably curative one, emblematized by the therapeutic trinity of 'relief', 'restoration', and 'replace[ment]'. The same need to legitimize plastic techniques can be seen in MacCormac's appeal to the standing of the 'many famous surgeons who [have] devoted their best attention to the matter'. Taken together, this series of apologies, reassurances, and legitimations ultimately serves to reveal the hidden difficulty that MacCormac was intent on evading, even to the extent of being reluctant to acknowledge its existence: the prospect that plastic operations might be more directly relevant to the art of beauty than to the art of healing.

For many fin de siècle practitioners, the direction of medical knowledge towards purely aesthetic – rather than restorative – ends seemed a contravention of medicine's basic Hippocratic principles. 'By,' as Elizabeth Haiken points out, 'placing healthy patients at risk, cosmetic surgery contradicted the fundamental tenets of the medical profession'.[73] Even if the actual risk involved was close to nil, there were still difficult questions surrounding the moral weight of interfering with a healthy, undamaged body. In a discussion of the use of cocaine to assist in circumcision, one correspondent to the *Lancet* cautioned his more enthusiastic peers: 'I think we should be sure we are on very safe ground before we counsel any attempts to improve upon nature by mutilation.'[74] The word 'mutilation' suggestively recurs throughout fin de siècle criticisms of aesthetic surgery. When

---

[71] Johann Friedrich Dieffenbach (1792–1847), pioneering rhinoplastic and maxillofacial surgeon.
[72] William MacCormac, 'Abstract of an Address on Plastic Operations and Their Place in Surgery', *BMJ*, 2.1456 (24 November 1888), 1158.
[73] Elizabeth Haiken, *Venus Envy: A History of Cosmetic Surgery* (Baltimore, MD: Johns Hopkins University Press, 1997), 5.
[74] Herbert Snow, 'The Use of Cocaine in Circumcision', *Lancet*, 128.3287 (28 August 1886), 429.

George Gould and Walter Pyle came to pen their encyclopaedic cornucopia of *Anomalies and Curiosities of Medicine* (1898), they grouped all modern aesthetic procedures together under the entry headed 'Cosmetic Mutilations'. Wrote Gould and Pyle:

> **Cosmetic Mutilations.** – In modern times there have been individuals expert in removing facial deformities, and by operations of various kinds producing pleasing dimples or other artificial signs of beauty. … It is quite possible that some of our modern operators have over-stepped the bounds of necessity, and performed unjustifiable plastic operations to satisfy the vanity of their patients.[75]

This entry articulates a morally forceful but, in practice, conceptually slippery distinction between the 'necess[ary]' repair of facial deformities and the 'unjustifiable' indulgence of 'vanity'. The passage is curiously inconsistent in how it defines its logic of artificiality. 'Correcting a disagreeable contour of the nose' and the 'manufacture of charming dimples' are ranked as 'artificial' additions to the human face, while the 'removal of facial deformity' suggests the excision of aberrant structures that are alien to the natural, healthy human countenance. While near-identical plastic procedures might be used in each case, the distinguishing factor is how far these operations conformed to an existing medical model of curative action. Effacing the effects of damage or disease was necessary and justifiable since this action returned the face to its natural condition. Overtly beautifying the face, however, risked deviating from nature and 'over-stepping' moral limits into falseness and mutilation. In this way, the cosmetic practitioner could be construed as surrendering the profession's true principles in order to earn the approval of his patient's self-destructive vanity.

These ethical problems were further aggravated by pragmatic considerations. Fin de siècle practitioners who struggled to determine the moral defensibility of aesthetic surgery found it equally difficult to arrive at a clear set of criteria for measuring such operations' success or failure. By the year 1900 even the cautious Sir William MacCormac could agree that 'plastic methods [had] been perfected in an extraordinary degree'.[76] Technical sophistication was only one facet of aesthetic surgery, however. As a writer for the *British Medical Journal* remarked in 1901, cosmetic surgery was a discipline that perennially seemed – Janus-like – to have 'two aspects' to it. Wrote the *BMJ*:

---

[75] Gould and Pyle, *Anomalies and Curiosities of Medicine*, 746.
[76] William MacCormac, 'Centenary Festival of the Royal College of Surgeons of England – An Address of Welcome', *BMJ*, 2.2065 (28 July 1900), 212.

> There are always two sides to the question of plastic surgery to the face. The surgeon is often extremely well satisfied with the results he has obtained under circumstances of great difficulty, while the patient is equally dissatisfied because when the original defect is remedied traces of the means employed remain permanently, and these two aspects of facial surgery should not be lost sight of.[77]

The journal's remarks highlight the disconcerting disparity of perspectives that could exist between the operating practitioner and the patient. More than in any other branch of surgery, it was possible for both parties to embark on a plastic procedure with drastically different expectations and standards of success. Viewed from a merely technical and profession perspective, an operation might be judged to have fully achieved its ends, while the patient might construe the same outcome as little better than abject failure. Thus, the confusing duality of the discipline: the field of plastic (or aesthetic) surgery appeared, in the *BMJ*'s view, to have a peculiar, two-faced quality to it; a successful result was perpetually elusive and uncertain, dependent not only on the appraisal of the practitioner but also (and perhaps more importantly) on the unrealized hopes and anticipations of the patient. Aesthetic surgery was, as such, distinguished in fin de siècle medical practice by the extent to which the patient implicitly sat in judgement on the work of the surgeon.

Discussions of plastic surgery frequently alerted practitioners to the gap that existed between their own perspectives and those of their clients. One writer counselled practitioners to remain cautious of the frequency with which 'the ultimate result' of plastic surgery tended to 'fall very far short of the ideal aimed at, [which] often leads to much disappointment on the part of the patient'.[78] Operations undertaken for purely aesthetic reasons were even more liable to this problem. In 1911, the German-American surgeon Frederick Strange Kolle lamented that: 'Patients who beg us to make them more beautiful … are the most difficult to please, and often complain, after a few days of constant mirror study of the parts changed by methods that are the result of years of hard-earned experience, that the nose or the eyes or the ears have not been changed as much as they desired.'[79] This pervasive wariness of potential 'complaints' and 'disappointment' stems, in large part, from an underlying consciousness of the fact that the main criterion for operative success in cosmetic cases was a distinctly undependable one: the patient's own satisfaction.

---

[77] 'Reviews', *BMJ*, 2.2130 (26 October 1901), 1272.
[78] 'Reviews', *BMJ*, 1.2307 (18 March 1905), 603.
[79] Frederick Strange Kolle, *Plastic and Cosmetic Surgery* (London: D. Appleton, 1911), 491.

Consequently, cosmetic surgery appeared to fin de siècle observers to be both ethically and practically unreliable – located in a precarious hinterland of medical morals and authority. Advocates for the emerging discipline attempted to recuperate their work by positioning it within an existing medical framework of curative action. In 1907, Charles Miller produced a textbook for facial aesthetic surgery entitled *The Correction of Featural Imperfections*, wherein he described how: '[Imperfection] revolts sensitive people so that unfortunates so afflicted earnestly desire relief, if such is attainable.'[80] Miller's strategy was to legitimize cosmetic surgery by rhetorically pathologizing ugliness and imperfection. Folds, wrinkles, and other 'featural imperfections' become, in Miller's rendering, 'afflict[ions]' which 'unfortunate' patients are forced to endure and which demand medical 'relief'. In this way, cosmetic surgeons could portray themselves as curing a disease-like ugliness that 'revolt[ed]' the sensitive person. However, even if cosmetic surgery could be excused as remedying a 'disease of ugliness', it was still a disease whose symptoms were highly subjective and dependent on the opinion of the patient. The symptoms of the disease of imperfection were, in the words of Elizabeth Haiken, 'individualised, defined by the patient before [being] diagnosed by the surgeon, and impossible to quantify'.[81] These individualized, subjective attributes of cosmetic medicine made it obviously troubling to the ethos of fin de siècle medical science as a whole: aesthetic medicine seemed to cure no obvious disease and could offer no reliable diagnoses. This was the other aspect inherent to the surgical fancies articulated in works like 'Changed at Will' and in practices like tattooing. Applied to aesthetics, fin de siècle medical science offered the prospect that the body might be reworked and tailored to suit individual preferences and desires. Such a changeable, highly individualized, and autonomous body, however, also threatened to erode the idea of a dependably fixed human form. The new body produced by cosmetic surgery was at once liberated but also capricious, apparently no longer receptive to objective medical recognition. Cocaine was similarly implicated in this uncertainty. In advancing the practical techniques of cosmetic medicine, cocaine anaesthesia also advanced the epistemological questions such operations provoked. By the end of the century, the cosmetic application of cocaine seemed to have acted to erode the governing restraint of the natural body. This axis of cocaine, cosmetic medicine, and anxious bodily mutability forms the central conceit of W. C. Morrow's 1897 short story 'Two Singular Men', a work which impishly relocates the cosmetically

---

[80] Charles Miller, *The Correction of Featural Imperfections* (Chicago: Oak Printing, 1907), 40.
[81] Haiken, *Venus Envy*, 6.

modified and cocainized bodies of its characters into the grotesquely comic realm of the freakish.

Bodies of lies: W. C. Morrow's 'Two Singular Men'

William Chambers Morrow (1854–1923) lived most of his adult life in California, working at various times as a short story writer, novelist, journalist, and writing teacher. In 1897 he produced a collection of short stories called *The Ape, the Idiot and Other People*. Published in Britain by Grant Richards, early reviews highlighted both Morrow's love of 'the horrible' and of 'morbid [and] grim fantasy' (traits which apparently marked him as a striking – though less artistically coherent – 'disciple of [Edgar Allan] Poe' and Robert Louis Stevenson) as well as his tendency to 'dwell much on medical details'.[82] This medical preoccupation in Morrow's writing is readily observable in 'Two Singular Men' – one of the final stories in the collection, and one which rather neatly captures contemporary feelings of disquietude occasioned by cocaine and developments in cosmetic medicine. 'Two Singular Men' centres on the simultaneously gothic and comic trope of the body alienated from itself. The spine of the plot is reasonably straightforward: two men – the sensitive and intellectual Sampey and the muscular and boorish Bat – are both in love with a beautiful young woman named Muggie and must compete to win her hand. This basic scenario, though, is complicated by the fact that all three of the participants are (or will become in the course of the story) star performers in a hugely popular freak show. As professional freaks, the romance between the three main characters is deeply implicated in the key motif of the story: the strangeness, instability, and even deceptiveness, of its characters' bodies.

Morrow's story begins with Bat having his nose cut off in a fight. Desperate to restore the missing member, Bat visits a surgeon who attempts to recreate the appearance of the lost nose by folding down and reshaping a flap of skin from his patient's forehead.[83] Unfortunately, Bat's scalp is unusually low and covered by particularly thickly matted hair, so that, when the transplant is effected, Bat is left with a substantial black mane surrounding his nose and bristling aggressively

---

[82] See 'Literature', *Glasgow Herald*, 115 (14 May 1898), 4; 'Fiction' *The Saturday Review*, 85.2224 (11 June 1898), 785; and 'Literary Notes', *Pall Mall Gazette*, 11042 (20 August 1900), 1.

[83] This operation was, by the time of Morrow's story, one of the most frequent and routine types of plastic procedure performed by practitioners, its most common application being to disguise the extensive nasal abscesses produced by syphilitic infection. (See Gilman *Making the Body Beautiful*, 49–60 and Haiken, *Venus Envy*, 20–4 for more details.)

upwards towards his eyes. This, the narration laconically informs the reader, gives him a uniquely 'grotesque and hideous appearance'.[84] Under threat of violent revenge from Bat, the surgeon introduces him to Muggie's father and his freak show, guaranteeing him a lucrative new career as 'the Marvellous Tuft-Nosed Wild Man, Hoolagaloo … the greatest curiosity in the world' (256–8). From this opening scene, Morrow draws a distinct line of connection between cosmetic medicine and the freakish. Bat's conversion into an artificial 'wild man' mirrors the processes by which tattoos and other 'fashionabl[y] savage'[85] forms of bodily modification might seem to reconstitute 'civilised'[86] subjects into 'cave-dweller[s]'[87] and 'Red Indian[s]'.[88] In Morrow's presentation, cosmetic surgery has the potential to become both monstrous and ironically self-defeating, since techniques which aim to restore normal, healthy bodies leave traces that are just as – if not more – disturbing than the original defects. The main action of cosmetic medicine in 'Two Singular Men' is to destabilize the body, rather than to restore it to a more conventional order. While the circumstances leading to Bat's 'marvellous tuft nose' are Morrow's own invention, they are based on real-world side effects that could follow fin de siècle cosmetic surgery. In 1897, the same year that *The Ape, the Idiot and Other People* appeared in print, the *BMJ* carried an article on an experimental rhinoplasty that had been carried out on a patient whose nose had been completely lost to rodent ulcer.[89] Since the tissues around the nasal cavity were either completely absent or badly scarred, the operating surgeon, Thomas Annandale, had had to reconstruct the nose partly by using skin taken from the patient's upper lip. Annandale concluded that, while the operation was 'entirely successful in closing the opening … one trouble remained, and it was that the lower flap [of the nose] having been taken from the upper lip, was covered with hair, but the patient preferred this to the unsightly gap which had previously existed'.[90] The fact that the alarming transfiguration of Bat's face is extrapolated from actual cosmetic medical effects implies that, in Morrow's thesis, there is something potentially (maybe even

---

[84] W. C. Morrow, *The Ape, The Idiot and Other People* (Philadelphia, PA: J.B. Lippincott, 1897), 258. All further references in parentheses.
[85] 'Fashionable Savages', *The Globe*, 3.
[86] 'Tattooers and Tattooed', *Pall Mall Gazette*, 1
[87] Scott, 'Tattooing in Japan', *The Illustrated London News*, 287.
[88] 'A Visit to a Professional Tattooer', *Chums*, 485.
[89] In modern pathology, rodent ulcer is synonymous with basal cell carcinoma (non-melanoma skin cancer). Pamela Gilbert, however, notes that, 'In the late nineteenth century, such skin lesions were widely identified with advanced venereal disease and with tuberculosis as permutations of the same pathology' (Gilbert, *Victorian Skin: Surface, Self, History*, 120).
[90] Thomas Annandale, 'Practical Suggestions in Connection with the Treatment of Some Deformities of the Nose', *BMJ*, 2.1927 (4 December 1897), 1626.

unavoidably) grotesque about the action of cosmetic medicine in general. In 'Two Singular Men', the ease with which the body can be remade by modern medical techniques ramifies outwards into a wider sense of somatic instability and confusion.

'Two Singular Men' essentially begins with an exaggerated pantomime of bodily destruction and remoulding. When Bat first arrives at the surgeon's consulting room, his face heavily wrapped in blood-soaked cloths, he begins by pathetically fumbling in his pockets, only to realize that he has lost the severed nose that he hoped the surgeon might reattach. The burlesque rapidity with which Bat's nose is cut off, pocketed, carried about, lost, and eventually remade into a new (and ludicrously hairy) image prefigures the experiences of the other characters in the story, whose bodies are ultimately revealed to be even more susceptible to rapid, unpredictable change. Muggie, the daughter of the freak show's owner and the object of Bat's affections, appears in the show under the name 'Mademoiselle Zoë, the Severed Lady' because she is 'apparently non-existent below the waist' (258). The note of hesitation sounded by Morrow's use of the qualifier 'apparently' returns when the narrator later observes that Muggie is seemingly never 'depressed by the apparent absence of all below the lower edge of her gold belt' (260). The real condition of Muggie's body is never explicitly articulated and is only indirectly conveyed in the finale when, over dinner, Sampey bends down to pick up a dropped napkin and accidentally brushes 'one of her daintily slippered feet' (271). Muggie's body is, as such, defined by its evasive presentation. For the bulk of the story Muggie appears to genuinely be (in Morrow's words) a 'half-person' (263) who 'end[s] at the waist' (259–60) and the truth is only obliquely revealed to us in the conclusion. (The story never explains how exactly Muggie and her father have accomplished the illusion of making her appear legless.) Muggie's body is, as such, represented to the reader as obscure, changeable, and difficult to unambiguously recognize. This ambiguousness also extends to Muggie's name: she is first introduced under her professional pseudonym of 'Mademoiselle Zoë' before Morrow tells us, in parentheses and with an air of obfuscatory tentativeness, that she is 'known in private life as Muggie (formerly Muggy, and probably originally Margaret)' (259). Muggie/Zoë is a confusing and illusory creation, her body and identity seemingly compounded of transitory falsehood and misdirection.

The perspicacious Sampey – the third axis of the narrative's love triangle – is more successful in mastering both illusion and medical technology to change his appearance and his fortunes in love. To win Muggie's heart, Sampey has not only to reckon with Bat's rivalry, but with Muggie's one specific requirement in a husband: that he possess eyes of a unique soft, limpid amber colour. Having spent most of her life as an exhibit in her father's show, Muggie has become transfixed by the multitude of eyes that regard her every day. In Morrow's words: 'As it was eyes only that she saw, it was of eyes only that she dreamed' (260). Consequently, Muggie imagines her future husband as the one man who will look upon her with the luminescent, amber-coloured eyes of 'princes, knights, and heroes'. This colour is the sign by which she believes she will recognize: 'my hero, my master, my love!' (261) Sampey's eyes are naturally grey, but when Muggie confides her dream of the amber eyes to him he nevertheless senses that the opportunity to win his beloved has arrived at last. The next time Sampey appears before Muggie in her crowd of observers she is amazed to see Sampey's eyes temporarily transform into the eyes of her dreams. Sampey explains this extraordinary change by suggesting that his love for Muggie has stirred the 'strange whisperings of heroism in [his] soul' (264) and that the change in his eyes is the outward sign of this new inspiration in his character. Finding her longed-for hero at last, Muggie and Sampey are married, and the conclusion of the story reveals how Sampey has worked his illusion: Sampey has in his possession a phial of cocaine and 'a number of curious, small, cup-shaped trinkets' made of different coloured glass and arranged in pairs – effectively, 'artificial eyes which Sampey had made to cover his natural eyeballs on occasion' (272). Thanks to this power of changing his eyes at will and his new status as a son-in-law, Muggie's father makes Sampey a partner in his freak show, and the young man – performing as 'the Mysterious Man with the Spectre Eyes' – goes on to 'become the happiest husband and the most prosperous freak and showman in the world' (274).

Bat's tufted nose provides an early illustration of the connection between medical technology and bodily metamorphosis in 'Two Singular Men', and this connection is deepened and elaborated on with Sampey's 'artificial eyes'. Cocaine was, as we have seen, both a technically and ideologically foundational substance for cosmetic medicine – the removal of pain was connotative of the removal of the body's aesthetic limitations and of the promise that (to paraphrase 'Changed at Will') the length of a nose would no longer determine the destiny of its owner.[91] Cocaine plays a similarly essential role for Sampey. By permitting him to change his features as the occasion demands, cocaine allows the young man to attain both financial success and to successfully romance the woman he loves. Sampey's triumph at the end of the story rests directly upon cocaine anaesthesia. While the story is vague as to specifics, 'Two Singular Men' heavily

[91] See 'Changed at Will', *Hampshire Telegraph*, 11.

implies that Sampey's multi-coloured eyes of glass are meant to be read as an original invention of his own. The German ophthalmologist Adolf Eugen Fick had developed a glass 'contact-lens' to correct astigmatism in the late 1880s, and a translated version of his research appeared in *Archives of Ophthalmology* in 1888 under the title 'A Contact-Lens'. Early reviewers of Fick's invention were uncomplimentary, however, pronouncing the lens to be 'utterly inapplicable to actual practice'. Neither Fick himself nor the commentary that appeared in the *British Medical Journal* suggested using cocaine to ameliorate the 'discomfort' of wearing the lens, though Fick's article ends with the intriguing remark that: 'An inquiry from one of [my] patients led me to believe that possibly contact-lenses will be often worn for purely cosmetic reasons [in the future].'[92] Despite seeming to fulfil Fick's prediction of a cosmetic contact lens, 'Two Singular Men' persistently refers to Sampey's discovery as an 'artificial eye' (rather than a 'contact-lens'), emphasizing the invention's apparent originality.

On one level, the depiction of cocaine in 'Two Singular Men' seems to realize the distinctly utopian and individualistic possibilities of cosmetic medical science: through his own inventiveness and by selectively changing his appearance, Sampey is able to achieve love, affluence, and fame as 'the happiest husband and the most prosperous freak and showman in the world' (274). However, the apparently unalloyed positivity of this ending conflicts with the more cynical presentation of cocaine and its cosmetic application that occurs throughout the rest of the story. However happy the ending might seem to be, the story continually manoeuvres the reader towards the realization that it is based on artifice. Before Sampey's 'artificial eyes' come to light, he maintains to Muggie that the changes in his appearance occur spontaneously in response to passing emotions. He tells his love that: 'When the essence of true heroism is breathed into [a man], his eyes, without his knowledge of the fact, may assume the amber hue of your dreams. Sometimes, in the development of the spirit of heroism, this colour is only transient; in time it may become permanent' (262). In lying to Muggie about why his eyes have changed colour, Sampey not only deceives her but also recasts his body as fundamentally mutable. Sampey's romancing of Muggie is enabled by the cocaine anaesthesia which allows him to slip different eyes in and out of his face from moment to moment. But their relationship is also predicated on her accepting the idea that his body is fluid, likely to spontaneously reform its appearance in ways which may be 'transient'

---

[92] See A. Eugen Fick, 'A Contact-Lens', *Archives of Ophthalmology*, 17.2 (1888), 215–26; and 'Novel Suggestion for the Correction of Irregular Astigmatism', *BMJ*, 2.1453 (3 November 1888), 1002–3.

or 'permanent' but which are, in either case, hard to reliably predict. Sampey's body is – like Muggie's own – oddly inconstant and illusory.

Sampey's use of cocaine is emblematic of the wider portrayal of cosmetic medicine in 'Two Singular Men'. In Morrow's rendering, the potential for easy medical modification of the body also engenders a sense of the body as impermanent and unstable. The promise of bodily autonomy also results in an extreme and (literally) freakish variety of bodily singularity. Morrow's title playfully conveys this. While the two singular men dominate the story's action, by the end it is heavily implied that all three of the main characters may have become *too singular* for their own good. One circumstance worth observing is that there are no congenitally disabled performers in Morrow's freak show; apart from the core trio, the only other member of the troupe that the narrative mentions (even in passing) is 'the Remarkable Tattooed Lady' (258). Freakishness, in the story's conception, is exclusively a product of illusion abetted by medical science.

Conclusion: Monstrosities of surgery

The year after the publication of *The Ape, the Idiot and Other People*, another (more infamous) late-nineteenth-century medical monster-maker was to commence his own reminiscences in very similar style to the beginning of Morrow's story. H. G. Wells's *The Island of Doctor Moreau* (1896) narrates how the gifted anatomist of its title has peopled his island with a race of surgically hybridized beast-people. When he comes to explain the techniques he has used to produce his creations, Moreau begins (like Morrow) with a description of cosmetic rhinoplasty. The doctor coldly describes how:

> Surgery can ... [accomplish] building up as well as breaking down and changing. You have heard, perhaps, of a common surgical operation resorted to in cases where the nose has been destroyed. A flap of skin is cut from the forehead, turned down on the nose, and heals in the new position. This is a kind of grafting in a new position of part of an animal upon itself.[93]

Both Morrow and Moreau imagine that the procedures of cosmetic surgery might lead to the radical transformation of the body – even unto the point of monstrousness. In the late-Victorian and Edwardian period, cocaine could be regarded as having cleared surgery of the obstruction of pain and opened the body

---

[93] H. G. Wells, *The Island of Doctor Moreau* (London: Penguin 2005), 71.

up to new forms of alteration. Thanks to the drug, each individual's garment of flesh might now be shaped, trimmed, and patterned according to desire. Behind these opportunities, though, there remained the fear that cosmetic medicine might rebound upon itself, turning recognizable and healthy bodies into illusory and hideous ones – an 'artificial simulacrum of a human being'[94] whose body was based not in the authenticity of nature but in 'cosmetic mutilation'.[95] Moreau, whose only emotions and desires are the 'strange, colourless' ones produced by scientific inquiry, cares nothing about pain, but one of his remarks on the subject has a peculiar resonance: 'Pain gets needless', Moreau states. 'I never yet heard of a useless thing that was not ground out of existence … sooner or later.' As the fin de siècle passed into the twentieth century, it appeared that pain – if not exactly needless – was no longer as inexorable as once it was, and that, thanks to cocaine, it might be possible (for better or worse) to realize Moreau's only real desire: 'to find out the extreme limit of plasticity in a living shape'.[96]

---

[94] Gilman, *Making the Body Beautiful*, 25.
[95] Gould and Pyle, *Anomalies and Curiosities of Medicine*, 746.
[96] Wells, *The Island of Doctor Moreau*, 74–5.

4

Cocaine bugs and the horrors of addiction

In the 1890s, as the approaching twentieth century came more immediately into view, some fin de siècle commentators began to question the prevailing mood of optimism with which their contemporaries seemed determined to greet the new era. The outgoing century might, as its enthusiasts maintained, have been characterized by an upward arc of ever-increasing social and technological complexity, but had the end results really justified the effort?

The *British Medical Journal* in July 1891 wrote:

> Not many years ago European civilisation was in an optimistic phase, and people went about saying that, what with railways, steamers, and telegraphs, we might thank Heaven that we were born in the nineteenth century. Satiety, disillusion, and the increase in population have thrown a gloom over these old and happy notions. Thoughtful people wish to know if we are really better than our ancestors.[1]

This 'thoughtful' (not to say sceptical) tenor to the *BMJ*'s prognosis is less surprising than it might at first appear. Indeed, throughout the 1890s and the first years of the twentieth century, devotees of medical science were more likely than average to be confronted by the 'disillusion[ing]' effects of the nineteenth century's surfeit of new discoveries. A peculiar paradox underlies contemporary perceptions of medical science in this transitional period from the 1890s to the 1900s. Medical advancement meant that not only was the fin de siècle a time in which 'unprecedented numbers of [professional] people got to work on other people's bodies', it also witnessed 'a dramatic rise in the range of surgical procedures that doctors, especially full-time surgeons, were prepared to attempt'.[2] Nineteenth-century medical progress had, by the turn of the century,

---

[1] 'Are We Too Clean?', *British Medical Journal*, 2.1593 (11 July 1891), 84.
[2] Sally Wilde and Geoffrey Hirst, 'Learning from Mistakes: Early Twentieth-Century Surgical Practice', *Journal of the History of Medicine and Allied Sciences*, 64.1 (January 2009), 40; Sally Wilde, 'Truth, Trust, and Confidence in Surgery, 1890–1910: Patient Autonomy, Communication, and Consent', *Bulletin of the History of Medicine*, 83.2 (June 2009), 302–3.

made therapeutic procedures more common, more varied, and more likely to lead to a productive outcome. However, as the curative potency of medicine increased in these years, there was also a corresponding increase in concern that medical science might – whether by careless practitioners or ill-informed patients – be misapplied to destructive ends; the more powerful medicine became, the more substantial seemed the possibility that its administration might go awry. Thus, to paraphrase Clair Brock, there developed a paradox wherein fin de siècle surgery simultaneously became objectively safer, yet could also be perceived to be more severely risky. As Brock states, 'At the turn of the century, according to late Victorian and early Edwardian surgeons, surgery could be seen simultaneously as possessing "so little risk" and surrounded with "special anxieties."'[3] The more effective medical techniques became in this era, the more circumspect were practitioners called upon to be in how they exercised their craft. This chapter considers these fin de siècle disputes about medical progress, risk, and responsibility through the medium of cocaine – a drug widely seen by contemporaries (as discussed in previous chapters) as one of the most emblematic medical technologies of the age.

Cocaine's usefulness to fin de siècle surgery meant that it had ascended 'like a meteor'[4] to a place of pre-eminence among modern therapeutic discoveries. By the 1890s, however, while cocaine's star was still far from being on the wane, it had begun to diminish somewhat. The potential addictiveness of the drug came to feature increasingly prominently in medical conversations, often in conjunction with the suggestion that medical professionals as a body were alarmingly uninformed about those risks. In 1898, the editorial pages of the journal *Laryngoscope* warned that: 'physicians in general do not understand the possibilities of this drug for evil'.[5] Consequently, alongside the characterization of cocaine as a medical triumph in this period, a counter-rhetoric also began to develop. In this alternative formulation, cocaine came to represent the destructive overconfidence of fin de siècle science, and the possibility that technological advancement might itself prove to be a barrier to truer, more substantial forms of progress. Towards the end of the year 1900, *The Spectator* published an article critiquing the modern social optimist's tendency to 'people the future with bright though rather nebulous imaginings'. Wrote *The Spectator*: '[The optimist tells us that] science will kill all epidemics and to a great extent rid us of all pain, even

---

[3] Clair Brock, 'Risk, Responsibility, and Surgery in the 1890s and Early 1900s', *Medical History*, 57.3 (July 2013), 318.
[4] 'Cocaine', *Chambers's Journal*, 3.114 (6 March 1886), 145.
[5] W. Scheppegrell, 'Editorial', *Laryngoscope*, 5.6 (December 1898), 374.

toothache disappearing before some wonderful cocaine. ... Science, we are told, is to save us; but suppose science grows inhuman, as other creeds have done.'[6] The same year, an article on 'The Coming Man' offered what it maintained to be a scientifically informed prognostication of the character of the man of the future. 'The coming man,' it predicted 'will shun morphia, chloral, cocaine, and similar agents as he does smallpox. In fact, the coming man will use few drugs, but he will know more about the powers and limitations of those few ... he will not be caught by the sensational exploitations of serums.'[7] In many ways the predictions contained on 'The Coming Man' represent exactly the kind of bright but nebulous imaginings that *The Spectator* objected to. The two works were, however, much more obviously aligned in their portrayal of cocaine: for both optimist and cynic, cocaine could now be read as a substance which conveyed the limitations of contemporary science and the imperative for society to evolve past such anticipatory fantasies. Cocaine, the 'revolution[ary]'[8] discovery of fin de siècle medicine, might also represent the overconfidence of contemporary innovation, and the suggestion that the utopian expectations of science might forever exceed attainable reality.

This chapter examines this figuration of cocaine and overconfidence in the context of fin de siècle medicine. It focusses on representations of cocaine addiction and habituation to determine how cocaine's effectiveness as a stimulant and as a household remedy contributed to emerging debates about the dangerous side effects of medical innovation, and the possible blame that practitioners might have to shoulder for fostering its destructive consequences. Many critics have illuminated the wider evolution of (both popular and medical) addiction discourses in this period, but – I argue – cocainism is persistently distinguished in late-nineteenth- and early-twentieth-century descriptions as a unique and unprecedentedly horrifying affliction. Widespread use of cocaine was still a relatively new innovation in these years, and this sense of radical newness colours contemporary responses to its addictiveness. Dependence on the drug seemed to come upon its victims suddenly, with a ferocious and unforeseen rapidity; its aphrodisiac and stimulant action – in explicit contrast to the dreamy lethargy of morphine or chloral – apparently flogged its users into delirious, sexualized viciousness; and its final, most horrible result was a condition that came to be known as the 'cocaine bugs' – a compulsion to constant

---

[6] 'Social Optimism', *The Spectator*, 85.3780 (8 December 1900), 837.
[7] 'The Coming Man – As the Scientist looks for Him', *Hampshire Telegraph*, 6197 (30 June 1900), 10.
[8] Simeon Snell, 'Presidential Address on Some Points of Progress in Ophthalmic Surgery', *BMJ*, 2.1489 (13 June 1889), 58.

self-mutilation and a delusional conviction that the user's own skin was full of incessantly crawling insects.[9]

For fin de siècle observers, cocaine seemed the bête noire of addictions: more compulsive and more abhorrent than any drug previously encountered. Susan Zieger has chronicled the early development of medical models of addiction in this period as practitioners and temperance campaigners began to articulate the nascent concept of 'inebriety' (which was, from the early twentieth century, to be superseded by 'addiction' as the preferred term-of-art for medical specialists). Inebriety represented 'an umbrella term conceptually uniting the compulsion to consume alcohol and drugs such as morphine, chloral hydrate, opium, ether, and cocaine, as variations on single disease or disorder'.[10] Under this model, cocainism (like morphinism and chloralism) signified one of a number of individual variations on an overarching pathology. Contemporary observers, however, often stress the ways in which cocaine appeared to have distinguished itself among its peers. Writers in the late nineteenth and early twentieth centuries tend to treat cocaine as unprecedently seductive: the newest, fastest, and 'most deadly form of narcotism known'.[11] Despite being diagnostically enfolded under the umbrella of inebriety (or addiction), cocaine was nevertheless rhetorically set apart, framed as a singularly original and threatening manifestation of the disease of addiction.

The initial sections of this chapter examine how this rhetoric of unparalleled newness was applied to cocaine addiction and cocaine toxicosis, showing how the technologically transformative effects of cocaine were reimagined as grotesque physical transformations inflicted upon the body by careless medical science. These sections take Arthur Machen's 1895 work 'The White Powder' as their primary literary case study. The chapter concludes by examining a particular strategy that medical authorities deployed to parry the criticisms levelled at them over cases of cocainism. It analyses the relationship between cocaine and the first generations of women doctors, arguing that – among proponents of their inclusion in the profession – women practitioners were framed as a moral and intellectual elite within medicine who might reassert a sense of responsible control and oversight over the problem of drug addiction. In this way, the newest and best incarnation of the profession might serve as a counter to its newest danger.

---

[9] 'Cocainomania', *Scottish Medical and Surgical Journal*, 5.5 (November 1899), 471.
[10] Susan Zieger, *Inventing the Addict: Drugs, Race, and Sexuality in Nineteenth-Century British and American Literature* (Amherst: University of Massachusetts Press, 2008), 5.
[11] 'The Cocaine Habit', *Cornishman*, 1206 (15 August 1901), 2.

'The Newest Born of All the Drug Cravings'

After the revelation of cocaine anaesthesia in 1884, it did not take long for the drug to become established as a commonplace painkiller and household remedy for minor complaints such as cold and flu, hay fever, and seasickness. 'There seems to be little doubt,' enthused *Myra's Journal of Dress and Fashion* in 1886, 'that a fairly reliable remedy has at last been found for sea-sickness. This is cocaine, the newly introduced alkaloid of Peruvian Coca leaves.'[12] 'The Home' column of *Lloyd's Weekly* advised its readers that 'the best applications for the throat cough of [the tickling and harassing] kind are the tabloids of cocaine'.[13] Thus was it possible for the respectable middle-class heroine of F. Woodward Neele's 'On-the-Rack' (1899) to exclaim, in casual conversation and without the further comment: 'Oh wait one minute, father, while I fetch my cocaine. I know it will cure [Charlie's] toothache.'[14] In the same vein, the unfortunate Miss Hall from R. S. Hichens's 'Broken Faith' (1893) suffers so badly from seasickness that she spends an entire voyage from Southampton to the West Indies immured in her cabin: 'I feel,' she quavers, 'we are at sea. I am not a good sailor, and I know it is going to be rough. Would you kindly reach me the cocaine lozenges?'[15] Cocaine's ubiquity, however, also contributed to serious concerns about its addictiveness. Writers for both lay and medical papers frequently warned their readers about the risks of over-employing cocaine to deal with comparatively minor health problems. 'A little cocaine', wrote the *Wiltshire Times* in 1901, might effectively 'allay the pain' of conjunctivitis (or 'cold in the eye') but its columnist scrupled that: 'I almost dread recommending this, so terrible in its effects is the cocaine habit.'[16] According to *The Quiver*, it was all too easy for the uninformed to succumb to the chemist's cocainized 'lotion or powder' that 'certainly removes all the unpleasant stuffiness and dull pain [of a cold]' but which might imperceptibly ensnare its user in 'the toils of [addiction's] fatal vice'.[17] Writing to the *British Medical Journal* in 1889, Lennox Browne observed that 'patients are frequently prescribed or obtain without prescription, cocaine solutions of considerable potency, for constant use by brush or spray with the purpose of relieving quite slight symptoms'. Given the dangers of the drug, Browne felt obliged to 'warn against [the profession's]

---

[12] 'Mal-De-Mer', *Myra's Journal of Dress and Fashion*, 12 (1 December 1886), 646.
[13] 'The Home', *Lloyd's Weekly London Newspaper*, 2613 (18 December 1892), 6.
[14] F. Woodward Neele, 'On-the-Rack', *The Windsor*, 9.52 (April 1899), 610.
[15] R. S. Hichens, 'Broken Faith', *Hearth and Home*, 104 (11 May 1893), 821. See also, R. S. Hichens, 'Broken Faith', *Hearth and Home*, 105 (18 May 1893), 21.
[16] 'Cold in the Eye', *Wiltshire Times*, 2335 (12 October 1901), 2.
[17] H. H. Riddle, 'The Drug Habit', *The Quiver* 47.5 (March 1912), 489.

growing inclination to cultivate a cocaine habit'.[18] In this way, perceptions of cocaine's dangerousness were often closely allied with perceptions of the drug's effectiveness as a remedy: cocaine's extreme potency and widespread usefulness apparently made it all the more liable to misuse by incautious practitioners and patients. As such, the narrative of cocaine addiction in this period was often one of a 'useful but dangerous drug',[19] one which instanced how medical technology might, if recklessly applied, inflict more harm than it healed.

The struggle to accurately understand and correctly apportion responsibility for addiction was a common feature of wider fin de siècle drug discourse. For contemporary observers, unpicking the question of culpability meant confronting several vexed and closely interconnected moral problems. The most immediate was the question of whether the 'physician-supplier' was to blame by reason of 'nefarious, careless, or naïve' behaviour or whether medical professionals were the 'dupes' of unscrupulous patients bent on self-medication and abuse.[20] It was, for instance, simultaneously possible for journalists to complain of the medical profession's failure to 'stand forth as one man and denounce the unnatural practice [of addiction] with all the emphasis at their command', and for practitioners themselves to bemoan how often they were deceived by their patients' tendency to 'speak through the symptom *at* [a particular] remedy, and with the object of getting it'.[21] In discussions of cocaine addiction, though, these questions of direct responsibility were often subsumed into a broader suspicion of the products of medical innovation more generally. For *The Spectator*, as we have seen, the disappointments of cocaine served as an example of the 'bright' but 'nebulous' promises of scientific optimism.[22] In 1890, T. S. Clouston (lecturer on mental diseases at Edinburgh University) described the essentially modern, technological preconditions that had enabled the spread of cocaine addiction.

---

[18] 'On the Cocaine Habit in Diseases of Throat and Nose', *BMJ*, 1.1478 (27 April 1889), 973.

[19] W. Scheppegrell, 'The Uses and Abuses of Cocaine', *Laryngoscope*, 7.3 (September 1899), 202.

[20] Susan Zieger, *Inventing the Addict: Drugs, Race, and Sexuality in Nineteenth-Century British and American Literature* (Amherst: University of Massachusetts Press, 2008), 138–9. As a corollary to this, the addict's own behaviour was frequently framed as similarly morally ambiguous, since it was often unclear whether they were merely the helpless victims of their addiction or whether their actions could be said to still be governed by their own deliberate decisions. In the early 1900s, for example, *The Speaker* meditated that: 'The subject of narcomania is not merely one of moral and social justice ... it opens up the much-debated question – that eternal subject of contention between the lawyer and the physician – of civil and criminal responsibility.' (A. R., 'The Cocaine Habit', *The Speaker*, 7 (8 November 1902), 142.) For a more extensive commentary on the question of responsibility and addiction in relation to fin de siècle morphine consumption see Zieger, *Inventing the Addict*, 138–42.

[21] 'Another Abuse in Society', *Dundee Courier*, 15020 (14 August 1901), 4; G. H. R. Dabbs, 'A Note on the Inebriate in the Making', *British Journal of Inebriety*, 1.4 (April 1904), 287.

[22] 'Social Optimism', *The Spectator*, 85.3780 (8 December 1900), 837.

According to Clouston: 'The newest born of all the drug cravings is that for cocaine. It required two of the latest discoveries of science – the hypodermic needle and the extraction of cocaine from the coca-leaf – combined, to create this new vice-disease.'[23] For fin de siècle observers, cocaine could easily illustrate the imperfection and overconfidence of modern technological medicine – a newly born 'vice-disease' that was the unintended offspring of 'the latest discoveries of science'. Other artificially produced drugs (most notably morphine and chloral) had already followed a similar trajectory from technological *dernier cri* to addictive danger earlier in the century,[24] but this characterization was at its most pronounced in the case of cocaine because of the drug's prevalence as both an everyday remedy and an icon of heroic medical endeavour. It did not take long for the disappointments of cocaine to begin to be keenly felt. In November 1886, the *Court Journal* and the *American Register* stated (in a piece that made its way through several other regional papers over the following weeks) that:

> Cocaine at first was claimed to be a universal panacea for all pains – the only stimulant that was followed by no reaction, the one anaesthetic that was harmless in its results. Its price was in accord with its supposed virtues, it being sold at something more than twenty times the price of gold, weight for weight. In less than a year, however, there came a reaction. ... The 'cocaine habit' [is] contracted by the habitual use of the drug, asserted to be much more destructive in its effects on mind and body than opium or alcohol.[25]

Cocaine is distinguished here mainly by the depth of disenchantment it provokes. The drug's sparkling promises, once esteemed beyond the price of gold, have apparently collapsed into leaden reality, and the sad reaction of cocainism has settled upon its devotees.

This passage offers an early example of another image that was to quickly become an established trope of cocaine addiction: the notion that cocaine was both a newer drug and a more fatally 'destructive' drug than familiar compounds like opium and alcohol. Descriptions of cocainism from this period often emphasize both the drug's unprecedented danger and its extreme contemporaneousness. In 1895, *Chambers's Journal* proffered cocaine (legitimately applied to medical ends) as 'a brilliant example of a remedy for the relief of pain that has become widely popular in a very short time, not

---

[23] T. S. Clouston, 'Diseased Cravings and Paralysed Control: Dipsomania; Morphinomania; Chloralism; Cocainism', *Edinburgh Medical Journal*, 35.2 (March 1890), 806.
[24] See Zieger, *Inventing the Addict*, 131–3, and 143.
[25] 'Cocaine', *The American Register*, 19.971 (13 November 1886), 8. See also: 'Notes from the Court Journal', *Isle of Wight Observer*, 1784 (27 November 1886), 8.

from much advertising, but mainly by its own intrinsic worth.'[26] As the new century drew near, cocaine could be celebrated as much for its newness as for its therapeutic effectiveness. Discussions of cocaine addiction also partook of this same imagery, though, accentuating cocaine's rapid emergence and hitherto unparalleled danger. In 1898 *The Laryngoscope* warned: 'There is no drug which has been on the market for such a comparatively short time in which the abuses have become so formidable.'[27] Conolly Norman's 'Note on Cocainism' (1892) observed that cocaine was 'a comparatively new drug' and that 'the dangers to be apprehended from the abuse of [it] are probably hardly yet quite realised'. Imperfectly appreciated as the menace of cocaine might still be, it was clearly a compound surrounded by 'special dangers' – 'Cocaine,' wrote Norman, 'is more seductive than morphia; it fastens upon its victim more rapidly, and its hold is at least as tight.'[28] Other writers on cocainism shared Norman's assessment, and it was common to see cocaine's newer and more terrible dangers contrasted with the better-known, and now banalized, effects of other addictions. In 1907, a correspondent to the *British Medical Journal* cautioned that, 'by the side of the cocaine habit, the morphine habit is comparatively insignificant'.[29] An article from the *Lakes Herald* on 'The Deliriums of Cocaine' provided a similar estimate of the drug's dangers: 'Opium, other narcotics and intoxicants used to excess, cause persons to become absolutely indifferent to all relations, duties and obligations; they even become brutal but not nearly so brutal or depraved as the cocaine slaves.'[30] In 1899, H. G. Wells complained of 'black coffee [and] cocaine' as 'thug helpers ... alkaloids that stifle natural fatigue and kill rest'.[31] The *Manchester Times* was firmer still in its pronouncements: 'Cocaine is unquestionably the most dangerous, because the most fascinating and the most deadly, of all vice-drugs.'[32] For fin de siècle observers, then, cocaine appeared to be the *enfant terrible* of modern drugs: the sense of its special newness combined with the belief in its singular, 'thug[gish]' destructiveness so that each accentuated the other. As a tool of modern medicine, cocaine promised to enact a 'revolution'[33] in therapeutic technology but, as its potential for abuse became more apparent, the drug often seemed to forebode a new and revolutionary danger.

[26] 'Some Popular Remedies', *Chambers's Journal*, 12.577 (19 Jan 1895), 45.
[27] W. Scheppegrell, 'Editorial', *Laryngoscope*, 5.6 (December 1898), 373.
[28] Conolly Norman, 'A Note on Cocainism', *Journal of Mental Science*, 38.161 (April 1892), 195.
[29] 'On the Use of Cocaine in the Morphine Habit: A Warning', *BMJ*, 2.2435 (31 August 1907), 556.
[30] 'The Deliriums of Cocaine', *Lakes Herald*, 802 (8 January 1886), 7.
[31] H. G. Wells, 'When the Sleeper Wakes', *The Graphic*, 1519 (7 January 1899), 9.
[32] 'Scraps', *Manchester Times*, 1554 (23 April 1887), 8.
[33] See: 'Recent Advances in Surgery and Medicine', *Edinburgh Review*, 168.344 (October 1888), 506; and Snell, 'Presidential Address on Some Points of Progress in Ophthalmic Surgery', *BMJ*, 58.

The apparently sudden newness and prevalence of cocaine addiction were further heightened by a sense of the speed with which the craving might take hold. Medical analyses of cocaine addiction in the fin de siècle period frequently concluded that it was a uniquely dangerous drug because it was possessed of a peculiarly treacherous celerity. Cocaine's pleasures were intense and quick to pass off, demanding that the user renew their dosage at ever shorter intervals. Cocaine in turn lacked the lingering after-effects of morphine, or the hangover of strong drink, so there was nothing to slow the user's rapid descent into addiction. T. S. Clouston's 1890 article in the *Edinburgh Medical Journal* on 'Diseased Cravings and Paralysed Control' succinctly enumerated this pattern in its concluding summary of cocaine's 'chief facts'. 'The dose,' Clouston wrote, 'requires to be increased faster than that of any [other] such drug to get the same effect'; 'its immediate effects are more transient than any other such drug, but this does not apply to the craving set up'; 'the morbid craving set up is very intense … [and] it is the acutest and most absolute destroyer of inhibition and of the moral sense generally that we yet know.'[34] The *Scottish Medical and Surgical Journal* preached a similar lesson:

> The cocaine habit is much more seductive and rapid in its effects in breaking down the mental powers than is morphine and is more insidious from the fact than in the early stage there are none of the unpleasant effects that attend the taking of morphine, such as morning headache and bad taste in the mouth. At first … the mental and bodily vigour is increased, but the system gradually becomes tolerant and the habit is established in from four to six weeks. Then an intense craving for the drug comes on.[35]

Conolly Norman based his appraisal of cocaine's dangers both on its rapidity of action and on the aphrodisiac effects that it produced. 'Sexual troubles' like 'undue sexual excitement, voluptuous sensations … violent erotic delirium … and sexual hallucinations' were, according to observations made by Norman and his colleagues, 'frequent' and 'distinctive traits arising from the misuse of cocaine'. Norman's assessment was that: 'Very probably the occurrence of these disturbances in the sexual region contribute further to the rapid mental degradation which marks this vice. … Thus cocaine is probably the most agreeable of all narcotics, therefore the most dangerous and alluring.'[36] Perceptions of cocaine's superlative dangerousness and 'allure'

---

[34] Clouston, 'Diseased Cravings and Paralysed Control', 809.
[35] 'Cocainomania', *Scottish Medical and Surgical Journal*, 471.
[36] Norman, 'A Note on Cocainism', 196–9.

were, consequently, closely connected with images of its speed and expediency. Cocaine was a swift seducer – a drug of transient exhilaration, immediate renewal, and massive destruction. Cocaine abuse was, in the late nineteenth and early twentieth centuries, characterized by a rhetoric of extremity, originality, and quickness. As a 'vice-disease'[37] it had emerged without warning, claimed its victims more hastily, and wrought greater 'destruct[ion] on mind and body'[38] than any existing intoxicant. 'Cocaine,' wrote one American doctor, 'sends its victims to shipwreck with all the engines in full blast. They find the rocks very quickly.'[39] In this framework, the onset of cocaine addiction implied the imminent danger of an aggressively accelerated modernity and the damage it might inflict upon the body.

Cocaine bugs and corrupted skin

Victorian sources dwelt not only upon the terrible speed with which cocaine addiction might assert itself but also on the hideous (and sometimes baroquely elaborated) symptoms produced by cocaine toxicosis. The most flamboyantly represented effect of cocaine habituation was one which Victorian observers named after the drug itself, and which is still (colloquially) known by that name today: the 'cocaine bug'. Usually identified in modern medical literature as 'Delusional Parasitosis'[40] – and more formally known to Victorian and Edwardian observers as 'Magnan's Sign'[41] – cocaine bugs are a tactile hallucination of itching, crawling sensations in the skin, combined with the delusion that insects (or worms, or some other small parasite or irritant) are lodged inside the skin and constantly moving about. Graphic accounts of this 'gruesome' condition circulated through several papers in the summer of 1889: 'One patient was always scraping his tongue, and thought that he was extracting from it little black worms; another made his skin raw in the endeavour to draw out cholera microbes; and a third, a physician, is perpetually looking

---

[37] Clouston, 'Diseased Cravings and Paralysed Control', 806.
[38] 'Notes from the Court Journal', *Isle of Wight Observer*, 1784 (27 November 1886), 8.
[39] George Wheelock Grover, *Shadows Lifted, or, Sunshine Restored in the Horizon of Human Lives: A Treatise on the Morphine, Opium, Cocaine, Chloral, and Hashish Habits* (Chicago: Stomberg, Allen, 1894), 68.
[40] See Amber Elliott, Tashfeen Mahmood, and Roger D. Smalligan, 'Cocaine Bugs: A Case Report of Cocaine-Induced Delusions of Parasitosis', *American Journal on Addictions*, 21.2 (March–April 2012), 180–1.
[41] Named after the French addiction specialist Valentin Magnan who described the condition in 1889. See G. Norman Meachen, 'The Cutaneous Affections of the Inebriate', *British Journal of Inebriety*, 1.4 (April 1904), 279.

for cocaine crystals under his skin.'[42] One of T. S. Clouston's most severely afflicted patients persistently 'imagined he had a skin disease [and] affirmed he felt sensations in the skin that could only be caused by living germs'.[43] The Anglo-Australian physician J. W. Springthorpe documented some of the most vivid accounts of the condition in 'The Confessions of a Cocainist' in 1895. The eponymous cocainist (and former medical man) interviewed by Springthorpe recounted how:

> Before long begins the 'hunting of the cocaine bug'. You imagine that in your skin worms or similar things are moving along. If you touch them with wool (especially with absorbent wool) they run away and disappear. ... You see small animals running about your body, and feel their bites.[44]

By 1899, it seemed clear to medical authorities that 'the "cocaine bug" or the "cocaine jigger"'[45] ... is observed in almost all advanced cases of cocainomania' and that the condition might 'be said to be pathognomonic of cocainomania'.[46]

Skin afflictions already occupied a conspicuous place in Victorian addiction discourse, and the spread of cocainism led to a significant expansion and elaboration of these images. In the late nineteenth and early twentieth centuries, morphine – and later cocaine – was usually administered by hypodermic injection, and the result of this was that the skin discolourations, lesions, and scars resulting from frequent (and improperly sterilized) injections came to be identified as the characteristic stigmata of the addict. Susan Zieger narrates how: 'The marks of [the morphinist's] obscene pleasure were [regarded as] accordingly ugly. ... Medical writers catalogued the signs of hypodermic abuse so that they might be easily detected [and] fictional accounts convert these clinical descriptions of sepsis into depictions of personal filth.'[47] In time, the cocainist was thought to be similarly recognizable by their 'tell-tale arm ... dotted with hypodermic punctures'.[48] Medical accounts meticulously enumerated the various marks of the cocaine addict's self-destructive pleasure, often with a peculiar emphasis on the sheer variety of different effects and afflictions the drug could

---

[42] See 'A New Form of Intoxication', *Trewman's Exeter Flying Post*, 6870 (25 May 1889), 8; 'What the Modern Use of Poisons Leads To', *The Blackburn Standard*, 55.2784 (22 June 1889), 2; 'A New Intoxicant', *The Dundee Courier & Argus*, 11266 (16 August 1889), 4.
[43] Clouston, 'Diseased Cravings and Paralysed Control', 808.
[44] J. W. Springthorpe, 'The Confessions of a Cocainist', *Australasian Medical Gazette*, 14 (20 September 1895), 371.
[45] 'Jiggers', or 'chiggers', are the biting parasitic larvae of mites related to ticks.
[46] 'Cocainomania', *Scottish Medical and Surgical Journal*, 471; Clarence G. S. Godfrey, 'Cocainomania', *Australasian Medical Gazette*, 18 (20 April 1899), 148.
[47] Zieger, *Inventing the Addict*, 144.
[48] 'The Literary Week', *The Academy*, 1506 (16 March 1901), 219.

produce. One 1888 account described a young dentist who had succumbed to the 'agreeable sensations and sexual desire' produced by cocaine injections. The examiner documented 'the following lesions on the skin':

> There was a peculiar crusty eruption, consisting of pustules the size of a pea, covered with a blackish-grey dry scab, on the anterior external surface of the two arms and on the anterior part of the legs and thighs. This eruption resembled the scabs of syphilitic rupia. ... At the spot where the injections were made there were white patches insensible to the touch ... which seemed to be due to localised gangrene.[49]

A woman addicted to both cocaine and morphine was noted to have heavily 'tattoo[ed]' herself 'by hypodermic injection'; small 'dark patches' resembling 'China ink' being found 'on all parts of [her] body accessible to the right hand, save the exposed parts'. The medical analyst suggested that these spots had most probably been produced by iron left in the skin by rusted needles and dryly noted that, 'their diagnosis should be easy; their situation and the lack of signification will be sufficient to distinguish them from ordinary tattoo marks'.[50] J. W. Springthorpe lamented the extent and number of the mutilations that his acquaintance, the cocainist, had inflicted upon himself: 'Frequently his needle would be fastened to his syringe by sealing wax, shellac, etc., and when he had no needle at all he would cut an opening with his knife, and insert the end of the syringe direct. Almost the whole of his body except the face was marked with needle scars.'[51]

The cocainist's maculated skin was likewise a familiar trope of the drug's representation in fiction. In Arthur Conan Doyle's *The Sign of Four* (1890) Dr Watson famously observes Sherlock Holmes's 'sinewy forearm and wrist' to be 'all dotted and scarred with innumerable puncture-marks' left behind by injections of his favourite 'seven-per-cent solution' of cocaine.[52] Reviews of Arthur Rickett's play *The Charmer* (1907) noted that the play's unfortunate, cocaine-addicted heroine Stella Hamerton was made up and costumed with 'sleeves loose enough for anyone to see the marks upon her arm'.[53] (Contemporary reviews of the play noted that, in fact, the 'Charmer' of the title referred not to 'a fascinating heroine with an easy way' but the 'deadly fascination for its victims possessed by the

---

[49] 'Cocaine Poisoning', *BMJ*, 1.1417 (25 February 1888), 438.
[50] 'Tattooing by Hypodermic Injection', *BMJ*, 2.2434 (24 August 1907), 29.
[51] Springthorpe, 'The Confessions of a Cocainist', 372.
[52] Arthur Conan Doyle, *The Sign of Four*, edited by Peter Ackroyd and Ed Glinert (London: Penguin, 2001), 5.
[53] 'The Play Actors', *The Stage*, 1387 (17 October 1907), 15.

cocaine habit.'⁵⁴) By the 1910s, cocaine sniffing started to come into fashion as an alternative to injection. Though this method left users with 'no scars resulting on the skin'⁵⁵ it produced a new variation on the familiar image nonetheless. Papers called attention to 'the disease of the nostrils commonly called "Cocaine Creeper"' that had recently joined 'the coke-bug' as a characteristic affliction of the addict:

> Apparently the cocaine powder prevents tissues of the nostrils from performing their proper functions, and so causes the matter to clog. Occasionally the poison thus set in will eat through the nose. Poisoning is often set up by the habit cocaine fiends have of using knives, hairpins, &c., to free their nostrils from the coagulated matter.⁵⁶

Cocaine addiction was thus imagined to be recognizable through a pattern of self-inflicted mutilation. However, where the skin of the morphinist was defaced purely as a side effect of constant injections, the cocainist's skin was regarded as being marked not only by the intrusion of the needle but also by frighteningly obsessive acts of self-destruction. Such acts were most often occasioned by the onset of 'cocaine bugs'. Suffers were not only marred by the administration of the drug itself, but seemed compelled to ceaselessly worry, scrape, and prick at their own flesh in an effort to dig out the imaginary contaminants in their skin. 'The sight,' wrote Springthorpe, 'presented by such a patient "hunting the cocaine bug" is one which, once seen, can scarcely ever be forgotten.'⁵⁷ One sufferer, 'scraped off pieces of his skin in the endeavour [to extract the parasites]'.⁵⁸ Maddened by the squirming of the 'Cocaine Microbe', the addict was reputed to 'mutilate his body, especially his hands and fingers, trying to dig out [the imaginary body] with the point of a penknife or other suitable sharp-pointed instrument'.⁵⁹ Clarence Godfrey's 1899 article on 'Cocainomania' described a physician's wife who: 'Sees insects in her skin and clothes, and feels them creeping over her. Is always cutting holes in her clothes and burning the pieces to destroy the insects. Has numerous sores on her hands and face from picking at the insects.' Based on this and other accounts, Godfrey concluded that 'The patient will attempt to pick out the [cocaine bug] with a needle or a scalpel wherever he sees or feels it, and

---

⁵⁴ See 'The Charmer', *The Referee*, 1575 (20 October 1907), 2; and 'The Play Actors', *The Stage*, 1387 (17 October 1907), 15.
⁵⁵ W. Starkey, 'The Cocaine-takers of Paris', *Journal of Mental Science*, 59.246 (July 1913), 524.
⁵⁶ 'Cocaine Creeper', *Heywood Advertiser*, 3098 (23 May 1913), 6.
⁵⁷ Springthorpe, 'The Confessions of a Cocainist', 371.
⁵⁸ 'A New Intoxicant', *The Dundee Courier & Argus*, 11266 (16 August 1889), 4.
⁵⁹ Stephen Lett, 'Cocaine Addiction and Its Diagnosis', *Canada Lancet*, 31.4 (December 1898), 830.

as a result is often covered with sores ... and holes ... on the body and head.'[60] It was in the skin, then, that the most tangible signifier of cocaine addiction was to be found. Godfrey's parallel descriptions of the addict's tattered clothing and ulcerated skin offer a particularly concise illustration of how the physical effects of cocainism were figuratively rendered in fin de siècle discourse: the addict's skin appears here as a rent surface, a bodily fabric that is ripped, disfigured, and holed by hallucinatory illusion and obsessively introverted 'picking'. The abscessed and pitted skin of the addict suggested (especially in concert with the parasitical delusions of cocaine bugs) a deeper and more metaphorical type of wounding: the notion that spiritual deformation might be reflected in the skin's superficial destruction.

Both Pamela K. Gilbert and William A. Cohen identify the ambiguous but powerful metaphysical associations that skin possessed for Victorian commentators. In much nineteenth-century medical discourse (particularly, as Gilbert notes, in the field of venerology) the patient's skin was assumed to convey a superficial representation of their inner healthiness and moral composition. Pamela Gilbert describes the tenacious 'persistence ... of the belief that a person's virtue shone forth in his or her personal beauty – that virtue itself was skin deep, or put a different way, that skin operated as an index of the condition of human "depth," not merely of the hidden [medical] aspects of the body, but of the condition of the soul'.[61] On its most basic level, then, skin could function as a visible surface upon which was manifested the image of a deeper interior constitution. Fin de siècle discourses of addiction largely follow this same logic: that the sin of addiction was necessarily written upon the skin of its perpetrator. In 1904, G. Norman Meachen (Tottenham Hospital's physician for diseases of the skin) turned his attention to 'The Cutaneous Affections of the Inebriate', writing that: 'cutaneous disorders resulting from any form of intemperance are something more than "skin-deep" – in other words, they are frequently associated with ... disease in the internal organs'. By reason of its 'ready visibility', Meachen concluded the skin 'affords undeniable proof of the mischief which the intoxicating agent, whatever it may be, is subtly but surely working in the system of its chain bound victim'.[62] A similar sentiment can be seen in Harry Campbell's 1903 presidential address to the Society for the Study of Inebriety. Urging the members of the society to unceasing watchfulness in

---

[60] Godfrey, 'Cocainomania', 148–9.
[61] Pamela Gilbert, *Victorian Skin: Surface, Self, History* (Ithaca: Cornell University Press, 2019), 115.
[62] G. Norman Meachen, 'The Cutaneous Affections of the Inebriate', *British Journal of Inebriety*, 1.4 (April 1904), 274 and 280.

their struggle with 'drug inebriety', Campbell affirmed that: 'New soporific and anodyne preparation are continually being put upon the market, and new drug habits continually being acquired. We must be on the alert for these leper-spots, and do what we can to prevent their spread.'[63] For Campbell, the leprous affliction of inebriety could be imagined to spread not only across the addict's own skin but (symbolically) also across the face of society as a whole.

Beyond this diagnostic significance, though, skin also acquired a nebulous but powerfully felt supernatural quality in the nineteenth century. William A. Cohen describes the skin's 'peculiar status as both physical embodiment and psychical envelope – both a surface projected from inside and a mask immediately comprehensible from without'. Cohen emphasizes the skin's 'sometimes conflicting psychological, spiritual, and social functions' in Victorian culture – capable of acting simultaneously as 'the integument that encloses the visceral interior of the body, yet also [as] the membrane within which, mysteriously and ethereally, the human essence is supposed to reside'.[64] Skin was (to quote Gilbert and Cohen) at once 'the site of interaction between self and world' and 'the physical embodiment of the imagined boundaries of the self'.[65] In this context, skin operated not only as a surface upon which medical and moral symptoms might play out but also as a point of contact (and even confusion) between the outer territory of the physical and the interior territory of selfhood and soul. These metaphysical connotations were to heavily inform the representation of skin in Arthur Machen's short story 'Novel of the White Powder' – one of the late nineteenth century's most gruesomely disturbing addiction narratives, and one which elevates the cocainist's ulcerated skin into an image of distinctively infernal ghastliness.

Under the skin: Arthur Machen and the phantasmagoria of addiction

'Novel of the White Powder' first appeared as one of the narratives contained in Machen's 1895 work *The Three Impostors* (originally fully titled *The Three Impostors or The Transmutations*). Partway between a collection of short stories

---

[63] Harry Campbell, 'The Study of Inebriety: A Retrospect and A Forecast', *British Journal of Inebriety*, 1.1 (July 1903), 11.
[64] William A. Cohen, *Embodied: Victorian Literature and the Senses* (Minneapolis: University of Minnesota Press, 2009), 65.
[65] Gilbert, *Victorian Skin*, 108 and Cohen, *Embodied*, 65.

and an episodic novel,⁶⁶ *The Three Impostors* is made up of a variety of shorter narratives (referred to in the text as 'Novels') linked by a framing account of the protagonists' encounters with three agents of a mysterious secret society and the 'young man with spectacles'⁶⁷ who the three pursue and eventually murder. 'Novel of the White Powder' is narrated by Miss Helen Leicester who relates how her student brother Francis, after succumbing to overwork and mental strain in his studies of the law, starts taking an unidentified but apparently innocuous white powder prescribed by their family doctor. At first the powder – which Francis dissolves in a glass of water and drinks off each day after lunch and dinner – seems to greatly improve his condition: he becomes more cheerful, less obviously studious and weary, and more willing (in the text's elusively coded language) to 'be young and a man' abroad in London. Miss Leicester observes a 'transmutation' in her brother's character – over the course of a few days 'he become[s] a lover of pleasure, a careless and merry idler of western pavements, a hunter out of snug restaurants, and a fine critic of fantastic dancing' (157–9). Francis's metamorphosis into a flâneur is, however, only the first of the powder's effects. The young man shortly becomes evasive and estranged from his sister. One evening over dinner, Helen Leicester happens to glance down at her brother's hand and sees a strange, disfiguring mark on it, the flesh of which is not only badly discoloured but which seems to exude an unnatural illumination, 'as of black fire' (162). After this, Francis quickly leaves the room and the next time his sister sees him his hand is wrapped in a handkerchief to conceal his affliction. Over the following weeks Francis stops eating, acquires a look in his eye that is 'scarcely human' (162), and eventually locks himself up in his room seeing no one. The family physician, Dr Haberden, pays Francis one brief visit, but he emerges horribly shaken and refuses to elaborate before leaving.

Miss Leicester comes home from a walk one day to see, briefly, some hideous thing staring out through the window of her brother's study. She describes: 'two eyes of burning flame ... in the midst of something as formless as my fear, the symbol and presence of all evil and all hideous corruption' (167–8). The climax of the story comes about when, not long after this, Miss Leicester and the servants discover a black liquid seeping through the floor of Francis's chambers and into the room below. Spurred by this discovery, Miss Leicester begs Dr Haberden to

---

⁶⁶ A format which Molly C. O'Donnell refers to as the '"tales novel" ... a hybrid form that includes attributes of the novel and tales collection' (Molly C. O'Donnell, 'Mirrors, Masks, and Masculinity: The Homosocial Legacy from Dickens to Machen', *Victoriographies*, 6.3 (2016), 258.)
⁶⁷ Arthur Machen, *The Three Impostors or The Transmutations* (London: John Lane, 1895), 8. (All further references in parentheses.)

help her break into Francis's room. Inside, they discover that Francis has decayed into 'a dark and putrid mass, seething with corruption and hideous rottenness, neither liquid nor solid, but melting and changing before our eyes, and bubbling with unctuous oily bubbles like boiling pitch' (171–2). Confronted with the sight of his unfortunate patient's fate, Dr Haberden, 'in a fury of loathing' (172), beats Francis to death with a poker.

In a postscript to the story, Miss Leicester receives a letter from Dr Haberden (now retreated abroad) where he informs her that he has had Francis's white powder chemically analysed by a friend of his. The letter reveals that the original drug which Haberden prescribed has (thanks to years of neglect in the chemist's storeroom) been gradually transmuted into 'the wine of the Sabbath' (176) – an ancient mystical substance that was long ago consumed in rituals of black magic and/or 'evil science' (177). The chemist's report elliptically hints at the effects of this 'wine' on its users:

> By the power of that Sabbath wine, a few grains of white powder thrown into a glass of water, the house of life was riven asunder, and the human trinity dissolved, and the worm which never dies, that which lies sleeping within us all, was made tangible and an external thing, and clothed with a garment of flesh. And then in the hour of midnight, the primal fall was repeated and re-presented, and the awful thing veiled in the mythos of the Tree in the Garden was done anew. (177–8)

The story concludes with the analyst confirming that the final effect of the powder is the 'corruption' and 'defilement' of the body already seen in the person of the unfortunate Francis. 'What began with corruption,' the chemist epitomizes, 'ended also with corruption' (178).

While the exact nature of Machen's white powder – both before and after its transformation – is left deliberately vague, a number of critics have identified a potential symbolic 'correspondence' between it and cocaine.[68] The exact nature of this correspondence is harder to define, however. For the purposes of this present reading, I want to reject the idea that the white powder represents a direct allegory or substitution for cocaine in Machen's narrative. Rather, I suggest that 'Novel of the White Powder' fantastically embellishes the more frightening and grotesque aspects of cocaine's depiction in popular discourse. We have already seen how in the 1890s cocaine was widely viewed as both

---

[68] See Brenda Mann Hammack, 'Phantastica: The Chemically Inspired Intellectual in Occult Fiction', *Mosaic: A Journal for the Interdisciplinary Study of Literature*, 37.1 (2004), 91; and Julia Briggs, *Night Visitors: The Rise and Fall of the English Ghost Story* (London: Faber, 1977), 71.

the 'newest' and most 'brutal' of all drug cravings.[69] Shockingly seductive and with the power to inflict a uniquely horrible blend of physical and psychical destruction on its victims, cocaine seemed to prophesy the arrival of a new epoch of addiction: one whose drugs were both technologically unparalleled and unprecedentedly destructive. (Writing several decades later in the 1920s, Machen himself identified the 'coming of cocaine' as synonymous with the rise of a characteristically modern 'nasty, underground, poisonous gaiety that is not gaiety at all, but rather ghastliness'.[70]) I want to argue, therefore, that Machen's story responds not so much to cocaine itself, as to the imagery of cocaine in the fin de siècle imagination: the 'ghastliness' of cocaine provides an imaginative lexicon through which to articulate the features of the demonic white powder.

The basic scenario of 'Novel of the White Powder' bears a considerable similarity to Robert Louis Stevenson's *The Strange Case of Dr Jekyll and Mr Hyde*. In the words of the *Pall Mall Gazette*'s reviewer:

> The incident of the powder, strangely altered from its pure condition until it obtain[s] the power of 'riving asunder the house of life and dissolving the human trinity,' and giving a human form to 'that which lies sleeping within us all,' argues an uncommon boldness in the man who ventures to use it after its being worked into 'Dr. Jekyll.' However, if Mr Machen thinks he can wear the armour of Achilles with grace, that is his affair.[71]

'Novel of the White Powder' might very well be said to have borrowed 'the armour of Achilles' by reproducing several key concepts from Stevenson's earlier novella, though there are important differences between the two works.[72] For our present purposes, the most important point of contrast is that Machen's story is much more apparently invested in the physically horrific and degrading aspects of Francis's transmutation. In 'The White Powder', the drug user's ontological fragmentation (the refashioning of the user's interior evil into 'a tangible and an

---

[69] T. S. Clouston, 'Diseased Cravings and Paralysed Control: Dipsomania; Morphinomania; Chloralism; Cocainism', *Edinburgh Medical Journal*, 35.2 (March 1890), 806; and 'The Deliriums of Cocaine', *Lakes Herald*, 802 (8 January 1886), 7.

[70] Arthur Machen, *Dreads and Drolls* (London: Martin Secker, 1926), 154.

[71] 'Reviews', *Pall Mall Gazette*, 9592 (21 December 1895), 4.

[72] Machen, for his part, later articulated what he took to be the main aesthetic flaw in Stevenson's composition: 'The plot, [of *Jekyll and Hyde*] in itself, strikes me as mechanical – this actual physical transformation, produced by a drug, linked certainly with a theory of ethical change, but not linked at all with the really mysterious, the really psychical – all this affects me, I say, as ingenious mechanism and nothing more'. See: Arthur Machen, *Hieroglyphics* (London: Grant Richards, 1902), 82. Machen's disappointment with the lack of 'psychical mystery' in *The Strange Case of Dr Jekyll and Mr Hyde* heavily implies that the symbolically resonant but ambiguous description of the Sabbath Wine's effects in 'Novel of the White Powder' is intended as a response to this aspect of Stevenson's work.

external thing') is consistently represented in the guise of bodily decay and sexual transgression. To give one example, the analytical chemist's final description of the white powder's effects leans heavily on erotic symbolism and metaphor:

> [He who drank the solution] found himself attended by a companion, a shape of glamour and unearthly allurement, beckoning him apart to share in joys more exquisite, more piercing than the thrill of any dream, to the consummation of the marriage of the Sabbath. It is hard to write of such things as these, and chiefly because that shape that allured with loveliness was no hallucination, but, awful as it is to express, the man himself. (177)

While the exact nature of these events is left deliberately mysterious, there is a clear sexual framing to the processes of physical and moral dissolution initiated by the white powder. The manifestation of the user's inner corruption, the 'worm which never dies' (177) – a phrase which Machen takes from a biblical account of hell in the book of Mark[73] – is described as 'alluring' the user and 'beckoning them apart' to 'consummate the marriage of the Sabbath'. This repetition of the 'primal fall', we are told, represents the underlying 'awful thing veiled [behind] the mythos of the Tree in the Garden' (177) – another biblical allusion, this time to Genesis and the expulsion from Eden. In this way, Machen uses the language of sexual sinfulness to convey a more abstract sense of moral and existential defilement; the exact nature of the 'awful thing' that the powder enacts can (it is implied) never be precisely articulated, only translated indirectly into the imagery of sexual 'allure' and revulsion. The chemist's final summary reiteration that 'Such was the *nuptiæ Sabbati*' (178) confirms the degree to which the white powder's metaphysical effects are meant to be interpreted through the language of sexual horror as the consummation of some monstrous wedding right.

Machen's sexualization of the white powder obviously resonates with the widespread belief in cocaine's special seductiveness and desirability. Indeed, it was not uncommon for fin de siècle writers to conflate the sense of cocaine's particular dangerousness with its function as a sexual stimulant and aphrodisiac. We have previously seen how Conolly Norman equated the 'rapid mental degeneration' of cocainism with the drug's power to produce 'sexual excitement [and] abnormal voluptuous sensations'.[74] In many accounts, the onset of compulsive eroticism and sexual delusion was taken to mark the cocainist's final, most abject degradation – a nadir which would either spur them to seek help

---

[73] See Mark 9.48.
[74] Norman, 'A Note on Cocainism', 198.

or signify their condemnation to irredeemable ruin. Thus, according to J. W. Springthorpe's anonymous cocainist:

> On [the addict] goes, taking more and more; and then enters a new kind of illusion, which finishes him up for the mad-house. I mean the revolting, dirty, sensuous illusions. The remembrance of it is for me so awful that I only tell you that one day every person I saw, near or far, appeared to be naked, and in the most lascivious positions, alone or with others. ... In terror, I took fright, ran to a medical friend at a lunatic asylum, and was placed under restraint.[75]

A similar example can be seen in the reportage surrounding the 1892 trial of Dr Thomas Neill Cream. Tried and executed in the autumn of that year for the poisoning of several women in the Lambeth area of London, newspaper descriptions of Cream's behaviour and personality drew clear parallels between his murderous impulses and his frequent abuse of cocaine. An anonymous acquaintance of Cream's told papers that:

> His principal characteristic was his never-ending talk about women, upon whom his entire thoughts seemed to run, and I confess his language about them was far from tolerable or agreeable; and he carried a number of pornographic photographs which he once forced upon my notice ... I have constantly seen him swallow some three or four pills which he stated were composed of strychnine, morphia, and cocaine, which he did not disguise had aphrodisiac properties. Indeed, he was exceedingly vicious, and seemed to live for nothing but the gratification of his passions.[76]

Cream's 'constant' use of cocaine as an 'aphrodisiac potion' is here enfolded into his 'vicious', murderous desire for women. In this way, accounts of Cream's crimes define him as a monster of exaggerated and distended appetites, since his compulsive desires for sexuality and for drugs both maintain and reflect each other. While other forms of fin de siècle drug addiction could be interpreted according to patterns of erotic behaviour,[77] descriptions such as these meant that cocaine was often seen as a drug with a distinctly sexual dimension all of its own. Metaphors of cocaine's addictive seductiveness could easily bleed over into factual descriptions of the drug's aphrodisiac effects. In this way cocaine addiction could be interpreted as a process in which acceptably normal erotic

---

[75] Springthorpe, 'The Confessions of a Cocainist', 372.
[76] 'The Poisoner Neill', *St James's Gazette*, 25.3858 (24 October 1892), 9.
[77] See Susan Zieger, *Inventing the Addict*, 162–95 for a more detailed analysis of fin de siècle addiction discourses and their potential parallels with masturbation, queer desire, and sexual submission/dominance.

desire was both artificially aggravated and misdirected, producing – as can be seen in W. Starkey's 'The Cocaine-takers of Paris' – a kind of eroticism that was both intensely hyperactive and incoherent: 'The drug acquires a personality for its victims – they love it or abuse it, have scenes with the box containing it, pressing it to their breasts, or throwing it out of the window, cursing it, and then asking pardon of it.'[78] In this rendering, cocaine appears as both lover and aphrodisiac. Like Machen's white powder (the demoniac wine of the Sabbath) cocaine seemingly both creates and receives the delirious sexuality of its users; the 'consummation of the marriage of the Sabbath' (177) follows closely upon the tempestuous seductions of cocaine.

The sexual 'awful[ness]' (177) of the white powder is, Machen takes pains to remind us, before long succeeded by the 'corruption and hideous rottenness' of Francis's transformation into 'a dark and putrid mass' (171). Intriguingly, the first readily detectable sign of Francis's affliction also qualifies as one of the story's central images – the weirdly luminescent mark that Miss Leicester observes on Francis's hand:

> Between the thumb and forefinger of the closed hand, there was a mark, a small patch about the size of a sixpence, and somewhat of the colour of a bad bruise. Yet, by some sense I cannot define, I knew that what I saw was no bruise at all. Oh, if human flesh could burn with flame, and if flame could be black as pitch, such was that before me! (160–1)

Francis's mark affords the reader their first indication that there is set to be some physical – indeed, pathological – consequence for his consumption of the white powder, and Machen reiterates its importance by recurring to the image of a despoiled hand at key points throughout the rest of the story. When his sister happens to catch a glimpse of Francis's malevolently altered form through his bedroom window, we are told that the one sight that most vividly 'remains forever engraved on [her] brain' is the picture of the distorted appendage with which he grips the window blind: 'It was not a hand: there were no fingers that held the blind, but a black stump pushed it aside; the mouldering outline and the clumsy movement as of a beast's paw had glowed into my senses before the darkling waves of terror had overwhelmed me' (168–9). The putrid, mouldered remains of Francis's hand are here described in terms which recall the disconcertingly shadowed radiance of his first bruise-like mark, seeming to 'glow' into Miss Leicester's senses while also submerging her in a 'darkling' terror. Later, Francis's

---

[78] W. Starkey, 'The Cocaine-takers of Paris', *Journal of Mental Science*, 59.246 (July 1913), 524.

final liquefaction is heralded by the maid's panicked discovery that some black substance has seeped through the ceiling of her mistresses' bedroom and spattered her hand. According to Helen Leicester:

> The servant maid staggered into the room and faced me, white and trembling.
>
> 'O Miss Helen', she whispered. 'Oh, for the Lord's sake, Miss Helen, what has happened? Look at my hand, miss; look at that hand!' I drew her to the window, and saw there was a black wet stain upon her hand. (169)

In this way, the story's 'climax' (the word that Miss Leicester herself uses to describe the discovery of Francis's final condition) is presaged by the maid's wetly blackened and stained hand – a curious repetition of the besmirching mark that first alerts the household to Francis's supernatural malady.

Most critical commentary on Francis's mark has tended to read it as a generalized signifier of impending degeneration and disease.[79] Given the demonically sexual suggestiveness of the story's end, it is similarly tempting to regard the black stain either as a symbolic rendering of syphiloma or as simply a reworking of the traditional concept of the witches' mark. Based on the imagery associated with it, however, I want to argue for a different reading: that the precise form of Francis's mark is dictated by an interconnected set of ideas drawn from late-Victorian discourses on cocaine, skin, and hallucination. We have already seen how, in cases of cocainism, the contamination of the skin acquired powerful metaphorical and metaphysical implications. Cocaine bugs, by virtue of their peculiarly mixed status as both a dermatological and hallucinatory disorder, tapped into and intensified the potent spiritual associations that the skin possessed in Victorian discourse. The cocaine bug was a malady poised disconcertingly between the bodily and the supernatural – a disease of strangely manifest illusion and etherealized decay. The mysterious patch that appears on Francis's hand represents an elaborated version of these same associations.

In this context, one subtle aspect of the mark which rewards careful analysis is its association with light, particularly with abnormal, spectral light. Helen Leicester's first frightened description of the mark relates that: 'If human flesh could burn with flame, and if flame could be black as pitch, such was that before me!' (161) A confused-sounding double conditional which implies that the diseased suppuration of Francis's skin is somehow also both vitally alive with

---

[79] See, for example, Adrian Eckersley, 'A Theme in the Early Work of Arthur Machen: "Degeneration"', *English Literature in Transition*, 35.3 (1992), 280, and Kimberly Jackson, 'Non-Evolutionary Degeneration in Arthur Machen's Supernatural Tales', *Victorian Literature and Culture*, 41.1 (2013), 125.

motion and alight with an unnatural 'black fire' (162). Immediately before noticing her brother's hand, though, Miss Leicester has been concentrating her attention on the setting sun outside their dining room windows:

> As I thought of what I would say to Francis, the sky began to flush and shine … and in the gap between two dark masses that were houses an awful pageantry of flame appeared. Lurid whorls of writhed cloud, and utter depths burning, and gray masses like the fume blown from a smoking city, and an evil glory blazing far above shot with tongues of more ardent fire, and below as if there were a deep pool of blood. I looked down to where my brother sat facing me, and the words were shaped on my lips, when I saw his hand resting on the table. (160)

Miss Leicester's two descriptions – first of the 'lurid' sunset and then of Francis's sickly patch of skin – draw an obvious parallel between the nightmarish lights and colours of the sky, and the ghastly 'black flame' that seemingly inhabits her brother's flesh. Indeed, the rapid transition between the two intimates the possibility that Francis's skin has somehow acquired or been tainted by the 'evil glory' of the sunset (in this regard, the story obliquely hints that both effects may be otherworldly auguries of the fact that the Sabbath wine has claimed a new victim). When, immediately after this, Helen Leicester turns to Dr Haberden for help, the medical man dismissively suggests another possibility – that it is not Francis's flesh that has been 'coloured' by the approaching twilight but his sister's perceptions:

> 'My dear Miss Leicester', he said … 'you know, of course, what a queer thing the brain is?'
>
> 'I understand what you mean; but I was not deceived. I saw what I have told you with my own eyes'.
>
> 'Yes, yes, of course. But your eyes had been staring at that very curious sunset we had tonight. That is the only explanation. You will see it in the proper light tomorrow, I am sure'. (161–2)

While we are clearly supposed to recognize Haberden's remarks as obtuse and unhelpful, his comments nevertheless reiterate one of the major thematic associations of Francis's mark – that uncanny illumination is somehow inherently linked with corrupting and deranging influences. Haberden's attempt to reassure Miss Leicester by promising her that she will 'see it in the proper light tomorrow' is calculated to recall readers to the distinctly improper light exuding from Francis's hand, as well as the light of the sunset which (according to Haberden's explanation) has 'glamour[ed]' (162) Helen's senses. From Miss Leicester's point of view, then, she leaves the meeting with her doctor 'but little comforted' (162), faced with the alarming notion that either Francis's body or her mind has been contaminated by the effects of some unnatural illumination.

While Dr Haberden's advice that the brain is a 'queer thing' has an air of nebulous evasiveness about it, his suggestion nevertheless draws upon a well-established paradigm in nineteenth-century discourses on thought and hallucination – one which is in turn directly relevant to Machen's framing of the accursed mark. In her analysis of 'Phantasmagoria: Spectral Technology and the Metaphorics of Modern Reverie' Terry Castle famously identifies a 'spectralisation of mental space'[80] that began in the early nineteenth century and which maintained its cultural currency into the fin de siècle. According to Castle's account, many medical and rationalist thinkers of the early-to-mid-century argued against the objective reality of ghosts and spectral phenomena, concluding instead that such images were merely delusional, hallucinatory products of the mind. This rationalizing project, however, resulted 'through a kind of epistemological recoil'[81] in a relocation of the spectral into the realm of thought itself:

> The rationalists did not so much negate the traditional spirit world as displace it into the realm of psychology. Ghosts were not exorcized – only internalized and reinterpreted as hallucinatory thoughts. Yet this internalisation of apparitions introduced a latent irrationalism into the realm of mental experience. ... The paradoxical effect of the psychological argument was to subvert the boundary between ghost-seeing and ordinary thought ... thought itself [came to be regarded as] a spectral process, and as such, easily modulated into hallucination.[82]

The reinterpretation of the ghost as a purely hallucinatory, 'internal' phenomenon of the brain introduced (by reflex) a new anxiousness into conceptions of thought and sensory perception, producing (to quote Helen Groth), 'a persistent anxiety about the fragility of the mind'.[83] The brain might, under these conditions, be viewed as alarmingly vulnerable to irrational and 'eerie'[84] alienation from itself;

---

[80] Terry Castle, 'Phantasmagoria: Spectral Technology and the Metaphorics of Modern Reverie', *Critical Inquiry*, 15.1 (1988), 29.
[81] Ibid.
[82] Castle, 'Phantasmagoria: Spectral Technology and the Metaphorics of Modern Reverie', 52–9.
[83] Helen Groth, 'Reading Victorian Illusions: Dickens's "Haunted Man" and Dr. Pepper's "Ghost"', *Victorian Studies*, 50.1 (2007), 59.
[84] Castle, 'Phantasmagoria: Spectral Technology and the Metaphorics of Modern Reverie', 50.

in these circumstances it was possible to imagine that, 'one's inmost thoughts might at any moment assume the strangely externalised shape of phantoms'.[85] Castle further suggests that the principal cultural metaphor through which these ethereal anxieties were captured was the image of the magic lantern 'phantasmagoria'. Originally a display of artificial phantasms and horrors produced by means of darkness, light projection, and other luminescent or ethereal illusions, the phantasmagoria also gradually came to signify (according to its full OED definition): '(A vision of) a rapidly transforming collection or series of imaginary (and usually fantastic) forms, such as may be experienced in a dream or fevered state, or evoked by literary description.'[86] Beginning in the earliest years of the century, the deranged – and deranging – 'spectral parade' of the phantasmagoria was 'translated into a metaphor for the imagery produced by the mind'.[87] This image retained its relevance until the early decades of the twentieth century and the assimilation of the magic lantern (the primary visual technology of the phantasmagoria) into early cinema.[88] Consequently, throughout the nineteenth century, phantasmagorical effects of abnormal light, darkness, luminosity, and colour came to be seen as inherently connotative of the mind's own spectrality – its liability to spontaneous, disordered, and unpredictable illusion.

The corrupted sunset and Francis's disease-like mark draw heavily upon these phantasmagorical associations. Both appear to manifest a contradictory and incomprehensible radiance. They emit a light that is at once 'black', 'lurid', 'blazing', and 'writh[ing]' (160–1), a distinctly phantasmagorical form of illumination that implies the frailness of rationality, and the mind's susceptibility to derangement; the 'black fire' within Francis's flesh blazes with the light of hallucination. If, however, Francis's mark is comprised of phantasmagorical light, then what are we to make of its situation on the physical surface of his skin? To answer this, it is worth recalling the peculiar condition of the cocaine bug as a disorder compounded of both physical destruction and hallucinatory disturbance. For fin de siècle observers, the cocaine bug represented a process by

---

[85] Ibid., 58.
[86] NB: More extensive histories of the invention of the phantasmagoria, its history, and the evolution of its practical effects can be found in Mervyn Heard, *Phantasmagoria: The Secret Life of the Magic Lantern* (Hastings: Projection Box, 2006); and Laurent Mannoni, *The Great Art of Light and Shadow: Archaeology of the Cinema*, translated by Richard Crangle (Exeter: University of Exeter Press, 2000).
[87] Castle, 'Phantasmagoria: Spectral Technology and the Metaphorics of Modern Reverie', 30.
[88] See Castle, 'Phantasmagoria: Spectral Technology and the Metaphorics of Modern Reverie', 42, 47–8, and 57 for examples of the employment of the phantasmagoria metaphor in the late nineteenth century.

which an internal, mental (or spiritual) ailment might seem to be transferred – or projected – onto the exterior surface of the body. Descriptions of cocaine bugs were sometimes quite explicit in using language that equated the organic functioning of the disease with the mechanical operation of the magic lantern and the phantasmagoria. According to Springthorpe's 'Confessions of a Cocainist': '[The cocaine bugs and] worms are projected on to the cocainist's own person and clothing. He sees them on his washing, in his skin, [and] creeping along his penholder.'[89] Springthorpe's conclusion to his article uses a similar image to extol the value of the cocainist's account as 'proceed[ing] from a skilled observer, who has himself been behind the scenes and watched the phantasmagoria from the subjective as well as the objective side'.[90] In the context of this phantasmagorical figuration, Machen's image of a darkly shining, disturbingly animated skin lesion becomes more comprehensible. The cocaine bug created a paradigm in which skin could be imagined to both express the stigma of disease and the horrors of a hallucinatory imagination – the addict's flesh becoming parasitized by their own disordered thoughts. 'Novel of the White Powder' innovates on this pattern so that Francis's skin becomes a surface which simultaneously manifests both a diseased canker and the spectral luminescence of the phantasmagoria. In parsing the imagery that Machen uses to characterize Francis's mark, it is worth keeping in mind that (to quote William A. Cohen) one of the most persistent convictions associated with skin in Victorian culture was its capacity for 'raising [the individual's] interior qualities to the surface'.[91] As such – while it might at first appear contradictory or even paradoxical – there is nevertheless a basic metaphorical kinship between the 'flatten[ing]' out of interior psychological and spiritual depth into the 'two-dimensional surface'[92] of skin, and the projection of illusory but apparently real images onto the flat surface of the magic lantern screen. In both cases, imaginary or supernatural forms could seem to acquire the veneer of reality by being projected onto physical substance; both phenomena imply the uncomfortable ambiguation of the real and the unreal, the substantial and the imaginary. This interweaving of images – of surface and depth, mind and material – underlies Machen's reimagining and embellishment of cocaine addiction and its signifiers. In 'Novel of the White Powder', the necrotized 'hole'[93] in the cocainist's flesh is transfigured into a type

---

[89] Springthorpe, 'The Confessions of a Cocainist', 371.
[90] Ibid., 374.
[91] Cohen, *Embodied*, 80.
[92] Gilbert, *Victorian Skin*, 111.
[93] Godfrey, 'Cocainomania', 149.

of abyssal void – a disease wound that burns with phantasmagorical light and infernal darkness.

Women of nerve and brain: Cocaine addiction and the medical woman

Even accepting that he has to deal with a situation far beyond the remit of conventional medicine, Dr Haberden can hardly be said to emerge from 'Novel of the White Powder' with much credit. Given that he (in order) 'unwittingly prescribes [Francis] the poison that condemns him to an awful death', 'tells the distressed Miss Leicester that she is imagining her brother's disease', and attempts to disavow all involvement in Francis's case when the powder begins to take effect,[94] it is not difficult to interpret his character as an indictment of medical authority and the medical profession's cavalier irresponsibility in overseeing the drugs it administers to its patients. Much of this chapter has concerned itself with the use of cocaine as an image of medical–technological 'disillusion[ment]', either as a result of the direct misapplication of cocaine or the perceived negligence of the medical profession in its handling of the drug.[95] I want to close, however, with a brief account of one particular discursive strategy that fin de siècle medical commentators employed to try to redeem the profession and its interactions with cocaine: the suggestion that the relatively new figure of the professionally qualified female doctor might afford a solution to the problems produced by the drug.

One of the major themes of the story of cocaine abuse in this period is the recurring suggestion of medical culpability. Not only were practitioners themselves suspected to be exceptionally vulnerable to the allure of cocainism, but they were also regarded as largely responsible (whether directly or indirectly) for inculcating the habit among their most vulnerable patients – particularly their female patients.[96] In a 1908 article on 'Doctor's Diseases' the *BMJ* noted that 'the cocaine habit [is] very common among members of the profession', a circumstance that could easily be explained by 'the anxieties caused by responsibilities which must weigh heavy on every man of right feeling; [by] the amount and trying nature of the work the doctor has to do; [by] irregularity in meals and broken

---

[94] See O'Donnell, 'Mirrors, Masks, and Masculinity', 272.
[95] 'Are We Too Clean?', 84.
[96] For a more sustained commentary on the relationship between physicians and female patients in the context of addictive drug use, see Zieger, *Inventing the Addict*, 127–48.

sleep; ... and [by] the scanty remuneration which his labour too often brings him'.⁹⁷ The hostile circumstances of the profession meant that the medical man was all the more exposed to the attractions of cocaine. Among the laity, women were similarly regarded as highly likely to be betrayed into cocainism by the attractions of fashionable pick-me-ups and medicaments. The 'chief victims' of medicinal coca wines were thought to be 'women and children'.⁹⁸ By the 1890s medical authorities became increasingly concerned that: 'Originally coca wine was made from coca leaves, but it is now commonly a solution of the [cocaine] alkaloid in a sweet and usually strongly alcoholic wine. ... [The mother and the] school mistress as a rule have a deep-rooted belief in the efficacy of the popular drug, and give it to their pupils on the slightest provocation'.⁹⁹ The prospect that cocaine addiction might be brought on by incautious self-medication (such as for seasickness, colds and flu, etc.) has already been discussed earlier in this chapter, and commentators were inclined to tie this growth in reckless 'self-prescribing' to the public's loss of conviction in medical expertise:

> As the natural consequence of the public's dwindling faith in the profession, self-prescribing is daily becoming more usual, particularly for commonplace ailments such as headaches, liver attacks, anaemia, nerves, and indigestion. The man in the street often says that the doctors know no more about this sort of thing than he himself does. Perhaps he is right.¹⁰⁰

At the same time, cocaine's stimulant effects also threatened to make the drug acutely alluring to female users. 'It is said,' wrote the *Dundee Courier*, 'that a dose of cocaine often enables a "hard-worked" society woman to get through her season all right, though at a heavy cost to her nerves in the end.'¹⁰¹ Jocelynne Joye, author of *The Outlook*'s 'A Woman's Week' column, recounted how:

> Women have earned the reputation of being the greatest offenders in the wholesale taking of injurious and often dangerous drugs. This is so, particularly amongst the class whose time is taken up in the pursuit of social pleasures. Women resort to these drugs from over-exhaustion, when the need of a stimulant is felt ... In a certain section of society one is astounded at the number of women one meets

---

⁹⁷ 'Doctor's Diseases', *BMJ*, 1.2461 (29 February 1908), 522. See also, Conolly Norman, 'A Note on Cocainism', *Journal of Mental Science*, 38.161 (April 1892), 195; and J. J. Graham Brown, 'Notes on the Treatment of the Diseases of the Nervous System', *Scottish Medical and Surgical Journal*, 4.6 (January–June 1899), 499 for similar remarks on the medical man's unique susceptibility to addiction.
⁹⁸ 'The Dangers of Coca Wines', *BMJ*, 2.1927 (4 December 1897), 1666.
⁹⁹ 'Coca Wine and its Dangers', *BMJ*, 1.1884 (6 February 1897), 353.
¹⁰⁰ H. H. Riddle, 'The Drug Habit', *Quiver*, 47.5 (March 1912), 488.
¹⁰¹ 'Another Abuse in Society', *Dundee Courier*, 15020 (14 August 1901), 4.

who carry 'restoratives' in their *bonbonnières*. To illustrate this, some little time back a lady at a fashionable 'at-home' was heard to offer a friend a tabloid from a small silver box – just as one might offer a cigarette to another – with the words, 'Do have one, dear – they're only cocaine. Personally I find them a necessity, and I don't know how I should get through the day without my "tabs" '.[102]

In this way 'the imperious dictates of social custom' represented a substantial danger of fostering 'cravings for alcohol, and pick-me-ups, and morphine and cocaine'[103] among 'the decidedly weaker sex'.[104]

Given the widespread assumption in this period that both women and doctors were especially vulnerable to the seductions of cocainism, there is a certain irony to the fact that the woman doctor was advocated as a potential answer to the problems of cocaine. Female practitioners had (to a more limited extent) participated alongside their male colleagues in the first phase of cocaine experimentation in the 1880s: in 1887 the *Ophthalmic Review* recorded the ophthalmologist Elizabeth Sargent's use of cocaine to treat pain and high tension in glaucoma;[105] and outside of the specialized medical press, *The Englishwoman's Review* excitedly observed that a medical student by the name of Mrs Davis had been awarded the first honour for her thesis on 'The Use of Cocaine in Obstetrics' by the New York Medical College. Beyond simply noting the fact of her victory, though, *The Englishwoman's Review* was keen to celebrate the scale of Davis's achievement: 'Mrs Davis, the youngest member of her class in New York Medical College, carried off all the honours – made the highest record on all examinations, and took the first honour for [her] Thesis.' All this was accomplished under the eye of 'Dr Mary Jacobi, the most severe examiner on the continent … In examination on surgery, [Davis] answered all questions on one branch, while eight male graduates, examined by the same professor, "knew nothing about it" '.[106] Davis's achievements are depicted as exceptional not only by virtue of her comparative youth and her triumph over the majority of her male classmates but also as having met the standards of an equally exacting female examiner. Both Davis and Jacobi are characterized as superior, even elite, individuals – a presentation which in turn mirrors wider representations of female doctors in the late nineteenth and early twentieth centuries.

---

[102] Jocelynne Joye, 'A Woman's Week', *The Outlook*, 2.38 (22 October 1898), 380.
[103] 'The 'Prodigy' Question', *The Scotsman*, 19081 (13 August 1904), 10.
[104] Joye, 'A Woman's Week', 380.
[105] See 'Recent Literature' *Ophthalmic Review*, 6 (1887), 279; and Elizabeth Sargent, 'Cocaine in Glaucoma', *Archives of Ophthalmology*, 16.2 (1887), 205.
[106] 'Foreign Notes and News', *The Englishwoman's Review*, 161 (15 September 1886), 427.

Both Vanessa Heggie and J. F. Geddes note that the early woman doctor's self-identity was (often by necessity) formulated as a mixture of exceptional cleverness, ambition, and talent.[107] Motivated by the need to distinguish themselves from subordinate nurses on the one hand and from socially superior amateur philanthropists (or 'Lady Bountifuls') on the other, fin de siècle women doctors arrived at an identity that emphasized 'the centrality of intellect, brains, and ambition'.[108] In order to differentiate their calling from other groups of medically involved women, the strategy of female doctors and surgeons was effectively to represent themselves as a feminine elite: exceptionally intelligent, professionally steadfast, and rigorously practically minded. This superior framing of the medical woman also extended to comparisons with their male confreres. In part, this was the outcome of making a virtue of necessity – both senior women practitioners and those medical men who supported female inclusion in the profession were aware that a newly qualified woman was likely to be judged more harshly than a man of the same level. Anne Digby remarks on the tensions inherent in the fact that female practitioners tended to be pushed towards lower status specializations 'focused particularly on children and on women' while also being subject to 'constant scrutiny' of their work.[109] As such, it was important that their professional judgement and behaviour be always scrupulously maintained at the highest level. Flora Murray, one of the co-founders of the Women's Hospital Corps during the First World War, frequently reminded her subordinates of the obstacles they faced in gaining public recognition for their skills: 'You not only have got to do a good job but you have got to do a superior job. What would be accepted from a man will not be accepted from a woman. You have got to do better.'[110] The same imperative to superior standards was expressed even more weightily by the physician and surgeon J. Walter Carr (later to be elected president of the Medical Society of London) in his introductory address to the Royal Free Hospital's School of Medicine for Women in 1898:

> Amongst male practitioners the public recognise that there are sure to be some failures. some doubtful characters, some foolish or ignorant persons, some disreputable individuals, and the existence of a few such does not materially

---

[107] Vanessa Heggie, 'Women Doctors and Lady Nurses: Class, Education, and the Professional Victorian Woman', *Bulletin of the History of Medicine*, 89.2 (2015), 290.
[108] Heggie, 'Women Doctors and Lady Nurses', 291.
[109] Anne Digby, *The Evolution of British General Practice, 1850–1948* (Oxford: Oxford University Press, 1999), 173–4.
[110] Quoted in J. F. Geddes, 'The Doctors' Dilemma: Medical Women and the British Suffrage Movement', *Women's History Review*, 18.2 (2009), 212.

injure the reputation or position of the profession as a whole; but, for the present at any rate, whilst the women's movement is still young, were there to be any serious falling off in the character and quality of the students, were we to send out into the world practitioners ill-qualified or unsuited for their work, were any medical women to be guilty of serious moral or professional indiscretion or to show themselves unworthy of the responsibility thrown upon them, then we may be assured that a thoughtless and indiscriminating public would at once jump to the conclusion that female practitioners were a failure. Once again, therefore, I would most earnestly impress the immense responsibility which rests upon each one here … [to avoid] any untimely frivolity, any want of tact or discretion, [and] any carelessness or dereliction of duty.[111]

The one benefit of such exhaustive difficulties was that they had and would in future continue to forge the sorority of medical women into 'a strong and indomitable race' – a movement guided by their 'genuine love of medicine' and their 'earnest purpose of work'.[112]

Advocates for women doctors thus defined them as an intellectual and vocational elite; while their numbers might still be small, and while they might face even greater 'professional difficulties'[113] than their brother medicos, they nevertheless represented the very *nonpareil* of the profession as a whole. Mary L. Breakell in her 1903 article on 'Women in the Medical Profession' was emphatic in the contrasts she drew between the qualifications and character of the average medical women and the average medical man:

Do people realise that out of the list of two hundred and forty-nine qualified medical women no fewer than sixty-six hold the high degree M.D., and some of them that of M.S.? and is it not a higher percentage (in proportion to their number, of course) than that held by medical men?

'But these are exceptional women,' someone will exclaim. Well, we may reply that is only exceptional women who even think, in the first place, of entering the medical profession, and still more exceptional women who pass successfully their five years or more of training. The man who enters the medical profession may, or may not, have special aptitude… but the woman must feel intensely that it is her vocation or she would never attempt its (to her) special difficulties. … [The prejudiced] say something vague about 'nerve' and 'nerves' as though men invariably held a monopoly of one, in the good sense, and women a

---

[111] J. Walter Carr, 'Royal Free Hospital: School of Medicine for Women', *Lancet*, 152.3919 (8 October 1898), 928.
[112] Ibid.
[113] Digby, *Evolution of British General Practice*, 165.

superabundance of the other, in the bad sense, forgetting that there can be nervous men and also women of nerve. ... We may imagine, indeed realise, that it took some 'nerve' as well as brain to win those distinctions.[114]

The medical woman was then (almost by definition) an 'exceptional' entity – a women who had been tempered by special difficulties, who was (indeed, had to be) more professionally committed, better learned, braver, and more collected than the average man in her field. And, as the elect of their profession, the woman doctor was also ideally suited to resolve the problem of feminine indulgence in dangerous medicines such as cocaine. Breakell's reasoning, for instance, was that there were many women – 'particularly unmarried women' – who resorted to such compounds because of their reluctance to submit themselves to masculine medical inspection and supervision:

> Thinking that have no alternative [these women] indiscriminately take drugs, in the form of one advertised patent medicine after another, reckless of the effect of the continued habit of using preparations of cocaine, kola, etc., etc.; drugs, some of them no doubt good, when taken at the right time, in due proportion, under medical advice; but ... In how many cases may we not suspect that [these drugs] have helped those who trusted in them down the dim, dreary ways of insanity to its ultimate asylum?[115]

Only under proper 'medical advice' could cocaine and its ilk be used for the patient's good – unrestrained, and outside of the practitioner's supervision they could lead only to a 'dim' and 'evil' end. Breakell's solution was to formalize – and, indeed, even to regiment – this supervision in the person of the female doctor. Boards of Health and local authorities might: 'appoint in every township of importance a qualified medical woman Officer of Health ... [moreover], instead of dressing like ordinary folk, might [lady doctors] not wear some quiet, distinctive uniform, that would in time come to carry to the public min a very true and strong conviction of its wearer's proved efficiency and ability in every fold?'[116] Here, the modern and definitively superior female physician is offered as a solution to the modern problem of cocaine and feminine self-medication. The medical woman is, in this vision, institutionalized and sanctioned as a separate, uniformed presence in national life. It is not difficult to equate the distinctive (even faintly ceremonial) garbing of the medical woman with the belief in

---

[114] Mary L. Breakell, 'Women in the Medical Profession', *The Nineteenth Century*, 54.321 (November 1903), 823–4.
[115] Breakell, 'Women in the Medical Profession', 824.
[116] Ibid., 825.

her exceptional status – while the uniform serves as a demonstration of her abilities to the wider public, it also illustrates her distinctiveness, an 'efficiency and ability' that is beyond the average and conveyed 'in every fold' of her 'quiet, distinctive' regalia. Contained in this image, there is the suggestion that one of the great problems of modern medicine – the ready availability of the kind of powerful, addictive drugs of which cocaine was the most emblematic – might be resolvable by empowering the best, most modern part of the profession to repair the damage done by medical science. In these lines, we can see a dual strategy at play: the female practitioner might be rescued from her undeserved marginalization and lifted to a new prominence in national life, and at the same time therapeutic innovation might be redeemed as a restorative force. Thus, 'the public's dwindling faith in the profession'[117] might be revitalized and medical optimism might be once again invigorated by the profession's newest and brightest members.

---

[117] Riddle, 'The Drug Habit', 488.

5

Sherlock Holmes and cocaine in canon and comedy: Profession, pleasure, and the Zany

Sherlock Holmes could claim to surpass even Sigmund Freud as the nineteenth century's most famous taker of cocaine.[1] The second of the Holmes novels, *The Sign of Four* (1890), begins with the detective taking his hypodermic syringe from its trim leather case on the mantelpiece, methodically scanning his arm, and injecting himself with a 7 per cent solution of cocaine. This incident represents Arthur Conan Doyle's only sustained description of Holmes's drug habit, but it was destined to make an impression, nevertheless. For late-nineteenth- and early-twentieth-century fans of the great detective, cocaine seemed as much a part of Holmes's character as the masterful deductions, endless disguises, and the cadences of a Stradivarius violin. In 1902 the *Torquay Times* enthused that: 'Dr. Conan Doyle set the world detective mad with the creation of Mr. Sherlock Holmes, with his passion for violin and hypodermic syringe, his great contempt of Scotland Yard and his wonderful mastery of the mysteries of round, stray pins, and buttonless coats with respect to crime.'[2] Slight as it might seem in comparison with the bulk of the Holmes canon, *The Sign of Four*'s 'mysterious hypodermic needle'[3] was to go on to prick the curiosity of decades-worth of readers. 'There are few ordinary readers who have not made Sherlock Holmes' acquaintance', wrote one reviewer in 1910,

---

[1] As an aside, it is worth noting that – while it has since become a critical commonplace to draw a 'parallel between [Freudian] psychoanalysis and Holmesian methods of detection' (Janice M. Allan and Christopher Pittard, 'Introduction', in *The Cambridge Companion to Sherlock Holmes*, ed. Janice M. Allan and Christopher Pittard (Cambridge: Cambridge University Press, 2019), 5.) – comparisons between the two men, their methods, and their shared consumption of cocaine were made almost as soon as psychoanalysis began to become popularized in the late 1910s. In the words of one analyst in July 1918: 'Behind Sherlock Holmes (the detective) stands Freud (the analyst). They are connected by the cocaine association.' (Alice Johnson, 'Dream-Analysis', *Proceedings of the Society for Psychical Research*, 30 (1920), 99.)
[2] 'Stray Thoughts', *Torquay Times*, 38.1453 (14 March 1902), 8.
[3] 'The Theatres', *Hamilton Daily Times*, 57.251 (23 October 1915), 14.

Sir Arthur Conan Doyle managed to endow his sleuthhound hero very liberally with ... a full share of that reasoning power, that quick perception even of trifles which, of course, all detectives must possess, and to crown it all he managed to surround him with an atmosphere almost uncanny in its effects, making him an inveterate smoker and a devotee to the cocaine habit.[4]

So thoroughly was Holmes ensorcelled with the 'uncanny atmosphere' of cocaine that it was not uncommon to see it suggested that it was through the fictional detective – rather than through real-world medicine – that the public was most likely to make their acquaintance with the drug. In August 1893, while the second series of Sherlock Holmes stories (later republished in volume form in 1894 as *The Memoirs of Sherlock Holmes*) was still underway in the *Strand Magazine*, the *Manchester Evening News* remarked that: 'Many people derive their practical acquaintance with cocaine from the part it plays in the career of the renowned Sherlock Holmes'.[5] The same sentiment was still current two and a half decades later: 'Most people,' according to a 1919 article on 'The Drug Habit', 'first became aware that there was such a thing as the cocaine habit from the pages of "Sherlock Holmes", just as they first learned of the opium habit from De Quincey's "Confessions".[6] Thus, we encounter the curious (possibly even paradoxical) circumstance that the era's 'most popular of paper detectives'[7] was also widely understood to be its foremost cocainist. For many years after the publication of *The Sign of Four*, Holmes dwelt in the collective imagination as – in the words of one 1930 memorial to Arthur Conan Doyle – a man who 'took cocaine before cocaine was fashionable'.[8]

This chapter focusses on the distinctive relationship between Sherlock Holmes and cocaine in the cultural imaginary of the late nineteenth and early twentieth centuries. The conventional critical interpretation of Holmes's cocaine habit is that it demonstrates his 'exotic'[9] sensibilities and 'eccentric, languid Bohemian[ism]'.[10] In relation to *The Sign of Four*, the contention is most often that the detective's blithe cocainism represents a colonial corruption of his body, just as the Agra treasure and the Anglo-Indian returnee Johnathan Small represent a foreign infiltration into the British homeland. The predominant

---

[4] 'Theatre Royal – "The Speckled Band"', *Dublin Daily Express*, 20052 (4 October 1910), 6.
[5] 'The Evening News', *Manchester Evening News*, 7625 (11 August 1893), 2.
[6] 'The Drug Habit', *Aberdeen Press and Journal*, 19989 (24 January 1919), 2.
[7] 'The Literary Week', *The Academy*, 1506 (16 March 1901), 219.
[8] 'Salute to Sherlock Holmes', *Yorkshire Post*, 25892 (11 July 1930), 8.
[9] Yumna Siddiqi, *Anxieties of Empire and the Fiction of Intrigue* (New York: Columbia University Press, 2008), 27.
[10] Russell Miller, *The Adventures of Arthur Conan Doyle* (London: Harvill Secker, 2008), 121.

view, as articulated by Benjamin D. O'Dell, is that the 7 per cent solution effectively dissolves colonial boundaries, that, 'Holmes's injection collapses the distinction between foreign and domestic, dismantling Victorian gentility to illustrate a savage core'.[11] This interpretation tends to rest on a parallel reading of cocaine and opium as similar chemical 'contaminations emanating from alien and primitive lands'.[12] But cocaine – as we have seen from previous chapters – was characterized by its own distinct set of discourses and associations in the late-Victorian popular imagination. Rather than threateningly Orientalized 'primitivism', cocaine signified a highly technologized therapeutic modernity. Such was cocaine's renown as the first successful local anaesthetic that – even after the risks of cocaine addiction and toxicosis began to be more widely known about – the alkaloid was still commonly regarded as coming as near as possible to a 'perfect ideal' among modern drugs.[13] With these associations in mind, then, how do we interpret Holmes's use of cocaine? How are we to respond to the detective's drug use when what we find suspended in the 7 per cent solution is not poisonous exoticism, but scientific ascendancy?

I want to suggest that cocaine is, in reality, intimately bound up with the nature of Holmes's work and operates as a powerful synecdoche for the focussed perfection of Holmes's professional life. At the outset, it is important to note that Sherlock Holmes is not a drug addict, or – to be more specific – Doyle never portrays him as conforming to conventional Victorian discourses of addiction.[14]

[11] Benjamin D. O'Dell, 'Performing the Imperial Abject: The Ethics of Cocaine in Arthur Conan Doyle's The Sign of Four', *Journal of Popular Culture*, 45.5 (2012), 980. Joseph Childers makes the related argument that Holmes's injections of cocaine function like a metaphorical 'vaccine', allowing the detective to inoculate himself against foreign (or Imperial) contamination and safely 'push the limits of Englishness, mov[ing] about the London cesspool with relative immunity'. (Joseph W. Childers, 'Foreign Matter: Imperial Filth', in *Filth: Dirt, Disgust, and Modern Life*, ed. William A. Cohen and Ryan Johnson (Minneapolis: University of Minnesota Press, 2005), 217.) For a further development of the interconnections between Holmes's cocaine, foreignness, and the vaccine metaphor see: Lorenzo Servitje, *Medicine Is War: The Martial Metaphor in Victorian Literature and Culture* (Albany: State University of New York Press, 2021), 161–3.

[12] Lawrence Frank, 'Dreaming the Medusa: Imperialism, Primitivism, and Sexuality in Arthur Conan Doyle's The Sign of Four', *Signs: Journal of Women in Culture and Society*, 22.1 (Autumn 1996), 58. See also Caroline Reitz, 'The Empires of a Study in Scarlet and The Sign of Four', in *The Cambridge Companion to Sherlock Holmes*, 128. Patricia Comitini draws a similar parallel between opium and coca as correspondingly 'fear[ful]' products of 'the Orient and South America'. (Patricia Comitini, 'The Strange Case of Addiction in Robert Louis Stevenson's "Strange Case of Dr. Jekyll and Mr. Hyde"', *Victorian Review*, 38.1 (Spring 2012), 114.)

[13] 'The Operation for Cataract', *Newcastle Weekly Courant*, 11447 (9 June 1894), 5.

[14] Both Douglas Kerr and Susan Zieger touch in brief upon Holmes's non-addiction to cocaine as part of a larger argument that Holmes might be seen as being more substantially addicted to the acquisition of information than he is to the consumption of drugs. As Kerr puts it, '[Holmes's] addiction is to knowledge, and specifically to those strings or sequences of information that constitute a story'. In Zieger's framing, Holmes's hunger for knowledge is indexed by his constant consumption of print literature – his compulsive and constant reading of newspapers, journals, and sensational accounts of crime demonstrating that, for Holmes, 'print proves more potent than cocaine'. See Douglas Kerr, *Conan Doyle: Writing, Profession, and Practice* (Oxford: Oxford University Press, 2013), 144;

Holmes, Watson tells us in 'The Yellow Face' (1893), only makes 'occasional use of cocaine ... and he only turned to the drug as a protest against the monotony of existence when cases were scanty and the papers uninteresting'.[15] Cocaine enlivens and stimulates Holmes's existence but he is not dependent on it; he only resorts to cocaine when deprived of a more fulfilling excitement: his work. For Holmes, cocaine is not a distraction from work but a compensation for the 'monotony' produced by its temporary absence. He cares little for the pleasures that cocaine might offer him on its own account, only taking it to afford him some intellectual 'interest' in lieu of deciphering the apparently insoluble mysteries that are his trade. Strange as it might at first appear, then, cocaine actually illustrates the extent to which Holmes values nothing in his life so highly as his profession. Coldly cerebral, unemotional, and ceaselessly reasoning, the technological associations of cocaine serve as a model for the almost machine-like optimization of Holmes's entire being for his chosen field of industry.

Holmes's character represents a complex synthesis between the apparently opposing poles of work life and drug life. This idea was quickly taken up and reworked by other contemporary writers, but with its moral and ideological emphases provocatively inverted. Over the decades, the richest and most consistent set of responses to Holmes's cocainism were to come from the realm of comedy. In the hands of satirists from the fin de siècle to the First World War and beyond, Holmes's pocket-sized bottle of cocaine was destined to enlarge to ludicrous extremes as legions of mock-detectives began to guzzle the drug by the gallon from buckets, casks, flasks, and bicycle pumps.[16] Taken together, these parodies afford us a rare opportunity to examine the figuration of drug use as a comic trope in this period. In most mainstream Victorian accounts of habituation, the longing for drugs was represented as fundamentally pathological – a 'morbid impulse to intoxication', destined to end with the 'ghastly and horrible' destruction of victim's entire being.[17] In caricaturing Sherlock Holmes's cocaine habit, however, Victorian writers hit upon a less resolutely ghoulish formula: a means – under the veil of comedy – to talk more light-heartedly about the desire

and Susan Zieger, 'Holmes's Pipe, Tobacco Papers and the Nineteenth-century Origins of Media Addiction', *Journal of Victorian Culture*, 19.1 (March 2014), 24.

[15] Arthur Conan Doyle, *The Memoirs of Sherlock Holmes*, ed. Christopher Roden (Oxford: Oxford University Press, 2009), 53.

[16] See, 'Sherlock Holmes Burlesqued at Terry's Theatre', *The Tatler*, 28 (8 January 1902), 72; Peter Todd, 'The Case of the Biscuit-Tin!', *Greyfriars Herald*, 1.2 (27 November 1915), 4; and Peter Todd, 'The Adventure of the Brixton Builder!', *Greyfriars Herald*, 1.9 (15 January 1916), 3.

[17] See: 'The Deliriums of Cocaine', *Lakes Herald*, 802 (8 January 1886), 7; 'The Relation of Alcoholism to Inebriety', *Freeman's Journal*, 121 (5 August 1887), 5; 'The Cocaine Habit', *Sheffield Weekly Telegraph*, 1729 (1 June 1895), 12.

for drugs and the joys of their unrestrained consumption, to toy with the idea that the technological and pharmacological progress of the nineteenth century could be applied to augment and optimize human pleasure as never before. These parodies similarly upend Arthur Conan Doyle's carefully constructed relationship between Holmes and his work. Alongside a delight in cocaine, the many Holmes parodies show the detective exulting in an extravagant ineptitude. While Doyle's Holmes is presented as a fantasy of instinctive and unflagging professional energy, the parody Holmes articulates an equally appealing (though much less respectable) fantasy: that merely pretending to work might lead to just as much practical success as actually working. The parody Holmes is – to use the terminology of cultural theorist Sianne Ngai – a fundamentally 'zany' creation: a comic aesthetic that is essentially (in Ngai's words) 'an aesthetic about work', 'about precariousness', and about the 'ambiguous erosion of the distinction between playing and working'.[18] Pleasure-loving, hyperactive, nakedly avaricious, and perpetually coked-up, this parody Holmes clowns his way through newspapers, cartoons, comic novels, and silent cinema, always seeking out most technologically modern of pleasures, and the most elaborate ways to avoid putting in a hard day's work. Tracing his footprints reveals a surprisingly playful reception of cocaine in the era of Sherlock Holmes.

'My own particular profession': Work and cocaine in the Holmes stories

Cocaine made a remarkable debut on the world's stage in September 1884. For month after month, newspapers and medical journals were full of accounts of the drug and its potential uses. Its effects seemed 'wonderful' and 'profound', sufficient 'within a week's time to raise it from an obscure position in the list of useless alkaloids to an importance and utility hardly exceeded in the materia medica'.[19] In 1885, the *Dublin Journal of Medical Science*'s twice-yearly 'Report on Materia Medica and Therapeutics' concluded that:

> With such a character so suddenly acquired, [cocaine] seems practically to have sprung into existence fully armed for a great amount of future good in the art

---

[18] Sianne Ngai, *Our Aesthetic Categories: Zany, Cute, Interesting* (Cambridge, MA: Harvard University Press, 2012), 188.
[19] Walter G. Smith, 'Report on Materia Medica and Therapeutics', *Dublin Journal of Medical Science*, 79.4 (April 1885), 323.

of medicine. Already it has been applied to many purposes ... [and] it is far too well tried to be classed with the doubtful novelties of the time, or have an uncertain importance in the future.[20]

The *Dublin Journal*'s sense that cocaine had 'sprung into existence fully armed' ascribes something of a divine resonance to the compound – cocaine manifests like a splendid new Athena, bursting from the forehead of Zeus-like nineteenth-century innovation. Cocaine's acute newness (not to say sacralization) and status as the medical–technological à la mode of the 1880s and 1890s gives us important background for understanding its inclusion in *The Sign of Four*. The first lines of the novel run:

> Sherlock Holmes took his bottle from the corner of the mantelpiece and his hypodermic syringe from its neat morocco case. With his long, white, nervous fingers he adjusted the delicate needle, and rolled back his left shirt-cuff. For some little time his eyes rested thoughtfully upon the sinewy forearm and wrist all dotted and scarred with innumerable puncture-marks. Finally, he thrust the sharp point home, pressed down the tiny piston, and sank back into the velvet-lined arm-chair with a long sigh of satisfaction.[21]

The overarching tenor of this passage is one of precise, rational detachment, the narration's most distinct feature being its simplicity and matter-of-factness. Concurrently, the unflinching clarity of Doyle's prose intensifies the passage's apparent preoccupation with physical vulnerability and frailness. Holmes's fingers are 'nervous' and the needle 'delicate': words which evoke not only his activeness of spirit but also the sensitivity of his flesh and the brittleness of the needle, the potential for material breakage and bodily pain. The 'sinewy' arm is 'dotted and scarred' with enduring indications of physical damage, and its eventual 'puncturing' reiterates the narration's mixture of the coldly precise and the tactile. At the moment of injection, the syringe becomes a 'tiny piston', removing the act from the context of sensory gratification and converting it into a mechanical and hydrodynamic process. Throughout, Holmes is distant and thoughtful, ignoring his damaged skin and looking only for a place to press home the needle. As a depiction of drug use, this description is at once bland but also uncomfortable – irritating but impassive. Holmes's consumption of cocaine is framed as mechanistic and unromantic rather than sensual or anticipatory. From the beginning, Holmes's encounters with cocaine look less

---

[20] Ibid., 323–4.
[21] Arthur Conan Doyle, *The Sign of Four*, ed. Peter Ackroyd and Ed Glinert (London: Penguin, 2001), 5.

like the dissipation of the voluptuary and more like the meticulousness of the technician.

It is not long before we are given a more complete explanation for these events. Watson – irked by his friend's deliberation and by his own sense of medical responsibility – confronts Holmes with the risks of his habit. He warns the detective that cocaine's effect on the brain is a 'morbid process which involves increased tissue change, and may at least leave a permanent weakness'. He directly asks Holmes: 'Why should you, for a mere passing pleasure, risk the loss of those great powers with which you have been endowed?'[22] Watson's assumption that Holmes is interested in 'mere pleasure' is a natural one, but Doyle has Watson articulate this interpretation specifically so that Holmes can rebuff it.[23] The detective counters that:

> I suppose that its influence is physically a bad one. I find it, however, so transcendently stimulating and clarifying to the mind that its secondary action is a matter of small moment. ... My mind rebels at stagnation. Give me problems, give me work, give me the most abstruse cryptogram or the most intricate analysis, and I am in my own proper atmosphere. I can dispense then with artificial stimulants. But I abhor the dull routine of existence. I crave for mental exaltation. That is why I have chosen my own particular profession, or rather created it, for I am the only one in the world.[24]

The Sign of Four emphasizes that what Holmes demands is not pleasure but mental excitation. Just as Doyle's description of the initial injection is intellectual and detached, instead of dissipatedly pleasurable, the appeal that the drug has for Holmes is shown to be primarily a cerebral one; his passions are passions of rationality and the drug 'clarifies' the rational mind. Critically, the drug is positioned as a mere substitute, an 'artificial' and inferior replacement for his most emphatic passion: the business of detection. We can easily observe how rapidly Holmes's explanation of his drug habit segues into a discussion of the nature of his work. Holmes affirms that he takes cocaine for the same reason that he has chosen his profession: both activities fundamentally satisfy his needs – which are not the needs of appetite but the needs of intellectual exertion.

---

[22] Doyle, *Sign of Four*, 6.
[23] Douglas Kerr suggests that this kind of frequently recurring structure – Watson's initial (incorrect) hypothesis followed by Holmes's correction and clarification of it – is 'paradigmatic' of the underlying 'epistemological hierarchy' of the Holmes stories: 'Some data are presented. Watson offers a tentative epitome. Holmes supplements and corrects Watson's account with a definitive statement of the case. ... Watson knows something, but Holmes knows more, as he always does.' (See Kerr, *Conan Doyle: Writing, Profession, and Practice*, 41.)
[24] Doyle, *Sign of Four*, 6.

Indeed, Holmes's intelligence is so potent a force that it threatens to overflow the bodily vessel containing it. While Watson cautions his friend against the 'pathological' consequences of cocainism, Holmes's attitude is that the 'mental exaltation' it brings is so 'transcendentally stimulating' that nothing else matters.[25] This is not the hedonistic disregard of the addict, but something more complex. Holmes is unmoved by the condition of his body so long as his brain is energized. Counterintuitive as it may seem, Holmes's cocaine habit actually indicates the depths of his indifference to physical pleasure, and his preference for the delights of the mind. As the first chapter of *The Sign of Four* draws to a close, Watson and Holmes helpfully summarize the conclusions of their dialogue on cocaine and the profession of the consulting detective. 'May I,' says Watson, 'ask whether you have any professional inquiry on foot at present?' To which the detective replies: 'None. Hence the cocaine. I cannot live without brain-work. What else is there to live for?'[26] In the years prior to the publication of *The Sign of Four*, cocaine had appeared to index a highly rarefied – even celestial – type of intellectual triumph. Holmes's 7 per cent solution acts similarly as a means by which to depict Holmes as a sort of stylite of the intellect, a man devoted only to the business of work and to the work of the mind. Cocaine illustrates Holmes's specific blend of totalizing cognition and total commitment to work.

Contemporary reviews of *The Sign of Four* were largely unphased by its hero's casual cocainism. Those critics who drew attention to the drug appear to have taken their cue from the detective's own explanations, and been intrigued by the notion that Holmes's proclivity for cocaine really signified his passion for work.[27] *The Saturday Review* remarked: 'Mr Holmes shows forth all the gifts of his calling in high perfection. He never sleeps when he has a case on hand … and he subjects his nerves to [cocaine] when he has no appalling mystery to unravel.'[28] Sherlock Holmes's commitment to detection also underpinned the review in the *Graphic*, which observed that Doyle's hero 'must be either engaged in unravelling a first-class mystery, or in consoling himself for the want of one with cocaine.'[29] *The Morning Post* went a step further and illustrated

---

[25] Ibid.
[26] Ibid., 12.
[27] For a cross section of contemporary reviews of *The Sign of Four*, see: 'New Novels', *The Scotsman*, 14763 (27 October 1890), 3; 'Novels', *The Saturday Review of Politics, Literature, Science and Art*, 70.1827 (1 November 1890), 512; 'Novels of the Week', *The Athenaeum*, 3293 (6 December 1890), 773; 'New Novels', *The Academy*, 971 (13 December 1890), 561; 'A Batch of Novels', *The Liverpool Mercury*, 13405 (24 December 1890), 7; 'New Novels', *The Graphic*, 1106 (7 February 1891), 150; and 'The Sign of Four', *The Morning Post*, 37029 (18 February 1891), 4.
[28] 'Novels', *The Saturday Review of Politics, Literature, Science and Art*, 70.1827 (1 November 1890), 512.
[29] 'New Novels', *The Graphic*, 1106 (7 February 1891), 150.

the point not only by referring its readers to the detective's cocaine use but also to his 'monographs upon such subjects as "The Distinction between the Ashes of the Various Tobaccos"'.[30] The idea that cocaine dramatized Holmes's professional excellence and expertise was, then, broadly accepted by the book's initial reviewers. The first readers of *The Sign of Four* seem to have recognized a fundamental distinction between the configuration of Holmes's cocainism and other more conventional narratives of inebriety: while the run-of-the-mill drunkard or drug-taker was traditionally imagined to forsake productive work for selfish pleasure, Holmes would clearly choose to do nothing but work if he could. Cocaine 'consol[es]' and fortifies Holmes during those intervals of 'scanty cases' when he is denied the professional exertion and 'brain-work' that he desires above all else.[31] In this sense, Holmes's employment of cocaine conforms to the 'non-addictive', and 'instrumentalised' pattern of drug use articulated by Gunter Schumann and Christian Müller.[32] Rather than being a pleasurable diversion, cocaine functions as a mechanism by which Holmes can manage the abrupt and demanding 'transition[s] from professional to private behaviour[s]' that his work necessitates.[33] For Holmes, cocaine is as much a professional tool as his 'magnifying lens' and the 'formidable array of bottles and test-tubes' that crowd the Baker Street sitting room.[34]

Cocaine and the 'calculating machine'

The first chapter of *The Sign of Four* makes at least one direct attempt to contrast Holmes's cocaine injections with another, more pitifully familiar, pattern of intoxication. Watson, hoping to put his friend's observational abilities to an 'impossible' test, presents him with a watch owned by Watson's late brother and asks him to read the 'character and habits' of its former owner. Under Holmes's keen analysis, one particularly fatal habit stands out: Watson's brother has taken to drink, and at length died of his drunkenness. At first glance, we might assume that Watson's 'unhappy brother' is intended as a warning example of Holmes's future. The elder Watson brother remains largely anonymous in the novel, though he is

---

[30] 'The Sign of Four', *The Morning Post*, 37029 (18 February 1891), 4.
[31] 'New Novels', *The Graphic*, 150; Doyle, *The Memoirs of Sherlock Holmes*, 53; Doyle, *Sign of Four*, 12.
[32] Christian P. Müller and Gunter Schumann, 'Drugs As Instruments: A New Framework for Non-Addictive Psychoactive Drug Use', *Behavioural and Brain Sciences*, 34.6 (December 2011), 295.
[33] Ibid., 298.
[34] Arthur Conan Doyle, *The Adventures of Sherlock Holmes*, ed. Richard Lancelyn Green (Oxford: Oxford University Press, 2008), 43–4.

identified – and connected to Holmes – by the suggestive initial 'H' imprinted on the back of the watch. But there are more differences than similarities between the two identically initialled, substance-using men in Watson's life. Watson's brother's watch is permanently defaced by its owner's 'careless' actions – it is 'cut and marked all over' by H's 'cavalier' treatment. Sherlock invites Watson to: 'Look at the thousands of scratches all round the hole – marks where the key has slipped. What sober man's key could have scored those grooves? But you will never see a drunkard's watch without them. He winds it at night, and he leaves these traces of his unsteady hand.'[35] The 'thousands of scratches' inflicted on the watch casing by its ebrious owner replicate the 'innumerable' dots and scars left on Holmes's skin by hypodermic injections. These superficially similar marks of habituation are very differently characterized, however. We are repeatedly and insistently told that Watson's brother was a thoroughly careless man: 'A man,' as Holmes deduces, 'of untidy habits – very untidy and careless.'[36] Where Watson's brother 'slip[s]' and fumbles his watch key with an 'unsteady hand', Holmes manipulates his syringe 'thoughtfully', minutely adjusting it with 'extreme deliberation'.[37] Holmes's cocainism is not only closely associated with rational intelligence, but with a meticulous exactitude and self-control.

In some ways, similarly 'marked' as they are, Holmes appears to have a closer and more substantial kinship with the machinery of the watch than he does with the human failings of its owner. This is the first indication in the novel of a related cluster of ideas that Doyle goes on to more fully enclose around Sherlock's cocaine habit. In the second chapter of *The Sign of Four*, we are introduced to Holmes's client and Watson's eventual fiancé, Miss Mary Morstan. Watson is immediately taken with her and remarks as much to Holmes:

> 'What a very attractive woman!' I exclaimed, turning to my companion.
>
> He had lit his pipe again, and was leaning back with drooping eyelids. 'Is she?' he said languidly; 'I did not observe'.
>
> 'You really are an automaton – a calculating machine', I cried. 'There is something positively inhuman in you at times'.[38]

The opening of *The Sign of Four* uses Sherlock Holmes's cocaine habit to clearly establish his preference for professional exertion over physical pleasure. In these lines this concept is elaborated and extended: Holmes's claim that he has not

---

[35] Doyle, *Sign of Four*, 10–12.
[36] Ibid., 10.
[37] Ibid., 5.
[38] Ibid., 17.

observed Miss Morstan's attractiveness suggests his wider indifference to any prospect of erotic, domestic, or even emotional gratification (or at least his ability to expel such factors from his mind because of their irrelevance to his immediate enquiry).[39] Holmes so vehemently declares that 'the emotional qualities are antagonistic to clear reasoning' that Watson suspects his friend of having a wholly computational nature. These mechanical and 'inhuman' associations return at the end of the novel. When Watson informs Holmes of his engagement, the detective reacts dismally to the news: 'I really cannot congratulate you ... love is an emotional thing, and whatever is emotional is opposed to that true cold reason which I place above all things. I should never marry, myself, lest I bias my judgement.'[40] The novel concludes with Watson's amused observation:

> 'You have done all the work in this business. I get a wife out of it ... pray what remains for you?'
>
> 'For me', said Sherlock Holmes, 'there still remains the cocaine bottle'. And he stretched his long white hand up for it.[41]

Sherlock's immediate return to cocaine at the end of the investigation reiterates his disdain for anything outside the boundaries of his working life – particularly for the feminine realms of marriage and emotional intimacy. Cocaine explicitly dramatizes Doyle's description of his protagonist (from an interview with *The Bookman* in 1892) as: 'utterly inhuman, no heart, but with a beautifully logical intellect'.[42]

The overtly technological associations of cocaine were likewise uniquely appropriate to support the image of Holmes as a perfectly calibrated detecting machine. It took very little time after its introduction into medical practice for the uses of cocaine to become 'almost indefinitely multiplied'.[43] Medical journals observed that: 'Many practitioners are inclined to smile at new remedies ... [but] the new anæsthetic cocaine should teach a lesson to the sceptics'. Such were the drug's incredible effects that it seemed assured of a lasting place in the nineteenth century's medical–technological pantheon: 'since the introduction of chloroform into surgical practice, there is no discovery which equals in importance the effects which are found to follow the use of this new preparation'.[44] Holmes's

---

[39] See Kerr, *Conan Doyle*, 44.
[40] Doyle, *Sign of Four*, 117.
[41] Ibid., 118.
[42] Raymond Blathwayt, 'A Talk with Dr. Conan Doyle', *The Bookman*, 2.8 (May 1892), 50.
[43] Walter G. Smith, 'Report on Materia Medica and Therapeutics', *Dublin Journal of Medical Science*, 84.6 (December 1887), 507.
[44] 'A New Anaesthetic', *Chambers's Journal*, 2.61 (28 February 1885), 144.

preferred mode of administration is another important factor. While not as new an invention as cocaine, by the end of the century the hypodermic syringe was still regarded as an almost 'magical'[45] device, a modern contrivance 'in the same technological echelon as gaslight and the railway'.[46] In this way, Sherlock's repeated injections of cocaine signify a rigorously mechanistic quotient in his personality – one which is carried to such an extent that human passions serve only to occlude his apparatuses of deduction and analysis.

These three concepts – Holmes's disregard for physical or emotional enjoyment (metonymically conveyed via his indifference to women), his use of cocaine, and his resemblance to a thinking machine – all recur in even closer proximity in the introduction to *The Sign of Four*'s sequel story, 'A Scandal in Bohemia' (1891). Watson begins the story by comparing his own romantic contentment with Holmes's unfailingly dispassionate outlook: 'All emotions, and [love] particularly, were abhorrent to his cold, precise but admirably balanced mind. He was, I take it, the most perfect reasoning and observing machine that the world has seen.' While Watson delights in his newly married life of 'complete happiness, and home-centred interests', Holmes has elected to 'remain in our lodgings in Baker Street, buried among his old books, and alternating from week to week between cocaine and ambition'.[47] The main points of this introduction – recycled and condensed from *The Sign of Four* as they are – seem to have appealed to Doyle as an essential outline of Holmes's personality. Holmes's professionally orientated life of 'cocaine and ambition' is explicitly juxtaposed with Watson's marriage and 'home-centred' enjoyments. Emotion, Watson imagines, would only effect Holmes like 'grit in a sensitive instrument, or a crack in one of his own high-power lenses'[48] – a comparison which suggests that Sherlock is best understood as another such 'instrument' of detection himself, though infinitely more elaborate and finely attuned than any microscope. Throughout the Holmes stories, the 7 per cent solution of cocaine – the most celebratedly technological of modern drugs – serves to condense both Holmes's magisterial devotion to his work and his automaton-like specialization to perform that work. For contemporary readers, the detective simultaneously appeared to be 'the Newton of detectives' and a 'bloodless ... cocaine driven machine'.[49] Sublimely focussed

---

[45] 'Recent Advances in Surgery and Medicine', *The Edinburgh Review*, 168.344 (October 1888), 514.
[46] Susan Zieger, *Inventing the Addict: Drugs, Race, and Sexuality in Nineteenth-Century British and American Literature* (Amherst: University of Massachusetts Press, 2008), 143.
[47] Doyle, *The Adventures of Sherlock Holmes*, 5.
[48] Ibid.
[49] 'A Medico-Literary Causerie: Our Medical Novelist', *The Practitioner: A Journal of Practical Medicine*, 55 (November 1895), 475; 'Mr Sherlock Holmes at Home', *Bournemouth Graphic*, 15.479 (19 May 1911), 9.

and mechanically optimized, Holmes takes on a markedly cybernetic aspect in these early stories, acquiring the semblance of a 'beautifully logical' engine attuned to the execution of his 'own particular profession'.[50]

Evading addiction

The twenty-four Sherlock Holmes stories published in the *Strand Magazine* between June 1891 and December 1893, had the double effect of making their hero 'a household name' and of initiating 'one of the most mutually profitable relationships between author and publisher in literary history'.[51] When, in the summer of 1893, the comic writer Israel Zangwill heard an early rumour that Doyle intended to kill off Holmes before the end of the year, he was confident in predicting that the detective was already far too famous to be easily done away with. Dr Doyle might, 'like Frankenstein', ruminate upon his creature's destruction as much as he liked. 'But,' wrote Zangwill, 'I doubt his ability to kill him … the violin-playing, cocaine-bitten genius has been definitely added to the gallery of fiction.'[52] Zangwill was ultimately proved correct. After pitching Holmes over the Reichenbach Falls in 'The Final Problem' in December 1893, Doyle was persuaded (thanks to the 'astronomical sum of $45,000 promised by the US magazine *Collier's Weekly*'[53]) to fish him out again a decade later in 1903s 'The Empty House'. Despite its obvious financial and popular success, however, Holmes's resurrection brought with it one potentially troubling question: raised from death, returned to Baker Street, to Watson, Mrs Hudson, and to his beloved investigations, was the 'cocaine-bitten genius' also destined to return to his 7 per cent solution?

The years that Holmes spent interred beneath the waters of the Reichenbach saw a subtle but important reconfiguration of the discourses surrounding cocaine. While the drug was still widely perceived as a technological miracle and as an essential part of modern therapeutics, this was balanced against a more widespread sense of the dangers associated with its unrestrained consumption. Thus, by the late 1890s and early 1900s, popular discussions of Holmes's cocainism increasingly began to pivot towards asking whether or not such a

---

[50] Blathwayt, 'A Talk with Dr. Conan Doyle', *Bookman*, 50; Doyle, *Sign of Four*, 6.
[51] See Clare Clarke, 'Doyle, Holmes and Victorian Publishing', in *The Cambridge Companion to Sherlock Holmes*, 35–8 for more details on the publishing success of the early Holmes stories.
[52] Israel Zangwill, 'Without Prejudice', *Pall Mall Magazine*, 1.2 (June 1893), 268.
[53] Clarke, 'Doyle, Holmes and Victorian Publishing', 38.

potentially 'insidious' habit was really appropriate for a character who occupied such 'a high position among the heroes of fiction'.⁵⁴ One particularly striking incident was reported by *The Academy* in March 1901. Dr John Wyllie, professor of clinical medicine at Doyle's alma mater, the University of Edinburgh Medical School, described in one of his lectures how:

> He was called one day to see a young man. As he was entering the house the patient's sister exclaimed: 'Oh, it's all that horrid book!' Inquiry elicited the fact that the patient's favourite reading was *Sherlock Holmes*. The young man was in a very low state, and his tell-tale arm was dotted with hypodermic punctures. His admiration for the most popular of paper detectives had betrayed him into the cocaine habit. Taking this case as text, Dr. Wyllie permitted himself a sentence or two of severe stricture on Dr. Conan Doyle's knowledge of the action of drugs: 'If such a man as Sherlock Holmes had existed, dosing himself as depicted by his creator, in a few weeks his opinion on anything would not have been worth having'.⁵⁵

The report was picked up a week later by the *British Medical Journal* which implied that – like Thomas DeQuincy before him – Arthur Conan Doyle might have 'much to answer for' by encouraging the casual taking of dangerous drugs.⁵⁶ The *Quarterly Review*, by contrast, took a more light-hearted swipe at both Sherlock's cocaine habit and the repetitiveness of Doyle's plots:

> The adventures of Sherlock are too brief to permit much study of character. The thing becomes a formula, and we can imagine little variation, unless Sherlock falls in love, or Watson detects him in blackmailing a bishop. This moral error might plausibly be set down to that over-indulgence in cocaine which never interferes with Sherlock's physical training or intellectual acuteness.⁵⁷

For all their differences in tone, these sources put their finger on the same idiosyncrasy in Holmes's character, the same issue that contemporary readers now had to navigate in understanding the great detective's relationship with cocaine: despite 'dosing' himself prolifically, Holmes remained oddly invulnerable to the expected hazards of cocainism. However much he might 'over-indulge' the detective seemed never to decline from his regular pitch of 'physical ... [and] intellectual acuteness'.

---

[54] 'Proposed Additions to the Poisons Schedule'. *Lancet*, 165.4259 (15 April 1905), 1013.
[55] 'The Literary Week', *The Academy*, 1506 (16 March 1901), 219.
[56] 'Literary Notes', *BMJ*, 1.2099 (23 March 1901), 733. See also: 'The Literary Lounger', *The Sketch*, 429 (17 April 1901), 518, for another description of this incident.
[57] 'The Novels of Sir Arthur Conan Doyle', *Quarterly Review*, 200.399 (Jul 1904), 176.

The month after the *Quarterly Review*'s article appeared, Doyle made an effort to resolve this problem. 'The Missing Three Quarter' (1904) begins with Holmes experiencing a fallow period for cases, a circumstance which greatly alarms Watson:

> I had learned to dread such periods of inaction, for I knew by experience that my companion's brain was so abnormally active that it was dangerous to leave it without material upon which to work. For years I had gradually weaned him from that drug mania which had threatened once to check his remarkable career. Now I knew that under ordinary conditions he no longer craved for this artificial stimulus, but I was well aware that the fiend was not dead, but sleeping; and I have known that the sleep was a light one and the waking near when in periods of idleness.[58]

On the surface this passage seems to fairly straightforwardly amend the presentation of Holmes's drug habit from *The Sign of Four*. Cocaine is here presented as a 'mania' and a 'fiend'. Cocainism has apparently led Holmes into a perdition from which Watson has only gradually delivered him after years of difficult work. On closer inspection, though, this passage reads less like a full revision of the opening of *Sign* and more like a partial reweighting of it. Holmes's 'drug-mania' is a curiously equivocal kind of addiction. As readers, we never witness it directly: it happens at some indeterminate point in the past and is over-and-done-with by the time we ever hear of it. By the same token, it seems to have no particularly definite long-term (or even short-term) consequences. All we know is that it 'threatened once to check [Holmes's] remarkable career' – a description that underscores the vagueness and transitoriness of cocaine's effects upon the detective; whatever debility cocaine might 'once' have inflicted on Holmes's body, his business, or his character is left up to the reader's imagination and confined definitively to the past. Most importantly, this description firmly reasserts that Holmes's craving for cocaine is wholly contingent upon his work; cocaine is still but an 'artificial simulant', a synthetic replacement for the cerebral exertions of detection. Holmes, then, remains more dependably professional than dependent on drugs. For all Watson's protestations, the 'fiend' would appear to be really quite soundly asleep after all, and to be almost entirely a bedevilment of the past.

A similar strain of evasiveness can be seen in those fin de siècle adaptations and pastiches that delt with Holmes and cocaine. Like Doyle himself in

---

[58] Arthur Conan Doyle, 'The Adventure of the Missing Three-Quarter', *Strand Magazine*, 28.164 (August 1904), 123.

'The Missing Three Quarter', these works often visibly struggle with the awkwardness of simultaneously acknowledging the risk of cocaine addiction, while also being reluctant to actually show Holmes suffering any of its mental or physical effects. The second act of William Gillette's 1899 play *Sherlock Holmes* (which loosely adapts and combines various elements of Doyle's works into an original narrative) once again reworks the iconic opening scene of *The Sign of Four*; once again (as shown in the play's publicity photographs) Holmes meditatively injects himself with his 7 per cent solution while Watson looks on disapprovingly (see Figure 5.1)

The play's Watson is, however, much more obviously concerned with the risk of addiction than his book counterpart. Likewise, Gillette's Holmes is more disdainfully fatalistic:

Watson: (*Goes to table, resting hand on upper corner looking at* **Holmes** *seriously.*) Holmes, for months I have seen you use these deadly drugs – in ever-increasing doses. When they lay hold of you there is no end! It must go on, and on, and on – until the finish! … These are poisons – slow but certain. They involve tissue changes of a most serious nature.

Holmes: Just what I want! I'm bored to death with my present tissues, and I'm trying to get a brand-new lot!

Watson: (*going near* **Holmes**) Ah, Holmes – I am trying to save you! (*Puts hand on* **Holmes's** *shoulder.*)

Holmes: (*Earnest an instant; places hand on* **Watson's** *arm.*) You can't do it, old fellow – so don't waste your time.[59]

Much as Watson and Holmes might pronounce on the inevitability of cocaine addiction and self-destruction, the action of the play conspires to keep any tangible symptoms of cocainism resolutely off-stage. According to this dialogue, Holmes must – if he persists in taking the drug – slowly but certainly become an addict, but he is not addicted *right now*. Cocaine addiction may be a terrible danger, but it is a prospective danger of the future, never realized in the time frame of the play itself. And, indeed, by the drama's end, Holmes seems certain to have evaded the threat altogether: the arrival of Alice Faulkner, the one woman whom Holmes loves and longs to marry, apparently prompts him to give up the delights of cocaine in favour of the joys of wedded life.

---

[59] William Gillette, 'Sherlock Holmes: A Drama in Four Acts', in *Plays by William Hooker Gillette*, ed. Rosemary Cullen and Don B. Wilmeth (Cambridge: Cambridge University Press, 2008), 226–7.

Figure 5.1 Holmes (played by William Gillette) injects himself with cocaine, 1900.

A similar intervention occurs in the *English Illustrated Magazine*'s Anthony Jones stories. Claiming to be both written and narrated by 'Inspector Hyram Vedder of the New York Detective Service', this pair of stories appeared in the magazine in October 1894 and August 1895 (during the period of Holmes's 'death' at the hands of Professor Moriarty) and chronicle Vedder's encounters with a brilliant, mysterious amateur detective named Anthony Jones. Throughout the first story, 'Mr Anthony Jones of New York', Vedder comes to believe that Jones is, in fact, heavily disguised and using a fake name. The story ends with him wondering: 'WAS SHERLOCK HOLMES REALLY KILLED, or had he his OWN MOTIVES FOR DISAPPEARING? ... Can my amateur, who evinces such an extraordinary power of reasoning by deductive process, and such unparalleled sagacity in following up the criminal trail, be Sherlock Holmes in disguise?'[60] The mystery of Jones's identity is never fully answered, and he remains an ambiguous entity. Contemporary reviews referred to him as both 'something resembling the ghost of Sherlock Holmes' and 'a sort of resurrection' of him.[61] The publication of Vedder's stories led some journalists to speculate whether the author was really Arthur Conan Doyle himself operating under a false name, for, as *Lloyd's List* put it: 'if "Hyram Vedder" be not synonymous with Conan Doyle, this writer is the possessor of, to put it pleasantly, considerable enterprise'.[62] Whether or not Anthony Jones is truly Sherlock Holmes in disguise (the character's name may well be intended to recall 'Athelney Jones', the blusterous Scotland Yard detective from *The Sign of Four*), he retains the original Holmes's penchant for cocaine. Visiting the detective in his 'luxurious' Madison Avenue flat, Vedder finds his acquaintance sipping the drug in the form of 'a clear yellow liquor' from 'a flat crystal flask, silver-topped'. Here again, the narrative visibly struggles with how precisely to engage with the issue of addiction. Jones asks his visitor: 'You have never tried cocaine? No? The better for you then! It grows upon a man –.'[63] Jones abruptly breaks off as Vedder interrupts with a question about their detective work, and we never learn exactly how (or to what degree) the cocaine habit has 'grow[n]' upon him.

Across all these various realizations of Holmes's character – Doyle's own stories, Gillette's stage adaptation, and Vedder's mysterious 'ghost'[64] – we see gestures towards the question of addiction, but little willingness to concretely engage with it. Enslavement to the drug is given lip service as a possibility, but it never arrives in the present tense of the story; Holmes's addiction to cocaine is constantly parried, interrupted, deflected into an uncertain future or into a

---

[60] Hyram Vedder, 'Mr Anthony Jones of New York', *English Illustrated Magazine*, 133 (October 1894), 28.
[61] 'Reviews', *Salisbury and Winchester Journal*, 29 September 1894, 3; 'August Magazines', *Oxford Times*, 1717 (27 July 1895), 6.
[62] 'The English Illustrated Magazine', *Lloyd's List*, 17807 (27 September 1894), 12. For a similar speculation see: *London Daily News*, 15123 (19 September 1894), 6.
[63] Hyram Vedder, 'Mr Swagg of London', *English Illustrated Magazine*, 143 (August 1895), 451.
[64] 'Reviews', *Salisbury and Winchester Journal*, 6.

non-specific past. We never directly witness Holmes's body being ravaged or abjected by cocaine. Equally, we never see him struggle with the pains of recovery or withdrawal. He retains the 'cool, nonchalant air' and 'masterly manner' that he enjoys at the very start of *The Sign of Four*.[65] To quote Susan Zieger: 'Traditionally, nineteenth-century narratives about habitual drunkenness and inebriety ended in the protagonist's death or, less frequently, recovery.'[66] Holmes, however, represents a potentially tantalizing departure from this conception. Holmes's cocaine habit is characterized neither by moral degradation nor by physical ruin. Throughout the late nineteenth and early twentieth centuries, Sherlock is surprisingly consistently represented as a drug-taker who can never become an addict: a consumer impervious to the ill-effects of consumption. To comic writers – who were less constrained by the moral seriousness of mainstream addiction discourse – this was an idea with powerful attractions. Again and again in this period, we encounter comic authors who, in place of meeting the detective's drug habit with contemptuous derision and moralizing, instead found themselves irresistibly drawn in by Holmes's potential for energetic hedonism.

Posthuman pleasures

Even in *The Sign of Four* itself, Holmes manages to put away a not inconsiderable quantity of cocaine. Watson claims to have watched his friend inject himself 'three times a day for many months' (possibly varying his regular 7 per cent solution with occasional doses of morphine), and even before the end of their conversation, Holmes is contemplating taking 'a second dose of cocaine'.[67] The many Sherlock Holmes parodies that appeared over the following decades convert these markers of Holmes's professional industriousness into the thrill of eagerly self-indulgent consumption. Doyle's Holmes demands nothing more from life than that it should 'give me problems, give me work'.[68] His caricatures, by contrast, encode the jaunty seductiveness of a life lived on an unashamed and perpetual bender. When, for example, in the pages of the *Greyfriars Herald*, 'Inspector Pinkeye of Scotland Yard' comes to call on 'Herlock Sholmes', he can confidently expect the generous offer to: 'Take a cigarette, my dear Pinkeye, and a gallon of cocaine.'[69] In 'The

---

[65] Doyle, *Sign of Four*, 5.
[66] Zieger, *Inventing the Addict*, 201.
[67] Doyle, *Sign of Four*, 5.
[68] Ibid., 6.
[69] Peter Todd, 'The Case of the Biscuit-Tin!', *Greyfriars Herald*, 1.2 (27 November 1915), 3–4.

Duke's Feather' (1893) – the second of *Punch*'s 'Adventures of Picklock Holes' stories – the hero requests nothing except an exquisitely bejewelled hypodermic, 'a richly-chased little gold instrument, tipped with a ruby', as a reward for his professional services to the Tzar of Russia.[70] The mystery of the missing golf balls from 'Sherlock Holmes Satirised' (1905) begins with the great detective amusing himself while waiting for his client: 'Slitting open his left forearm with a razor, Holmes was about to inject a bicycle pumpful of cocaine when the light of battle gleamed in his eyes and caused the cat to think dawn had come. "Someone is coming upstairs, Watson", he said.'[71] The image of Holmes taking his drug of choice by bicycle pump and bucketful also appears in *Sheerluck Jones; Or, Why d'Gillette Him Off?*, a 1902 burlesque of William Gillette's stage play (see Figure 5.2).[72] Twenty years later, the joke was still going strong. In 1923 in *The Yale Record*, 'the great Sherlock Holmes' appears laboriously crawling across the floor, eyes fixed on his magnifying glass, and 'closely followed by Watson, bearing a hypodermic syringe and a bucket of cocaine' (see Figure 5.3).[73]

While these parodies fairly straightforwardly express the joys of uninhibited consumption, they also gesture towards the possibility of even more audacious pleasures, transforming Holmes's professionally orientated existence into one of louche and irresponsible appetite. In 1915's 'The Mystery of the Orange Pips', for example, 'Sherlaw Kolmes' only agrees to 'go out and find a mystery' so that 'Dr Whatson' will stop 'nagging [him] about [his] cocaine habit'.[74] (Whatson's complaints turn on the particular issue that Kolmes's drug money could, in the doctor's opinion, be much better used to upgrade their breakfast kippers to Dover sole.) Where the authentic Holmes's life was devoted entirely to work, the many Sherlaw Kolmes, Herlock Sholmes, and Sheerluck Joneses that followed him exhibit a similarly totalizing relationship with pleasure. Just as Sherlock's 7 per cent solution was satirically enlarged – first to 'seventy per cent' and then to 'seven-hundred-per cent'[75] – so too did Holmes's patterns of consumption expand to ever more colossal proportions until his entire existence seemed to be subordinated to enjoyment.

We have already witnessed the extent to which Holmes's working life is so diligent and technologically supplemented as to make him into a somewhat

---

[70] Cunnin Toil, 'The Duke's Feather', *Punch*, 105 (19 August 1893), 76.
[71] 'Sherlock Holmes Satirised', *Wellington Journal and Shrewsbury News*, 2612 (4 March 1905), 3.
[72] 'Sherlock Holmes Burlesqued at Terry's Theatre', *The Tatler*, 28 (8 January 1902), 76.
[73] W.B.K., 'When Detectives Disagree', *The Yale Record*, 51.12 (11 April 1923), 595.
[74] N.K., 'The Mystery of the Orange Pips', *Sporting Times*, 2697 (29 May 1915), 18.
[75] See 'Sherlock Holmes Americanised', *Hartlepool Northern Daily Mail*, 5274 (11 May 1895), 3; and Peter Todd, 'The Adventure of the Brixton Builder!', *Greyfriars Herald*, 1.9 (15 January 1916), 3.

SHEERLUCK INJECTS COCAINE

Figure 5.2 Sheerluck Jones (played by Clarence Blakiston) parodies Holmes's cocaine habit, 1902.

cybernetic figure. Watson's account of him from 'A Scandal in Bohemia' compares him to 'a sensitive instrument' or a 'high-power lens' focussed solely on the business of detection.[76] But what if that lens were trained, instead, on the art of pleasure? This unspoken question lies behind many of the parodies that

---

[76] Doyle, *The Adventures of Sherlock Holmes*, 5.

Figure 5.3 Dr Watson faithfully dogs Sherlock Holmes with syringe at the ready. Peter Arno, 1923.

followed in the wake of Doyle's original creation. What might be the result if a being such as Holmes – genius, technologically augmented, and apparently immune to the damaging effects of addiction – were to devote themselves to such a seemingly superficial and comical objective as self-indulgence? The parodic framing affords these works the licence to speculate as to the kind of byzantine pharmacological amusements that might be possible for an individual more akin to 'a machine rather than a man'.[77] Such images of elaborately technologized pleasure can be seen in, for example, the *Yale Record*'s 'Sherlock's "At Homes"' series. At the beginning of 'The Dreihoff Poisoning Case' (1899),

---

[77] Doyle, *The Memoirs of Sherlock Holmes*, 157.

Dr Batson finds his friend: 'seated before the fire in his favourite rocker, taking laudanum through a straw, while a simple device, operated by the motion of the chair injected morphine into this arm as he rocked'. The case ends similarly, with Sherlock having 'mixed himself a cock-tail of laudanum and cocaine, and dropped in it reflectively an opium cherry'.[78] While parodying *The Sign of Four*'s structure of beginning and ending with Holmes's drug use, the story also suggests the convergence and multiplication of a diverse suite of pleasures in Sherlock's own person. Snuggly cocooned near the fire, Holmes is simultaneously plumbed into multiple delivery systems for multiple different drugs; his 'favourite rocker' is both an appurtenance of domestic cosiness and a massive extension of his hypodermic syringe, constantly and automatically renewing his morphine high. Encircled and permeated by a complex of different technological delights, Holmes's body is presented to us as a comfortable, stimulated, networked, and flamboyantly intoxicated body.

The apogee of this type of Holmesian technological hedonism is to be found in the 1916 Douglas Fairbanks silent film comedy *The Mystery of the Leaping Fish* (directed by John Emerson).[79] Fairbanks plays the role of Coke Ennyday, 'the world's greatest scientific detective'. Despite being set in America in the early twentieth century, Ennyday is clearly identifiable as part of the wider lineage of Holmes caricatures not only by virtue of his extravagant cocaine habit but also by his costume of loudly patterned inverness cape and deer-stalker hat. The name 'Coke Ennyday' gives an early (and not particularly subtle) indication that the main comedic engine of the film is the sheer relentlessness of its hero's drug habit. The first shot of Ennyday's office shows an enormous, cake-tin-sized container of cocaine sitting on the corner of his desk (see Figure 5.4). Across his chest, Ennyday wears a bandolier of syringes from which he regularly injects himself – Fairbanks does this at least three times in the first ninety seconds of the film, grinning hugely and casually chucking aside the spent hypodermics afterwards (see Figure 5.5). In-between doses, Coke's butler makes use of the flat's extensive chemical apparatus to mix his master a cocktail of gin, laudanum, and prussic acid (aka, hydrogen cyanide), which he dispenses into the detective's open mouth using an enormous, syringe-like hand pump. Coke spends the last third of the film, according to an intertitle, 'full of hop' after polishing off an entire brick of raw opium he recovers from a crime scene. Ennyday's progress through the film

---

[78] 'The Dreihoff Poisoning Case', *Yale Record*, 28.2 (28 October 1899), 16.
[79] John Emerson, *The Mystery of the Leaping Fish* (Culver City, CA: Triangle Film Corporation, 1916), Film.

Figure 5.4 Coke Ennyday (Douglas Fairbanks) in his office, *The Mystery of the Leaping Fish*, 1916.

is thus accompanied by a constantly evolving parade of different substances and different means of consumption: he is never more than moments away from smoking, eating, drinking, injecting, or sniffing *something* psychoactive.

This multitude of intoxicants is, however, only the most obvious of the systems of technological gratification with which Coke Ennyday surrounds himself. In his role as the ultimate 'scientific detective' (British papers advertised the film as a comedy of 'scientific absurdity'[80]) Ennyday is constantly enveloped by seemingly endless masses of gadgetry and recreational machinery. When Ennyday wants to relay instructions to his butler, he does so via an electric bell and a four-way switch wired up to a dial on the wall that indicates his present requirement. The dial is equally dividing into Coke's four most essential needs: Eats, Sleep, Dope, and Drinks. When his investigations take Ennyday away from his flat and out to the seaside, he encounters the 'Leaping Fish' of the film's title. Large, inflatable beach toys hired out to tourists so they can ride the waves, these appliances were actually patented by J. P. McCarty and F.W. Falck as 'Surf Diving and Skimming Device[s]',[81] the same year that the

---

[80] 'The Hall', *Donegal Independent*, 1310 (20 October 1917), 2.
[81] J.P. McCarty & F.W. Falck, 'Surf Diving and Skimming Device', US Patent 1,222,114, filed 16 February 1916 and issued 10 April 1917.

Figure 5.5 Coke Ennyday's collection of syringes, 1916.

film was released. The inclusion of the leaping fish does much to suggest the narrative's integration into a wider milieu of immediately contemporaneous, early-twentieth-century mechanical amusements. In the film's presentation, the main outcome of scientific innovation is the faster and more efficient production of enjoyment: *The Mystery of the Leaping Fish* is crowded with devices to help people play in the sea, machines to make them more comfortable at home, toys and games they can take with them on the road, and (most prominently) newly multiplied and complicated cocktails of drugs.

Significantly, the many technologies that Coke Ennyday encounters during the film are almost always in motion: always folding, unfolding, reacting, and transforming. Ennyday observes visitors to his flat through a 'scientific periscope', a kind of closed-circuit television camera (to use modern terminology) whose control system elaborately unfolds from the wall around Ennyday's desk, opening multiple doors and nested cabinets to finally expose the device's screen. Clothes and disguises automatically slide in and out of the flat's wardrobe on wires, and Ennyday has in his possession a powerful telescope that rapidly compresses down into a top hat for when the detective has to conceal his identity. In this way, Ennyday's own delirious, drugged-up energy seems to extend to the film's characterization of technology as a whole. Unphased, bounding through the film on a constant cocaine high, both Ennyday and his machines convey a feeling of hugely accelerated plasticity and adaptability.

The Mystery of the Leaping Fish provides us with a particularly vibrant example of a central motif that recurs throughout many Sherlock Holmes parodies of the late nineteenth and early twentieth centuries: the fanciful interaction between technology, desire, and pleasure. For Arthur Conan Doyle, Holmes's character could be summed up in the image of the detective as 'a calculating machine' industriously oscillating between 'cocaine and ambition'.[82] Exaggerating and caricaturing this idea, however, afforded other authors the opportunity to imagine the potential joys of unfettered drug use, and to delve into the complex chemical delights that might be afforded to an individual so comprehensively cybernetic as Sherlock Holmes. Freed from the expected narratives of addiction and degradation, and covered by the aegis of comedy, these works envision the extravagant forms of diversion, dissipation, stimulated activity, and composed self-satisfaction that might be available to such a 'perfect', cocainized 'machine'[83] as Arthur Conan Doyle's master detective.

Cocaine zanies: Work and pretending to work in the Holmes comedies

Coke Ennyday is a man who takes, putting it mildly, a great deal of cocaine. The most obvious consequence of this radical cocainization is that he is also a man who is near-constantly in motion. Throughout *The Mystery of the Leaping Fish*, Coke is a continually fleeting, hyperactive presence: he is always overwrought, always buzzing, jigging, falling in the sea, bounding out of the sea, leaping into the rafters of a beach-house (the film frequently plays its footage backwards so that Coke seems to defy gravity by effortlessly launching himself to great heights), dancing around henchmen, having a fight with the villain in a pitch-black room, changing disguises, pausing briefly to refill his cocaine high, and then abruptly taking off again. In this way, *The Leaping Fish* bases its appeal to the viewer not only upon the vicarious allure of highly technologized drug use but also upon the invocation of a particular comic aesthetic: the zany. In *Our Aesthetic Categories: Zany, Cute, Interesting*, Sianne Ngai describes zaniness as a 'style of incessant activity ... an aesthetic of action pushed to strenuous and even

---

[82] Doyle, *Sign of Four*, 17; Doyle, *Adventures of Sherlock Holmes*, 5.
[83] Doyle, *Adventures of Sherlock Holmes*, 5.

precarious extremes'.⁸⁴ 'Zany performers,' Ngai tells us, 'are constantly in motion and in flight'; for a comedian, to perform zaniness means acting out, at great speed, 'an unremitting succession of activities' until the many individual actions of the zany blur together into 'an undifferentiated, chaotic swirl'.⁸⁵

Ennyday's style of coked-up, manic (not to say meteoric) clownishness marks him as a definitively zany figure, but the aesthetic of zaniness goes beyond mere unrelenting physicality. Outwardly defined by constant, overheated performance – by unremitting exertion and an amorphous but feverish and continuous 'doing' – the zany is also a form that speaks to the many ambiguous and ill-defined exertions of modern work. In Ngai's words: 'this playful, hypercharismatic aesthetic is really an aesthetic about work'; the zany performance dramatizes the 'ambiguous intersection between cultural and occupational performance, acting and service, playing and labouring'.⁸⁶ For Ngai, the zany's over-taxed 'chaotic swirl' serves to instantiate the hectic confusion and arduousness of employment itself – zaniness plays out the precarious and uncertain overlap between working a job, play-acting a part, and performing a role. This aspect of zaniness speaks directly to another important element in the comic reception of Sherlock Holmes's cocaine habit: the parodic reversal of the relationship between the 7 per cent solution and Holmes's working life. We began this chapter by examining the extent to which Sherlock's fondness for cocaine in fact indicates the depths of his devotion to his job as a consulting detective. I want to conclude by arguing that the Holmes parodies recast this professional competence into zany performance: the comic Sherlock manifests the same 'splendid energy and vigour'⁸⁷ as Doyle's original, but this wildly cocainized dynamism is dedicated not to work but to propagating the illusion of work. In doing so, these parodies articulate the humorous (and potentially subversive) idea that *pretending* to work might be just as productive as actually working.

On a basic level, cocaine and the zany would seem to be a natural fit for each other. Sianne Ngai's analysis does not delve into the implications of drug use for the aesthetics of zaniness, but, as a stimulant, cocaine appears admirably suited to the performative requirements of the zany character.⁸⁸ This alignment

---

⁸⁴ Sianne Ngai, *Our Aesthetic Categories: Zany, Cute, Interesting* (Cambridge: Harvard University Press, 2012), 185.
⁸⁵ Ngai, *Our Aesthetic Categories*, 182, 193, and 197.
⁸⁶ Ibid., 182 and 188.
⁸⁷ Doyle, *Sign of Four*, 117.
⁸⁸ As an aside regarding the comedic appeal of the drug user, it may also be worth bearing in mind Walter Benjamin's typically elliptical remark that one of the 'most important social effects' of drugs

goes some way towards explaining the ease with which comic writers could convert Holmes's 7 per cent solution into a source of zany vitality. To return briefly to the example of Coke Ennyday, the detective's jacked-up exuberance isn't merely confined to his own person but is also infused into his interactions with other characters and objects. While riding one of the 'leaping fish' down at the beach, Coke sights a suspect and takes off in pursuit. When his prey begins to outdistance him, Coke responds by injecting the fish with some of his cocaine, causing the inflatable to frantically accelerate through the waves. Later, Coke overcomes the villain's henchmen by the same method: as each man tries to attack him, the detective adroitly seizes their arm and pricks them with a hypodermic. Overcome by sudden massive infusions of cocaine, the men cartwheel their way out of windows or vibrate their way off of the ground and out of the top of shot, never to be seen again. In this way, cocaine operates in *The Mystery of the Leaping Fish* like a kind of injectable anarchy – zaniness by transfusion.

There is, however, more to the zaniness of the comedic Holmes than just the stimulant effects of Sherlock's drug of choice; while not immediately obvious, these parodies draw upon a grain of thematic zaniness incipit in Doyle's own stories. Many critics have identified the nature of work as a central concern not only of the Holmes stories themselves but of the *Strand Magazine* as a whole, the publication displaying a seemingly inexhaustible 'preoccupation with defining, knowing, and theorising the professional'.[89] More specifically, Doyle's stories are particularly preoccupied with the nature of self-employment, consultancy, and other forms of economic autonomy in the late-nineteenth-century marketplace. Douglas Kerr writes that the Holmes stories represent a 'drama of consultancy' in 'the age of the consultant'.[90] Towards the end of the nineteenth century, self-employment was increasingly held up as an ideal of 'personal autonomy, freedom and perpetual change: freedom of capital; [and] freedom from the ties of custom and deference'.[91] Doyle's stories, however, depict another side to this model of economic liberty. Many of Holmes's clients (particularly those encountered in

---

'consists in the charm displayed by addicts under the influence'. See Walter Benjamin, *Charles Baudelaire: A Lyric Poet in the Era of High Capitalism*, trans. Harry Zohn (London: Verso, 1997), 56.

[89] Clare Clarke, *Late Victorian Crime Fiction in the Shadows of Sherlock* (London: Palgrave Macmillan, 2014), 82.

[90] Kerr, *Conan Doyle*, 44 and 42. For more discussion of the precise details of Holmes's work and its relationship with late-Victorian models of medical consultancy, see Nicki Buscemi, 'The Case of the Case History: Detecting the Medical Report in Sherlock Holmes', *Journal of Victorian Culture*, 19.2 (2014), 216–31; and Kerr, *Conan Doyle*, 41–78.

[91] Elizabeth Wilson, *Bohemians: The Glamorous Outcasts* (New York: Tauris Parke, 2003), 18.

the early stories collected in *The Adventures* and *The Memoirs of Sherlock Holmes*) are self-employed people and their work is often represented as a contradictory, precarious, sometimes even eccentric phenomenon. The work of the self-employed person is – in Holmes's world – often unreliable and difficult to define or to properly differentiate from idleness. In 'The Engineer's Thumb' (1892), for example, Holmes's client Victor Hatherley (a self-employed engineer) describes his strained professional circumstances to the detective: 'I suppose that everyone finds his first independent start in business a dreary experience. To me it has been exceptionally so. During two years I have had three consultations and one small job… Every day, from nine in the morning until four in the afternoon, I waited in my little den, until at last my heart began to sink.'[92] Hatherley's main occupation consists of a frustrating type of mandatory inactivity: a rote performance of the working day but without productive outcome. Here, the definition of work is disconcertingly eroded and vague – Hatherley is nominally *at* work while also (confusingly) waiting *to* work.

A similar scenario occurs in the case of Violet Hunter, a governess whose urgent need of employment leads her to accept a position in the family of Mr. Rucastle. Beyond the work of educating the Rucastles' child, she is asked to cut her striking red hair very short, 'wear any dress which [they] might give [her]', and 'obey any little commands which [Rucastle or his] wife might give'. Despite these requirements, Rucastle initially insists he wants to hire her because she has 'the bearing and deportment of a lady',[93] highlighting the ambiguity of her position: to obey like a servant, dress herself like a doll, but comport herself like a lady. Rucastle in fact wants to employ her because he has imprisoned his daughter in order to force her to make over her inheritance to him, and he needs Hunter (without her knowledge) to play the part of the missing daughter and allay suspicion. Violet Hunter's job thus consists of a curious matryoshka doll of multiple, non-specific roles, only some of which she is really aware of enacting.

Hatherley and Hunter's jobs – with their ostentatious confusion of performance and selfhood, activity and drudgery – recall the similarly ambivalent situations of both Neville St Clair from 'The Man with the Twisted Lip' (1891) and Jabez Wilson from 'The Red-Headed League' (1891). The first of these men makes a comfortable living by pretending to be a badly scarred London beggar named Hugh Boone – an activity that seemingly represents the ultimate form of indolence (sitting still and begging for money) but which also demands that

---

[92] Doyle, *Adventures of Sherlock Holmes*, 202.
[93] Ibid., 274–5.

St Clair exercise his skills with theatrical make-up and keenly honed 'facility in repartee'. Wilson, apparently on account of nothing more substantial than his 'blazing, fiery red hair', is offered the 'purely nominal' work of laboriously copying out the Encyclopaedia Britannica in exchange for four pounds a week.[94] These characters illustrate a persistent issue in Doyle's writing: how to categorically delineate work in the modern era – whether or not it is possible to disentangle skilled and unskilled forms of labour, recognize industriousness from indolence, or distinguish the subject who is authentically performing a service from one who is only 'nominally' play-acting the superficialities of work.

Parodies of the Holmes stories project this thematic preoccupation with the vague and obfuscatory nature of work onto the detective himself, depriving him of his 'god-like manner and insight as swift and lucid as lightning'[95] and reconfiguring him into a zany illusionist. These works suggest the same doubts and uncertainties about modern working conditions as Doyle's stories, but they approach the topic with an air of facetiousness. In these comedies, the imperious consulting detective of Baker Street is revealed to be more concerned with acting like he is working than with actually achieving anything – his successes come from continually, hyperbolically pretending to work, rather than from real results. For comedians, Holmes's cocaine habit was the ideal vector to convey this manic yet oddly attractive style of professional legerdemain.

One particularly zany iteration of Holmes appears in *The Bohemian* magazine's 'Ideal Interview' series in October 1893. The article opens with Holmes asking the interviewer to pass him 'a bottle which was labelled cocaine but smelt like whiskey … the singular man drank a pint or more of it and said he felt better'. After 'repeated applications of the drug (?)', Holmes – already none too stable – becomes increasingly erratic and confidential. 'You see,' he confesses, 'I must practice effect. … [Watson] taught me when to look bored, when to yawn, and when to let my eyes light up with the fire of enthusiasm. When I had mastered all that, he taught me those bad manners of mine which are taken for the eccentricity of genius.' Over the course of the interview – and as he takes 'more cocaine (?)' – Holmes's actions become even wilder. He attempts to write his name on the wall with revolver bullets but is too bad of a shot to pull it off, he cries, screams, sinks into despair and rebounds volcanically, he intends to board a train for the North

---

[94] Ibid., 55, 57, 147. For a different reading of these characters which emphasizes their subjection to the 'effects of greed' and the 'temptations of easy money' rather than the inherent precariousness and instability of self-employment, see Clarke, *Late Victorian Crime Fiction*, 87–95.
[95] George Edgar, 'The Unromantic Detective', *The Living Age*, 49.4368 (24 December 1910), 827.

Pole, tries to strangle the interviewer, and pathetically winds up playing 'Daddy wouldn't buy me a Bow-Wow' on the violin.[96]

Throughout the interview Holmes is (in definitively zany style) both self-consciously performing and wildly out of control of his own performance. He is constantly labouring to produce the various poses, 'eccentricit[ies]', and affectations taught to him by Watson, but he is also over-invested in these performances to the point where it is not clear that he could stop performing even if he wanted to. Like other quintessentially zany characters, he seems 'to perform without enough distance from his emotions'.[97] This muddled, unhinged blend of complete emotional sincerity and acknowledged artifice underscores the wider ambiguity of performance and work in the late-Victorian and early-Modernist period. Holmes's constant tippling of 'cocaine (?)' encapsulates this confusion: both an affectation and a real intoxicant (whiskey masquerading as cocaine), it acts as a prop in Holmes's performance, but it also impels that performance beyond the limits of self-control. As he remarks: 'When I have taken plenty of whi – cocaine, I mean – I am a real, regular, rightdown, rampant, viceexterminating, blasé, cynical, callous, keenscented, readywitted, neverthwarted, demoniacal detective, with melodramatic effects.' This sudden, chaotic proliferation of adjectives, images, and 'effects' suggests that the more 'cocaine (?)' Holmes takes, the less control he has over the act of pretending.

Between doses, Holmes recounts his life story to the interviewer:

> I started my professional career as a quickchange variety artist, and the experience I then acquired has served me well in my present work. I developed a liking for cocaine, a distaste for the commonplace, and a large bump of mendacity. So large did this latter become, that I left the stage and became an advertisement canvasser. From that the transition to my present position was rapid.[98]

Following on from the insinuation that his character is largely a product of Watson's instruction, Holmes's previous jobs as 'a quickchange variety artist' and 'advertisement canvasser' suggest that his present work is simply a fresh phase in a long career of dubious boosterism and performativity. In *The Bohemian*'s rendering, the main work of Holmes's life is implied to be the exhausting, incoherent, immersive, and inebriated business of playing the role that is Sherlock Holmes. Here, the forms of play and the forms of real labour become both appealingly and disconcertingly blurred together.

---

[96] Anyhow, 'Ideal Interview: Sherlock Holmes' *The Bohemian*, 1.5 (October 1893), 214–16.
[97] Ngai, *Our Aesthetic Categories*, 190.
[98] Anyhow, 'Ideal Interview: Sherlock Holmes' *The Bohemian*, 214.

This maniacally performative figuration of Holmes and his work recurs in Frank Richardson's 1905 comic novel *The Secret Kingdom* where it is brought into an even more explicit alignment with cocaine. Finding himself in the grip of a particularly perplexing family mystery, the novel's hero, Paul Peterson, takes the natural step of rushing to London to consult the eminent detective of Baker Street. When he arrives, however, Holmes seems much more easily distracted than Paul had envisioned from the stories in the *Strand Magazine*. Watson seems to regard his associate with an eye 'more professional than friendly'.[99] When Holmes withdraws for a moment, Watson takes the opportunity to disclose the truth to Paul:

> 'The case is very simple, but very sad. My poor friend's mind is totally unhinged. Years ago he became a victim to cocaine, and while under the influence of the drug his brain evolved extraordinary criminal mysteries. Of course, they stood in no sort of relation to life. But they had a certain fascination of their own … at any rate, to me, his friend. To humour him, I … wrote them down. And, as you are aware, they had a considerable vogue with the public. … The whole thing, the crimes, the criminals, the arrests … all inventions, the marvellous inventions of a shattered brain!'
>
> Watson was overcome with emotion.
>
> 'Except the deer-stalker cap?'
>
> 'Except that. But, of course, the wearing of that sort of cap is in itself a symptom of disease'.[100]

This passage (like *The Bohemian*'s 'Ideal Interview' before it) impishly reframes the relationship between drug consumption and work, so that the pleasures of unrestrained cocainism end up leading to unexpectedly productive outcomes. Rather than wrecking his career, Holmes's excessive indulgence has, in fact, been the making of him. Watson too has managed to come out ahead in spite of his own lack of ability. When Paul indignantly accuses him of having relinquished his duty as a doctor and 'made capital out of the terrible condition of your poor friend!' Watson shamefacedly responds: 'Yes, in a sense. But I am not precisely … what shall I say? … a great genius. … I often think that I am somewhat of a … can I say? … chump head.'[101] This configuration upends what John Tosh refers to as the 'characteristically Victorian valorisation of work as both a moral

---

[99] Frank Richardson, *The Secret Kingdom* (London: Duckworth, 1905), 84.
[100] Richardson, *Secret Kingdom*, 108–9.
[101] Ibid., 108.

duty and personal fulfilment'.¹⁰² Paid remuneration and productivity come not from a commitment to work and to the ethics of work but from performing something that looks enough like work to pass muster. Watson is a 'chump head' who has bumbled into creating a publishing sensation from his friend's cocaine delusions; Holmes is a drug maniac who dresses loudly enough (so loudly, in fact, that his deer-stalker hat can be recognized as a 'symptom of disease') and acts confidently enough to convince the public that he is 'the greatest detective the world has known'.¹⁰³ In this context, the representation of Holmes's 'shattered brain' that produces money and renown recalls the essentially fragmented personality pattern of the zany character: their fractured status as a simultaneous 'virtuoso/loser'.¹⁰⁴ In *The Secret Kingdom*, both Holmes and Watson are moral and professional failures, but they carry their cocainism and chump-headedness to such consummate degrees that they wind up prospering from them.

Thus, beyond their humorous façade, the Holmes parodies express an element of longing for unrealizable ideal: the yearning for acts of indulgence, play, pretence, drug taking, and elaborated forms of idleness that can lead to the same productive outcomes as industry and temperance. For Arthur Conan Doyle, cocaine served as a means to illustrate Holmes's complete, mechanistic devotion to working life – more finely and sincerely stimulated by work than by the 7 per cent solution, Holmes observes of himself: 'I never remember feeling tired by work, though idleness exhausts me completely.'¹⁰⁵ Holmes represents a beguiling paradox in which work assumes the effortlessness of enjoyment, while the 'exhaustion' of inactivity has to be fought back with constant injections of cocaine. In the numerous parodies and skits that followed the success of Doyle's detective, Holmes's cocaine habit became instead a means by which to puncture the moral austerity of work. The parodic Holmes flirts with the kind of joys that might come from discarding the rigid obligations of self-restraint and industry; his love of cocaine (whether in 7 per cent, 70 per cent , or 700 per cent solutions) holds out the possibility that the body might be reworked into a kind of engine for perpetual pleasure and that the moral centrality of work might be redirected into a zany and endlessly extravagant playtime.

---

[102] John Tosh, 'Masculinities in an Industrialising Society: Britain 1800–1914', *Journal of British Studies*, 44.2 (April 2005), 332.
[103] Richardson, *Secret Kingdom*, 85.
[104] Ngai, *Our Aesthetic Categories*, 191.
[105] Doyle, *Sign of Four*, 68.

6

White powder, White fears: Race, sex, and masculinity in the jazz age[*]

Aleister Crowley, the occultist, writer, and mountaineer famously styled by *John Bull* magazine as 'the Wickedest Man in the World … [a] degenerate poet and occultist, traitor, drug fiend, and Master of Black Magic',[1] was the author of some of the most baroquely romantic descriptions of cocaine to appear in the early twentieth century. Crowley, though a British citizen, had spent most of the Great War living abroad in America, and it was there in 1917 that he produced his paean 'Cocaine' for *The International*:

> Look at this shining heap of crystals! They are Hydrochloride of Cocaine. The geologist will think of mica; to me, the mountaineer, they are like those gleaming feathery flakes of snow, flowering mostly where rocks jut from the ice of crevassed glaciers, that wind and sun have kissed to ghostliness. To those who know not the great hills, they may suggest the snow that spangles trees with blossoms glittering and lucid. The kingdom of faery has such jewels.[2]

Crowley's adulation imbues cocaine with a crystalline otherworldly perfection, the icy flower of some higher plane tenderly cultivated by more ethereal conditions than those of earth. Yet, as the article goes on, it becomes increasingly clear that if cocaine is aesthetically beautiful, it is only because of the spiritual beauty of its effects. 'There was never any elixir so instant magic as cocaine', writes Crowley. 'Give it to no matter whom … [and] melancholy vanishes. … The man is happy.'

> To one the drug may bring liveliness, to another languor; to another creative force, to another tireless energy, to another glamor, and to yet another lust. But

---

[*] See pp. 17–18 for a fuller rationale of the decision to capitalize 'White' as an identifier of racial identity.
[1] 'The Wickedest Man in the World', *John Bull*, 33.877 (24 March 1923), 10.
[2] Aleister Crowley, 'Cocaine', *The International*, 11.10 (October 1917), 291.

each in his way is happy. Think of it! – so simple and so transcendental! The man is happy!³

In Crowley's eyes, the true 'miracle' of cocaine – the secret 'marvel' behind its ghostly loveliness and faery glimmer – is the transcendent simplicity of its power to summon up happiness. In some ways, this elaborately ornamented depiction recalls the technologizing confidence that cocaine commanded in the 1880s and 1890s. The 'instant magic' with which the drug takes effect might well elicit memories of cocaine's one-time status as the 'magic drug'⁴ that 'flashed'⁵ across the horizon of fin de siècle medicine. Here, though, cocaine's medicinal application is completely obscured by its much more expansive capacity to make its user 'happy'; for Crowley, cocaine's curative power is wholly subsumed into its power for pleasure.

At first blush, the Crowley's efflorescent description seems like an obvious outlier in the cocaine discourse of the early twentieth century. The 1910s and 1920s marked a period where, across Britain and North America, the consumption of cocaine was heavily curtailed and criminalized by legislation such as the United States's Harrison Narcotics Act (1914). In Britain, wartime concern over the misuse of drugs by soldiers and civilians led in 1916 to the introduction of section 40b of the Defence of the Realm Act (DORA), whose provisions (that cocaine could now only be purchased with a doctor's prescription and could only be sold, carried, or given to others by 'authorised persons' such as pharmacists, veterinary surgeons, dentists, and recognized medical practitioners) were later adapted into the Dangerous Drugs Act of 1920.⁶

The recreational use of cocaine became severely castigated and racially inflected during this time. Marek Kohn, for instance, describes the formulation

---

³ Ibid.
⁴ Marian Von Glehn, 'A Day in a Hospital', *The Leisure Hour*, February 1890, 279.
⁵ See Walter G. Smith, 'Report on Materia Medica and Therapeutics', *Dublin Journal of Medical Science*, 80. 6 (December 1885), 506; and 'Cocaine', *Chambers's Journal*, 3.114 (6 March 1886), 145.
⁶ 'The Regulations with Respect to the Sale of Cocaine', *Lancet*, 188.4849 (5 August 1916), 238. See P. E. Caquet, 'France, Germany, and the Origins of Drug Prohibition', *The International History Review*, 42.4 (2020), 207–9, for a more detailed overview of the progress of national and international drug legislation during this period. For a further account of the legislative history of DORA 40b and the military anxieties that presaged it see Virginia Berridge, 'War Conditions and Narcotics Control: The Passing of Defence of the Realm Act Regulation 40B', *Journal of Social Policy*, 7.3 (July 1978), 285–99; and Marek Kohn, *Dope Girls: The Birth of the British Drug Underground* (London: Granta Books, 2001), 28–44. Formal regulation of cocaine in Britain and North American was preceded by some years by the British introduction of colonial laws in India to restrict the sale of cocaine to officially regulated medical channels – 'mak[ing] the Government of India the first to attempt such geographically comprehensive controls on the drug'. For more information on these early colonial moves towards drug prohibition and their influence on later legal measures, see James H. Mills, 'Cocaine and the British Empire: The Drug and the Diplomats at the Hague Opium Conference, 1911–12', *Journal of Imperial and Commonwealth History*, 42.3 (2014), 411.

of a 'demonology of dope' that was inscribed onto cocaine in these decades – the spread of recreational cocaine consumption and addiction becoming 'a symbolic issue in which larger national crises [were] reworked in microcosm'.[7] A key tenet of this 'demonology' was the conjuration of a new image of the typical drug addict. Victorian and fin de siècle narratives of addiction and habituation had tended to prioritize the tragic image of a hopeful, useful life gone astray.[8] By the first years of the twentieth century, however, the concept of the inadvertent addict – the professional, respectable addict brought low by their own naiveté or lack of proper medical supervision – began to be displaced by a newly conceived-of 'Vicious Group'[9] who were, according to Caroline Acker, regarded as 'fundamentally different from individuals who had become addicted medically'.[10] This 'Vicious' class, as the physician Sir William Henry Willcox defined them in 1923, were imagined to 'devote their lives to so-called pleasure seeking and the search for new excitements and sensations'.[11] Cocaine was suggested to be used largely to 'stimulate the flagging appetite for pleasure' and the spread of such viciously motivated addiction was met with the suggestion that cocaine debauchees 'should be isolated like cases of infectious disease, thus removing a source of infection of others with the cocaine habit'.[12] In this way, the pitiful 'cocainist'[13] of the fin de siècle was imaginatively transformed into the brutal and pathologically pleasure-seeking 'cocaine fiend' of the twentieth century.[14]

As well as acquiring an aura of barbarous hedonism, this era also marked a shift in the racial associations of cocaine. Across Europe and North America, the early decades of the century were characterized by 'the creation of a racial drama of drug use'[15] that portrayed drugs (particularly cocaine) as instruments that racially minoritized populations might use to corrupt and destroy unwary White subjects. Young White women were thought to be especially susceptible to

---

[7] Kohn, *Dope Girls*, 4–7.
[8] Susan Zieger, *Inventing the Addict: Drugs, Race, and Sexuality in Nineteenth-Century British and American Literature* (Amherst: University of Massachusetts Press, 2008), 234.
[9] W. H. Willcox, 'Norman Kerr Memorial Lecture on Drug Addiction', *BMJ*, 2.3283 (1 December 1923), 1013.
[10] Caroline Acker, *Creating the American Junkie: Addiction Research in the Classic Era of Narcotic Control* (Baltimore, MD: Johns Hopkins University Press, 2002), 2.
[11] Willcox, 'Norman Kerr Memorial Lecture on Drug Addiction', 1013.
[12] 'Cocaine Addiction', *Lancet*, 204.5278 (25 October 1924), 857–8.
[13] J. W. Springthorpe, 'The Confessions of a Cocainist', *Australasian Medical Gazette*, 14 (20 September 1895), 370.
[14] Joseph F. Spillane, *Cocaine: From Medical Marvel to Modern Menace in the United States* (Baltimore, MD: Johns Hopkins University Press, 2000), 106.
[15] Catherine Carstairs, *Jailed for Possession: Illegal Drug Use, Regulation, and Power in Canada, 1920–1961* (Toronto: University of Toronto Press, 2006), 20.

the dangerous allure of cocaine. In 1923, Sidney Felstead claimed to be shocked by the horrible frequency with which 'some pleasure-sated girl dies from an overdose of cocaine or morphia, supplied to her by of some black or yellow parasite'.[16] Cocaine was assumed to be the product of other races – a 'black or yellow' contaminant that threatened to poison British womanhood. The Chinese community in Britain was often associated with cocaine, largely because of its historical links with opium smoking and the press attention given to infamous underworld figures like the Regent Street restaurant-owner and drug dealer Brilliant Chang.[17] But it was African American and Afro-Caribbean subjects who were most readily connected with the pollution of cocainism. Since the first years of the century, cocaine had largely featured in the British imagination as a drug of Black America (a concept which was elastic enough in practice to be extended to Black Caribbean subjects as well) and British newspapers in the late 1910s and 1920s were wont to fret over 'the marked increase in London of that disastrous and degrading habit which students have hitherto associated with the American negro'.[18] In post-war drug discourse, cocaine appears as an essentially Black drug – a malicious device that 'facilitated the seduction of young white women by men of colour'.[19]

Both of these factors – the racialization and vicious characterization of the cocaine user – contribute to the sense that cocaine enjoyed an almost 'uniformly sinister reputation'[20] in the public consciousness of this period. Much of the critical commentary on recreational cocainism in the early twentieth century has tended to concentrate on reconstructing the mechanisms by which, to quote Joseph F. Spillane, 'the social or moral stigma [of cocaine use] … [became] magnified through lenses of fear, racism, and class prejudice' and how these prejudices were, in turn, instantiated into acts of law.[21] It is, though, worth bearing in mind the observation made by Kiran Pienaar and her co-authors that not only does the stigmatization of a given drug not automatically 'imply an absence of pleasure … [but] stigma can in fact give rise to particular forms of pleasure'.[22] This

---

[16] Sidney Theodore Felstead, *The Underworld of London* (London: John Murry, 1923), 2.
[17] See John Burrows, '"A Vague Chinese Quarter Elsewhere": Limehouse in the Cinema 1914–36', *Journal of British Cinema and Television*, 6.2 (2009), 286–95; and Kohn, *Dope Girls*, 125–31, 143–9, and 161–75 for more extensive analyses of Chang, and the assumed links between Chinese communities and drug trafficking in 1920s popular culture.
[18] C. W. Saleeby, 'The Curse of Cocaine', *Liverpool Daily Post*, 19075 (19 July 1916), 7.
[19] Kohn, *Dope Girls*, 20.
[20] Caquet, 'France, Germany, and the Origins of Drug Prohibition', 220.
[21] Spillane, *Cocaine*, 161–2.
[22] Kiran Pienaar, Dean Anthony Murphy, Kane Race, and Toby Lea, 'Drugs as Technologies of the Self: Enhancement and Transformation in LGBTQ Cultures', *International Journal of Drug Policy*, 78 (April 2020), 2.

chapter examines the cultural and ideological functions of cocaine pleasure in the period that straddles the drug's criminalization. Indulgence in cocaine might signal the threat of 'white racial degeneration'[23] and illustrate the sybaritically 'frazzled nerves' of the post-war generation,[24] but – I argue – it could also be used to assert the potential of an omnipotent White masculine dominance over the remainder of the century. This chapter details an alternative configuration of cocaine, wherein – precisely because of its racially pejorative and pathological associations – a nonchalant familiarity with the drug's pleasures could be taken as proof of the inner verities of a White man's character, and of his fitness to master the technological and social challenges of an uncertain future.

James Donald describes a complex of imaginative connotations attached to Black American culture and to individual Black people in Europe in the early Modernist period. To many observers in 'post-war Paris, Berlin, and London'[25] Black subjects appeared to simultaneously epitomize the futuristic allure of American modernity, as well as the primordial energy and vigorousness of Africa. Black individuals could as such be represented as the emissaries of 'a fantasied Black America' that comprised a 'combination of supposed African primitivism and manifest American modernism'.[26] Black-aligned cultural products like jazz, modern dance, and, I argue, cocaine could be subjected to this same framing – 'recognised as product[s] of machine-age modernity, but at the same time as something elemental or natural or primitive that might redeem the abstraction and rationality of the age'.[27] The over-wrought character of these almost entirely White-authored racial fantasies was famously summed up in a remark of Josephine Baker's in 1931: 'It's really something, the white imagination, when it comes to Blacks.'[28]

This chapter reveals how Black cocainism could easily be enfolded into this imaginative schema of modernity and 'vitalist primitivism'.[29] The drug retained its former identity as an advanced technological product, but its pleasures were rendered as emphatically vigorous, social, and sexual. This discursive formulation of Black pleasure and its supposed appeal for White women

---

[23] Zieger, *Inventing the Addict*, 52.
[24] Rebecca Cameron, ' "Syncopated Nerves": Jazz and the Pathology of Modern Youth in Noël Coward's 1920s Theatre', *Modernist Cultures*, 15.2 (2020), 187.
[25] James Donald, *Some of These Days: Black Stars, Jazz Aesthetics, and Modernist Culture* (Oxford: Oxford University Press, 2015), 36.
[26] Ibid., 25 and 66.
[27] Ibid., 65.
[28] 'C'est quelque chose l'imagination blanche quand il s'agit des Noirs'. Josephine Baker and Marcel Sauvage, *Voyages et Aventures de Joséphine Baker* (Paris: Marcel Sheur, 1931), 16.
[29] Donald, *Some of These Days*, 5.

represented an implied challenge to White masculinity in the early twentieth century. To retain his former position of cultural mastery and security, it was reasoned, the White man would have to acquire a commanding familiarity with the dynamically modern and primitively carnal pleasures of cocaine. These futurist and hegemonic functions of cocaine are most clearly represented in the fiction and journalism of Aleister Crowley – notably his 1923 novel *The Diary of a Drug Fiend*. Cocaine appears in Crowley's works as a technology of pleasure – a 'marvel' and 'formula of magic'[30] that can, if properly controlled and brought to heel, allow its White user to re-incise his own image on the destiny of the coming age.

American modernity

Since the late nineteenth century it had been common practice for British newspapers and journals to depict cocaine as a definitively American drug. 'The use of cocaine is a growing habit in the United States', wrote the *Manchester Courier* in 1898:

> Immense quantities are sold to the most ignorant of persons … In some stores, so they say, it is kept ready done up in 5-cent packages, and the customers are so well known that they do not need to tell what they want. They simply throw down the five cents, and get the cocaine just as easily as they would a glass of beer in a saloon.[31]

The explanation for cocaine's 'excessive use in America'[32] was often located in the country's equally excessive advancement. 'America,' wrote one observer in 1890 'is a go-ahead nation, in the van of human progress, and the strife after the almighty dollar is increasing.'[33] The growth of the cocaine habit 'to amazing proportions'[34] in the country was assumed to be synonymous with its over-developed and violently disorientating modernity. 'We have it on authority,' wrote the *Bristol Mercury* in 1895, 'that the cocaine habit, the ever-growing conflicts between capital and labour, and the excessive thirst for wealth which exists in the United States, tends very considerably to enfeeble the mind and

---

[30] Crowley, 'Cocaine', 291.
[31] 'Cocaine in America', *Manchester Courier*, 74.13042 (27 August 1898), 9.
[32] 'The Cocaine Habit', *Belfast Telegraph*, 44.14654 (28 July 1916), 3.
[33] 'Chit-Chat', *Sheffield Evening Telegraph*, 803 (7 January 1890), 2.
[34] 'The Cocaine Habit', *Belfast Telegraph*, 3.

dethrone reason.'[35] The same year, another article on the subject of 'Drink and Drugs' stated that: 'The cocaine habit is a recognised fact in America where our Teutonic race, subjected to an intenser climate and an intenser pace of life than in Europe, has developed a quicker sensibility and more irritable nerves.'[36]

Many reporters in the UK maintained that the habit of abusing cocaine was one that had been introduced into the Old World from her precocious offspring across the Atlantic. On 15 August 1901, the *Cornishman* newspaper reminisced that 'The first alarm of the growth of the cocaine habit came from New York 14 years ago.'[37] Only the day prior, the *Dundee Courier* had claimed that, 'Like bridge', the most demoralizing of the modern card games, 'the cocaine habit is an importation from New York.'[38] This idea persisted well into the twentieth century. According to the *Belfast Telegraph* in 1913: 'The pernicious habit of cocaine-sniffing, which originated in America and then reached Paris, is now spreading in London.'[39] Through the fin de siècle and up into the war years, stories (often incorporating first-hand material recycled from papers in the United States) proliferated in the British press about the cocaine 'menace' that had swallowed 'many big American cities'.[40] *The Globe* claimed that: 'the city of Chattanooga has been thoroughly demoralised solely by the use of cocaine.'[41] In the heart of New York there was supposed to be a district 'known as "Poison Row", for the ease with which [cocaine] can be obtained in the neighbourhood'.[42] Reports of these kinds of American drug plagues had been widely circulated going back to the 1890s:

> It is stated that at Manchester, Kentucky, the cocaine habit has recently assumed the proportions of a veritable epidemic, and that thousands of people are suffering from it. The evil commenced with a local druggist, who advertised a popular remedy for catarrh, which was found on investigation to be a mixture of menthol and cocaine. There was a sudden demand for it, and it was taken to such an extent that many of the victims had to be accommodated in the public lunatic asylum.[43]

---

[35] 'Drink and Insanity', *Bristol Mercury and Daily Post*, 14826 (16 November 1895), 8.
[36] 'Drugs and Drink', *Huddersfield Daily Chronicle*, 8789 (30 September 1895), 4.
[37] 'The Cocaine Habit', *Cornishman*, 1206 (15 August 1901), 2.
[38] 'Another Abuse in Society', *Dundee Courier*, 15020 (14 August 1901), 4.
[39] 'Cocaine Creeper', *Belfast Telegraph*, 43.13651 (7 May 1913), 5.
[40] 'The Cocaine Evil', *Dundee Evening Telegraph*, 12236 (15 February 1916), 4.
[41] 'The "Cocaine" Habit', *The Globe*, 32952 (11 January 1901), 6.
[42] 'The Cocaine Habit', *Shoreditch Observer*, 2696 (5 September 1908), 7.
[43] 'The Cocaine Habit', *BMJ*, 1.1882 (23 January 1897), 219. Reports of this event were widely circulated through various papers in 1897, with some early accounts misidentifying the town as Manchester, Connecticut. See, for example, 'Chips', *North-Eastern Daily Gazette*, 2 January 1897, 2.

By the early decades of the twentieth century, observers were wont to commiserate that: 'it would appear that there are more "drug fiends" in the United States than in any other country in the world'.[44]

For Aleister Crowley, cocaine's effects were an ideal shorthand with which to capture a specifically American manifestation of hectic, urbanized modernity. In 1918, Crowley wrote ecstatically of 'Manhattan, most loved, most hated, of all cities, whose soul is a Delirium beyond Time and Space'. To experience the city was to encounter 'cloudless, definite, physiological pleasure' and to excite every nerve in the body at once: 'The daily rush of New York resembles the effect of Cocaine; it is a universal stimulation'. Immersion in New York, according to Crowley, could effect the same kind of systemic nervous acceleration as the consumption of cocaine: a rapid 'physiological' hit of raw energy, followed by a speeding onward towards the hyperactive 'transcendental delights of pure madness'.[45] In 1886, while cocaine was still in the pink of its success as a newly discovered local anaesthetic, the *BMJ*'s correspondent in America had recorded that: 'Cucaine [sic] is being used in this country for nearly everything'.[46] By 1916 and the passage of DORA regulation 40b, it had become an accepted truism to say that: 'The United States has witnessed more cocainism than any other country hitherto'.[47]

Black pleasures and White anxieties

It was not long before the prospect of America's national cocainization began to batten itself onto a more general ambience of White racial unease, both in Britain and the United States. Around 1900, observers began to document the spread of cocaine into Black populations in both the southern and northern states. 'The cocaine habit appears to be extremely prevalent among negroes in the United States', wrote the *British Medical Journal* in 1902. These early accounts of Black cocainism were mostly concerned with the prevalence of the drug among the longshoremen of the Louisiana waterfronts and the plantation hands of Mississippi cotton country. In search of something to help 'put in a big day's work' the drug was allegedly sometimes 'kept in stock' and doled out to Black labourers by White employers, and sometimes bought and taken by the

[44] 'The Drug Habit in America', *Western Times*, 19002 (4 June 1910), 4.
[45] Aleister Crowley, 'Drama Be Damned!', *The International*, 12.4 (April 1918), 127.
[46] 'Special Correspondence', *BMJ*, 1.1305 (2 January 1886), 40.
[47] C. W. Saleeby, 'The Curse of Cocaine', *Liverpool Daily Post*, 19075 (19 July 1916), 7.

workers on their own initiative. 'The negroes,' summarized the *BMJ*, 'found that the drug enabled them to work longer and to make more money, and so they took to it.'[48] Later descriptions, though, took a much more obviously alarmist tone in response to the growth of recreational cocaine use in working-class Black communities. In 1903, *The Globe* published an account by an American observer who decaled himself completely 'satisfied that many of the horrible crimes committed by the coloured people can be traced directly to the cocaine habit'.[49] The idea that Black drug use was inextricable from Black violence and criminality was – as we shall see – to become an almost endemic feature of cocaine discourse over the following decades.

Unbiased descriptions of Black experiences with cocaine and its pleasures are not easy to locate. The cultural–historical record of the early twentieth century trends towards, as Michael M. Cohen remarks, 'a dependence upon a White written record, intent on demonising the Black user, that failed to document [their] experiences of escapism and suffering, of pleasure and warning'.[50] One consistently useful vein of information, though, can be found in the blues and folk song lyrics of the period. Over the fin de siècle and early twentieth century, the genres of jazz and blues music developed out of a mix of older musical forms and solidified into their own separate but interconnected entities.[51] An important 'hallmark' of this emerging culture was, according to R. A. Lawson, its self-conscious mixture of music and intoxication: 'In the "Black places" where blues were performed, sexuality often mixed with drug use. Blues lyrics evidence both the realities of drug use among blues musicians and patrons as well as the celebratory attitude with which 'blues people' considered their narcotic and alcohol use.'[52] In Memphis, Tennessee, in the early 1900s, 'The coke craze coincided with high tide for the so-called coon song genre [of Black folk music].'[53] In this context, descriptions of cocaine use illustrate not only the direct enjoyment of the drug itself but its proximity to other mutually enhancing

---

[48] 'The Cocaine Habit Among Negroes', *BMJ*, 2.2187 (29 November 1902), 1729. See also, 'The Excessive Use of Cocaine in the States', *Bournemouth Daily Echo*, 2.701 (29 November 1902), 2.
[49] 'Cocaine Inhalers', *The Globe*, 33751 (8 August 1903), 5.
[50] Michael M. Cohen, 'Jim Crow's Drug War: Race, Coca Cola, and the Southern Origins of Drug Prohibition', *Southern Cultures*, 12.3 (Autumn 2006), 71.
[51] See Gerald Horne, *Jazz and Justice: Racism and the Political Economy of the Music* (New York: Monthly Review Press, 2019), 7–12 and 30–37 for a more in-depth discussion of the origins and evolution of these genres.
[52] R. A. Lawson, *Jim Crow's Counterculture: The Blues and Black Southerners 1890-1945* (Baton Rouge: Louisiana State University Press, 2010), 72. See pages 70–74 for a more general discussion of the overlap between blues and experiences of intoxication.
[53] Preston Lauterbach, *Beale Street Dynasty: Sex, Song, and the Struggle for the Soul of Memphis* (New York: W. W. Norton, 2015), 127.

pleasures such as music, sex, and sociability. Looking back from the 1930s, the jazz musician Jelly Roll Morton (aka Ferdinand Morton) recalled his youth amidst the night life of early 1900s New Orleans:

> Hundreds of men were passing through the streets day and night. The chippies in their little-girl dresses were standing in the crib doors singing the blues. Then you could observe the fancy Dans, dressed fit to kill, wearing their big diamonds. ... These guys were all big gamblers, and had all the best women and a lot of them smoked hop or used coke. In fact those days you could buy all the dope you wanted in the drug store. Just ask for it and you got it.[54]

In Tennessee in 1910, Gus Cannon of the band 'Gus Cannon's Jug Stompers' first met his future band mate, the harmonica player Noah Lewis:

> Lawd, he used to blow the hell outa that harp [ie. harmonica]. He could play two harps at the same time ... through his mouth and nose, same key and same melody. Y'know he could curl his lips 'round the harp and his nose was just like a fist. Noah, he was full of cocaine all the time – I reckon that's why he could play so loud and aw, he was good![55]

For both Cannon and Morton, cocaine could be remembered with a feeling of nostalgic affection and hedonistic awe – the drug was a catalyst for pleasure, evocative of the wild spectacles of street parties, women, loud music, and big money. The comparative ease with which working-class Black subjects could access cocaine was also a factor in this celebration. Cocaine, as Jelly Roll Morton said, was there for the asking: in a friendly drug store, 'there was no slipping and dodging. All you had to do was to walk in to be served.'[56]

Alongside the reminiscences of musicians, numerous songs about cocaine also circulated through the repertoires of early-twentieth-century balladeers and blues singers. Works like 'cocaine blues' and 'coco blues' were sung and recorded by various artists.[57] As the American sociologist Howard W. Odum somewhat

[54] Alan Lomax, *Mister Jelly Roll: The Fortunes of Jelly Roll Morton, New Orleans Creole and 'Inventor of Jazz'* (New York: Grosset and Dunlap, 1950), 49–50. Interestingly, George Cochran's 1924 glossary of American underworld slang describes a 'chippy' as 'young girl' but also records the phrase 'to get chippy with coke', suggesting cocaine's use as an aphrodisiac and its association with casual sex in the early twentieth century. See George Cochran, *Keys to Crookdom* (New York: D. Appleton, 1924), 400.
[55] Quoted in Giles Oakley, *The Devil's Music: A History of the Blues* (New York: Da Capo Press, 1997), 137.
[56] Lomax, *Mister Jelly Roll*, 25.
[57] Rupert Till, *Pop Cult: Religion and Popular Music* (London: Continuum, 2010), 39. The use of 'coco' as a slang term for cocaine seems to have migrated into English from French (where it means 'coconut') in the early 1920s. In 1922, 'O.M.S', the Paris correspondent for *The Graphic*, narrated an anecdote where he had 'had an opportunity to purchase some "coco", as it is called in France' in the night-time streets near Montmartre. See 'The Cocaine Trafficker in Paris', *The Graphic*, 105,2725 (18

fastidiously remarked in *The Negro and His Songs* (1925): 'The Negro singer pays his respects to the cocaine habit and whiskey. The majority of these songs are indecent in their suggestion.'[58] One of the clearest articulations of cocaine's use as a euphoriant and disinhibitant comes from 'Cocaine Habit Blues' released in 1930 by the 'Memphis Jug Band' with the singer Hattie Hart:

> I love my whiskey, and I love my gin,
> But the way I love my coke is a doggone sin,
> Hey, hey, honey take a whiff on me.
> ...
> It takes a little coke to give me ease,
> Strut my stuff long as you please,
> Hey, hey, honey take a whiff on me.[59]

Performers frequently modified elements of lyric and melody from earlier songs, so that a core set of images and motifs recirculated (with superficial modifications) through a variety of musical works about cocaine. The progenitor of many of these cocaine ballads and blues tunes (including 'Cocaine Habit Blues') was the song 'Take a Whiff on Me' – sometimes also known as 'Take a One on Me' or 'Take a Sniff on Me'. Based on the work of Preston Lauterbach it is possible to infer a potential origin for this song in the communal 'chants' sung by Black party-goers in the early 1900s. One chant documented in 1903 included the lines:

> The quickest action and the most satisfaction is a little sniff of coke,
> It make me feel like ridin' on a cloud, floating through the air on wings,
> And I hear sweet voices a'singin' loud, and this is the song they sings:
> Honey take a sniff on me.[60]

In the late 1920s, the folk musicologists John and Alan Lomax transcribed a version of 'Take a Whiff on Me' patch-worked together from verses sung by the musicians Iron Head (James Baker) and Lead Belly (Huddie William Ledbetter), and other verses that the authors heard in New York city prisons. Like 'Cocaine Habit Blues', 'Take a Whiff on Me' suggests the basically communal significance of recreational cocaine consumption, the shared experiences of dance, sociality, and the collective enjoyment of intoxicants. One of the rhymes used by Lead

---

February 1922), 180. See also, 'Perforation of the Nasal Septum in Cocaine Takers', *BMJ*, 2.3178 (26 November 1921), 917, which documents both the French slang terms 'coco' and 'prise de blanc'.

[58] Howard W. Odum, *The Negro and his Songs: A Study of the Typical Negro Songs in the South* (Chapel Hill: University of North Carolina Press, 1925), 218.

[59] Memphis Jug Band, 'Cocaine Habit Blues', Victor Records V-38620-A, 1930.

[60] Preston Lauterbach, *Beale Street Dynasty*, 126.

Belly and Iron Head runs: 'I'se got a nickel, you's got a dime, / You buy de coke an' I'll buy the wine. / Ho, ho, honey, take a whiff on me.'[61] Other verses that appear in both the Lomaxs' and Howard Odum's transcripts of the song describe the drug's use to heighten the experiences of sex and desire. (In this context it is interesting to note that, like Odum, the Lomaxs refer to further verses of the song that they overheard but which were, in their view, 'unprintable'.) John and Allan Lomax include the lines:

> Comin' down State Street, comin' down Main,
> Lookin' for a woman dat use cocaine.
> Honey take a whiff on me![62]

Odum's copy follows this with:

> Goin' down Peter Street, comin' down Main,
> Lookin' for de woman ain't got no man.
> Honey take a one on me![63]

In these kinds of working-class (and criminal underclass) Black accounts, cocaine appears primarily as a party drug: 'ridin' on a cloud' of cocaine and conviviality, the user could strut, sing, dance, and go looking for sex. Dealing out 'the quickest action and the most satisfaction', cocaine seemed the optimal enhancer of collective friendliness, eroticism, and joy.

It was precisely these effects, however, that were to quickly make cocaine into a 'focus of white anxieties over black working-class pleasures'.[64] The quantity of historical material from this period detailing Black enjoyment of cocaine is dwarfed by that dealing with White racial unease centred on the drug. Throughout the early part of the century, it was common practice for American authorities (particularly in the southern states) to attribute Black criminality to the action of cocaine: 'Whites perceived cocaine taking as the manifestation of a newer, bolder attitude on the part of a "new generation" of young, urban blacks. ... The effects of the drug were often described as transforming otherwise law-abiding blacks into beasts.'[65] These attitudes and assumptions were duly repeated by British reporters. 'It is general knowledge,' wrote the *Scotsman* in 1913, 'that the use of drugs among the negroes of the South is constantly increasing. ...

---

[61] John A. Lomax and Alan Lomax, *American Ballads and Folk Songs* (New York: Macmillan, 1934), 187.
[62] Ibid.
[63] Odum, *The Negro and His Songs*, 193.
[64] Adam Gussow, *Seems Like Murder Here: Southern Violence and the Blues Tradition* (Chicago: University of Chicago Press, 2002), 178.
[65] Spillane, *Cocaine*, 95.

Ninety-nine percent of the race conflicts, it is said, are the direct result of the abuse of cocaine.'⁶⁶ In 1914, the *Lancet* and several other newspapers in the UK republished the assertions of the American doctor E. Huntington Williams: 'The negro who has once formed the habit, declares Dr. Williams, is absolutely beyond redemption. His whole nature is changed by the habit. Sexual desires are increased and perverted; peaceful men become quarrelsome and timid ones courageous.'⁶⁷

British public attention was most seriously engaged in the question of African American cocainism in the late summer and autumn of 1906. On 20 August of that year, a young Englishwoman named Ethel Lawrence described how – while visiting her brother in Atlanta – she had been attacked and severely beaten by an unidentified Black man. British newspapers such as *The People* luridly detailed the perpetration of this 'horrible outrage on an English girl'. When help arrived: 'Miss Lawrence was found in an awful condition. Her right eye was gouged out, her right arm broken, her nose bitten off, and she was otherwise SHOCKINGLY MALTREATED.'⁶⁸ Over the next month White violence in Atlanta was to build until the evening of 22 September and the start of the 1906 Atlanta race riot.⁶⁹ With the newspapers' attention already captured by the Lawrence assault, the September riots were widely reported in the UK. And while some papers deplored the prejudice and 'uncontrollable' violence of the White mob 'which was simply mad to kill ... to gratify racial hatred',⁷⁰ other papers repeated the rioters' assertion that the lynchings were the consequence of: 'a tidal wave of crime [that] has swept over the negroes due to the torrid weather, the increase of the cocaine habit, and cheap liquor in low saloons on whose walls are placarded pictures of white women.'⁷¹ Thus, while British newspapers maintained that the vice of cocainism was one that had arrived on their shores from the new world, they had also begun to acquire their own versions of American racial and

---

⁶⁶ 'The Harrison Tragedy', *Scotsman*, 21904 (1 October 1913), 10.
⁶⁷ 'Cocainism in the Southern United States', *Lancet*, 183.4727 (4 April 1914), 980. See also, 'A Worse Evil', *Western Mail* 1400 (4 April 1914), 6.
⁶⁸ 'A Black Fiend', *The People*, 1298 (26 August 1906), 14. See also: 'Negro Runs Amok', *Daily Telegraph*, 16952 (25 August 1909), 11; and 'A Fiendish Assault', *Belfast Telegraph*, 35.11205 (22 August 1906), 5.
⁶⁹ See David Fort Godshalk, *Veiled Visions: The 1906 Atlanta Race Riot and the Reshaping of American Race Relations* (Chapel Hill: University of North Carolina Press, 2005), 35–9 for more on the lead-up to the riots and the reporting of the Ethel Lawrence case.
⁷⁰ 'Massacre of Negroes in Georgia', *Morning Post*, 41913 (25 September 1906), 7.
⁷¹ 'Reign of Terror in Georgia', *Pall Mall Gazette*, 83.12937 (25 September 1906), 7. See also: 'The Race War in Georgia', *Edinburgh Evening News*, 10435 (25 September 1906), 4; 'Anti-Negro Riots', *Birmingham Daily Gazette*, 86.11706 (26 September 1906), 5; and 'Georgia Race Feud', *Leeds Mercury* 21368 (26 September 1906), 5.

sexual prejudices linked to cocaine. These attitudes were to become even more obviously pronounced in the years following the First World War.

'A subtle influence over White women'

The DORA 40b regulations had been initially introduced in 1916 with the intention of protecting wartime national discipline, but after the war was over their enforcement – and the enforcement of the Dangerous Drugs Act which succeeded them – was to become heavily enmeshed in fears of sexual and racial transgression. In American accounts, cocaine had for decades been freely associated with the nightmare of Black sexual menace – the prospect that the drug might turn normally passive Black subjects into monsters intent on violently 'outraging' the White women they secretly lusted after as their 'sexual desires [were] increased and perverted'.[72] In post-war Britain, this fear of assault evolved into a less explicitly violent but more insidious fear of seduction.

Of all potential drug-takers (or 'dopers') the young White woman was imagined to be the most tragically vulnerable to the temptations of cocaine. By 1921, newspaper reports on 'Girls and Cocaine' began to appear, warning that: 'The number of young girls in the West End who are cocaine takers is quite appalling.'[73] Sidney Felstead's sensational exploration of metropolitan criminality, *The Underworld of London* (1923) provides several helpfully concise examples of the gendered narratives that sprang up around cocaine in the 1920s. Felstead's concluding chapter deals almost entirely with cocaine and its exceptional allure for the young ladies of the capital: 'There is fast springing up in London a horde of female "dopers", women who regularly drug themselves with cocaine … Within the last twelve months the [cocaine] habit has become known all over the West End of London. From being a vice practised by the few, it has spread to all classes of Englishwomen.'[74] From his observations, Felstead theorized that 'the soothing and at the same time exhilarating effects of cocaine'[75] made it an ideal drug for the energetic, pleasure-seeking young woman about town:

> It is easy enough to understand women who live the gay life taking to cocaine as a means of producing brightness and abandon. … How easy is the path of

---

[72] 'Cocainism in the Southern United States', *Lancet*, 980.
[73] 'Girls and Cocaine', *Daily Herald*, 1701 (11 July 1921), 5.
[74] Felstead, *Underworld of London*, 264 and 290.
[75] Ibid., 273.

temptation! Midnight suppers and early-morning dances, bodily lassitude and sleeplessness, all to be banished by 'dope'.[76]

Cocaine, as the archetypal drug of 'exhilaration' and self-assurance, was particularly fitted to the enjoyments of the 'fast' modern girl, the frequenter of nightclubs and fashionable restaurants, the hunter-up of parties and 'wild pleasures'.[77] Intriguingly, while Felstead never draws explicit attention to cocaine's aphrodisiac effects, his book often emphasizes the gendered rituals attached to cocaine pleasure. Cocaine, as represented in Felstead's book, is a drug that is almost always 'discreetly obtained'[78] for the lady cocainist 'by some male acquaintance'. The 'high class "doper"' rarely purchases her cocaine in the club or in the street: 'A male friend does that for them; he pays for his barely tolerated devotion by purchasing his lady-love little luxuries unattainable by the uninitiated. The lady will tell him that she feels off-colour; she thinks a little cocaine might pull her round.'[79] Cocaine addiction is similarly presented as a perverse version of erotic fixation. 'The despicable creatures,' wrote Felstead, 'who hawk the cocaine round know only too well that a drug-sodden woman will sell body and soul to maintain a supply of "dope".'[80] In this framing, cocaine is itself not only addictively seductive but also synonymous with the act of seduction: the giving and receiving of the drug implies a ceremony of flirtation as its supply and demand takes on the aspect of romantic devotion. Cocainism was, in the night life of the 1920s, inherently connected with coupling. This dynamic of gendered pleasure, subjection, and control was all the more disturbing when the 'male acquaintance' (or 'despicable creature') was a man of colour.

The generally assumed connection between cocaine and Black subjects is most succinctly evidenced in a remark made by one anonymous policeman in 1923. In August of that year the London police arrested Jack Kelson, 'a coloured American seaman' for cocaine dealing. (Kelson was also subsequently identified as Jack Delzim, a British subject born in Trinidad.[81]) While he was being held in police custody, one of the officers allegedly said to his charge: 'Come on, darkie, you coloured fellows know where the cocaine comes from. Tell me where you fellows get it, and I will let you go.'[82] Throughout the early 1920s, it was common

---

[76] Ibid., 284.
[77] Ibid., 264.
[78] Ibid.
[79] Ibid., 286.
[80] Ibid., 269.
[81] 'London Rid of a Cocaine Pest', *Dundee Evening Telegraph*, 14574 (10 August 1923), 3.
[82] See 'Negro in Cocaine Charge', *Sunday Post*, 938 (5 August 1923), 2; and 'Negro and Cocaine', *Westminster Gazette*, 9381 (6 August 1923), 5.

for papers to claim that, while London's 'opium shops' were concentrated in the Chinese neighbourhoods of Limehouse, the cocaine dealers of the metropolis were to be found in 'the negro communities in Soho and near Tottenham Court Road, as it is believed that a great part of the traffic has now passed into the hands of negro agents'.[83] Just as young White women were assumed to be 'the chief victims' of the cocaine traffic, the main perpetrators were most commonly imagined to be Black men. Out of the environs of Whitfield Street and Tottenham Court Road, 'known as the Black Man's Colony', it was claimed that, 'large quantities of [cocaine] have changed hands and have been conveyed westward, there to be sold to the unfortunate young women and girls whose craving for the "snow" has brought them to the lowest depths of degradation'.[84] Coverage of Jack Kelson's arrest demonstrates many of the era's well-worn tropes of cocaine and Black sexual peril: the *Dundee Evening Telegraph*'s subheadline called him the 'Coloured Man Who Tempted White Women'; Kelson was, 'a cocaine fiend and a bully of the worst kind … He would entice white women to try cocaine, selling them packets at 5s apiece, and once they became addicted to the drug he would raise his prices to £1 and £2 a packet'.[85] Given cocaine's flirtatious connotations, the supply of the drug could be easily integrated into narratives of erotic seduction. Cocaine features in the British popular imagination of this period as an engine for miscegenation, a contrivance by which superficially charming Black men might 'entice' White women into drugged and sexualized degradation.

As frightening as Jack Kelson and the anonymous denizens of Tottenham Court Road might be, the public's most enduringly fearsome bogeyman of Black cocainism was Edgar ('Eddie') Manning, the Jamaican-born restaurateur, jazz musician, and so-called 'Dope King' of London.[86] Manning was arrested twice for selling cocaine, once in 1922 and again in 1923, and both incidents were sensationally reported. Manning's mien was, according to contemporary papers, overwhelmingly one of chic predatory debauchery. He affected a modish Malacca cane, 'of the latest fashionable type of straight stick. It was of the light variety, and silver-mounted.' Screwed apart, 'The Drug Stick' as the papers called it, contained a hidden glass tube that could 'be used to carry large quantities of

---

[83] See 'Crime Streets', *Nottingham Evening Post*, 14041 (22 June 1923), 4; and 'Negro Dope Dealers', *Shields Daily News*, 20061 (22 June 1923), 1.
[84] 'Who Is the New Dope King?', *The People*, 2276 (31 May 1925), 1.
[85] 'London Rid of a Cocaine Pest', *Dundee Evening Telegraph*, 3.
[86] 'Capture of "Dope King"', *Dundee Evening Telegraph*, 14556 (20 July 1923), 4.

cocaine or morphia' hidden in plain sight.⁸⁷ Articles described Manning playing host to 'all-night orgies' complete with 'cocaine cocktails', opium, and high-stakes poker. 'For injections of cocaine,' wrote *The People*, 'Manning received his clients in a luxuriously-furnished apartment, and charged 10s for the operation.'⁸⁸

Accompanying these accounts of stylish dissipation was the constant threat of the pernicious attraction that he exercised over White women. According to Manning's neighbours, 'he had a great many visitors, most of them being women, who called from about 2 o'clock in the morning, and ran up and down the stairs up to about 6 a.m.'⁸⁹ His all-night parties 'were attended by black men and women. Over white women Manning had a subtle influence.'⁹⁰ Both of Manning's arrests were marked by a surge of journalistic and judicial outrage at the racial and sexual dangers embodied in cocaine. *The Times*' coverage of Manning claimed that: 'There is reason to believe that he employed Chinese agents to bring the drugs into the country, that he made a practice of teaching innocent girls how to take cocaine, and that he forced these girls to sell his wares by a system of terrorization of the most abominable kind.'⁹¹ The image of Manning and his Chinese agents (whether real or not) collaborating to corrupt and enslave their female victims draws on the same reservoir of racist anxiety as Sidney Felstead's drug-dealing 'black or yellow parasite[s]'⁹² and the image of a hostile 'Black Man's Colony'⁹³ in the heart of London – the spectre of a racially monstrous conspiracy to invade and attack the body of England. In July 1923, the Recorder at Manning's trial was described as saying that: 'He was determined to assist Parliament all he could to excise this moral cancer from the social system. The prisoner had supplied this horrible self-destroying drug to unfortunate women, and it was more than likely that innocent women had suffered in the same way.' In these remarks, the sexual peril of cocainism is transfigured into a disease that had to be aggressively, even painfully eradicated. Manning's first arrest in 1922 occasioned demands – both in newspapers and in parliamentary debates – for the penalty of flogging to be applied to cocaine traffickers.⁹⁴

⁸⁷ See 'Trafficker in Cocaine', *Western Daily Press*, 128.19,924 (1 May 1922), 8; 'The Drug Stick', *Nottingham Journal*, 30087 (1 May 1922), 2; and 'Important Drug Trafficker', *The Times*, 43019 (1 May 1922), 9.
⁸⁸ 'Opium Party Revels', *The People*, 2179 (22 July 1923), 9.
⁸⁹ 'Cocaine Raid', *Lincolnshire Echo*, 9474 (23 June 1923), 2.
⁹⁰ 'Opium Party Revels', *The People*, 9.
⁹¹ 'Cocaine Debauchery', *The Times*, 43019 (1 May 1922), 19.
⁹² Felstead, *Underworld of London*, 2.
⁹³ 'Who Is the New Dope King?', *The People*, 1.
⁹⁴ See, 'Cocaine Debauchery', *The Times*, 19; 'Soho Drug Merchant', *Western Times*, 22710 (1 May 1922), 4; and *Hansard Parliamentary Debates*, HC Deb, 4 May 1922, vol.153, c.1549. For a wider examination of the use of flogging by cat o' nine-tails in British prisons in the interwar years,

Numerous letters appeared in the pages of *The Times* warning 'fathers of young girls' to beware 'the coloured man['s] ... debauchery of girls with cocaine' and demanding that harsher punishments be meted out in future: 'Men who traffic in these poisons ... want flogging. They fear nothing but physical pain, and they should have it.'[95] The overall mood of these letters approaches one of violent retributive hysteria: the feeling that the nation's 'young womanhood'[96] needed to be rescued, and that cocaine needed to be aggressively, even brutally, purged from society. In this way, cocaine's white powder came to signify a specifically sexualized manifestation of White anxiousness.

Technologies of pleasure in the age of jazz

The aggressiveness with which Black cocainism was stigmatized, however, reflects the extent to which Black pleasure was also imagined to be more potent and – even – more technologically advanced than its White equivalent. Cocaine had long been associated with a distinctly American modernity and, as the first decades of the twentieth century wore on, it also came to be increasingly explicitly linked with newer African American artefacts of cultural innovation. The most obvious point of comparison was with jazz music. Though the cocaine habit was much more obviously hazardous than the jazz craze, cocaine nevertheless seemed to offer its early twentieth-century devotees a similarly revitalizing vision of futurity; the drug, like jazz, 'promised a sensual and experimental way of living in the present as well as creating the future.'[97] By the 1920s (and much to the alarm of some White observers), cocaine crystals came to materialize the vision of a Modernist, energized, and technologized Black America.

This futuristic representation of cocaine pleasure began to appear almost as soon as inhalation became the default mode of taking the drug. In 1903, the British newspaper *The Globe* published an account of Black American 'Cocaine Inhalers' by the Georgian colonel J. W. Watson. The article approaches its subject

---

see: Alyson Brown, 'The Sad Demise of z.D.H.38 Ernest Collins: Suicide, Informers and the Debate on the Abolition of Flogging', *Cultural and Social History*, 15.1 (2018), 100–1 and 108–11.
[95] 'Cocaine Debauchery – An Alien Traffic', *The Times*, 43021 (3 May 1922), 17; and 'Cocaine Debauchery – Present Penalties No Deterrent', *The Times*, 43020 (2 May 1922), 17. For further letters and articles debating cocaine and corporal punishment in the immediate aftermath of the first Manning trial, see: 'Cocaine Traffic', *The Times*, 43023 (5 May 1922), 17; 'Cocaine Traffic – Limited Police Powers', *The Times*, 43024 (6 May 1922), 17; 'The Rally Against Cocaine', *The Times*, 43026 (9 May 1922), 17; and 'The Real Cocaine Criminals', *The Times*, 43029 (12 May 1922), 7.
[96] 'Who Is the New Dope King?', *The People*, 1.
[97] Donald, *Some of These Days*, 7.

with fascinated horror, emphasizing the perverse innovation and accelerated action of 'cocaine sniffing'. Cocainized snuffs had been freely available as remedies for nasal congestion since the mid-1890s,[98] but in Watson's description cocaine sniffing is taken as evidence of the baffling, aberrant ingenuity of Black subjects: 'The cocaine crystals are pulverised and mixed with sugar and reduced to the right strength. … It has mystified our physicians and men of medicine to know how the negroes learned the art of mixing and pulverising the crystals.'[99] Equally disturbing was the frenetic speed and intensity of pleasure that cocaine sniffing provided, far outstripping the older procedures of injection and ingestion. Watson's writing is – for all its horror at the 'evil' of its subject – oddly precise in delineating the characteristic pleasures of cocaine sniffing:

> By sniffing the cocaine up the nostrils it reaches the brain quicker, and the effect is more lasting than if swallowed or administered by hypodermic injection. … A small pinch of the pulverised stuff goes further than seven times the same amount swallowed or injected by the user. Its effects are said to be similar to those of morphine, but it gives a feeling of a jag produced by large drinks of whisky. Like opium, too, it produces visions of wealth, beauty, and happiness. There are no menageries and snakes in a drink from cocaine; it is full of genuine joys, it is claimed, until the effects begin to die out, when it requires another dose or two to start the machinery of joy and good feeling. Unquestionably the drug affects the brain rapidly.[100]

Cocaine sniffing apparently combines the joy of morphine, the composure of opium, and the 'jag' of whisky; it is 'full of genuine joys' unmixed with dread or *delirium tremens*; it strikes the brain faster and lasts longer than if used in any other way. Black cocaine sniffing is also figured as an emphatically technologized practice of pleasure. The art of mixing the drug is described as having 'mystified' White medical expertise, obliquely suggesting its emergence from some previously unfamiliar, alien trajectory of innovation. Likewise, the assumed primitivity of popular Black medical understanding jars against the recurring images of mechanized acceleration that Watson uses to describe

---

[98] The 1897 outbreak of cocaine addiction in Manchester, Kentucky, had been blamed on the sale of one such 'snuff' and in 1896 the *London Journal*'s 'Home Notes' column had carried a recipe for a similar home-made medicine compounded of cocaine, ground coffee, menthol, and powdered sugar. ('Chips', *North-Eastern Daily Gazette*, 2; 'Remedy for Head Cold', *London Journal*, 25.631 (18 January 1896), 60.)

[99] 'Cocaine Inhalers', *The Globe*, 5. *The Globe*'s account was extracted from a longer piece by Watson that appeared in American papers in June 1903. See 'Cocaine Sniffers', *New-York Tribune*, 63.20671 (21 June 1903), 11.

[100] 'Cocaine Inhalers', *The Globe*, 5.

the action of cocaine sniffing. Cocaine snuff, he concludes, 'is a brain wrecker of the worst kind', a sentiment which sets up the shock of cocaine inhalation as a kind of cerebral train wreck. Powdered cocaine is, as such, envisioned as a form of *express* pleasure: it is fast, expedient, and runs direct to its destination. In adopting the use of cocaine for their own enjoyment Black subjects had, it seemed, managed to engineer for themselves a new and disconcertingly advanced 'machinery of joy'.

The mechanized associations of cocaine taking became yet more evident as the fin de siècle gave way to the Modernist era. Life in the aftermath of the Great War was – according to an article on Britain's new 'Cocaine Cult' from December 1918 – a matter of: 'living furiously; unless in motoring phrase "a certain number of revolutions per minute are attained there is no development of power". When the stimuli acting from without fail to whip the organism to its wonted speed, other means are apt to be adopted'.[101] Cocaine was the ideal synthetic 'excitement' to counteract post-war weariness, a fierce emotional gasoline powering a generation recalibrated to run at a higher nervous horsepower. Jazz seemed to address this same modern requirement for frenetic stimulation. 'Jazz', wrote the African American philosopher Alain LeRoy Locke, 'is the spiritual child of this age ... [the] emotional exhaust and compensation ... of a machine-ridden, extroverted form of civilisation'.[102] Jazz, like cocaine, was defined not only as an essential manifestation of twentieth-century modernity but also as an essentially Black American product (regardless of the actual ethnicity of its performers).[103] The style seemed to capture in music the chaotic energy and 'jag'[104] that cocaine infused into the bloodstream. In 1927 Italian composer Pietro Mascagni (writer of the 1890 operatic sensation *Cavalleria rusticana*) was reported as having contemptuously declared: 'Modern music is the cocaine of our times, and just as dangerous as poison'.[105] The following year he returned to the idea, this time underscoring its more racially menacing aspect: jazz, said Mascagni, 'is the

---

[101] 'The Cocaine Cult', *The Times*, 41974 (16 December 1918), 5.
[102] Alain Locke, *The Negro and His Music* (Washington, DC: The Associates in Negro Folk Education, 1936), 88–9.
[103] James Donald remarks: 'Jazz was heard and felt as not European, even when it was made by Europeans, but rather as American (that is, as modern) and, at the same time, however speciously, because of the Blackness of some of its performers, as African' (Donald, *Some of These Days*, 7). Alain Locke made a similar assertion, writing that jazz manifested 'a distinctive racial intensity of mood and a peculiar style of technical performance, that can be imitated, it is true, but of which the original pattern was Negro. ... The Negro, strictly speaking, never had a jazz age; he was born that way' (Locke, *The Negro and his Music*, 72 and 87).
[104] 'Cocaine Inhalers', *The Globe*, 5.
[105] 'Attack on Jazz', *Aberdeen Press and Journal*, 22707 (12 October 1927), 7; 'Cocaine of Music', *Liverpool Echo*, 14910 (12 October 1927), 6.

musical cocaine of the white races'.[106] More conservative middle-class Black commentators drew the same comparisons. In 1925, the American doctor E. Eliot Rawling (author of the Harlem-published *Amsterdam News*'s 'Keeping Fit' column) wrote that: 'The form of music called jazz is just as intoxicating as morphine or cocaine … In fact, jazz, as a drug, is being universally used, and its effect as a drug on the mind, the brain, the personality of the people, is a factor of great importance in these modern days.' Jazz, the medical man warned his readers, 'stimulates first, and then it over-powers'.[107]

In White eyes, Jazz and cocaine were frequently conjoined as threatening manifestations of a racialized Modernism – a modernity that incongruously contained within it the seeds of an evolutionary degeneration. The contemporary preference for 'raucous "Jazz"', with its heathenish noise, its shimmery slippery movements, its cocktails and cocaine', implied a modern regression to the level of 'the chimpanzee' or the 'sponge-like jelly-fish mixture … [of] a thousand million years ago'.[108] H. Rootham's 1924 article 'Jazzomania and Devil Dances' prophesied that the music's engine-like 'jerking', 'vibration', and 'frenzied syncopation' would lead inexorably to the over-stimulation and destruction of its listeners:

> In this diabolical music we do not get the apparent speed and quickened breath of Schumann, but a deliberate jerking of the breath, a repeated dislocation of the personal rhythm that connects together the organic structures that we name body. What should be the vital energy in the body is thus transformed into a hideous potency of destruction, and it is highly significant that the abuse of cocaine (a drug which stimulates physically without in any sense even temporarily ennobling or heightening the mental vision) should have become appallingly prevalent at a time when such an insidious assault is being made on the body.[109]

For Rootham, cocaine and jazz were alike in their debased physicality. The appetite for cocaine and syncopated melody testified to the 'patently impure' character of the age, the hunger for some frantic stimulant that would 'excite individual desire into veritable bestial frenzy'.[110]

The pleasures of jazz and cocaine thus appeared to be derived from the same underlying blueprint: the energized kick of the machine age, with its rash velocity,

---

[106] 'Musical Dope', *Belfast Telegraph*, 6 December 1928, 6.
[107] E. Eliot Rawling, 'Jazz – a Drug', *Amsterdam News*, 1 April 1925, 16.
[108] 'Religion and Sacred Art', *Hastings and St Leonards Observer*, 4560 (19 November 1927), 2.
[109] H. Rootham, 'Jazzomania and Devil Dances', *English Review*, January 1924, 111.
[110] Ibid.

self-confidence, and high-pitched sexuality. While the comparison with cocaine was an easy (and emotive) one for critics of jazz to draw, even defenders of the music found themselves falling into involuntary echoes of the drug's action. Looking back on the 'Jazz Age' from the 1930s, Alain Locke fascinatedly recalled the contemporary idea that the genre 'was a marvellous antidote to Twentieth Century boredom and nervous exhaustion, a subtle combination of narcotic and stimulant'.[111] Locke's formulation of jazz as simultaneously narcotic and stimulant unconsciously reiterates Sidney Felstead's more lustrous descriptions of cocaine – that 'shining feathery substance, almost incredibly light, and fearfully expensive' with its 'soothing and at the same time exhilarating effects'.[112] Both cocaine and jazz could be understood as fabulous 'tonic[s]' innately 'tinctured with modernism'.[113] To some observers then, it seemed possible that the 'Jazz Age' might (in some alarming but also potentially thrilling way) be likewise interpreted as the Cocaine Age, and that the Black subjects who popularized both of these innovations might have conclusively proved themselves to be the newest, most superlative technicians of modern 'light and pleasure'.[114]

Barry Pain's 'The Reaction' – dope and diminished manhood

The assumed superiority of this Black 'machinery of joy' – and its apparent attractions for White women – engendered a powerful sense of White masculine insecurity centred on cocaine. One conceptual solution to this anxiety was, as we have seen, to ferociously (even violently) stigmatize the drug and its users: to position cocaine's White British consumers as innocents and 'dupes' and the 'foreigners and coloured men' who supplied it as 'human tigers ... bent on the ruin of our boyhood and girlhood'.[115] It was possible, however, for an alternative discourse to stem from these conditions. The Black man's especial relationship with cocaine suggested, to some White observers, the possibility of a more general masculine superiority; a greater familiarity with cocainized pleasure could be read as a tangible instance of greater modernity, confidence, and sexual proficiency. Against this background, familiarity with cocaine could look like demonstrable proof of masculine competency, and puritanical fear of

---

[111] Locke, *The Negro and His Music*, 89–90.
[112] Felstead, *Underworld of London*, 267 and 284.
[113] Locke, *The Negro and His Music*, 90.
[114] 'The Cocaine Cult', *The Times*, 5.
[115] 'Who Is the New Dope King?', *The People*, 1; and 'Cocaine Debauchery', *The Times*, 19.

it seems like craven submission and unmanly hesitation – positive proof that such a man was (in Sidney Felstead's words) one of the 'uninitiated'.[116] Some hint of this attitude can be seen in the pharmacologist and neurologist W. E. Dixon's assertion in 1923 that, though it might be a 'rapid and exhilarating intoxicant' those men who tried sniffing cocaine 'in the spirit of adventure or bravado' were most likely proof against the danger of 'true addiction'.[117] By this logic, rather than being coded as a marker of deviant or degenerate masculinity, cocaine could be used to signal a manly insouciance and worldliness; a casual, knowing relationship with cocaine might denote the fundamental continence of a man's character. This idea is directly dramatized – and explicitly racialized – in Barry Pain's short story, 'The Reaction', published in May 1923, only a few months after Dixon's lecture on cocaine.

Pain's protagonist is Ernest Purdon, a young assistant pharmacist working in the Whitechapel area of London. Despite his pharmaceutical training, Purdon is timid of intoxicants. Pain tells us that: 'Purdon had never taken any dope before [although], in his profession he had seen something of it' – he likewise keeps a full eight-ounce bottle of brandy in his room, 'for emergencies', which has remained untouched for two years.[118] This wariness of drink and drugs is indicative of Purdon's slightly feeble character and of the narrative's repeated imaging of his emasculation. In his work he is respectable but unintelligent, having barely passed his qualifying exams. The 'clumsy, ill-dressed' dockworkers who visit the pharmacy 'earn more money than our Mr. Purdon ever did or could'.[119] He is 'heartily afraid' of his tyrannical landlady, and goes to church every Sunday with his sweetheart Ethel, for whom he feels little real affection, but consoles himself: 'It was of no use to cry for the moon, and if he lost Ethel, he might not get another.'[120] Ethel, for her part, is seeing at least two other young men. Near the end of the story Ethel's mother coyly remarks to Purdon that her daughter, 'knows how to take care of herself. She can put a man in his place all right',[121] strongly implying that the spiritless Purdon has been 'put in his place' by Ethel's determined management.

Ernest's friend Harry Bates, by contrast, is 'popular with the ladies' and lives a life of carefree amusement:

---

[116] Felstead, *Underworld of London*, 286.
[117] W. E. Dixon, 'A British Medical Association Lecture on the Drug Habit', *BMJ*, 1.3248 (31 March 1923), 544.
[118] Barry Pain, 'The Reaction', *Nash's Pall Mall Magazine*, 71.361 (May 1923), 112.
[119] Pain, 'The Reaction', 51.
[120] Ibid., 111.
[121] Ibid., 116.

> Bates was a man of good appearance and manner, knew how to talk, and was sometimes dryly humorous. He was in the same profession as Purdon and no better qualified. But he was making considerably more money. Bates was employed by a man who kept a very well-known and very discreet druggist's shop in Mayfair. Wealthy young men, suffering from the night before, consulted Bates, took what he gave them, and were not ungenerous. Some of Bates's caustic sayings were quoted in the West End clubs.[122]

Working out of fashionable Mayfair in the West End, Bates is an intimate of the fun-loving late-night world of parties, wealth, and drugs that Purdon can only regard with repressed envy.[123] Bates and the shop where he works have 'a great reputation with the big racing men and the stars of the theatrical world. Such people had money to spend and were willing to spend it.'[124] Bates exists in a world of jollity and affluence; his understanding of 'dope' and its various uses seems, in Pain's description of him, to be part and parcel of his dissolute charm, attractiveness, and moneyed affluence.

Recreational drug use forms the core of 'The Reaction's plot'. One day, a ship's steward and casual acquaintance of Purdon's brings him a small packet of mysterious brown powder that he has taken off the body of a recently deceased passenger:

> Got it from a negro who died of pneumonia this trip and was buried at sea. He wasn't the ordinary sort. Mr E. Matthews he was on the passenger-list, and letters after his name. An educated man I should say, and got money. Travelling in first class he was. ... Showed me this powder, and said he was going to make a fortune with it.[125]

Purdon agrees to take the packet home and analyse its contents as far as he is able. While investigating the powder in his room, he accidentally introduces some of it into a cut on his hand and is immediately predicated into an ecstatic drug trip. Purdon decides to try to replicate the compound and make himself rich by marketing it to the kind of fast clientele known to Harry Bates. Before

---

[122] Ibid., 111.
[123] Christopher Hallam points to the advent of late-night (and all-night) pharmacies in London as an important factor in the city's evolving drug trade in the 1920s. Under DORA and the 1920 Dangerous Drugs Act, cocaine could be legally purchased with a doctor's prescription. As such, one viable tactic for recreational users was to gain the cooperation of a 'script doctor' or the connivance of a willing pharmacist. This nocturnal trade was 'conducive to making London the prescribing capital of the UK'. (Christopher Hallam, 'From Injudicious Prescribing to the Script Doctor: Transgressive Addiction Treatment in the Interwar Years', in *White Drug Cultures and Regulation in London, 1916-1960*, ed. Christopher Hallam (London: Palgrave Macmillan, 2018), 39.)
[124] Pain, 'The Reaction', 114.
[125] Ibid., 112.

he can write to Bates, however, the drug's reaction sets in. Purdon experiences a series of terrifying hallucinations that attack him and try to make him kill himself. The delirium passes off before he can throw himself out of his window, but Ernest's hopes of fame and fortune are lost along with the rest of the powder.

For our purposes, one of the most significant details of 'The Reaction' is the nature of the delusions that afflict Purdon. The two hallucinations that most vividly torment him are the voice of Harry Bates and the image of E. Matthews, the Black intellectual and originator of the brown powder. Neither of these two appear directly on page, but they haunt Purdon nevertheless – his insecurities manifest most intensely in the spectres of the two men who are not only superior to him but whose superiority is marked by their greater familiarity with the world of drugs. At his lowest ebb, Purdon imagines the voice of Harry Bates nonchalantly mocking his inexperience and teasing him with the prospect of death:

> 'A thousand pities you didn't come to me at the very first', said Bates. 'I could have warned you. I know about the stuff, and have seen two cases. Cocaine is a baby's toy to it. After one hypodermic, the reaction lasts as long as life lasts. Life doesn't last long, because suicide is inevitable. No human being can stand the damned torture of it. No known drug touches it. Nothing can alleviate it'.[126]

Purdon's imaginary Bates is one who is contemptuously knowledgeable, who is secure in his experience with cocaine, and knows to beware the new compound that Ernest has stupidly exposed himself to. In Purdon's fantasies, it seems natural that not only should Bates already know all about the new drug, but that his voice should be the one to articulate Purdon's sense of shame at his ignorance.

Matthews appears as a more directly physical threat, manhandling and beating Purdon. In life, we are told, Matthews was already wealthy and educated (travelling, as Purdon's friend observes, in first class, with letters after his name, and plenty of money and personal jewellery) and was seemingly poised to make even more money off of the powder. (Pain never clarifies whether or not Matthews is the inventor of the drug, but given his credentials it seems not implausible that he is.) Purdon's imagination exaggerates these traits. He appears in the White man's mind as 'a gigantic negro wearing a light tweed suit'. He wears 'a double watch chain with a bunch of seals pendant from it, over his protuberant stomach, and there was an enormous diamond in his emerald-green necktie. There were diamond rings too on the brown hands.'[127] Purdon's hallucination

---
[126] Ibid., 115.
[127] Pain, 'The Reaction', 114.

of Matthews recalls the suavely 'fashionable' representation of Edgar Manning with his silver-chased 'Drug Stick',[128] as well as other (even more flamboyantly racist) accounts of the stereotypical Black 'snow' seller with 'no fewer than eleven diamond rings on his fingers, to say nothing a large-sized tie pin, a heavy gold watch guard, and diamond studs in his shirt front'.[129] These contemporary images of Black cocainism ramify directly into the portrayal of Matthews: Pain's story was published almost exactly one year after Manning's first arrest in 1922 and three months before his second in 1923.

What Purdon's mind conjures up, then, is a threatening White caricature of the Black dandy and drug user – belligerently strong, opulently attired, and intellectually capable. The double-page illustration by Émile Verpilleux that begins the story shows the hallucinatory Matthews emerging from under Purdon's bed and gripping his ankle like a monster from a childhood nightmare. Like the spectral voice of Bates, Matthews directly enacts Purdon's insecurities: the Black man never speaks to Purdon, only 'laughing' at him.[130] As the original source of the powder, Matthews's vigorousness, wealth, and abilities are seemingly concentrated in a confident integration into the world of 'dope,' and suggest the possibility that Black intellects might be the ones best equipped to yield new forms of drug pleasure. Behind Ernest Purdon's haunted imaginings there lies the suspicion that a familiarity with drugs (particularly cocaine, the emblematic chemical propellant of the jazz age) is the modern mark of the better man, and that abstinence signals only enfeeblement and subjection.

'The pure snow of heaven' – race and eroticism in *Diary of a Drug Fiend*

Barry Pain had been willing to probe the outer edges of White male unease regarding cocaine, race, and pleasure, but Alistair Crowley was much bolder in proposing a definite plan to cut through these new complications: to regain his sense of unchallenged ascendancy, the White man would be required to rise to mastery over the pleasures of cocaine. Lordship of the future would go, in Crowley's reckoning, to he who acquired supremacy over that 'snow-white chalice … filled up with the red lusts of man'.[131]

[128] Lomax, *Mister Jelly Roll*, 49; 'Trafficker in Cocaine', *Western Daily Press*, 8; 'The Drug Stick', *Nottingham Journal*, 2.
[129] 'Black Man's Paradise', *Nottingham Evening Post*, 14494 (4 December 1924), 1.
[130] Pain, 'The Reaction', 114.
[131] Aleister Crowley, *The Diary of a Drug Fiend* (London: W. Collins, 1923), 24–5.

The most succinct articulation of Crowley's theorization of drug pleasure and its mastery is to be found in his 1922 article 'The Great Drug Delusion' which he published in the *English Review* under the pseudonym 'A New York Specialist'.[132] Crowley's logic echoes that of the self-doubting Ernest Purdon – that ignorance and fear of drugs indicates an inborn and shabby subjection:

There are three main classes of men and women.

1. Afraid to experiment with anything, lest –
2. Enslaved by anything that appeals to them.
3. Able to use anything without damaging themselves.

I hesitate to admit either of the two former classes to the title of Freeman.[133]

Crowley paints both drug addiction and abstinence as equally pernicious forms of enslavement. The only truly free individual is one who is unafraid of their own pleasure, and able to indulge in drugs without becoming overcome by them. Drug use (as Crowley explains in one of his later commentaries on *The Book of the Law*, the sacred text of his spiritual philosophy of 'Thelema') acts to 'reveal' a man's inner disposition, exposing whether he has a 'slave-soul' or not: 'If you are really free, you can take cocaine as easily as salt-water taffy. … If a man is simple, fearless, eager, he is all right; he will not become a slave. If he is afraid, he is already a slave.'[134] Cocaine, according to the magician, is harmless if given to the 'good citizen', a man who he describes as 'wise, schooled to the world, … a man of intelligence and self-control'.[135] Cocaine use, then, acts as a testimonial to a man's moral character; the 'citizen' (or master) remains strong while the 'slave' is broken and afraid.

The racial implications of Crowley's language are readily apparent, all the more so given his assumption of an American identity in authoring 'The Great Drug Delusion'. The image of drug enslavement was commonly used in the nineteenth and early twentieth centuries to characterize the degrading nature of addiction and to suggest its racially derogatory implications.[136] The parallel

---

[132] Virginia Berridge writes that, in 1922, Crowley produced two pseudonymous articles for the *English Review*: '"The great drug delusion", by "A New York specialist", and "The drug panic" by "A London physician", the latter supposedly a response to the first piece, although in fact also written by Crowley himself'. See: Virginia Berridge, 'The Origins of the English Drug 'Scene' 1890–1930', *Medical History*, 32 (1988), 62.

[133] Aleister Crowley, 'The Great Drug Delusion. By a New York Specialist', *English Review*, 34 (June 1922), 571.

[134] Aleister Crowley, *The Law Is for All*, ed. Louis Wilkinson and Hymenaeus Beta (Tempe: New Falcon, 1996), 110.

[135] Aleister Crowley, 'Cocaine', *The International*, 11.10 (October 1917), 294 and 292.

[136] See Zieger, *Inventing the Addict*, 55.

had deep roots in the United States where it was understood that: '[drug] slavery was anathematic to white manhood because addiction entailed a state of dependency… a condition of servitude analogous to that of enslaved blacks'.[137] In Britain by the 1910s and 1920s, this metaphorical representation of addiction had become heavily implicated in the cultural mythology of the 'white slave' – the tragic figure of a young White woman who was seduced, pressed into sexual slavery, and controlled by means of violence and drugs.[138] The architect of this degradation was most frequently presupposed to be a man of colour. In 1924, the *Nottingham Evening Post* described the 'brutal treatment' allegedly meted out to such unfortunates: 'The administration of a beating to these white girls is a nightly occurrence. If she does not earn sufficient money to satisfy the needs of her lord and master, she is brutally flogged. And scarcely ever are the black men charged in the police court.'[139] Consequently, on both sides of the Atlantic, it was implicitly assumed that 'addiction undermined the whiteness of addict[s]'.[140] Crowley's work subtly revises this basic tenet of drug slavery and its figuration of racial hierarchy. Here, the 'Freeman' is the cocaine user; Whiteness (construed primarily as a state of mastery over racial inferiors) is affirmed not by keeping the body pure and free of contaminating intoxicants but by a fearless and 'self-control[led]' enjoyment of such drugs. Drug pleasure, as such, becomes a means by which to assert White hegemony over a racially coded slave population – reversing the disconcerting connotations of cocaine as an inherently Black pleasure.

This alignment of drug pleasure with racial freedom and mastery is central to Crowley's first published novel *The Diary of a Drug Fiend* (1923). Split into three sections labelled (in a restructuring of Dante's cosmic progression) *Paradiso*, *Inferno*, and *Purgatorio*, the novel describes the knighted former flying ace Peter Pendragon and his wife Lou's experiences with drugs – first cocaine and subsequently cocaine and heroin together – and how these are bound up with their spiritual development and eventual realization of the tenets of Thelema. In parts one and two, Lou and Peter meet, are quickly married, and embark on a protracted 'cocaine honeymoon'[141] on the continent before returning to England and sinking into the hellish grind of addiction. The final part (*Purgatorio*) chronicles their recovery under the spiritual and medical guidance of Basil King

---

[137] Jonathan S. Jones, 'Opium Slavery: Civil War Veterans and Opiate Addiction', *The Journal of the Civil War Era*, 10.2 (June 2020), 189.
[138] See Kohn, *Dope Girls*, 31–2.
[139] 'Black Man's Paradise', *Nottingham Evening Post*, 1.
[140] Jones, 'Opium Slavery', 190.
[141] Crowley, *Diary of a Drug Fiend*, 44.

Lamus – a flattering and thinly disguised portrait of Crowley himself. Lamus instructs the Pendragons in the principles of Thelema and cultivates their self-realization until they are able to gain control over their drug use. In the end, the couple are pronounced to have 'conquered'[142] their addictions, continuing to employ drugs as they like, but remaining in command of their usage.

Lou narrates the *Inferno* section of the narrative, and one of her most important functions is to restate the ideological premise of 'The Great Drug Delusion' but with an added emphasis on sex and the performance of masculinity. Women, Lou thinks, 'expect a man to show himself superior. It will not do to kill passion … But he must refuse to surrender to his passions; he must make them serve him.'[143] Lou expands on this idea by an analogy:

> Who would kill a horse because he was afraid to ride him? It is better to mount, and dare the brute to bolt.
>
> After the man is thrown, we pick him up and nurse him, but we don't adore him. Most men are like that. But what every woman is looking for is the man with the most spirited horse and the most complete mastery of him.[144]

In Lou's mind, the ideal man – the man who Crowley imagines women will 'adore' more than any other – is the man whose passions are the most energetic but also most resolutely under his dominion. Lou's question of 'who would kill a horse because he was afraid to ride him?' recalls Crowley's contempt for those who are enslaved because they are 'afraid to experiment with anything'.[145] Abstinence is equated with cowardice, and the 'spirited' man, the 'unafraid' man, does not abstain. Pleasure, and the 'complete mastery' of pleasure, asserts a clear hierarchy of manliness.

Cocaine is closely connected with the novel's portrayal of this hierarchy, both in its sexual and racial dimensions. Throughout the novel Lou and Peter frequently have sex while high on cocaine, and (from Peter's point of view at least) the drug is associated with a triumphantly masculinized sexual omnipotence. The night the couple first meet is also the night of Peter's first experience with the drug. In the moments after inhaling the 'sparkling dust' he thinks of Lou: 'Now I was her man, her mate, her master!'[146] Finding himself alone with his lady and a fresh dose of cocaine in the taxi home, the young

---

[142] Ibid., 367.
[143] Ibid., 195–6.
[144] Ibid., 196.
[145] Crowley, 'The Great Drug Delusion', 571.
[146] Crowley, *The Diary of a Drug Fiend*, 25–6.

Pendragon is 'stimulated to male intensity'.¹⁴⁷ Cocaine is similarly integral to the couple's perception of their relationship and mutual attraction. Lou, in Peter's eyes, has 'a sparking quality' in everything she does: 'She was the spirit of cocaine incarnate; cocaine made flesh. Her mere existence made the Universe infinitely exciting.'¹⁴⁸ Likewise, Lou's pet name for Peter is 'Cockie'. Supposedly a reference to the crowing of the cockerel in the biblical denial of Peter, the name much more directly evokes the couple's shared love of 'coke'.¹⁴⁹ Lou and Peter's cocaine idyll is summarized in their plan of action the day after their first meeting: 'What we had to do was to get married as quickly as we could, and lay in a stock of cocaine, and go away and have a perfectly glorious time for ever and ever.'¹⁵⁰ Cocaine acts as an engine of eroticism in the novel. 'Until you've got your mouth full of cocaine,' Peter observes, 'you don't know what kissing is. … You never get tired! You're on fourth speed all the time, and the engine purrs like a kitten, a big white kitten with the stars in its whiskers.'¹⁵¹ The drug propels a more perfect version of romance and instils a more complete form of feminine love and devotion; the cocaine lover is, after all according to Lou, 'what every woman is looking for'.¹⁵² For the White English man, cocaine use suggests the possibility that he might recoup to himself the same kind of slavish devotion and 'subtle influence'¹⁵³ over White women that his cocainized Black rivals were imagined to commanded.

In these circumstances, it is hardly surprising that Peter and Lou's *affaire de cocaïne* easily transitions into acts of racialized sexual theatrics. Peter's knighthood and his 'Pendragon' surname connect him with the mythologized Ur-Englishness of Arthurian legend. Indeed, it is more than once suggested that Sir Peter is an actual descendant of the legendary Pendragons: 'We Pendragons are a pretty proud lot, especially since Sir Thomas Malory gave us that write-up in the time of Henry VIII.'¹⁵⁴ Peter's aristocratic lineage and his status as a war hero combine to suggest that he represents an idealized image of traditional White Britishness.¹⁵⁵ Locked in a Paris hotel room with Lou and a plentiful supply of

---

¹⁴⁷ Ibid., 28.
¹⁴⁸ Ibid., 50.
¹⁴⁹ Ibid., 55 and 47.
¹⁵⁰ Ibid., 41.
¹⁵¹ Ibid., 55.
¹⁵² Ibid., 196.
¹⁵³ 'Opium Party Revels', *The People*, 9.
¹⁵⁴ Crowley, *The Diary of a Drug Fiend*, 80.
¹⁵⁵ See Justin Sausman, 'Science, Drugs and Occultism: Aleister Crowley, Henry Maudsley and Late-Nineteenth Century Degeneration Theories', *Journal of Literature and Science*, 1.1 (2008), 47 for further commentary on Peter's embodiment of the health of the British nation.

cocaine, however, the couple's sexuality revolves around the performance of a variously racialized sexual drama:

> It pleased her to assume the psychology of the Oriental pleasure-making woman. I was her Pasha-with-three-tails, her Samurai warrior, her gorgeous Maharaja, with a scimitar across my knee, ready to cut her head off at the first excuse.
>
> She was the Ouled Näil with tattooed cheeks and chin, with painted antimony eyebrows, and red smeared lips.
>
> I was the masked Toureg, the brigand from the desert, who had captured her.[156]

In the playing out of these orientalized scenarios, cocaine comes to manifest a fantasy of totalizing racial and erotic confidence. At one point, Peter imagines that the experience of taking cocaine must be very like the feeling of having been an Englishman when the British Empire was still at its greatest potency: 'Cocaine removes all hesitation', he thinks, it reminds one what it is like to 'be a lord of creation'.[157] Taken up by the White male user, then cocaine could (in Crowley's conception) permit them to reacquaint themselves with a lost feeling of omnipotent control and imperious self-satisfaction; by conquering the drug themselves, they might banish the doubts produced by the insurrectionary advent of newly 'sophisticated' yet 'elemental' Black pleasures.[158] 'With cocaine', Peter reflects to himself, 'one is indeed master of everything'.[159]

Towards the dawn – *Diary of a Drug Fiend*'s cocaine future

Ultimately, *Diary of a Drug Fiend* also posits that this sense of absolute invulnerability might transcend the present and be impressed onto the uncertain aspect of the future itself. While the novel characterizes the experience of heroin as a 'spiritual' and 'calm beatitude', the pleasures of cocaine are 'definitely stimulating' and bombastically technological.[160] Ranging across Britain, France, and Italy in a whirl of cocaine and international travel, the Pendragons find themselves 'living at ten times the normal voltage'.[161] The couple's radically accelerated pace of living is maintained by keeping their 'furnace[s] full of coke', says Peter: 'The first hint of fatigue sent one's hand to

---

[156] Crowley, *The Diary of a Drug Fiend*, 50.
[157] Ibid., 44–5.
[158] Locke, *The Negro and His Music*, 88 and 90.
[159] Crowley, *The Diary of a Drug Fiend*, 62.
[160] Ibid., 61–2.
[161] Ibid., 46.

one's pocket. One sniff … and we were on fourth speed again!'[162] The purest of these images of modernized velocity draw on Peter's wartime experience in the flying corps. In the first heat of his passion for Lou the two make a mad sprint from the nightclub to a friend's flat, to a motorcar, and then into Peter's private aeroplane and out over the English Channel: 'We soared towards the dawn. I went straight to over three thousand. I could hear the beat of my heart. It was one with the beat of the engine. … It was an octave to cocaine; the same invigorating spiritual force expressed in other terms.'[163] Cocaine provides the couple a means by which to internalize the 'invigorating' energy of modern technologies – a 'perpetual stoking'[164] for the 'furnace' of the passions. The 'crystal glimmer'[165] of cocaine provides the motive power for the twentieth century's newly mechanized hedonism: a life of 'perfect pleasure' lived at 'tremendous pace'.[166]

On top of using cocaine to fuel Peter's orientalized sexual fantasies, Crowley's novel also maintains the wider early-twentieth-century association between the drug and an imaginative version of Black American Modernism. Lou and Peter encounter two other noteworthy cocainists in their travels across Europe. One is a Black American the couple meet in Naples, who warns them of the tendency of cocaine to make its devotees 'flighty and sceptical' (Lou later ponders whether by 'sceptical' the man really meant 'suspicious').[167] The other is: 'a girl in Paris, half a Red Indian, a lovely baby with the fascination of a fiend and a fund of the foulest stories that ever were told. She lived on cocaine.'[168] The couple's encounters with these American expatriates point towards the longstanding impression of the United States as simultaneously the most modern, the most racially cosmopolitan, and the most heavily cocainized of the world's nations. This imaginative combination of racial primitivism and American modernity recurs at key moments through the novel. Peter first tries the white powder in the dancing room of The Smoking Dog nightclub. As Lou dances and recites mystic poetry, Peter notes that:

> A wave of almost insane excitement swept through the club. It was like the breaking out of anti-aircraft guns. The band struck up a madder jazz.

[162] Ibid., 46–7.
[163] Ibid., 38.
[164] Ibid., 95.
[165] Ibid., 77.
[166] Ibid., 42.
[167] Ibid., 167.
[168] Ibid., 49.

The dancers raved with more tumultuous and breathless fury. ... Around us rang the shrieking laughter of the crazy crowd.¹⁶⁹

An instant later, 'the sudden, the instantaneous madness of cocaine swept from my nostrils to my brain'.¹⁷⁰ Jazz and cocaine exert a shared set of effects: an immediate, violent onset of action and a delirious 'madness'. Likewise, they both manifest themselves in the body through intensified respiration: jazz induces a 'breathless fury' while cocaine is inhaled 'in one long breath ... like a choking man'.¹⁷¹ This same combination of savage energy and breathless modernism reappears as the couple cross from France into Italy aboard the *train de luxe*. Not long after boarding the express the Pendragons begin 'automatically "coking up" without knowing that we were doing so'. When the train reaches the plains of Lombardy the pair begin 'breathing rapidly and deeply', feeling the pull of something 'savage in our souls'.¹⁷² Peter descends into a slew of visions and sensations that culminate in the impression that he has become:

> A Witch-Doctor presiding over a cannibal feast, driving the yellow mob of murderers into a fiercer Comus-rout, as the maddening beat of the tom-tom and the sinister scream of the bull-roarer destroy every human quality in the worshippers and make them elemental energies; Valkyrie-vampires surging and shrieking on the summit of the storm.¹⁷³

The 'elemental energies' of cocaine are here condensed into a hyperbolic vision of ogrish savagery. The thunderous beat of the tom-tom and bull-roarer replicate the maddening jazz that was the accompaniment to Peter's first dose of cocaine; the chaotic force of the drug and the 'stupendous speed and diabolical delight' of the express train are welded together into a lurid phantasm of race and modernity. Cocaine in *Diary of a Drug Fiend* not only suggests the technologically and culturally transcendent potential of the future but also encapsulates the suspicion that the White race might not be fated to be the progenitors of that future. The final thesis of Crowley's novel, though, is that it might be possible to resolve this hesitation – that in taking cocaine it might be possible for White subjects to imaginatively retake the twentieth century.

The conclusion of the novel comes when Lou and Peter learn – thanks to their instruction in Thelemic philosophy – to subordinate their addiction to the

---

¹⁶⁹ Ibid., 22.
¹⁷⁰ Ibid., 26.
¹⁷¹ Ibid., 25.
¹⁷² Ibid., 104–6.
¹⁷³ Ibid., 105.

maturity of their wills, completing their evolution into the kind of masterful souls who can 'use anything without damaging themselves'.[174] Basil King Lamas (who acts as both their teacher and Crowley's own self-insertion into the text) exemplifies the novel's ideal of drug use, able to 'use cocaine as a fencing-master uses a rapier, as an expert, without danger of wounding himself'.[175] Lamas frequently encourages the couple to view their individual recovery as part of a larger project of social and intellectual evolution. The master exhorts Lou and Peter to see themselves 'as pioneers of humanity undertaking a desperate adventure for the good of the race'.[176] In mastering their addictions, they are also ensuring humanity's continued mastery of the future:

> 'I encourage you to take drugs', he went on, 'exactly as I encourage you to fly. … You children are the flower of the new generation. You have got to fear nothing. You have got to conquer everything. You have got to learn to make use of drugs as your ancestors learnt to make use of lightning'.[177]

These lines illustrate the generational, futuristic implications that cocaine use carries in the novel. Peter and Lou, the children of the aftermath, are tasked with undertaking a mission of regeneration and conquest. Control of cocaine is bound up with an almost magical-sounding dominion of sky and lightning – a mystical arc of technological triumph that curves upward from their ancestral past into a reinvigorated future. At the lowest point of the couple's addiction Peter thinks of their rundown, wasted condition as being, 'like Europe after the war'.[178] By this same analogy, Peter and Lou's emancipation from drug slavery suggests a means by which to affect a broader resurgence of European – and particularly Anglo-Saxon – civilization.

While Lamas's utopian project of drug mastery is consistently framed as an undertaking for the benefit of all mankind, it is difficult to square this aspiration with the novel's larger motifs of racial control and hierarchy. The closing passages of *Diary of a Drug Fiend* describe the comforting notion that Lou and Peter have now been 'tried in the crucible and come out pure gold'; in attaining control over heroin and cocaine, they have demonstrably 'attained a higher stage of evolution' and found an 'absolute faith in the future'.[179] Cocaine appears in the text as the consolation and substantiation of a new faith, but Crowley's rendering

---

[174] Crowley, 'The Great Drug Delusion', 571.
[175] Crowley, *The Diary of a Drug Fiend*, 362.
[176] Ibid., 280.
[177] Ibid., 158.
[178] Ibid., 139.
[179] Ibid., 363 and 368.

of the drug is heavily dictated by the racial associations that it held in the wider culture of the early twentieth century. The pleasures of cocaine – its euphoria, eroticism, lightning energy, and transcendent confidence – were, at root, racially and sexually demarcated pleasures. In mastering its fierce ecstasies, the White man could imagine the redemption of his own manhood and feel his continued mastery of the future. Within the 'sheer bright infinite beauty' of cocaine we find the fantasy of an eternalized and immaculate Whiteness.[180]

---

[180] Ibid., 25.

Conclusion

Did you ever hear about Cocaine Lil?
She lived in Cocaine town on Cocaine hill,
She had a cocaine dog and a cocaine cat,
They fought all night with a cocaine rat.

She had cocaine hair on her cocaine head.
She had a cocaine dress that was poppy red;
She wore a snowbird hat and sleigh-riding clothes.
On her coat she wore a crimson, cocaine rose.

Big gold chariots on the Milky Way,
Snakes and elephants silver and grey.
Oh the cocaine blues they make me sad,
Oh the cocaine blues make me feel bad.

The comic ballad and 'song-sketch' of the character of 'Cocaine Lil' first appeared in the early twentieth century. Versions of the song made their way into print as early as 1918 before Carl Sandburg compiled it into his famous anthology, *The American Songbag* in 1927.[1] In 1938, the English poet W. H. Auden included it in *The Oxford Book of Light Verse* under the title 'Cocaine Lil and Morphine Sue', the same title used in Frank Shay's song-book *More Pious Friends and Drunken Companions* from 1928.[2]

As an endpoint for this study, 'Cocaine Lil' has a particular symbolic resonance. Throughout this book we have seen the extent to which cocaine in the late nineteenth and early twentieth centuries acquired a wide variety of both real-world and metaphorical applications. To observers in the 1880s, cocaine

---

[1] See: Frederick H. Martens, *The Phantom Drum* (New York: J. Fischer & Bro., 1918), 66; and Carl Sandburg, *The American Songbag* (New York: Harcourt, Brace, 1927), 206.
[2] W. H. Auden, *W. H. Auden's Book of Light Verse*, ed. Edward Mendelson (New York: New York Review Books, 2004), xvi and 280. See also: Frank Shay, *More Pious Friends and Drunken Companions* (New York: Macmillan, 1928), 77–8.

seemed to have struck out immediately on a course 'scarcely [to] be paralleled in the history of any other drug' with an 'almost indefinitely multiplied' number of uses.³ Cocaine was figured as a drug with a singularly fragmented and pluralized character. In this vein we might recall Henry Hallett Dale's observation that: 'the case of cocaine is in some respects unique. There are other drugs of addiction; but cocaine appears to be the only one in which the therapeutic value depends upon an action of a different type from that which leads to the vicious habit.'⁴ Peculiarly divided between its beneficent local anaesthetic action and its euphoric effects on the 'central nervous system', cocaine was further distinguished for contemporary commentators by the sheer multitude of ways in which it might be consumed.⁵ As Louis Lewin noted in 1924, 'No other substance has as many different modes of application as cocaine.'⁶ In this context, 'Cocaine Lil's chaotic proliferation of images reflects the distinctive multiplication of meanings and uses attached to cocaine across the period of this study. The main aesthetic effect of 'Cocaine Lil' is a sense of frenetic muddling and juxtaposition: the work is both comic and tragic, morbid and whimsical. The song ends with Lil coming home late one night from a 'snow party' and taking one last 'sniff' of cocaine that 'knock[s] her dead'.⁷ Cocaine, as it appears in the song, is fundamentally incoherent, oxymoronic, delirious, anarchically funny, and finally lethal. In trying to introduce the piece to readers of *The American Songbag*, even Carl Sandburg felt compelled to own that many of the song's images were 'hard to explain' and were probably best understood as being intended to 'symbolise a snarl'.⁸ This sense of confusion, of 'Cocaine Lil' as a fundamentally tangled, snarled up jumble of images, is emblematic of the contemporary confusion of views about cocaine more broadly. For observers across the late nineteenth and early twentieth centuries, cocaine could simultaneously register euphoria, fear, zany hyperactivity, the strengthening of the body, the slavery of addiction, and the generous gifts of medical science to a 'suffering humanity'.⁹

Cocaine was, as this work has demonstrated, a substance whose cultural and imaginative reception was enmeshed in multiple different discourses and

---

³ Walter G. Smith, 'Report on Materia Medica and Therapeutics', *Dublin Journal of Medical Science*, 80.6 (December 1885), 506; Walter G. Smith, 'Report on Materia Medica and Therapeutics', *Dublin Journal of Medical Science*, 84.6 (December 1887), 507.
⁴ H. H. Dale, 'The Possible Substitutes for Cocaine', *BMJ*, 1.3299 (22 March 1924), 511.
⁵ Ibid.
⁶ Louis Lewin, *Phantastica: A Classic Survey on the Use and Abuse of Mind-Altering Plants* (Rochester, NY: Park Street Press, 1998), 68.
⁷ Sandburg, *The American Songbag*, 206.
⁸ Ibid.
⁹ 'A New Anaesthetic', *Chambers's Journal*, 2.61 (28 February 1885), 144.

coloured by the many different ways in which it could be employed. This study has examined some of the most prominent imaginative connotations and metaphorical framings of the substance, as well as its integration into the tropes, genre conventions, and characters of fin de siècle and early-twentieth-century popular fiction. The chapters of this book have been intended to spotlight some of these distinct discourses, but by way of conclusion I want to briefly trace some larger arcs of interconnection between them – to follow some individual threads through the 'snarl' of cocaine discourse.

While cocaine has a seemingly discordant and conflicted presence in the popular imagination of this period, it also frequently serves to convey an image of discord itself. Cocaine often figures as a representation of societal energy, disorder, and rapid change – particularly the disorienting acceleration and sudden transformations of modernity. The analyses contained in the preceding chapters demonstrate the remarkable consistency with which, over a period of more than forty years, cocaine was used rhetorically to signal an abstractly conceived but vividly felt form of newness. The opening chapters of this work examine the manifestation of this discourse in the use of cocaine as an image of transformative medical–technological innovation. Chapter 2 argues that the discovery of cocaine anaesthesia in 1884 was framed as a final humanitarian crescendo for the life-altering effects of Victorian science before the arrival of a new century. Cocaine was positioned as a substance that had 'leapt into frame at one bound', a 'wonderful medicament' and 'magic drug' that had produced 'a complete revolution' in fin de siècle medicine.[10] The drug, with its power to rapidly and efficiently eliminate pain without resorting to general anaesthetics, seemed to capture the immaterial forces of scientific progress and their capacity to profoundly alter the conditions of individual lives. Later advocates for the use of the coca plant – popularized by the experiences of Edward Weston and Robert Christison documented in Chapter 1 – cultivated a similar language of transformative scientific ascendence. For William Golden Mortimer, author of *Peru: History of Coca, 'The Divine Plant' of the Incas* (1901), the evolution of the coca plant from a subject of Incan veneration to an industrially cultivated crop was emblematic of a deeper and more profound process of scientific transfiguration. According to Mortimer:

---

[10] See: 'Cocaine', *Glasgow Herald*, 310 (26 December 1884), 6; 'Occasional Notes', *Leeds Mercury*, 14703 (23 May 1885), 1; Marian Von Glehn, 'A Day in a Hospital', *The Leisure Hour*, February 1890, 279; and Simeon Snell, 'Presidential Address on Some Points of Progress in Ophthalmic Surgery', *BMJ*, 2.1489 (13 July 1889), 58.

In the study of any scientific problem the tales and traditions which associate it with an early race are always full of interest ... Influences which among a primitive people were regarded with superstitious awe, as of supposed miraculous origin, have often been developed by knowledge into important means. Many of the most useful inventions have thus been interpreted through the light of science. The amusing trifles of childhood's hour have become the absorbing powers of the present. Civilization has advanced by the adaption of primitive means.[11]

Here, coca exemplifies the power of science to 'interpret' and 'adapt' the primitive into the modern, to 'develop' the future from the raw materials found among the 'earl[ier] races' of the past. In this way, coca stands as an illustration of the capacity for 'higher civilization' to transmute the child-like knowledge of 'simple people' into a fuller mastery of 'the resources of the universe'.[12] Framed in this way, both cocaine and the coca plant were linked in the late nineteenth century with notions of scientific discovery, ascension, and the creation of the new. The cocaine alkaloid and the leaves that contained it implied the reforging of modern civilization and of individual bodies by the vast forces of technological and medical advancement.

This futurist imagery, as we have seen, also projected itself onto patterns of recreational cocaine consumption and abuse. Chapter 4 details how cocaine addiction was singled out, in the years following the drug's widespread introduction into medical practice, as a condition that might claim its victims more quickly and annihilate them more thoroughly than any previous drug. Depictions of cocaine as the most 'seductive and rapid' of all drugs of addiction convert the compound's transformative impact on therapeutic science into hitherto unimaged (and unimaginably swift) forms of bodily devastation.[13] Thus, cocaine's particular newness combined with a belief in its special destructiveness so that each heightened the other. Chapter 6 describes the discursive connection between the cocaine habit and the United States of America, demonstrating the extent to which the spread of cocainism in the United States was thought to express the young country's dynamic, but also potentially deranging, modernization. The 'amazing proportions' of American cocaine use were taken as evidence of its headlong flight towards an ever-more heavily urbanized, industrialized future, and the demands that this progress placed on its citizens.[14] The spread of the

---

[11] William Golden Mortimer, *Peru: History of Coca, 'The Divine Plant' of the Incas* (New York: J.H. Vail, 1901), 400.
[12] Ibid., 24.
[13] 'Cocainomania', *Scottish Medical and Surgical Journal*, 5.5 (November 1899), 471.
[14] 'The Cocaine Habit', *Belfast Telegraph*, 44.14654 (28 July 1916), 3.

cocaine habit and its status as 'a very serious menace in many big American cities' was attributed to 'a general belief in its lessening local nervous sensibility, and enabling greater mental and bodily labour being endured'.[15] Cocaine could, as such, be interpreted as both a symbol and a symptom of America's destabilizing modernity: the stimulation conferred by the drug appeared both to illustrate the day-to-day experience of modern American life and to be essential to endure it.

While cocaine was often represented in the late nineteenth and early twentieth centuries as a characteristically American drug, it was also used to illustrate – and, indeed, to stigmatize – other projects of rapid national modernization and change. Throughout the 1920s, critics of Soviet Russia not infrequently turned to cocaine as a figure for the country's seemingly relentless and insatiably brutal flight into a new political order. If maintaining the 'intenser pace of life' in modern America demanded the energizing effects of cocaine, then it likewise appeared as if the feverish violence and political transformation of Bolshevism could only be sustained by that most 'brutal [and] depraved' of all drugs.[16] One newspaper story from 1920 maintained that:

> One of the articles most needed in Russia and for which practically any price can be obtained is cocaine. This noxious drug is vitally necessary to a large number of men and women in Communist circles in Russia, especially in the Extraordinary Commission, where for some reason or other one finds a great number of neurasthenic, unbalanced individuals of both sexes, who cannot exist without sniffing the white poisonous powder.[17]

Other, more pruriently vicious stories circulated of the flamboyant (and eroticized) violence perpetrated by the 'young ... well turned out ... cocaine fiend[s]' of the Cheka. These men and women – dressed in the fashionable uniforms of the Red Army officer corps and with silver spurs on their boots – were said to amuse themselves with 'debaucheries', elaborate tortures, and by 'shoot[ing] prisoners with [a] revolver in the garden by moonlight'. The Bolshevik officer Rosa Schwartz was reputed to 'count her victims by hundreds, takes cocaine, and, while smoking, goes naked to see the prisoners in their cells, kills them with a blow from her revolver, or burns their eyes with her cigarette'.[18] In its alignment with cocaine, Soviet Russia was imagined as a ghastly reflection of

---

[15] 'The Cocaine Evil', *Dundee Evening Telegraph*, 12236 (15 February 1916), 4; 'The Cocaine Habit', *The Queen*, 101.2617 (20 February 1897), 332.
[16] 'Drugs and Drink', *Huddersfield Daily Chronicle*, 8789 (30 September 1895), 4; 'The Deliriums of Cocaine', *Lakes Herald*, 802 (8 January 1886), 7.
[17] 'Bribed by Cocaine', *Nottingham Evening Post*, 13231 (11 November 1920), 4.
[18] 'Where Women Live in Terror', *Beeston Gazette and Echo*, 1366 (22 November 1924), 3.

the United States of America: a chaotic, hyperactive society, 'doped' to frantic intensity by the crystallized chaos of its drug of choice.[19] More generally, we might draw a productive comparison between the technological 'revolution' of cocaine anaesthesia and the more literal revolutionary activities of the cocainized agents of the Extraordinary Commission.[20] We have seen how contemporary observers described cocaine as having a 'unique[ly]' split character, distinctively divided between a useful therapeutic action (anaesthesia) and a harmful addictive one (stimulus of the central nervous system).[21] Despite being biomechanically distinct, however, these two actions were nevertheless discursively aligned with each other. Both as an anaesthetic and as a stimulant/euphoriant, cocaine appeared to illustrate the excitement and rapidity of the modern. Across the period of this study, cocaine's white crystals could condense the energized confusion and the jarring, chaotic, sometimes violent impact produced by the advent of the new.

Cocaine's capacity to capture both the radiant and infernal prospects of modernity was reflected in another recurring aspect of the drug's discourse: its seemingly divine or supernatural character. Whether describing cocaine's effects as an aid to endurance or as a recreational stimulant, observers across the period of this study have a remarkable tendency to resort to images of the otherworldly, the seraphic, and the mystical. This book began with Ronald K. Siegel's 1983 report of his interview with the bank robber and cocaine devotee Eddie Love. Injecting cocaine for the first time, Love had experienced a revelation: that cocaine was 'the perfect drug', that it was 'God's gift', and that it was one substance with 'God himself'.[22] This devotional formula – the presentation of cocaine as some material imprint of the divine – echoes back into earlier nineteenth- and twentieth-century depictions of the drug. We have seen how nineteenth-century artists like Albert Robida and Alphonse Mucha repackaged the iconography of Incan religion (most obviously the Incan goddess 'Mama Coca') for consumption by modern subjects. William Golden Mortimer's *Peru: History of Coca, 'The Divine Plant' of the Incas* (1901) takes its subtitle from the consecrated status assigned to coca in Incan cosmology and religious practice. Throughout his book Mortimer continually reiterates the image of coca as a 'divine plant', a herb

---

[19] 'Dying Russia', *Nottingham Evening Post*, 13465 (15 August 1921), 1.
[20] Snell, 'Presidential Address on Some Points of Progress in Ophthalmic Surgery', *BMJ*, 58.
[21] Dale, 'The Possible Substitutes for Cocaine', 511.
[22] See Ronald K. Siegel, 'Cocaine and the Privileged Class', *Advances in Alcohol & Substance Abuse*, 4.2 (1984), 37; and Ronald K. Siegel, *Intoxication: The Universal Drive for Mind-Altering Substances* (Rochester, NY: Park Street Press, 2005), 249–50.

whose modern uses (as a tonic or as a fortifier of endurance) are fundamentally contiguous with its original, sacred condition. Writes Mortimer: 'Coca, has appealed alike to the archaeologist, the botanist, the historian, and traveller as well as to the physician. Its history is united with the antiquity of centuries, while its traditions link it with a sacredness of the past.'[23] *Peru: History of Coca* is replete with descriptions and details of coca's ritual significance in Incan culture. In one passage, Mortimer suggests that the perceived divinity of coca was derived from the divinity of the sun and that the plant was seen as inheriting the sun's divine vitalism and life-giving potency:

> From a regard of the sun as the creator of all things, it was but a single step [for the Inca] to look upon the several representatives of that element as symbols of life and generation ... It was in this same spirit that Coca was considered as the divine plant, because it was the means of force and strength as well as a stimulant to reproduction; and the Incan Venus was represented as holding a spray of Coca as typifying the power and fruitfulness of love.[24]

In harking back to the Incan past in passages like this, Mortimer reinforces the notion of coca as possessing a divine pedigree. The plant's effects are implied to be so miraculous and powerful – so capable of bringing joy, of strengthening the body, and of conferring life itself – that they can be viewed as materializing some otherworldly energy. The brilliance of the sun and the vibrancy of creation is figured as having been distilled down into the leaves themselves. Towards the end of the book, Mortimer asserts that in modern civilization coca 'must prove a boon to the weak and depressed, as divine as its substance was held among the Incas'.[25] Coca and its physical effects are, therefore, imaginatively invested with an aura of celestial communion.

Cocaine was, as we saw most directly in Chapter 6, also susceptible to this same fantasy. Aleister Crowley persistently figures the euphoria of cocaine as a moment of 'miraculous' contact with some higher, more transcendental realm of spiritual consciousness. To consume this 'radiant powder' is to be precipitated beyond the limits of earthy convention; the 'happiness' brought about by cocaine is: 'the miracle of miracles, as sure as death, and yet as masterful as life; a thing more miraculous, because so sudden, so apart from the usual course of evolution'.[26] Peter Pendragon, the protagonist of Crowley's 1923 novel *The Diary*

---

[23] Mortimer, *Peru: History of Coca*, 7.
[24] Ibid., 56.
[25] Ibid., 492.
[26] Aleister Crowley, 'Cocaine', *The International*, 11.10 (October 1917), 291.

of a Drug Fiend, narrates how, in taking cocaine, his thoughts and sensations become 'utterly etherealised'. Pendragon describes how:

> Everything soever is transmuted as by 'heavenly alchemy' into a spiritual beatitude. ... It is a blind excitement of so sublime a character that it is impossible to worry about anything. And yet, this excitement is singularly calm and profound. There is nothing of the suggestion of coarseness which we associate with ordinary drunkenness. The very idea of coarseness or commonness is abolished. It is like the vision of Peter in the Acts of the Apostles in which he was told, 'There is nothing common or unclean'.
>
> As Blake said, 'Everything that lives is holy'. Every act is a sacrament.[27]

For Crowley, cocaine registers as a form of divine transfusion, a sacramental substance that places the body in contact with the empyrean. Crowley's descriptions of cocaine pleasure repeat many of the images and motifs employed by Mortimer in his account of the strengthening effects of coca leaves: in both cases the action is so immediate and so potent as to suggest the operation of some 'heavenly alchemy'. This construction of coca and cocaine as forms of supernatural 'transmut[ation]' – the sudden impress of the otherworldly into the individual body of the user – also informs Arthur Machen's 1895 story 'The Novel of the White Powder' (examined in Chapter 4). Though Machen's weighting of these ideas is emphatically towards the demonic rather than the divine, the mysterious white powder that destroys Francis Leicester produces a similar supernatural ecstasy and otherworldly intrusion. The white powder that 'dissolve[s the] human trinity' and re-enacts 'the primal fall' of Eden springs from the same imaginative root as Mortimer's 'divine plant' and Crowley's cocaine 'sacrament' that summons up the visionary bliss of apostles, 'saints and martyrs'.[28]

The recurrence of these supernatural or pseudo-supernatural metaphors throughout this book suggests some of the complications that fin de siècle and early-twentieth-century observers faced in describing the experience of cocaine. This complexity extends both to the individual experience of taking the drug and to the way in which the drug was culturally experienced through its representation in fiction, popular and medical journalism, and other sources. The particular effects of cocaine – its anaesthetic action; its

---

[27] Aleister Crowley, *The Diary of a Drug Fiend* (London: W. Collins, 1923), 47–8.
[28] Arthur Machen, *The Three Impostors or the Transmutations* (London: John Lane, 1895), 177–8; Crowley, 'Cocaine', 291.

strengthening influence; the stimulation, confidence, and elation it produced – seemed to overshoot the boundaries of mundane reality. While cocaine could metaphorically signify the galvanizing disorder of modernity, it also performed a more complex metaphorical function: that of rendering modernity (especially medical–technological modernity) as a form of transubstantiation or possession. Cocaine's peculiar mix of actions suggested a peculiarly incongruous combination of images: the simultaneous suggestion of some mysterious external force impressing itself onto the body of the user, at the same time as the user was miraculously relieved from the weight of all burdens and inhibitions.

I want to finish by briefly tracing this curious contradiction in cocaine discourse of the late nineteenth and early twentieth centuries. Across these decades, cocaine has the peculiar property of making its users seem simultaneously more and less themselves, of making them appear at once more and less human. Chapter 1 of this book detailed Robert Christison's representation of coca as calibrating or harmonizing the body's various operations, restoring them to an inherently optimal alignment. In Christison's rendering, coca does not distort or artificially alter the body's functions, but acts to restore them to their most proper and naturally vigorous configuration. This representation of coca's effects was echoed by Sigmund Freud in his 1884 article on cocaine, 'Ueber Coca'. Freud describes the experience of taking cocaine as an 'exhilaration and lasting euphoria, which does not differ in any way from the normal euphoria of a healthy person. … One is simply normal and finds it difficult to believe that one is under the influence of any drug at all.'[29] In Christison and Freud's accounts, coca and cocaine produce a strange state of heightened normality: the 'euphoria' cocaine produces is defined as the 'normal' enjoyment of energetic good health and the strengthening of 'self-control', 'vigour', and 'capab[ility]'.[30] For both men, the main enjoyment of coca/cocaine comes from the feeling that (thanks to the drug) the body has become more fully and naturally itself.

A similar framing can be seen in the discourse that evolved around the contrast between cocaine anaesthesia and older general anaesthetics in the years after 1884. As documented in Chapter 2, the introduction of general anaesthetics into surgical practice occasioned the anxiety that operating surgeons might come to see the anaesthetized, unconscious patient as 'a mere object, … [deprived] of

---

[29] Sigmund Freud, *The Cocaine Papers*, ed. K. Donoghue and James Hillman (Vienna: Dunquin Press, 1963), 10.
[30] Ibid.

the beneficial limitations imposed by human empathy'.[31] The advent of cocaine anaesthesia, by contrast, promised to preserve the patient's agency, selfhood, and human identity throughout the surgical process. For the fin de siècle, cocaine offered a new, idealized form of surgery – one in which the patient would be invulnerable to pain but still remain empathetically and humanely connected to the practitioner. Complications, however, emerged within this discourse in response to the demands of the emerging field of cosmetic medicine. Chapter 3 examines the darkly comic and gothic undercurrents that accumulated around cocaine anaesthesia in relation to newly developed cosmetic surgeries. Works such as W. C. Morrow's 'Two Singular Men' (1897) raise the possibility that the bodies of modern subjects might (in this new anaesthetic age) begin to expand horribly beyond the restraining limits imposed by pain. In this sense, there is a deeper kinship between the grotesque inmates of Morrow's freak show and the horrifying 'transmutation' inflicted upon Francis Leicester in Arthur Machen's 'The Novel of the White Powder'.[32] Both Chapters 3 and 4 detail the possibility that cocaine – whether employed surgically or recreationally – might have the potential to radically precipitate its users beyond the threshold of the human.

This intersection between cocaine and the ambiguous construction of the human is perhaps most clearly illustrated in the character of Sherlock Holmes. Holmes's cocaine habit was used both to convey the extent of the detective's mechanized optimization for his profession, and – in parodies of Doyle's work – to explore the potential application of modern medical discoveries to the art of self-indulgence. Holmes's cocainism could be configured as evidence of his status as 'the most perfect reasoning and observing machine the world has seen' and as an extravagant fantasy of zany, technologized, posthuman pleasure.[33] Both in Doyle's original works and in their parodies, Holmes appears more like 'a machine rather than a man'; his cocaine use marks him as an individual who has been rigorously, even cybernetically, engineered to operate in either the world of work or in the realm of pleasure.[34] The final chapter of this book follows these images of cocaine pleasure, technology, and the human into the 1920s. For Aleister Crowley, the mastery of cocaine and the euphoria it brings is tantamount to the previous generation's mastery of flight and electricity.[35] Those

---

[31] Ian A. Burney, *Bodies of Evidence: Medicine and the Politics of the English Inquest, 1830–1926* (Baltimore, MD: Johns Hopkins University Press, 2000), 145.
[32] Machen, *The Three Impostors*, 159.
[33] Arthur Conan Doyle, *The Adventures of Sherlock Holmes*, ed. Richard Lancelyn Green (Oxford: Oxford University Press, 2008), 5.
[34] Doyle, *The Memoirs of Sherlock Holmes*, 157.
[35] Crowley, *The Diary of a Drug Fiend*, 158.

who use the drug are 'pioneers of humanity undertaking a desperate adventure for the good of the race'.[36] In this way, cocaine represents a route by which the post-war generation might ascend to a 'higher stage of evolution' while also continuing to reassert older hierarchies of racial hegemony and control.[37] Among all these case studies, there is the recurring sense of the ease with which the discursive complications of cocaine bleed over into the discursive complications of the human – the limits of the human body, of human identity, and of human evolution in the face of new medical–technological innovations.

The aim of this book has been not only to detail the cultural history of cocaine in the years before its criminalization and stigmatization, but to examine the 'fantasies', 'figure[s]', and 'metaphor[s]' that accumulated around the drug between the last decades of the nineteenth century and the first decades of the twentieth.[38] Following Susan Sontag's *Illness as Metaphor*, this book approaches cocaine – a particular substance and medical technology – as metaphor. I have attempted to foreground the variation and contradiction of cocaine discourse in this period: the long-enduring sense of cocaine as one of the most 'splendid triumphs of science' alongside the dread of addiction.[39] Across the period of this study, cocaine participates (perhaps more readily than any other contemporary drug) in fantasies of both disease and of cure, of pleasure and of productivity. In fictional narratives, whether literary, filmic, or dramatic, cocaine serves as a prop in the portrayal of individual characters, and is itself thus characterized by these portrayals. This book has analysed some of the diverse ways in which cocaine was 'aestheticize[d]' in these years, and some of the processes by which it was imbued with a diverse and complex sense of personality. In considering how cocaine functions as a 'trope for [different] attitudes towards the self' this book addresses the wider project of the medical humanities: it illustrates how the metaphors attached to an individual substance can become metaphors about ourselves, about our shared humanity, our doubts and confusion about this condition, and about who we do or do not accord the privilege of being seen as fully human.[40]

---

[36] Ibid., 280.
[37] Ibid., 368.
[38] Susan Sontag, *Illness as Metaphor and AIDS and its Metaphors* (London: Penguin Books, 2002), 3.
[39] 'Cocaine', *Chambers's Journal*, 3.114 (6 March 1886), 145; 'Coca and Cocaine', *Lancet*, 124.3198 (13 December 1884), 1063.
[40] Sontag, *Illness as Metaphor and AIDS and Its Metaphors*, 20, 28.

Bibliography

'The 500 Miles Walk', *Glasgow Herald*, 12098 (11 March 1876): 5.

Acker, Caroline. *Creating the American Junkie: Addiction Research in the Classic Era of Narcotic Control*. Baltimore, MD: Johns Hopkins University Press, 2002.

'Address by Professor Botkin on the Circumstances Attending the Suicide of the late Professor Kolomnin', *Lancet*, 128.3303 (18 December 1886): 1195–6.

'Against Benign Neglect', *New York Times*, 22 September 1974: 252.

A. L. 'A New Use for Coca', *Lancet*, 108.2769 (23 September 1876): 449.

Allan, Janice M., and Christopher Pittard. 'Introduction', in *The Cambridge Companion to Sherlock Holmes*, ed. Janice M. Allan and Christopher Pittard. Cambridge: Cambridge University Press, 2019, 1–12.

'The American Scandals', *Northern Echo*, 1929 (14 March 1876): 3. 'The Anglo-American Walking Match', *The Penny Illustrated Paper and Illustrated Times*, 755 (12 February 1876): 106.

Annandale, Thomas. 'Practical Suggestions in Connection with the Treatment of Some Deformities of the Nose,' *BMJ*, 2.1927 (4 December 1897), 1625–6.

'The Annus Medicus 1884', *Lancet*, 124.3200 (27 December 1884): 1151–61.

'Answers to Correspondents', *The Girl's Own Paper*, 1079 (1 September 1900): 767.

'Anti-Negro Riots', *Birmingham Daily Gazette*, 86.11706 (26 September 1906): 5.

Anyhow. 'Ideal Interview: Sherlock Holmes', *The Bohemian*, 1.5 (October 1893): 211–16.

'Another Abuse in Society', *Dundee Courier*, 15020 (14 August 1901): 4.

A. R. 'The Cocaine Habit,' *The Speaker*, 7 (8 November 1902): 142.

'Are We Too Clean?', *BMJ*, 2.1593 (11 July 1891): 84–5.

'The Art of Walking', *York Herald*, 5957 (13 March 1876): 8.

'Athletic Notes', *Sporting Gazette*, 14.718 (12 February 1876): 158.

'Attack on Jazz', *Aberdeen Press and Journal*, 22707 (12 October 1927): 7.

Auden, W. H. *W. H. Auden's Book of Light Verse*, ed. Edward Mendelson. New York: New York Review Books, 2004.

'Au Courant', *Eddowes's Shrewsbury Journal*, 4852 (9 June 1886): 4.

'August Magazines', *Oxford Times*, 1717 (27 July 1895): 6.

Bailkin, Jordanna. 'Making Faces: Tattooed Women and Colonial Regimes', *History Workshop Journal*, 59 (2005): 33–56.

Baker, Josephine, and Marcel Sauvage. *Voyages et Aventures de Joséphine Baker*. Paris: Marcel Sheur, 1931.

Ballin, Ada S. 'Health and Beauty', *Womanhood*, 7.40 (March 1902): 323.

Ballin, Ada S. 'Health and Beauty', *Womanhood*, 9.52 (March 1903): 299.

Barrows, C. M. 'Suggestion without Hypnotism', *Proceedings of the Society for Psychical Research*, 12 (1896–7): 21–44.

'A Batch of Novels', *The Liverpool Mercury*, 13405 (24 December 1890): 7.

Baudrillard, Jean. 'Modernity', *Canadian Journal of Political and Social Theory*, 11.3 (December 1987): 63–72.

Beerbohm, Max. 'A Defence of Cosmetics', *The Yellow Book*, 1 (April 1894): 65–82.

Benjamin, Walter. *Charles Baudelaire: A Lyric Poet in the Era of High Capitalism*, trans. Harry Zohn. London: Verso, 1997.

Berridge, Virginia. 'Opium Eating and Life Insurance', *Addiction*, 72.4 (April 1977): 371–7.

Berridge, Virginia. *Opium and the People: Opiate Use and Policy in Nineteenth and Early Twentieth Century Britain*. London: Free Association Books, 1999.

Berridge, Virginia. 'The Origins of the English Drug "Scene" 1890–1930', *Medical History*, 32 (1988): 51–64.

Berridge, Virginia. 'War Conditions and Narcotics Control: The Passing of Defence of the Realm Act Regulation 40B', *Journal of Social Policy*, 7.3 (July 1978): 285–304.

Bjelić, Dušan I. *Intoxication, Modernity, and Colonialism: Freud's Industrial Unconscious, Benjamin's Hashish Mimesis*. New York: Palgrave, 2016.

'A Black Fiend', *The People*, 1298 (26 August 1906): 14.

'Black Man's Paradise', *Nottingham Evening Post*, 14494 (4 December 1924): 1.

Blathwayt, Raymond. 'A Talk with Dr. Conan Doyle', *The Bookman*, 2.8 (May 1892): 50–1.

Boddice, Rob. 'Species of Compassion: Aesthetics, Anaesthetics, and Pain in the Physiological Laboratory', *19: Interdisciplinary Studies in the Long Nineteenth Century*, 15 (2015): https://doi.org/10.16995/ntn.628.

Bradley, S. M. 'Coca-Leaf on the Brain', *Lancet*, 107.2744 (1 April 1876): 519.

Bramwell, J. Milne. 'On the Evolution of Hypnotic Theory', *Brain: A Journal of Neurology*, 19.4 (1896): 459–568.

Breakell, Mary L. 'Women in the Medical Profession', *The Nineteenth Century*, 54.321 (November 1903): 819–25.

'Bribed by Cocaine', *Nottingham Evening Post*, 13231 (11 November 1920): 4.

Briggs, Julia. *Night Visitors: The Rise and Fall of the English Ghost Story*. London: Faber, 1977.

Brock, Clair. 'Risk, Responsibility, and Surgery in the 1890s and Early 1900s', *Medical History*, 57.3 (July 2013): 317–37.

Brown, Alyson. 'The Sad Demise of z.D.H.38 Ernest Collins: Suicide, Informers and the Debate on the Abolition of Flogging', *Cultural and Social History*, 15.1 (2018): 99–114.

Brown, J. J. Graham. 'Notes on the Treatment of the Diseases of the Nervous System', *Scottish Medical and Surgical Journal*, 4 (January–June 1899): 490–509.

Brown, J. J. Graham. 'Notes on the Treatment of Diseases of the Nervous System', *Scottish Medical and Surgical Journal*, 8 (January–June 1901): 481–503.

Brown, J. J. Graham. 'Notes on the Treatment of Diseases of the Nervous System', *Scottish Medical and Surgical Journal*, 12 (January–June 1903): 97–124.

Buklijas, Tatjana. 'Surgery and National Identity in Late Nineteenth-Century Vienna', *Studies in History and Philosophy of Biological and Biomedical Sciences*, 38.4 (December 2007): 756–74.

Burney, Ian A. *Bodies of Evidence: Medicine and the Politics of the English Inquest, 1830–1926*. Baltimore, MD: Johns Hopkins University Press, 2000.

Burrows, John. '"A Vague Chinese Quarter Elsewhere": Limehouse in the Cinema 1914–36', *Journal of British Cinema and Television*, 6.2 (2009): 282–301.

Buscemi, Nicki. 'The Case of the Case History: Detecting the Medical Report in Sherlock Holmes', *Journal of Victorian Culture*, 19.2 (2014): 216–31.

Buxton, Dudley W. 'Fifty Years of Anaesthetics', *British Medical Journal*, 2.1868 (17 October 1896): 1143–8.

Cameron, Rebecca. '"Syncopated Nerves": Jazz and the Pathology of Modern Youth in Noël Coward's 1920s Theatre', *Modernist Cultures*, 15.2 (2020): 179–201.

Campbell, Harry. 'The Study of Inebriety: A Retrospect and A Forecast,' *British Journal of Inebriety*, 1.1 (July 1903): 5–14.

'Capture of "Dope King"', *Dundee Evening Telegraph*, 14556 (20 July 1923): 4.

Caquet, P. E. 'France, Germany, and the Origins of Drug Prohibition', *International History Review*, 42.4 (2020): 207–25.

'Carl Koller and Cocaine', *British Journal of Ophthalmology*, 12.5 (May 1928): 262–3.

Carr, J. Walter. 'Royal Free Hospital: School of Medicine for Women', *Lancet*, 152.3919 (8 October 1898): 926–8.

Carstairs, Catherine. *Jailed for Possession: Illegal Drug Use, Regulation, and Power in Canada, 1920–1961*. Toronto: University of Toronto Press, 2006.

Castle, Terry. 'Phantasmagoria: Spectral Technology and the Metaphorics of Modern Reverie', *Critical Inquiry*, 15.1 (1988): 26–61.

'"Cat" for Cocaine Sellers', *Pall Mall Gazette*, 17754 (27 April 1922): 4.

'Changed at Will', *Hampshire Telegraph*, 5875 (31 March 1894): 11.

'The Charmer', *The Referee*, 1575 (20 October 1907): 2.

Chetwynd, George. *Racing Reminiscences and Experiences of the Turf*, Vol. 1. London: Longmans, Green, 1891.

Childers, Joseph W. 'Foreign Matter: Imperial Filth', in *Filth: Dirt, Disgust, and Modern Life*, ed. William A. Cohen and Ryan Johnson. Minneapolis: University of Minnesota Press, 2005, 201–21.

'Chips', *North-Eastern Daily Gazette*, 2 January 1897: 2.

'Chit-Chat', *Sheffield Evening Telegraph*, 803 (7 January 1890): 2.

Christison, Robert. 'Observations on the Effects of Cuca, or Coca, the Leaves of the Erythroxylon Coca', *BMJ*, 1.800 (29 April 1876): 527–31.

Clarke, Clare. 'Doyle, Holmes and Victorian Publishing', in *The Cambridge Companion to Sherlock Holmes*, ed. Janice M. Allan and Christopher Pittard. Cambridge: Cambridge University Press, 2019, 29–41.

Clarke, Clare. *Late Victorian Crime Fiction in the Shadows of Sherlock*. London: Palgrave Macmillan, 2014.
Clouston, T. S. 'Diseased Cravings and Paralysed Control: Dipsomania; Morphinomania; Chloralism; Cocainism', *Edinburgh Medical Journal*, 35.2 (March 1890): 793–809.
'Coca', *Lancet*, 81.2060 (21 February 1863): 222.
'Coca', *Lancet*, 99.2544 (1 June 1872): 746.
'Coca and Cocaine', *Lancet*, 124.3198 (13 December 1884): 1063–4.
'Cocaine', *The American Register*, 19.971 (13 November 1886): 8.
'Cocaine', *Chambers's Journal*, 3.114 (6 March 1886): 145–7.
'Cocaine', *Glasgow Herald*, 310 (26 December 1884): 6.
'Cocaine', *Lancet*, 125.3201 (3 January 1885): 43.
'Cocaine', *The Scotsman*, 29 August 1887: 7.
'Cocaine Addiction', *Lancet*, 204.5278 (25 October 1924): 857–8.
'Cocaine Creeper', *Belfast Telegraph*, 43.13651 (7 May 1913): 5.
'Cocaine Creeper', *Heywood Advertiser*, 3098 (23 May 1913): 6.
'The Cocaine Cult', *The Times*, 41974 (16 December 1918): 5.
'Cocaine Debauchery', *The Times*, 43019 (1 May 1922): 19.
'Cocaine Debauchery – An Alien Traffic', *The Times*, 43021 (3 May 1922): 17.
'Cocaine Debauchery – Present Penalties No Deterrent', *The Times*, 43020 (2 May 1922): 17.
'The Cocaine Evil', *Dundee Evening Telegraph*, 12236 (15 February 1916): 4.
'The Cocaine Habit', *Belfast Telegraph*, 44.14654 (28 July 1916): 3.
'The Cocaine Habit', *BMJ*, 1.1882 (23 January 1897): 219.
'The Cocaine Habit', *Cornishman*, 1206 (15 August 1901): 2.
'The "Cocaine" Habit', *The Globe*, 32952 (11 January 1901): 6.
'The Cocaine Habit', *Sheffield Weekly Telegraph*, 1729 (1 June 1895): 12.
'The Cocaine Habit', *Shoreditch Observer*, 2696 (5 September 1908): 7.
'The Cocaine Habit', *The Queen*, 101.2617 (20 February 1897): 332.
'The Cocaine Habit Among Negroes', *BMJ*, 2.2187 (29 November 1902): 1729.
'Cocaine in America', *Manchester Courier*, 74.13042 (27 August 1898): 9.
'Cocaine Inhalers', *The Globe*, 33751 (8 August 1903): 5.
'Cocaine in Sea-Sickness', *Lancet*, 126.3236 (5 September 1885): 451.
'Cocaine in Seasickness', *Manchester Times Supplement*, 19 September 1885: 8.
'The Cocaine Muddle', *Chemist and Druggist*, 89.1938 (17 March 1917): 51.
'Cocaine of Music', *Liverpool Echo*, 14910 (12 October 1927): 6.
'Cocaine Poisoning', *BMJ*, 1.1417 (25 February 1888): 438.
'Cocaine Raid', *Lincolnshire Echo*, 9474 (23 June 1923): 2.
'Cocaine Traffic', *The Times*, 43023 (5 May 1922): 17.
'Cocaine Traffic – Limited Police Powers', *The Times*, 43024 (6 May 1922): 17.
'The Cocaine Trafficker in Paris', *The Graphic*, 105.2725 (18 February 1922): 180.
'Cocainism in the Southern United States', *Lancet*, 183.4727 (4 April 1914): 979–80.

'Cocainomania', *Scottish Medical and Surgical Journal*, 5.5 (November 1899): 470–2.
'The Coca Leaf', *Dublin Evening Mail*, 5644 (21 February 1855): 1.
'Coca Wine and Its Dangers', *BMJ*, 1.1884 (6 February 1897): 353.
Cochran, George. *Keys to Crookdom*. New York: D. Appleton, 1924.
Cohen, Michael M. 'Jim Crow's Drug War: Race, Coca Cola, and the Southern Origins of Drug Prohibition', *Southern Cultures*, 12.3 (Autumn 2006): 55–79.
Cohen, William A. *Embodied: Victorian Literature and the Senses*. Minneapolis: University of Minnesota Press, 2009.
'Cold in the Eye', *Wiltshire Times*, 2335 (12 October 1901): 2.
'The Coming Man – As the Scientist looks for Him', *Hampshire Telegraph*, 6197 (30 June 1900): 10.
Comitini, Patricia. 'The Strange Case of Addiction in Robert Louis Stevenson's "Strange Case of Dr. Jekyll and Mr. Hyde"', *Victorian Review*, 38.1 (Spring 2012): 113–31.
'Commercial and Financial Notes', *Manchester Guardian*, 15474 (16 March 1896): 8.
'Corneal Tattoos', *BMJ*, 2.1923 (6 November 1897): 74.
Cowley, Abraham. *The Second and Third Parts of the Works of Mr Abraham Cowley*. London: Charles Harper, 1700.
Crespi, Alfred J. H. 'Some Recent Scientific Advances', *The Gentleman's Magazine*, 1906 (October 1889): 391–406.
'Crime Streets', *Nottingham Evening Post*, 14041 (22 June 1923): 4.
Crittenden, Ann, and Michael Ruby. 'Cocaine: The Champagne of Drugs', *New York Times*, 1 September 1974: 14–15.
Crowley, Aleister. 'Cocaine', *The International*, 11.10 (October 1917): 291–4.
Crowley, Aleister. *The Diary of a Drug Fiend*. London: W. Collins, 1923.
Crowley, Aleister. 'Drama Be Damned!', *The International*, 12.4 (April 1918): 127–8.
Crowley, Aleister. 'The Great Drug Delusion: By a New York Specialist', *English Review*, 34 (June 1922): 571–6.
Crowley, Aleister. *The Law Is for All*, ed. Louis Wilkinson and Hymenaeus Beta. Tempe: New Falcon, 1996.
Curry, Tommy J. 'Shut Your Mouth When You're Talking to Me: Silencing the Idealist School of Critical Race Theory through a Culturalogic Turn in Jurisprudence', *Georgetown Law Journal of Modern Critical Race Studies*, 3.1 (2012): 1–38.
Dabbs, G. H. R. 'A Note on the Inebriate in the Making', *British Journal of Inebriety*, 1.4 (April 1904): 287–9.
Dale, H. H. 'The Possible Substitutes for Cocaine', *BMJ*, 1.3299 (22 March 1924): 511–12.
Dallinger, W. H. 'Notes on Current Science', *Wesleyan-Methodist Magazine*, 9 (January 1885): 67–70.
Dallinger, W. H. 'Notes on Current Science', *Wesleyan-Methodist Magazine*, 9 (February 1885): 146–9.

'Dangerous Drugs Act Regulations', *Chemist and Druggist*, 94.2143 (19 February 1921): 49–56.

'The Dangers of Coca Wines', *BMJ*, 2.1927 (4 December 1897): 1666.

Dawson, Janis. 'Rivaling Conan Doyle: L. T. Meade's Medical Mysteries, New Woman Criminals, and Literary Celebrity at the Victorian Fin de Siècle', *English Literature in Transition*, 58.1 (2015): 54–72.

De Bertouch, Baroness. 'Mrs Ada S. Ballin and her Work', *Hearth and Home*, 13.338 (4 November 1897): 1035.

Deane, Bradley. *Masculinity and the New Imperialism*. Cambridge: Cambridge University Press, 2014.

'The Deliriums of Cocaine', *Lakes Herald*, 802 (8 January 1886): 7.

De Styrap, Jukes. *The Young Practitioner*. London: H.K. Lewis, 1890.

Digby, Anne. *The Evolution of British General Practice, 1850–1948*. Oxford: Oxford University Press, 1999.

Dimeo, Paul. *A History of Drug Use in Sport: 1876–1976: Beyond Good and Evil*. London: Routledge, 2007.

Dimeo, Paul. 'The Myth of Clean Sport and Its Unintended Consequences', *Performance Enhancement and Health*, 4 (2016): 103–10.

Dixon, W. E. 'A British Medical Association Lecture on the Drug Habit', *BMJ*, 1.3248 (31 March 1923): 543–5.

Dixon, W. E. 'Physiology the Basis of Treatment', *BMJ*, 2.3577 (27 July 1929): 138–43.

'Doctor's Diseases', *BMJ*, 1.2461 (29 February 1908): 522–3.

'The Dogs' Beauty Doctor', *Daily Mirror*, 57 (8 January 1904): 11.

Donald, James. *Some of These Days: Black Stars, Jazz Aesthetics, and Modernist Culture*. Oxford: Oxford University Press, 2015.

Donaldson, Henry Herbert. 'On the Temperature Sense', *Mind: A Quarterly Review of Psychology and Philosophy*, 10.39 (July 1885): 399–416.

Doyle, Arthur Conan. 'The Adventure of the Missing Three-Quarter', *Strand Magazine*, 28.164 (August 1904): 123–35.

Doyle, Arthur Conan. *The Adventures of Sherlock Holmes*, ed. Richard Lancelyn Green. Oxford: Oxford University Press, 2008.

Doyle, Arthur Conan. *The Sign of Four*, ed. Peter Ackroyd and Ed Glinert. London: Penguin, 2001.

Doyle, Arthur Conan. *The Memoirs of Sherlock Holmes*, ed. Christopher Roden. Oxford: Oxford University Press, 2009.

'The Dreihoff Poisoning Case', *Yale Record*, 28.2 (28 October 1899): 16.

'The Dress Question in Times Past', *The Ladies' Treasury: An Illustrated Magazine of Entertaining Literature*, 1 March 1895: 179–81.

'Drink and Insanity', *Bristol Mercury and Daily Post*, 14826 (16 November 1895): 8.

'The Drug Habit', *Aberdeen Press and Journal*, 19989 (24 January 1919): 2.

'The Drug Habit in America', *Western Times*, 19002 (4 June 1910): 4.

'Drugs and Drink', *Huddersfield Daily Chronicle*, 8789 (30 September 1895): 4.

'The Drug Stick', *Nottingham Journal*, 30087 (1 May 1922): 2.
'Dying Russia', *Nottingham Evening Post*, 13465 (15 August 1921): 1.
Eckersley, Adrian. 'A Theme in the Early Work of Arthur Machen: "Degeneration"', *English Literature in Transition*, 35.3 (1992): 277–87.
Edgar, George. 'The Unromantic Detective', *The Living Age*, 49.4368 (24 December 1910): 825–7.
'Editorial Notes', *Pick-Me-Up*, 46 (17 August 1889): 314.
'Educating a Nose', *Bow Bells*, 46.1200 (27 July 1887): 139.
Edwards, Harry Stillwell. 'Sons and Fathers', *Nottinghamshire Guardian*, 2682 (10 October 1896): 6.
E.J.W.F., 'Life & Labour without Fatigue, Without Food', *The Ladies' Treasury: An Illustrated Magazine of Entertaining Literature*, 1 August 1867: 355–6.
'Electric Pin-Pricks', *Weekly Telegraph*, 2427 (17 October 1908): 17.
Elliott, Amber, Tashfeen Mahmood, and Roger D. Smalligan. 'Cocaine Bugs: A Case Report of Cocaine-Induced Delusions of Parasitosis', *American Journal on Addictions*, 21.2 (March–April 2012): 180–1.
Emerson, John (Director). *The Mystery of the Leaping Fish* [Film]. Culver City, CA: Triangle Film Corporation, 1916.
'The English Illustrated Magazine', *Lloyd's List*, 17807 (27 September 1894): 12.
'An English Tattooer', *The Pall Mall Gazette*, 7525 (1 May 1889): 7.
Errol, J. 'A Visit to Professor Dr Hermann Pagenstecher's Augenklinik', *London Society*, 63.375 (March 1893): 291–9.
'Erythroxylon Coca', *Lancet*, 100.2555 (17 August 1872): 248.
'Erythroxylon: Trial of its Action by A.B. and R.B.L.', Notebook, Edinburgh University Library Special Collections, GB 237 COLL-237.
'The Evening News', *Manchester Evening News*, 7625 (11 August 1893): 2.
'Everybody's Column', *Illustrated Police News*, 1242 (3 December 1887): 2.
'Evils of Cocaine', *Illustrated Police News*, 2990 (2 June 1921): 6.
'The Excessive Use of Cocaine in the States', *Bournemouth Daily Echo*, 2.701 (29 November 1902): 2.
'Fact and Fancy', *Weekly Telegraph*, 1843 (7 August 1897): 15.
Farber, David. *Crack: Rock Cocaine, Street Capitalism, and the Decade of Greed*. Cambridge: Cambridge University Press, 2019.
'Fashionable Savages', *The Globe*, 30385 (21 October 1892): 3.
'The Fashion to be Tattooed', *Hull Daily Mail*, 2239 (11 November 1892): 3.
Felstead, Sidney Theodore. *The Underworld of London*. London: John Murry, 1923.
Fick, A. Eugen. 'A Contact-Lens', *Archives of Ophthalmology*, 17.2 (1888): 215–26.
'Fiction' *The Saturday Review*, 85.2224 (11 June 1898): 785.
'A Fiendish Assault', *Belfast Telegraph*, 35.11205 (22 August 1906): 5.
Fishman, Ronald S. 'Karl Koller: The Introduction of Local Anesthesia', in *Foundations of Ophthalmology: Great Insights that Established the Discipline*, ed Michael F. Marmor and Daniel M. Albert. New York: Springer, 2017, 117–28.

'Foreign Notes and News', *The Englishwoman's Review*, 161 (15 September 1886): 424–9.

Foy, George. *Anaesthetics Ancient and Modern*. London: Baillière, Tindall, and Cox, 1889.

Frank, Lawrence. 'Dreaming the Medusa: Imperialism, Primitivism, and Sexuality in Arthur Conan Doyle's The Sign of Four', *Signs: Journal of Women in Culture and Society*, 22.1 (Autumn 1996): 52–85.

Freud, Sigmund. *The Cocaine Papers*, ed. K. Donoghue and James Hillman. Vienna: Dunquin Press, 1963.

Freud, Sigmund. *The Interpretation of Dreams*, ed. A. A. Brill. New York: Macmillan, 1913.

Gay, George R., Darryl S. Inaba, Richard Tobin Rappolt, George F. Gushue, and John James Perkner. ' "An' Ho, Ho, Baby, Take a Whiff on Me": La Dama Blanca Cocaine in Current Perspective', *Anesthesia & Analgesia*, 55.4 (July 1976): 582–7.

Gay, G. R., and D. S. Inaba. 'Acute and Chronic Toxicology of Cocaine Abuse', in *Cocaine: Chemical, Biological, Clinical, Social, and Treatment Aspects*, ed. S. J. Mule. Cleveland, OH: CRC Press, 1976, 245–52.

Geddes, J. F. 'The Doctors' Dilemma: Medical Women and the British Suffrage Movement', *Women's History Review*, 18.2 (2009): 203–18.

Gilbert, Pamela. *Victorian Skin: Surface, Self, History*. Ithaca, NY: Cornell University Press, 2019.

Gillette, William. 'Sherlock Holmes: A Drama in Four Acts', in *Plays by William Hooker Gillette*, ed. Rosemary Cullen and Don B. Wilmeth. Cambridge: Cambridge University Press, 2008, 192–272.

Gilman, Sander L. *Making the Body Beautiful: A Cultural History of Aesthetic Surgery*. Princeton, NJ: Princeton University Press, 2000.

'Girls and Cocaine', *Daily Herald*, 1701 (11 July 1921): 5.

Gleaves, John, and Matthew Llewellyn. 'Sport, Drugs and Amateurism: Tracing the Real Cultural Origins of Anti-Doping Rules in International Sport', *Journal of the History of Sport*, 31.8 (May 2014): 839–53.

Godfrey, Clarence G. S. 'Cocainomania', *Australasian Medical Gazette*, 18 (20 April 1899): 147–50.

'Georgia Race Feud', *Leeds Mercury* 21368 (26 September 1906): 5.

Goerig, M. 'Aus dem Nachlass von Carl Koller: Aufzeichnungen zu seinen Experimenten mit Kokain', *Der Anaesthesist*, 64.6 (June 2015): 469–77.

Godshalk, David Fort. *Veiled Visions: The 1906 Atlanta Race Riot and the Reshaping of American Race Relations*. Chapel Hill: University of North Carolina Press, 2005.

Gould, George M., and Walter L. Pyle. *Anomalies and Curiosities of Medicine*. Philadelphia, PA: W. B. Saunders, 1900.

'The Great Walking Match', *Huddersfield Daily Chronical*, 2683 (13 March 1876): 3.

Groth, Helen. 'Reading Victorian Illusions: Dickens's "Haunted Man" and Dr. Pepper's "Ghost" ', *Victorian Studies*, 50.1 (2007): 43–65.

Grover, George Wheelock. *Shadows Lifted, or, Sunshine Restored in the Horizon of Human Lives: A Treatise on the Morphine, Opium, Cocaine, Chloral, and Hashish Habits*. Chicago: Stomberg, Allen, 1894.

'The Growth of Tattooing', *Pall Mall Gazette*, 7543 (22 May 1889): 2.

Gussow, Adam. *Seems Like Murder Here: Southern Violence and the Blues Tradition*. Chicago: University of Chicago Press, 2002.

'The Hall', *Donegal Independent*, 1310 (20 October 1917): 2.

Haiken, Elizabeth. *Venus Envy: A History of Cosmetic Surgery*. Baltimore, MD: Johns Hopkins University Press, 1997.

Hallam, Christopher. 'From Injudicious Prescribing to the Script Doctor: Transgressive Addiction Treatment in the Interwar Years', in *White Drug Cultures and Regulation in London, 1916-1960*, ed. Christopher Hallam. London: Palgrave Macmillan, 2018, 17–48.

Hammack, Brenda Mann. 'Phantastica: The Chemically Inspired Intellectual in Occult Fiction', *Mosaic: A Journal for the Interdisciplinary Study of Literature*, 37.1 (2004): 83–100.

Hansard Parliamentary Debates, HC Deb, 4 May 1922, vol. 153, c.1549.

Harris, Nick, Helen Harris, and Paul Marshall. *A Man in a Hurry: The Extraordinary Life and Times of Edward Payson Weston, the World's Greatest Walker*. London: deCoubertin Books, 2012.

'The Harrison Tragedy', *Scotsman*, 21904 (1 October 1913): 10.

Heard, Mervyn. *Phantasmagoria: The Secret Life of the Magic Lantern*. Hastings: Projection Box, 2006.

Heggie, Vanessa. 'Bodies, Sport, and Science in the Nineteenth Century', *Past and Present*, 231 (May 2016): 169–200.

Heggie, Vanessa. 'Women Doctors and Lady Nurses: Class, Education, and the Professional Victorian Woman', *Bulletin of the History of Medicine*, 89.2 (2015): 267–92.

Henne, Kathryn E. *Testing for Athlete Citizenship: Regulating Doping and Sex in Sport*. New Brunswick, NJ: Rutgers University Press, 2015.

Hichens, R. S. 'Broken Faith', *Hearth and Home*, 104 (11 May 1893): 821.

Hichens, R. S. Broken Faith', *Hearth and Home*, 105 (18 May 1893): 21.

Holt, Richard. 'The Amateur Body and the Middle-Class Man: Work, Health, and Style in Victorian Britain', *Sport in History*, 26.3 (2006): 352–69.

'The Home', *Lloyd's Weekly London Newspaper*, 2613 (18 December 1892): 6.

Horne, Gerald. *Jazz and Justice: Racism and the Political Economy of the Music*. New York: Monthly Review Press, 2019.

'Horticulture', *Hampshire Advertiser*, 1995 (23 November 1861): 2.

'Important Drug Trafficker', *The Times*, 43019 (1 May 1922): 9.

'The Improvement of Human Health', *The Spectator*, 2796 (23 July 1881): 11.

'International Legislation', *Chemist and Druggist*, 109.20 (17 November 1928): 604–6.

'International Walking Match', *Birmingham Daily Post*, 25.5486 (10 February 1876): 8.
'The International Walking Race', *Daily News*, 9298 (10 February 1876): 3.
'Irresistible Eyes', *Dundee Courier*, 14361 (6 July 1899): 4.
Jackson, Kimberly. 'Non-Evolutionary Degeneration in Arthur Machen's Supernatural Tales', *Victorian Literature and Culture*, 41.1 (2013): 125–35.
Jalland, Pat. *Death in the Victorian Family*. Oxford: Oxford University Press, 1996.
'A Japanese Tattooer', *Liverpool Mercury*, 13720 (26 December 1891): 6.
'John O' Gaunt', *The Sportsman*, 16971 (16 January 1924): 5.
Johnson, Alice. 'Dream-Analysis', *Proceedings of the Society for Psychical Research*, 30 (1920): 33–133.
Jones, Jonathan S. 'Opium Slavery: Civil War Veterans and Opiate Addiction', *The Journal of the Civil War Era*, 10.2 (June 2020): 185–212.
Joye, Jocelynne. 'A Woman's Week', *The Outlook*, 2.38 (22 October 1898): 380.
Karch, Steven B. *A Brief History of Cocaine*. London: Taylor and Francis, 2006.
Kerr, Douglas. *Conan Doyle: Writing, Profession, and Practice*. Oxford: Oxford University Press, 2013.
Kohn, Marek. *Dope Girls: The Birth of the British Drug Underground*. London: Granta Books, 2001.
Kolle, Frederick Strange. *Plastic and Cosmetic Surgery*. London: D. Appleton, 1911.
Koller, Carl. 'On the Use of Cocaine for Producing Anaesthesia of the Eye', *Lancet*, 124.3197 (6 December 1884): 990–2.
Koller, Carl. 'Personal Reminiscences of the First Use of Cocain as a Local Anesthetic in Eye Surgery', *Anesthesia and Analgesia*, 7.1 (February 1928): 9–11.
'Knicknacks', *Fun*, 43.1088 (17 March 1886): 121.
'Latest Cocaine Miracle', *Hampshire Telegraph and Sussex Chronicle*, 5454 (26 December 1885): 12.
'Latest News', *Freeman's Journal*, 9 April 1877: 6.
'Latest News', *Freeman's Journal*, 10 April 1877: 5.
Lauterbach, Preston. *Beale Street Dynasty: Sex, Song, and the Struggle for the Soul of Memphis*. New York: W. W. Norton, 2015.
Lawson, R. A. *Jim Crow's Counterculture: The Blues and Black Southerners 1890–1945*. Baton Rouge: Louisiana State University Press, 2010.
Lees, David B. 'The Neurotic Treatment of Catarrh', *Lancet*, 127.3261 (27 February 1886): 394.
Lett, Stephen. 'Cocaine Addiction and Its Diagnosis', *Canada Lancet*, 31.4 (December 1898): 829–32.
Lewin, Louis. *Phantastica: Die Betäubenden und Erregenden Genussmittel*. Berlin: Georg Stilke, 1924.
Lewin, Louis. *Phantastica: A Classic Survey on the Use and Abuse of Mind-Altering Plants*. Rochester, NY: Park Street Press, 1998.
'The Literary Lounger', *The Sketch*, 429 (17 April 1901): 518.
'Literary Notes', *BMJ*, 1.2099 (23 March 1901): 733–4.

'Literary Notes', *Pall Mall Gazette*, 11042(20 August 1900): 1.
'The Literary Week', *The Academy*, 1506 (16 March 1901): 219–22.
'Literature', *Glasgow Herald*, 115 (14 May 1898): 4.
Locke, Alain. *The Negro and His Music*. Washington, DC: The Associates in Negro Folk Education, 1936.
Lomax, Alan. *Mister Jelly Roll: The Fortunes of Jelly Roll Morton, New Orleans Creole and 'Inventor of Jazz'*. New York: Grosset and Dunlap, 1950.
Lomax, John A., and Alan Lomax. *American Ballads and Folk Songs*. New York: Macmillan, 1934.
'London Rid of a Cocaine Pest', *Dundee Evening Telegraph*, 14574 (10 August 1923): 3.
López-Valverde, A., J. de Vicente, L. Martínez-Domínguez, and R. Gómez de Diego. 'Local Anaesthesia through the Action of Cocaine, the Oral Mucosa and the Vienna Group', *British Dental Journal*, 217.1 (11 July 2014): 41–3.
MacCormac, William. 'Abstract of an Address on Plastic Operations and Their Place in Surgery', *BMJ*, 2.1456 (24 November 1888): 1158–9.
MacCormac, William. 'Centenary Festival of the Royal College of Surgeons of England – An Address of Welcome', *BMJ*, 2.2065 (28 July 1900): 209–12.
Machen, Arthur. *Dreads and Drolls*. London: Martin Secker, 1926.
Machen, Arthur. *Hieroglyphics*. London: Grant Richards, 1902.
Machen, Arthur. *The Three Impostors or the Transmutations*. London: John Lane, 1895.
'Making Women Beautiful', *Birmingham Daily Post*, 9396 (7 August 1888): 5.
'Mal-De-Mer', *Myra's Journal of Dress and Fashion*, 12 (1 December 1886): 646.
Mannoni, Laurent. *The Great Art of Light and Shadow: Archaeology of the Cinema*, translated by Richard Crangle. Exeter: University of Exeter Press, 2000.
Martens, Frederick H. *The Phantom Drum*. New York: J. Fischer & Bro., 1918.
'Massacre of Negroes in Georgia', *Morning Post*, 41913 (25 September 1906): 7.
Mattison, J. B. 'Cocaine Dosage and Cocaine Addiction', *Lancet*, 129.3325 (21 May 1887): 1024–6.
McCartney, J. L. 'Flash Lights on the Progress of the Century or the Scientific Horizon of 1800 to 1900'. *The New Century Review*, 46 (October 1900): 249–60.
McCarty J. P., and F. W. Falck. 'Surf Diving and Skimming Device', US Patent 1,222,114, filed 16 February 1916 and issued 10 April 1917.
Mcnamara, J. 'Deaths from Chloroform', *BMJ*, 2.1762 (6 October 1894): 795.
Meachen, G. Norman. 'The Cutaneous Affections of the Inebriate', *British Journal of Inebriety*, 1.4 (April 1904): 274–80.
Meade, L. T. 'The Red Bracelet', *The Strand Magazine*, 9 (January–June 1895): 545–61.
Meade, L. T. 'The Brotherhood of the Seven Kings', *The Stand Magazine*, 15 (January–June 1898): 649–64.
'Medical News', *Lancet*, 88.2242 (18 August 1866): 195.
'Medical News', *Lancet*, 88.2257 (1 December 1866): 625.
'A Medico-Literary Causerie: Our Medical Novelist', *The Practitioner: A Journal of Practical Medicine*, 55 (November 1895): 471–5.

Memphis Jug Band. 'Cocaine Habit Blues' [Musical Recording] Victor Records V-38620-A, 1930.
Miller, Charles. *The Correction of Featural Imperfections*. Chicago: Oak Printing, 1907.
Miller, John. *Memoirs of General Miller in the Service of the Republic of Peru*, Vol. 2. London: Longman, Rees, Orme, Brown, and Green, 1829.
Miller, R. Shalders. 'Remarks on the Employment of Cucaine', *BMJ*, 1.1314 (6 March 1886): 439–40.
Miller, Russell. *The Adventures of Arthur Conan Doyle*. London: Harvill Secker, 2008.
Milligan, Barry. 'Morphine-Addicted Doctors: The English Opium-Eater, and Embattled Medical Authority', *Victorian Literature and Culture*, 33.2 (2005): 541–53.
Mills, James H. 'Drugs, Consumption, and Supply in Asia: The Case of Cocaine in Colonial India, c. 1900–c. 1930', *Journal of Asian Studies*, 66.2 (May 2007): 345–62.
Mills, James H. 'Cocaine and the British Empire: The Drug and the Diplomats at the Hague Opium Conference, 1911–12', *Journal of Imperial and Commonwealth History*, 42.3 (2014): 400–19.
Møller, Kristian, and Jamie Hakim. 'Critical Chemsex Studies: Interrogating Cultures of Sexualized Drug Use beyond the Risk Paradigm', *Sexualities*, https://doi.org/10.1177/13634607211026223.
Morrow, W. C. *The Ape, The Idiot and Other People*. Philadelphia, PA: J.B. Lippincott, 1897.
Mortimer, William Golden. *Peru: History of Coca, 'The Divine Plant' of the Incas*. New York: J.H. Vail, 1901.
'Mr Sherlock Holmes at Home', *Bournemouth Graphic*, 15.479 (19 May 1911): 9.
'Mr. Weston's Feat', *Lancet*, 123.3160 (22 March 1884): 539–40.
Müller, Christian P., and Gunter Schumann. 'Drugs as Instruments: A New Framework for Non-Addictive Psychoactive Drug Use', *Behavioural and Brain Sciences*, 34.6 (December 2011): 293–310.
'Musical Dope', *Belfast Telegraph*, 6 December 1928: 6.
Myers, F. W. H. 'The Subliminal Consciousness: Chapter 2 – The Mechanism of Suggestion', *Proceedings of the Society for Psychical Research*, 7 (1891–1892): 327–55.
Neele, F. Woodward. 'On-the-Rack', *The Windsor Magazine*, 9.52 (April 1899): 605–10.
'Negro and Cocaine', *Westminster Gazette*, 9381 (6 August 1923): 5.
'Negro in Cocaine Charge', *Sunday Post*, 938 (5 August 1923): 2.
'Negro Dope Dealers', *Shields Daily News*, 20061 (22 June 1923): 1.
'Negro Runs Amok', *Daily Telegraph*, 16952 (25 August 1909): 11.
'A New Anaesthetic', *Chambers's Journal*, 2.61 (28 February 1885): 144.
'New Forms of Narcotism', *BMJ*, 1.1482 (25 May 1889): 1186.
'A New Form of Intoxication', *Trewman's Exeter Flying Post*, 6870 (25 May 1889): 8.
'A New Form of Intoxication', *Blackburn Standard and Weekly Express*, 22 June 1889: 2.
'A New Intoxicant', *The Dundee Courier & Argus*, 11266 (16 August 1889): 4.
'New Novels', *The Graphic*, 1106 (7 February 1891): 150.
'New Novels', *The Scotsman*, 14763 (27 October 1890): 3.

'New Preparations and Scientific Inventions', *Dublin Journal of Medical Science*, 98.3 (September 1894): 272.

'New Vegetable Stimulant', *Hampshire Advertiser*, 1995 (23 November 1861): 2.

Ngai, Sianne. *Our Aesthetic Categories: Zany, Cute, Interesting*. Cambridge, MA: Harvard University Press, 2012.

N.K. 'The Mystery of the Orange Pips', *Sporting Times*, 2697 (29 May 1915): 18.

Norman, Conolly. 'A Note on Cocainism', *Journal of Mental Science*, 38.161 (April 1892): 195–9.

'Notes and Notions', *Sporting Times*, 605 (16 February 1876): 91.

'Notes from the Court Journal', *Isle of Wight Observer*, 1784 (27 November 1886): 8.

'Novels', *The Saturday Review of Politics, Literature, Science and Art*, 70.1827 (1 November 1890): 512.

'The Novels of Sir Arthur Conan Doyle', *Quarterly Review*, 200.399 (July 1904): 158–79.

'Novel Suggestion for the Correction of Irregular Astigmatism', *BMJ*, 2.1453 (3 November 1888): 1002–3.

'Now and Then', *Evening Herald* (Dublin), 9.264 (12 January 1901): 5.

Oakley, Giles. *The Devil's Music: A History of the Blues*. New York: Da Capo Press, 1997.

'Occasional Notes', *Leeds Mercury*, 14703 (23 May 1885): 1.

O'Dell, Benjamin D. 'Performing the Imperial Abject: The Ethics of Cocaine in Arthur Conan Doyle's The Sign of Four', *Journal of Popular Culture*, 45.5 (2012): 979–99.

O'Donnell, Molly C. 'Mirrors, Masks, and Masculinity: The Homosocial Legacy from Dickens to Machen', *Victoriographies*, 6.3 (2016): 256–75.

Odum, Howard W. *The Negro and His Songs: A Study of the Typical Negro Songs in the South*. Chapel Hill: University of North Carolina Press, 1925.

'Opening Address by the President (Sir Robert Christison, Bart.)', *Transactions of the Botanical Society*, 12 (November 1873–July1876): 395–409.

'The Operation for Cataract', *Newcastle Weekly Courant*, 11447 (9 June 1894): 5.

'Old and New', *The Scots Observer*, 3.64 (8 February 1890): 334.

'On Tattooing', *Newcastle Courant*, 11677 (5 November 1898): 6.

'On the Use of Cocaine in the Morphine Habit: A Warning', *BMJ*, 2.2435 (31 August 1907): 556.

'On the Cocaine Habit in Diseases of Throat and Nose', *BMJ*, 1.1478 (27 April 1889): 973.

'Opium Party Revels', *The People*, 2179 (22 July 1923): 9.

Pain, Barry. 'The Reaction', *Nash's Pall Mall Magazine*, 71.361 (May 1923): 51, 110–16.

'Painless Surgery', *Daily News*, 17016 (6 October 1900): 5.

Pascal, Blaise. *Pensées*. London: Penguin, 1995.

Pavy, F. W. 'The Effect of Prolonged Muscular Exercise on the System', *Lancet*, 107.2739 (27 February 1876): 429–31.

'Perforation of the Nasal Septum in Cocaine Takers', *BMJ*, 2.3178 (26 November 1921): 917.

'Philosophical Periodicals, etc.' *Mind: A Quarterly Review of Psychology and Philosophy*, 3.11 (July 1894): 430–40.
Pienaar, Kiran, Dean Anthony Murphy, Kane Race, and Toby Lea. 'Drugs as Technologies of the Self: Enhancement and Transformation in LGBTQ Cultures', *International Journal of Drug Policy*, 78 (April 2020): 1–9.
Pilcher, James E. 'Cocaine as an Anaesthetic; Its Status at the Close of the First Year of its Use', *Annals of Surgery*, 1.3 (January 1886): 51–66.
'The Play Actors', *The Stage*, 1387 (17 October 1907): 15.
'The Poisoner Neill', *St James's Gazette*, 25.3858 (24 October 1892): 9.
Porter, Roy. *Disease, Medicine and Society in England, 1550–1860*. Basingstoke: Macmillan, 1993.
'Possible Substitutes for Cocaine', *Lancet*, 203.5247 (22 March 1924): 596–8.
Power, Henry. 'An Address Delivered at the Opening of the Section of Ophthalmology and Otology', *BMJ*, 2.1283 (1 August 1885): 206–8.
Primrose, Deborah. 'Health and Beauty', *Hearth and Home*, 308 (8 August 1897): 924–6.
Primrose, Deborah. 'Health and Beauty', *Hearth and Home*, 332 (23 September 1897): 784–6.
Primrose, Deborah. 'Health and Beauty', *Hearth and Home*, 336 (21 October 1897): 970.
Primrose, Deborah. 'Health and Beauty', *Hearth and Home*, 411 (30 March 1899): 846–8.
'Priti Patel Wants to "Make An Example" Out of Middle-Class Cocaine Users', *Independent*, 16 August 2021, https://www.independent.co.uk/news/uk/politics/priti-patel-middle-class-cocaine-b1903337.html
'The "Prodigy" Question', *The Scotsman*, 19081 (13 August 1904): 10.
'Progress of the Nineteenth Century', *The London Reader*, 78.2021 (25 January 1902): 377.
'Proposed Additions to the Poisons Schedule', *Lancet*, 165.4259 (15 April 1905): 1013–14.
'Questions and Answers', *The Musical Herald*, 515 (1 February 1891): 58.
'The Race War in Georgia', *Edinburgh Evening News*, 10435 (25 September 1906): 4.
'The Rally against Cocaine', *The Times*, 43026 (9 May 1922): 17.
Race, Kane. 'Thinking with Pleasure: Experimenting with Drugs and Drug Research', *International Journal of Drug Policy*, 49 (July 2017): 144–9.
Rawling, E. Eliot. 'Jazz – a Drug', *Amsterdam News*, 1 April 1925: 16.
'The Real Cocaine Criminals', *The Times*, 43029 (12 May 1922): 7.
'Recent Advances in Surgery and Medicine', *Edinburgh Review*, 168.344 (October 1888): 491–515.
'Recent Literature', *Ophthalmic Review*, 6 (1887): 278–81.
'Re-Colouring the Eyes', *Huddersfield Daily Examiner*, 11511 (8 February 1905): 2.
'The Regulations with Respect to the Sale of Cocaine', *Lancet*, 188.4849 (5 August 1916): 238.
'Reign of Terror in Georgia', *Pall Mall Gazette*, 83.12937 (25 September 1906): 7.

Reitz, Caroline. 'The Empires of a Study in Scarlet and The Sign of Four', in *The Cambridge Companion to Sherlock Holmes*, ed. Janice M. Allan and Christopher Pittard. Cambridge: Cambridge University Press, 2019, 127–39.

'The Relation of Alcoholism to Inebriety', *Freeman's Journal*, 121 (5 August 1887): 5.

'Religion and Sacred Art', *Hastings and St Leonards Observer*, 4560 (19 November 1927): 2.

'Remedy for Head Cold', *London Journal*, 25.631 (18 January 1896): 60.

Renton, J. Crawford. 'Cocaine in Ophthalmic Surgery', *Glasgow Medical Journal*, 23.1 (January 1885): 28.

'Restoring Broken Noses', *The Review of Reviews*, 25.146 (February 1902): 146.

'A Revival in Tattooing', *Yorkshire Evening Post*, 4379 (14 September 1904): 2.

'Reviews', *BMJ*, 2.2130 (26 October 1901): 1272–3.

'Reviews', *BMJ*, 1.2307 (18 March 1905): 602–3.

'Reviews', *Pall Mall Gazette*, 9592 (21 December 1895): 4.

'Reviews', *Salisbury and Winchester Journal*, 29 September 1894: 3.

Richardson, Benjamin Ward. 'The Mastery of Pain: A Triumph of the Nineteenth Century', *Longman's Magazine*, 19.113 (1 March 1892): 489–510.

Richardson, Frank. *The Secret Kingdom*. London: Duckworth, 1905.

Riddle, H. H. 'The Drug Habit', *The Quiver*, 47.5 (March 1912): 487–90.

Rogers, Blair O. 'John Orlando Roe – Not Jacques Joseph – The father of Aesthetic Rhinoplasty', *Aesthetic Plastic Surgery*, 10.1 (December 1986): 63–88.

Rootham, H. 'Jazzomania and Devil Dances', *English Review*, January 1924: 109–11.

'Rosy Cheeks', *Elgin Courant and Morayshire Advertiser*, 5328 (9 August 1904): 6.

'Rosy Cheeks', *Irish Independent*, 3679 (18 November 1904): 2.

'Round Lancaster Castle', *Lancaster Gazette*, 6052 (15 February 1890): 8.

Saleeby, C. W. 'The Curse of Cocaine', *Liverpool Daily Post*, 19075 (19 July 1916): 7.

'Salute to Sherlock Holmes', *Yorkshire Post*, 25892 (11 July 1930): 8.

Sandburg, Carl. *The American Songbag*. New York: Harcourt, Brace, 1927.

Sargent, Elizabeth. 'Cocaine in Glaucoma', *Archives of Ophthalmology*, 16.2 (1887): 205–6.

Sausman, Justin. 'Science, Drugs and Occultism: Aleister Crowley, Henry Maudsley and Late-nineteenth Century Degeneration Theories', *Journal of Literature and Science*, 1.1 (2008): 40–54.

Scheppegrell, W. 'Editorial', *Laryngoscope*, 5.6 (December 1898): 373–4.

Scheppegrell, W. 'The Uses and Abuses of Cocaine', *Laryngoscope*, 7.3 (September 1899): 202.

'Scientific Miscellany', *Manchester Times Supplement*, 24 November 1866: 375.

'Science Notes', *Pall Mall Gazette*, 9634 (10 February 1896): 1.

'Scraps', *Manchester Times*, 1554 (23 April 1887): 8.

Scott, Clement. 'Tattooing in Japan', *The Illustrated London News*, 103.2837 (2 September 1893): 287.

Servitje, Lorenzo. *Medicine Is War: The Martial Metaphor in Victorian Literature and Culture*. Albany: State University of New York Press, 2021.
Shay, Frank. *More Pious Friends and Drunken Companions*. New York: Macmillan, 1928.
'Sherlock Holmes Americanised', *Hartlepool Northern Daily Mail*, 5274 (11 May 1895): 3.
'Sherlock Holmes Burlesqued at Terry's Theatre', *The Tatler*, 28 (8 January 1902): 76.
'Sherlock Holmes Satirised', *Wellington Journal and Shrewsbury News*, 2612 (4 March 1905): 3.
Siddiqi, Yumna. *Anxieties of Empire and the Fiction of Intrigue*. New York: Columbia University Press, 2008.
Siegel, Ronald K. 'Cocaine and the Privileged Class', *Advances in Alcohol & Substance Abuse*, 4.2 (1984): 37–49.
Siegel, Ronald K. *Intoxication: The Universal Drive for Mind-Altering Substances*. Rochester, NY: Park Street Press, 2005.
'The Sign of Four', *The Morning Post*, 37029 (18 February 1891): 4.
'Skin Pictures', *Irish Independent*, 3819 (16 May 1904): 2.
Small, Douglas R. J. 'Primitive Doctor and Eugenic Priest: Grant Allen, M.P. Shiel, and the Future of the Victorian Medical Man', *Journal of Literature and Science*, 11.2 (2018): 40–61.
Smith, Walter G. 'Report on Materia Medica and Therapeutics', *Dublin Journal of Medical Science*, 79.4 (April 1885): 313–26.
Smith, Walter G. 'Report on Materia Medica and Therapeutics', *Dublin Journal of Medical Science*, 80.6 (December 1885): 312–26.
Smith, Walter G. 'Report on Materia Medica and Therapeutics', *Dublin Journal of Medical Science*, 84.6 (December 1887): 506–12.
Smith, Watson. 'The Cocaine Cure for Sea-Sickness', *Manchester Guardian*, 12531 (12 October 1886): 7.
Snell, Simeon. 'Presidential Address on Some Points of Progress in Ophthalmic Surgery', *BMJ*, 2.1489 (13 July 1889): 57–61.
Snow, Herbert. 'The Use of Cocaine in Circumcision', *Lancet*, 128.3287 (28 August 1886): 429.
Snow, Stephanie J. *Operations without Pain: The Practice and Science of Anaesthesia in Victorian Britain*. Basingstoke: Palgrave Macmillan, 2005.
'Social Optimism', *The Spectator*, 85.3780 (8 December 1900): 837–8.
'Soho Drug Merchant', *Western Times*, 22710 (1 May 1922): 4.
'Some Popular Remedies', *Chambers's Journal*, 12.577 (19 January 1895): 42–5.
Sontag, Susan. *Illness as Metaphor and AIDS and Its Metaphors*. London: Penguin Books, 2002.
'Special Correspondence', *BMJ*, 1.1305 (2 January 1886): 38–41.
Spillane, Joseph F. *Cocaine: From Medical Marvel to Modern Menace in the United States*. Baltimore, MD: Johns Hopkins University Press, 2000.

'Sporting Pictures on the Human Skin', *Country Life Illustrated*, 7.160 (27 January 1900): 108–10.

Springthorpe, J. W. 'The Confessions of a Cocainist', *Australasian Medical Gazette*, 14 (20 September 1895): 370–4.

Starkey, W. 'The Cocaine-takers of Paris', *Journal of Mental Science*, 59.246 (July 1913): 524–5.

Stevenson, Robert Louis. *The Letters of Robert Louis Stevenson to His Family and Friends*, ed. Sidney Colvin. London: Methuen, 1901.

Stiles, Anne. *Popular Fiction and Brain Science in the Late Nineteenth Century*. Cambridge: Cambridge University Press, 2014.

'Stray Thoughts', *Torquay Times*, 38.1453 (14 March 1902): 8.

Streatfeild, Dominic. *Cocaine*. London: Virgin Books, 2007.

'Taking Cocaine', *Burnley Express*, 4059 (31 July 1909): 2.

'Tattooed Countesses', *Hearth and Home*, 77 (3 November 1892): 821.

'Tattooers and Tattooed', *Pall Mall Gazette*, 8441 (9 April 1892): 1–2.

'Tattooing by Hypodermic Injection', *BMJ*, 2.2434 (24 August 1907): 29.

'Tattooing the Body', *Supplement to the Cork Daily Herald*, 40.1195 (16 May 1896): 2.

'Tattooing the Human Eye', *Hampshire Telegraph and Sussex Chronicle*, 6045 (24 July 1897): 12.

'Tattooing the Human Eye', *Northern Daily Mail*, 5931 (24 July 1897): 6.

'Theatre Royal – "The Speckled Band"', *Dublin Daily Express*, 20052 (4 October 1910): 6.

'The Theatres', *Hamilton Daily Times*, 57.251 (23 October 1915): 14.

Thompson, J. Ashburton, 'Physiological Memoranda on E. P. Weston's Third Walk', *BMJ*, 1.792 (4 March 1876): 297–8.

Thompson, J. Ashburton, 'Weston's Fourth Walk', *BMJ*, 1.793 (11 March 1876): 334–5.

Tibbits, Edward T. 'On Systematic Exercises; Their Value in the Prevention of Disease' *Lancet*, 112.2874 (28 September 1878): 435–6.

Till, Rupert. *Pop Cult: Religion and Popular Music*. London: Continuum, 2010.

'Tip-Tilted Noses', *BMJ*, 1.1381 (18 June 1887): 1345.

Todd, Peter. 'The Adventure of the Brixton Builder!', *Greyfriars Herald*, 1.9 (15 January 1916): 3–5.

Todd, Peter. 'The Case of the Biscuit-Tin!', *Greyfriars Herald*, 1.2 (27 November 1915): 3–5.

Toil, Cunnin. 'The Duke's Feather', *Punch*, 105 (19 August 1893): 76.

Tosh, John. 'Masculinities in an Industrialising Society: Britain 1800–1914', *Journal of British Studies*, 44.2 (April 2005): 330–42.

'To Tourists, Pedestrians, &c.' *Athletic News*, 2.65 (26 August 1876): 8.

'Trafficker in Cocaine', *Western Daily Press*, 128.19,924 (1 May 1922): 8.

Untitled Article. *Fun*, 23 (16 February 1876): 78.

Untitled Article. *London Daily News*, 15123 (19 September 1894): 6.

Untitled Article. *The Midland Medical Miscellany and Provincial Medical Journal*, 3.31 (1 July 1884): 208.

Untitled Article. *The Midland Medical Miscellany and Provincial Medical Journal*, 5.51 (1 March 1886): 125.

Valdez, Lidio M., Juan Taboada, and J. Ernesto Valdez. 'Ancient use of Coca Leaves in the Peruvian Central Highlands', *Journal of Anthropological Research*, 71.2 (January 2015): 231–58.

Vedder, Hyram. 'Mr Anthony Jones of New York', *English Illustrated Magazine*, 133 (October 1894): 17–28.

Vedder, Hyram. 'Mr Swagg of London', *English Illustrated Magazine*, 143 (August 1895): 451–8.

Verity, Richard. 'Erythroxylon Coca', *Lancet*, 100.2549 (6 July 1872): 31.

'A Visit to a Professional Tattooer', *Chums: An Illustrated Paper for Boys*, 2.81 (28 March 1894): 485.

Von Glehn, Marian. 'A Day in a Hospital', *The Leisure Hour*, February 1890: 277–81.

Wagner, Peter. *Modernity: Understanding the Present*. London: Polity, 2012.

'The Walking Match', *The Star*, 106 (16 March 1876): 1.

Waller, Augustus D. 'On the Influence of Reagents on the Electrical Excitability of Isolated Nerve', *Brain: A Journal of Neurology*, 19.2 (1896): 277–300.

Watson, Veronica T. *The Souls of White Folk: African American Writers Theorize Whiteness*. Jackson: University of Mississippi Press, 2013.

Watson-Williams, E. 'Cocaine and its Substitutes', *BMJ*, 2.3283 (1 December 1923): 1018–21.

W.B.K. 'When Detectives Disagree', *The Yale Record*, 51.12 (11 April 1923): 595.

Webb, J. Eustace. 'The Use of Hydro-Chlorate of Cocaine in Private Surgical Practice', *Scottish Medical and Surgical Journal*, vol. 7 (July to December 1900): 46.

Wells, H. G. *The Island of Doctor Moreau*. London: Penguin, 2005.

Wells, H. G. 'When the Sleeper Wakes', *The Graphic*, 1519 (7 January 1899): 9–11.

Weston, Edward Payson, 'Mr Weston on the Use of Coca Leaves', Lancet, 107.2742 (18 March 1876): 447.

'Weston in England', *Forest and Stream*, 6.4 (2 March 1876): 56.

'Weston's Attempt to Walk 500 Miles in Six Days', *Lancaster Gazette*, 4636 (15 March 1876): 4.

'Weston's Last Feat', *Daily News*, 9329 (17 March 1876): 6.

'Weston's Last Feat', *Lancet*, 107.2742 (18 March 1876): 339–440.

'What the Modern Use of Poisons Leads To', *The Blackburn Standard*, 55.2784 (22 June 1889): 2.

'Where Women Live in Terror', *Beeston Gazette and Echo*, 1366 (22 November 1924): 3.

'Who Is the New Dope King?', *The People*, 2276 (31 May 1925): 1.

'The Wickedest Man in the World', *John Bull*, 33.877 (24 March 1923): 10.

Willcox, W. H. 'Norman Kerr Memorial Lecture on Drug Addiction', *BMJ*, 2.3283 (1 December 1923): 1013–18.

Wilde, Sally. 'Truth, Trust, and Confidence in Surgery, 1890–1910: Patient Autonomy, Communication, and Consent', *Bulletin of the History of Medicine*, 83.2 (June 2009): 302–30.

Wilde, Sally, and Geoffrey Hirst. 'Learning from Mistakes: Early Twentieth-Century Surgical Practice', *Journal of the History of Medicine and Allied Sciences*, 64.1 (January 2009): 38–77.

Wilson, Elizabeth. *Bohemians: The Glamorous Outcasts*. New York: Tauris Parke, 2003.

'A Worse Evil', *Western Mail*, 1400 (4 April 1914): 6.

Young, William Semple. *Cocaine as a Local Anaesthetic: With Special Reference to its Use in Tooth Extraction*. Glasgow, 1898.

Zangwill, Israel. 'Without Prejudice', *Pall Mall Magazine*, 1.2 (June 1893): 263–70.

Zieger, Susan. 'Holmes's Pipe, Tobacco Papers and the Nineteenth-century Origins of Media Addiction', *Journal of Victorian Culture*, 19.1 (March 2014): 24–42.

Zieger, Susan. *Inventing the Addict: Drugs, Race, and Sexuality in Nineteenth-Century British and American Literature*. Amherst: University of Massachusetts Press, 2008.

Index

Acker, Caroline 177
addiction 9, 13, 16–17, 19, 47–8, 53, 76–7,
    109–21, 127, 132–5, 143, 143 n.14,
    153–9, 162, 166, 177, 189, 193 n.98,
    197, 201–3, 207–8, 212, 214, 221;
    see also cocainism; cocaine habit;
    degeneration
alcohol 10, 22, 25, 32–3, 53, 57, 93–4, 110,
    113, 134–5, 183, 185
    see also coca wine; drink; drunkenness
America, United States of 1–3, 6, 9,
    18, 21–3, 45, 48, 88–9, 116, 163,
    175–89, 192, 194–5, 201–2, 206,
    211–12, 214–16
anaesthesia
    by cocaine 6, 8–9, 11, 13–15, 18, 21,
        47–58, 61, 64–5, 72–3, 75–6, 79–85,
        87, 89–95, 99, 103–4, 111, 113, 143,
        151, 182, 212–13, 216, 218–20
    general 50–2, 52 n.20, 79–80, 213, 219;
    see also chloroform; ether; nitrous oxide
Annandale, Thomas 101
anti-Semitism 9
Atlanta Race Riot (1906) 187
Auden, W. H. 211

Baker, James (Iron Head) 185–6
Baker, Josephine 179
Ballin, Ada S. 83
Barnum's American Circus 27 n.36
Barrows, C. M. 73
Baudrillard, Jean 15 n.60
Beaumont, Edgar 69;
    see also Meade, L. T.
Beerbohm, Max 82, 85
Benjamin, Walter 167 n.88
blackness 17 n.67, 18, 178–9, 182–96,
    199–200, 202, 204–6
Blues Music 183–6, 211–12
    see also Jazz Music
Bolivar, Simon 22
Bolivia 23;

see also South America
Bradley, S. M. 29–30
brain 24, 29, 33–5, 54–6, 127, 129–30,
    133, 136, 138, 147–9, 155, 172–3,
    193–5, 207;
    see also mind
Breakell, Mary L. 137–8
Brettauer, Joseph 8, 49
British Empire 18, 90 n.45, 142–3,
    205
Brown, J. J. Graham 55
Browne, Lennox 111
Burney, Ian A. 52
Buxton, Dudley 79–80

Campbell, Harry 120–1
cancer 14, 52, 101 n.89, 191
Cannon, Gus 124
Carr, J. Walter 136–7
Castle, Terry 130–1
Chang, Brilliant 178
Chattanooga 181
chemsex 16;
    see also cocaine as aphrodisiac;
        pleasure; sex
Chetwynd, George (Baronet) 40
Chinese 178, 190–1
chloral 76, 109–10, 113
chloroform 15, 50–3, 55, 59, 62–4, 72,
    76, 151;
    see also anaesthesia
Christ 18–19
Christison, Robert 6–7, 23, 37–9, 41,
    213, 219
cigarettes *see* tobacco
cigars *see* tobacco
circumcision 52, 96
Cleopatra (Queen of Egypt) 85–6
Clouston, T. S. 112–13, 115, 117
coca
    chewing 2–4, 6, 14, 22–3, 25–32, 35, 37,
        39, 42, 44–6;

see also Christison, Robert; Weston, Edward Payson
as divine, see cocaine as divine
habit 27–30
as liquid 6, 38, 40, 42, 57
spelled 'cuca' 37–9
wine 3–4, 134
cocaine
as aphrodisiac 16, 53, 109, 115, 125–7, 184 n.54, 189; see also sex
as cold and flu remedy 57–8, 111–12, 134, 193
conflation with coca 7 n.26
criminalization 11, 13, 17, 176, 179, 221; see also Dangerous Drugs Act (1920); Defence of the Realm Act
dealing 19, 178, 189–91, 200; see also crime
as divine 1, 3–5, 18–19, 56, 61–2, 70, 146, 213, 216–19
drinking 12, 158
habit 10, 12, 16–17, 22, 25, 47, 109, 111–16, 119, 133, 138, 141–2, 144, 147–8, 150, 154–5, 158–63, 167, 170, 173, 177, 178, 180–5, 187–8, 192, 212, 214–15, 220; see also addiction; coca habit; cocaine fiend; cocainism
inhalation see cocaine sniffing
injection 1, 12, 53, 55, 57, 89, 117–19, 143, 143 n.11, 146–50, 152, 173, 191, 193; see also hypodermic needle
poisoning 10, 76, 119, 126
price fluctuations 53, 113
as sea-sickness cure 53, 57–8, 111
slang terms for 184, n.54, 184 n.57
smoking 12
sniffing 12, 119, 164, 181, 185, 192–4, 197, 206, 212, 215
snuff 12, 193–4; see also cocaine sniffing
as stimulant 1, 4, 7, 12, 14, 24–6, 39, 44–5, 53, 109, 113, 125, 134, 147, 167–8, 195–6, 216–17
toxicosis 10, 116, 143; see also cocaine bugs
cocaine bugs 16, 107, 109, 116–17, 119–20, 128, 131–3; see also cocaine toxicosis; hallucination
cocaine fiend 199, 155, 175, 177, 182, 190, 206, 215

cocainism 10, 16–17, 47, 76, 109–10, 111–17, 120, 125–8, 133–5, 142, 144–5, 148–50, 153–9, 172–3, 178–9, 182, 187, 188–92, 200, 214, 200; see also addiction; coca habit; cocaine habit
cocainomania 117, 119;
  see also addiction, cocainism; cocaine habit
cocktails 22, 163, 165, 191, 195;
  see also alcohol
coffee 114, 198 n.98
Cohen, Michael M. 183
Cohen, William A. 120–1, 132
contact lenses 103–4;
  see also cosmetic medicine; Fick, Adolf Eugen; Morrow, W. C.
cosmetic medicine 15–16, 79–87, 90–1, 100–2, 106, 220; see also cosmetics; Morrow, W. C.; plastic surgery
cosmetics 82, 85, 169
Cowley, Abraham 3
Cream, Thomas Neill 126
Crespi, Alfred J. H. 58–9, 68, 77
crime 1–2, 11, 88–9, 112 n.20, 126, 141, 158, 163, 172, 183, 186–8, 189–92;
  see also cocaine, dealing
Crowley, Aleister 7 n.26, 18, 175, 200–2, 217, 220
  The Book of the Law 201
  'Cocaine' 175–6
  The Diary of a Drug Fiend 18, 180, 200–8, 217–18, 220–1
  'Drama Be Damned!' 182
  'The Great Drug Delusion' 201
cybernetic 153, 161, 166, 220;
  see also posthumanism

Dale, Henry Hallett 12, 212
Dangerous Drugs Act (1920) 11, 176, 188, 198 n.123;
  see also Defence of the Realm Act
Dawson, Janis 69
Defence of the Realm Act (DORA) 11, 176, 176 n.6, 182, 188, 198 n.123;
  see also Dangerous Drugs Act
degeneration 11–12, 88, 125, 128, 175, 179, 203, 205
Delirium Tremens 193
delusional parasitosis 116;
  see also cocaine bugs; hallucination

De Quincey, Thomas 142
De Styrap, Jukes 51
Digby, Anne 136
Dimeo, Paul 25 n.25, 45
Dixon, W. E. 11, 197
Donald, James 179, 194 n.103
Donders, Franciscus Cornelius 9
dope 46, 164, 177, 184, 188–90, 196–200, 216
Doyle, Arthur Conan
  'The Copper Beeches' 169
  'The Empty House' 153
  'The Engineer's Thumb' 169
  'The Final Problem' 153
  The Man with the Twisted Lip' 169–70
  'The Missing Three Quarter' 155–6
  'The Red-Headed League' 169–70
  'A Scandal in Bohemia' 152, 161
  Sherlock Holmes (character) 17, 69, 141–3, 145, 151, 153–5, 158–9, 162, 166–8, 170, 173, 220
  Sherlock Holmes parodies 145, 161–8, 170–3; see also posthumanism; zany
  The Sign of Four 118, 141–3, 146–53, 155–6, 158–9, 163
  'The Yellow Face' 144
drink 22, 38, 88, 115, 149, 164, 181, 193, 197;
  see also alcohol; coca wine; drunkenness
drug fiend see cocaine fiend
drunkenness 149–50, 159, 211, 218;
  see also alcohol; coca wine; drink

Edinburgh 23, 37, 38, 53, 65, 112, 115, 154
Edwards, Harry Stillwell 62–3
electricity 59, 83, 85, 91–3, 164, 220, 205
electrolysis see cosmetic medicine
Emerson, John 163
  The Mystery of the Leaping Fish 163–8
endurance
  of aesthetic imperfection 79, 99; see also cosmetic medicine; plastic surgery
  of fatigue 6, 21, 23–5, 30, 34, 37–9, 42–3, 61, 215–17; see also coca chewing; cocaine as stimulant
  of pain 88, 90; see also anaesthesia; tattooing

enhancement 14, 24–6, 36, 41, 43, 45–6, 68, 84, 85, 183, 186
  see also sports doping
enslavement 67, 88, 114, 158, 191, 201–3, 208, 212;
  see also addiction; blackness; whiteness
epilepsy 55
Erlenmeyer, Friedrich Albrecht 10
Errol, J. 60
ether 15, 50–3, 59, 76, 110;
  see also anaesthesia
eye surgery see ophthalmology

Fairbanks, Douglas 163–4;
  see also Emerson, John
Falck, F. W. 164
fashion 16, 80–1, 87–91, 93–5, 101, 134–5, 142, 189–90, 200, 215;
  see also cosmetic medicine; cosmetics; tattooing
fatigue 4, 23, 27, 34, 37–9, 114, 205
Felstead, Sidney 178, 188–9, 191, 196–7
Fick, Adolf Eugen 104
First World War 11, 13 n.55, 18, 136, 144, 175, 188, 194, 204, 208, 221
flogging 19, 191–2, 202
Freud, Sigmund 6–8, 53, 141, 219

general practitioners 64–76;
  see also medical profession
Gilbert, Pamela K. 101 n.89, 120–1
Gillette, William 156–8, 160
Gilman, Sander L. 80
Glasgow 25, 39, 56, 57, 64
Gleaves, John 25–7
Godfrey, Clarence 119–20
gothic 16, 19, 81, 100, 220
Gould, George 97
Great War see First World War

Haiken, Elizabeth 96, 99
hallucination 24, 115, 128–33, 199–200
  symptom of cocaine toxicosis see cocaine bugs; cocaine toxicosis
  under general anaesthesia 51–2, 72–3
Hammack, Brenda Mann 24, 47 n.2
Harrison Narcotics Act (1914) 176;
  see also Dangerous Drugs Act; Defence of the Realm Act

Hart, Hattie 185
Heggie, Vanessa 25, 27 n.37, 136
Heidelberg 6, 8, 49, 52
Hichens, R. S. 111
Holt, Richard 36
Hori Chyo 89
horses 40, 59
hypnosis 70–5
hypodermic needle 53, 77, 89, 92, 113, 117–18, 141, 146, 150, 152, 154, 160, 162–3, 165, 168, 193, 199;
see also cocaine injection

Imperialism see British Empire
Inca Civilisation 2–4, 7, 23, 213, 216–17
India 13 n.55, 42, 142, 176 n.6
Indians see Native American Peoples
inebriety 110, 120–1, 149, 159;
see also addiction; cocaine habit
instrumentalization 23–4, 27, 149;
see also enhancement; modernity, drug use as adaptation to

Jacobi, Mary 135
Japan 87–8, 93–4, 205
Jazz Music 18, 179, 183–4, 190, 192–6, 200, 206–7;
see also Blues Music; modernity

Karch, Steven B. 25
Kelson, Jack 189–90
Kentucky 181, 193 n.98
Kerr, Douglas 143 n.14, 147 n.23, 168
Kohn, Marek 13 n.53, 176, 178 n.17
Kolle, Frederick Strange 98
Koller, Karl 6–9, 21, 49–50

Lauterbach, Preston 185
Lawrence, Ethel 187
Lawson, R. A. 183
Ledbetter, Huddie William (Lead Belly) 185–6
Lees, David B. 57
Lewin, Louis 12, 212
Lewis, Noah 184
life expectancy 60 n.54
Llewellyn, Matthew 25–7
Locke, Alain LeRoy 194, 196

Lomax, John and Alan 185–6
Lombroso, Cesare 88–9;
see also tattooing; primitivity, associated with tattooing
Louisiana 182
Love, Eddie 1, 216

MacCormac, William 95–7
MacDonald, Sutherland 81, 89, 91, 93, 95
Machen, Arthur
  Dreads and Drolls 124
  Hieroglyphics 124 n.72
  'Novel of the White Powder' 16, 110, 121–5, 127–33, 218, 220; see also cocaine bugs; hallucination
  The Three Impostors or the Transmutations see 'Novel of the White Powder'
Mahomed, Frederick Akbar 27
make-up see cosmetics
Mama Coca 3–5, 216;
see also cocaine as divine
Manning, Edgar (Eddie) 190–2, 200
masculinity 18, 68, 75, 138, 179–80, 196–200, 202, 203–5, 209
Mattison, J. B. 10
McCartney, J. L. 58, 60 n.54
McCarty, J. P. 164
McNamara, J. 51
Meachen, G. Norman 120
Meade, L. T. 68–9, 77
  The Brotherhood of the Seven Kings 69
  'The Red Bracelet' 15, 49, 68–76
medical profession
  and cosmetic operations 86–7, 90–100
  as middle class ideal 67–8, 75–6
  ideological investment in cocaine 48–50, 52–6, 60–77
  perceived responsibility for addiction 108–10, 112–13, 133–4
  special vulnerability to addiction 47–8, 133–5
  woman practitioners 110, 133–9
metabolism 27 n.37
Miller, Charles 99
Miller, William 22–3
mind 33–6, 56, 67, 70, 113, 116, 130–2, 147–9, 151–2, 172, 178, 180, 195;

see also brain
Mississippi 182
modernity 9, 15, 17–18, 23, 48–9, 58–60, 68, 86, 88, 90–3, 97, 102, 108, 112–16, 124, 138–9, 143, 145, 151–2, 167, 179–80, 182, 189, 192, 194–6, 206–7, 213–16, 219–20
   definition of 15 n.60
   drug use as adaptation to 23–3;
   see also instrumentalization
morphine 11, 53, 92, 109–10, 112 n.20, 113–15, 117–18, 135, 159, 163, 193, 195, 211;
   see also addiction
Morrow, W. C. 99–100
   'Two Singular Men' 82, 100–5, 220
Mortimer, William Golden 4, 7 n.26, 213–14, 216–18
Morton, Ferdinand (Jelly Roll Morton)184
Mucha, Alphonse 3–4, 216
Müller, Christian 23–4, 27, 149
Murray, Flora 136
Myers, F. W. H. 73

Native American Peoples 2–3, 7, 22–3, 37 n.72, 88, 101, 206;
   see also Inca Civilisation
Neele, F. Woodward 111
nerves 1, 6, 12, 35, 40–1, 54–5, 61, 71, 73, 75, 89, 133–4, 137–8, 146, 148, 179, 181–2, 194, 196, 212, 215–16
New York 9, 80, 89, 135, 157, 158, 181, 182, 185, 201
Ngai, Sianne 17, 145, 166–7;
   see also zany
Niemann, Albert 6
nitrous oxide 51–2;
   see also anaesthesia
Norman, Connolly 47, 114–15, 125
nursing 61, 84, 136;
   see also medical profession

O'Dell, Benjamin D. 143
Odum, Howard W. 184–6
ophthalmology 6, 8–9, 11, 49–50, 52, 61–3, 64, 71–2, 80, 91, 104, 135
opium 10, 110, 113–14, 142–3, 143 n.12, 163, 178, 190–1, 193;
   see also De Quincey, Thomas

Pachamama 3
Pagenstecher, Hermann (Professor) 60–1
pain 6, 8 n.30, 12, 15, 16, 19, 34, 49–61, 63, 65, 72–3, 79–81, 83–5, 88–93, 95, 103, 105–6, 108, 111, 113, 135, 146, 159, 191–2, 213, 220;
   see also anaesthesia
Pain, Barry 196–200
Pavy, Frederick William 27–9, 44–5
performance-enhancement *see* enhancement
Perkins, William 21, 23, 25, 27–8, 31
Peru 2, 22–3, 39–40, 58, 111, 213, 216–17;
   see also South America
phantasmagoria *see* hallucination
pharmacies 6, 176, 197–8
physiology 7, 27–9, 42, 45, 52 n.20;
   see also metabolism; sport
Pienaar, Kiran 178
plastic surgery 82, 85, 87, 95–8, 100 n.83;
   see also cosmetic surgery; H. G. Wells, *Island of Doctor Moreau*
   as distinct from cosmetic surgery 82, 95–6
pleasure 16–18, 94, 115, 117, 122, 144–5, 147–52, 159–66, 172–3, 176–86, 188–9, 192–7, 200–6, 209, 218, 220–1;
   see also cocaine as aphrodisiac; sex
Poe, Edgar Allan 100
Porter, Roy 66
posthumanism 95, 99, 106, 109, 149–53, 159–66, 207–9, 219–21
Power, Henry 9, 11
primitivity
   as aspect of modernity 179–80, 192–5, 206–7, 214, 216–17; *see also* jazz music
   associated with tattooing 88–90, 92–5, 101, 205; *see also* Lombroso Cesare
   and British Empire 143
Primrose, Deborah 83–4
prohibition *see* cocaine criminalisation
Psychical Research 73
Pyle, Walter 97

rhinoplasty *see* cosmetic medicine
Richardson, Frank 172–3
Rickett, Arthur 118
Robida, Albert 4–5, 216
Roe, John Orlando 80
Russia *see* Soviet Union

Sandburg, Carl 211–12
Sargent, Elizabeth 135
savagery *see* primitivity
Schumann, Gunter 23–4, 27, 149
Scott, Clement William 88, 93
selfhood 14, 27, 221
    medical 68, 77, 220
    and skin 121
    sporting 14–15, 26–7, 31–6, 43, 46
    and work 169
sex 1, 16, 18, 109, 115, 118, 125–8, 179, 183–4, 186–8, 190–2, 196, 202–6, 209;
    see also cocaine as aphrodisiac; pleasure
Shay, Frank 211
Sherlock Holmes *see* Doyle, Arthur Conan
Siegel, Ronald K. 1, 216
skin 12, 16, 31, 81, 83, 85, 89, 91–5, 100–1, 105, 110, 116–21, 128–33, 146, 150;
    see also hypodermic needle; tattooing
smoking *see* cocaine smoking; opium; tobacco
Snow, Stephanie J. 50
Sontag, Susan 13–14, 221
South America 2, 4, 22, 25, 45, 143 n.12;
    see also Inca Civilisation
Soviet Union 215–16
speed 60, 63, 115–16, 167, 182, 193–5, 204, 206–7;
    see also modernity
Spillane, Joseph F. 48, 178
sport 21–36, 39–46
    amateur 26–7, 36, 39–44, 46
    professional 26–7, 30–2, 35–6, 42–6
sports doping 14–15, 25–6, 44–6;
    see also enhancement
Springthorpe, J. W. 117–19, 126, 132
Stevenson, Robert Louis 57, 100
    Strange Case of Dr Jekyll and Mr Hyde 124

syphilis 53, 100 n.83, 118, 128
syringe *see* hypodermic needle

tattooing 15–16, 81, 87–95, 99, 101, 105, 118, 205;
    see also cosmetic medicine; primitivity; skin
teetotalism 22, 25, 32
temperance movement 25, 32–3, 110
Tennessee 183–4
Thelema 201–3, 207
Thompson, John Ashburton 27–31, 33–4, 44
Tibbits, Edward T. 34–5
tobacco 10, 22, 28, 93, 135, 142, 149, 159, 164, 206, 215
Tosh, John 172–3

Utrecht 9

vaccination 52, 92;
    see also hypodermic needle
Vedder, Hyram (pseudonym) 157–8
Verity, Richard 4–6
Von Glehn, Marian 60–1, 63

walking *see* Weston, Edward Payson
Watson, J. W. (Colonel) 192–4
Webb, J. Eustace 64
Wells, H. G. 114
    Island of Doctor Moreau 105–6
Weston, Edward Payson 6, 14, 21–37, 40, 42–6, 213
Weston, Maria 21
whiteness 17 n.67, 18, 177–80, 182–3, 186–97, 199–200, 202–9
Willcox, William Henry 177
Williams, E. Huntington 187
Williams, John 94
women
    and addiction 134–5, 138, 177–8, 189
    and racialised peril 177–8, 187–92, 196
women doctors *see* medical profession, women practitioners
work 17, 23–4, 48, 66, 68, 122, 133, 143–5, 147–52, 155, 159, 160, 166–73, 182–3, 220
    self-employment 168–70
Wyllie, John 154

Young, William Semple 64–5

Zangwill, Israel 153
zany (comic style) 17, 145, 166–8, 170–3, 212, 220;
see also Ngai, Sianne
Zieger, Susan 47 n.2, 110, 112 n.20, 117, 126 n.77, 133 n.96, 143 n.14, 159
Zinner, Friedrich 9

www.ingramcontent.com/pod-product-compliance
Lightning Source LLC
Chambersburg PA
CBHW071823300426
44116CB00009B/1416